**8TH
EDITION**

Cases in Collective Bargaining & Industrial Relations

A Decisional Approach

Raymond L. Hilgert
*Professor of Management
and Industrial Relations*

Sterling H. Schoen
Professor Emeritus of Management

*both of the
John M. Olin School of Business
Washington University
St. Louis, Missouri*

IRWIN

Chicago • Bogotá • Boston • Buenos Aires • Caracas
London • Madrid • Mexico City • Sydney • Toronto

© Richard D. Irwin, a Times Mirror Higher Education Group, Inc. company, 1969, 1974, 1978, 1982, 1986, 1989, 1993, and 1996

Senior sponsoring editor:	Kurt L. Strand
Project editor:	Karen J. Nelson
Production supervisor:	Lara Feinberg
Designer:	Matthew Baldwin
Cover illustration:	AM Design
Compositor:	Carlisle Communications, Ltd.
Typeface:	10/12 Times Roman
Printer:	Quebecor/Kingsport

Library of Congress Cataloging-in-Publication Data

Hilgert, Raymond L.
    Cases in collective bargaining and industrial relations : a decisional approach / Raymond L. Hilgert, Sterling H. Schoen.—8th ed.
        p. cm.
    ISBN 0-256-16214-X
    1. Collective labor agreements—United States—Cases. I. Schoen, Sterling Harry, 1918-   II. Title.
KF3408.A4S3   1996
344.73'0189—dc20
[347.304189]   95-806

Printed in the United States of America
1 2 3 4 5 6 7 8 9 0 QK 2 1 0 9 8 7 6 5

Preface

This eighth edition provides a convenient yet extensive set of cases in a variety of union-management problem situations. The book is probably most utilized as a supplementary text in survey courses in collective bargaining, labor economics, and industrial relations. The cases vary in length, complexity, and numbers of issues. The collection is of sufficient magnitude and depth that the book is appropriate for advanced courses or case courses in collective bargaining and labor relations.

Our major objective has been to provide a means by which students can apply principles, concepts, and legal considerations they have learned to real decision situations and confrontations between labor and management. We have used these cases in seminars and classes and have found them challenging and fascinating learning instruments.

The cases are representative of the types of problems that perennially confront management and labor unions. These cases test analytical ability in dealing with challenging human relations and union-management conflicts in a way useful even for students who do not have a management or labor relations career in mind.

In an effort to reflect the impact of recent trends, we have collected representative cases dealing with current issues both in the private and public sectors. About 35 percent of the cases in the eighth edition are new. Those we have retained from previous editions provide continuity and balance, and are "timeless" in their elucidation of union-management relations.

Part I of the book presents National Labor Relations Board cases as restructured from published reports of the NLRB and court decisions. Our intent has been to describe each situation from the perspective of impartial writers reporting the facts and issues of the case. For the most part the case formats are developed as follows: the background information of the case is presented, including relevant legal issues; the position of the union(s) or person(s) and the position of the management or company are then stated. An introductory discussion and important and substantive sections of the Labor Management Relations Act (as amended) are included at the outset of Part I to enable students to become famililar with the provisions of the Act applicable throughout the cases.

We believe that the legal obligations and responsibilities of unions and management under the Labor Management Relations Act continue to be among the most dynamic and important issues of collective bargaining today. Case studies such as those in the first section enable the student to appreciate the nature of this Act, its application in various union-management situations, and the duties and legal obligations of management and union representatives to carry out their bargaining responsibilities in good faith. These principles are applicable for the most part in public sector labor relations where other statutes provide the legal framework for collective bargaining.

Part II consists of cases adapted from grievance-arbitration decisions. We are grateful to the Bureau of National Affairs, Inc. (Judith Springberg, Permissions Manager), for permission to adapt certain published cases from *Labor Arbitration Reports*. Here, too, the approach has been to restructure these actual arbitration cases in a convenient format. The highlights and issues of each case are provided through relevant background information, including the contractual clauses, rules, practices, and the like that are pertinent. Principal arguments of the union and management sides are then presented. Cases in Part II demonstrate complexities and controversial areas that manifest themselves in the ongoing relationships between management and union personnel. We have included a brief introductory discussion of major considerations in the grievance-arbitration procedures from which these cases emanate.

In studying both the NLRB and labor arbitration cases—which have been selected without intent of presenting "good" or "bad" or "right" or "wrong" union-management practices—the student should ask, "What are the problems or principal issues?" "What is at stake between the parties?" "What is justice or equity in the situation?" "What does the law require?" "What does the contract say on the issue(s)?" "How have previous NLRB decisions or previous labor arbitration decisions handled similar circumstances?" These questions, and the more specific questions we have developed at the conclusion of each case, urge students toward analysis of issues. Decisions of the NLRB, the courts, and labor arbitrators for these cases are provided in an instructor's manual. It has been the authors' experience that most students want to compare their decisions and approaches with those of authorities in the field.

Index and classification tables open each part of the book. These tables cite the major issues of each case; for the NLRB cases, legal provisions are indicated. Selected bibliographies provide more detailed reading in areas either directly or indirectly involved in the case materials.

Although we cannot recognize everyone who has had a part in developing this book, we wish to acknowledge the following professors who reviewed the previous editions of the text and instructor's manual and who offered numerous helpful suggestions and insights:

David B. Balkin
University of Colorado–Boulder

Mei L. Bickner
California State University at Fullerton
Jeff E. Biddle
Michigan State University
David R. Bloodsworth
University of Massachusetts–Amherst
Grady L. Butler
University of Southwestern Louisiana
Donald A. Coffin
Indiana University Northwest at Gary
Howard M. Leftwich
University of Cincinnati
Michael P. Long
Oakland University
Karl O. Magnusen
Florida International University
Lynn Mercer
University of Findlay–Ohio
Julie A. Mobley
University of North Carolina–Charlottesville
Richard Tyson
University of Wisconsin–Stout

We are particularly grateful to Donald Gardiner of the St. Louis office of the National Labor Relations Board, and to John Hornbeck of the Office of the General Counsel of the NLRB, whose assistance in regard to materials for Part I was invaluable. The cooperation of James Kelly of the St. Louis office of the Federal Mediation and Conciliation Service and of Lawrence Babcock of the Washington, D.C., office of the FMCS in providing us with FMCS materials is similarly recognized. Karl A. Sauber, Labor Relations Attorney in St. Louis, again assisted us with a number of helpful suggestions for which we are most appreciative. Finally, the services of the Washington University Olin Business School administrative staff—particularly Leslie Stroker, Karen Busch, and Teresa Melton—who word processed the book and instructor's manual manuscripts are gratefully acknowledged.

Raymond L. Hilgert
Sterling H. Schoen

Contents

PART II

Case Problems in Union-Management Relations: Cases from Grievance Arbitration

PART I

Legal Aspects of Collective Bargaining: National Labor Relations Board Cases

Introduction to the Labor Management Relations Act (LMRA)

This introductory section will briefly explain the principal provisions of the Labor Management Relations Act (LMRA) of 1947 as amended. A partial text of the Act follows. For more detailed understanding of the provisions of the Act and its applications, a selected bibliography is included at the end of this introductory section. It also is recommended that the student of collective bargaining and industrial relations contact a regional or national office of the National Labor Relations Board (NLRB) to obtain various NLRB publications that explain detailed principles and procedures involved in administration of the law. For example, a publication included in the bibliography entitled, *A Guide to Basic Law and Procedures under the National Labor Relations Act,* is prepared by the Office of the General Counsel of the NLRB; this booklet is very helpful for understanding many of the day-to-day activities of the Board and some of its most recent thinking. Parts of this publication have been adapted and included here.

The LMRA of 1947, also known as the Taft-Hartley Act in recognition of the principal congressional authors of the law, is the principal labor legislation governing the "rules of the game" of collective bargaining for the private sector of the U.S. economic system.[1] The LMRA of 1947 constituted a major amendment and revision of the National Labor Relations (Wagner) Act of 1935. The Act since has been amended a number of times (1951, 1958, 1959, 1969, 1973, 1974, and 1980); the 1974 amendments focused primarily on health care institutions. As it stands today, the Act is the fundamental legislative basis for private sector union-management relationships in the

---

[1]The Railway Labor Act of 1926 (as amended) governs collective bargaining in the rail and airline industries. Although the Railway Labor Act is not widely applicable and some of its provisions are considerably different from those in LMRA, its premises and procedures were drawn upon by the framers of the National Labor Relations (Wagner) Act of 1935, upon which the Act of 1947 subsequently was based. The student is encouraged to study the provisions of the Railway Labor Act, as well as a history of labor laws in the railroad industries that led to the passage of the Railway Labor Act of 1926.

United States.[2] The LMRA is an extremely complex document in and of itself. Of even greater complexity, however, is the body of administrative laws and decisions that has evolved over the years in hundreds of thousands of union-management cases. The Act is constantly being tested, evaluated, and reevaluated by the NLRB, the courts, and by the Congress of the United States in the light of changing times, new confrontations, and new decisions. It is not the purpose of this section to completely interpret the Act or to present it in its entirety. Rather, selected parts of the Act will be discussed to underscore the major elements of the Act governing the collective bargaining process. An understanding of these parts of the Act should provide sufficient insights on which analysis of various aspects of specific union-management cases may be based.

Excerpts and Comments on the Text of the Labor Management Relations Act, 1947, as Amended

Section 1. The Statement of Findings and Policy

The LMRA begins with a statement to the effect that industrial strife interferes with the normal flow of commerce. The purpose of the Act is to promote the full flow of commerce by prescribing and protecting rights of employers and employees and by providing orderly and peaceful procedures for preventing interference by either with the legitimate rights of the other.

---

[2]A major component of public sector labor relations is at the federal government employee level. Executive Order 10988, originally signed by President Kennedy in 1962, was replaced by Executive Order 11491, issued by President Nixon in 1970. (Executive Orders 11616 and 11636 issued by President Nixon in 1971, and Executive Order 11838, issued by President Ford in 1975, amended Executive Order 11491.) These orders provided federal employees with union representation and collective bargaining rights. Subsequently, in 1978, Title VII of the Civil Service Reform Act replaced these Executive Orders and consolidated into law provisions for civilian federal government employees to govern collective bargaining in the federal sector. Title VII of the Civil Service Reform Act (Public Law 95–454) closely parallels the LMRA in many fundamental areas, with many of its provisions similar to various provisions in LMRA governing union-management relations in the private sector. Federal government employees do not have the right to strike or to have a "union shop," and a number of key areas remain outside the scope of bargaining in the federal sector. For example, general compensation levels, benefit entitlements, and certain general conditions of employment are largely determined by congressional legislation; many areas of employee concern are handled under federal and civil service regulations. The Civil Service Reform Act created a new administrative agency, the Federal Labor Relations Authority (FLRA), whose functions are similar to those of the National Labor Relations Board (NLRB). Some cases decided in the federal sector have drawn for precedent and policy from· decisions of the NLRB in the private sector. Included in the bibliography at the end of this introductory section are a number of sources to consult for public sector bargaining law, cases, and decisions.

The U.S. Postal Service was brought under partial coverage of the LMRA through enactment of the Postal Reorganization Act of 1970 (Public Law 91–375). This law granted the NLRB jurisdiction over the U.S. Postal Service for various aspects of bargaining unit determination, unfair labor practices, and related matters. The Postal Reorganization Act contains provisions for negotiation of collective bargaining agreements between the Postal Service and labor organization bargaining representatives. These provisions include a procedure for mediation and even binding arbitration of disputes when the parties are unable to reach a negotiated agreement.

This statement of public policy also points out that the labor law of the land is designed to regulate both unions and employers in the public interest. The Act encourages employees to exercise their right to organize labor unions and to bargain collectively with their employers as a means of balancing bargaining power. At the same time, the Act encourages union and employer practices that are fundamental to the friendly adjustment of industrial disputes, with the objective of eliminating some union and employer practices that impair the public interest by contributing to industrial unrest and strikes.

The NLRB, which is the federal agency administering the Act, has consistently interpreted this section to mean that the public policy of the United States is to promote and encourage the principle of unionism.

Section 2. Definitions

This section of the Act defines various terms used in the statement of the Act, and also outlines the coverage of the Act. By its terms, the Act does not apply to employees in a business or industry where a labor dispute would not affect interstate commerce. In addition, the Act specifically states that it does not apply to the following:

Agricultural laborers.

Domestic servants.

Any individual employed by one's parent or spouse.

Government employees, including those of government corporations or the Federal Reserve Bank, or any political subdivision such as a state or a school district.[3]

Independent contractors who depend upon profits, rather than commissions or wages, for their income.

Individuals employed by an employer subject to provisions of the Railway Labor Act.

Supervisors are excluded from the definition of employees covered by the Act. Whether or not a person is a supervisor is determined by authority rather than by title. The authority required to exclude an employee from coverage of the Act as a supervisor is defined in Section 2(11) of the Act.

---

[3]About half the states have laws—which vary widely in scope and coverage—to provide collective bargaining rights and procedures for state and local government employees, including teachers and employees of government-operated health care facilities. For example, in 1984 the state of Illinois enacted a comprehensive labor relations law for its public employees, which contains many provisions that are comparable to provisions within Title VII of the Civil Service Reform Act for federal employees.

The following sources are recommended for a review of legislation governing collective bargaining for state, local, and municipal government employees: Marvin J. Levine, *Labor Relations in the Public Sector: Readings and Cases,* 2nd ed. (Columbus, Ohio: Grid, 1985); Michael T. Leibig and Wendy L. Kahn, *Public Employee Organizing and the Law* (Washington, D.C.: Bureau of National Affairs, 1987); and Benjamin Aaron, Joyce Najita, and James L. Stern, *Public Sector Bargaining,* 2nd ed. (Washington, D.C.: Bureau of National Affairs, 1988).

All employees properly classified as "managerial," not just those in positions susceptible to conflicts of interest in labor relations, are excluded from the protection of the Act. This was the thrust of a decision of the Supreme Court in 1974.

The 1974 amendments to LMRA (Public Law 93–360) brought all private health care institutions, whether or not operated for a profit, under the coverage of the Act. Section 2(14) defines a private health care institution as "any hospital, convalescent hospital, health maintenance organization, health clinic, nursing home, extended care facility, or other institution devoted to the care of sick, infirm, or aged person."

An *employer* is defined in the law as including "any person acting as an agent of an employer, directly or indirectly." A *person* is defined to include "one or more individuals, labor organizations, partnerships, associations, legal representatives, trustees, trustees in bankruptcy, or receivers."

The term *labor organization* means any organization, agency, or employee representation committee or plan in which employees participate and that exists for the purpose, in whole or in part, of dealing with employers concerning grievances, labor disputes, wages, rate of pay, hours of employment, or conditions of work.

Section 2(12) defines the meaning of the term *professional employee,* for which specific organizational rights are guaranteed in a later section.

Sections 3, 4, 5, 6. The National Labor Relations Board

Section 3 creates the NLRB as an independent agency to administer the Act. The NLRB consists of five members appointed by the President of the United States.

Section 3 also authorizes the appointment of a General Counsel of the Board, who is given supervisory authority over the Board attorneys and officers and employees in the regional offices of the Board.

Sections 4 and 5 outline certain compensation, procedural, and administrative authorities granted to the NLRB by the Congress.

However, the key section is Section 6, which gives the Board authority to establish rules and regulations necessary to carry out provisions of the LMRA. In effect, this section empowers the NLRB to administer and interpret the labor law as it deems appropriate to the case situations encountered.

In order to do this, the Board has developed various standards—for the most part, dollar sales or volume standards—by which it determines whether or not a business or some other form of enterprise is deemed to be interstate commerce and thus covered under the provisions of the Act.[4] The Board has developed detailed rules, policies, and

---

[4]For example, the NLRB has used a standard of $500,000 total annual volume of business to determine whether a *retail enterprise* should be considered interstate. For *nonretail businesses* the Board uses two tests: *(a)* direct sales to consumers in other states or indirect sales through others, called outflow, of at least $50,000 a year; or *(b)* direct purchases of goods from suppliers from other states or indirect purchases through others, called inflow, of at least $50,000 a year.

Among the NLRB jurisdictional standards in effect at the time of writing this text are the following:

Office buildings: Total annual revenue of $100,000, of which $25,000 or more is derived from organizations that meet any of the standards except the indirect outflow and indirect inflow standards established for nonretail enterprises.

procedures by which it determines appropriate collective bargaining units, holds representational elections, investigates labor disputes, and conducts other such matters. The NLRB by its policies and rulings in effect can and does reshape the Act, subject to review of the federal courts. The Appendix to this introductory section will provide an overview of the operations of the NLRB and the magnitude of those operations.

Public utilities: At least $250,000 total annual volume of business, or $50,000 direct or indirect outflow or inflow.

Newspapers: At least $200,000 total annual volume of business.

Radio, telegraph, television, and telephone enterprises: At least $100,000 total annual volume of business.

Hotels, motels, and residential apartment houses: At least $500,000 total annual volume of business.

Transit systems: At least $250,000 total annual volume of business.

Taxicab companies: At least $500,000 total annual volume of business.

Law firms and legal assistance programs: At least $250,000 gross annual revenues.

Employers that provide social services: At least $250,000 gross annual revenues.

Privately operated health care institutions: At least $250,000 total annual volume of business for hospitals; at least $100,000 for nursing homes, visiting nurses' associations, and related facilities; and at least $250,000 for all other types of private health care institutions defined in the 1974 amendments to the Act.

Associations: These are regarded as a single employer in that the annual business of all association members is totaled to determine whether any of the standards apply.

Enterprises in the territories and the District of Columbia: The jurisdictional standards apply in the territories; all businesses in the District of Columbia come under NLRB jurisdiction.

National defense: Jurisdiction is asserted over all enterprises affecting commerce when their operations have a substantial impact on national defense, whether or not the enterprises satisfy any other standard.

Private universities and colleges: At least $1 million gross annual revenue from all sources (excluding contributions not available for operating expenses because of limitations imposed by the grantor).

Symphony orchestras: At least $1 million gross annual revenue from all sources (excluding contributions not available for operating expenses because of limitations imposed by the grantor).

Ordinarily, if an enterprise does the total annual volume of business listed in the standard, it will necessarily be engaged in activities that "affect" commerce. The Board must find, however, based on evidence, that the enterprise does in fact affect commerce.

The Board has established the policy that if an employer whose operations affect commerce refuses to supply the Board with information concerning total annual business, and so on, the Board may dispense with this requirement and exercise jurisdiction.

Section 14(c) (1) authorizes the Board, in its discretion, to decline to exercise jurisdiction over any class or category of employers where a labor dispute involving such employers is not sufficiently substantial to warrant the exercise of jurisdiction, provided that it cannot refuse to exercise jurisdiction over any labor dispute over which it would have asserted jurisdiction under the standards it had in effect on August 1, 1959.

Finally, the NLRB has adopted other standards and policies that it uses in determining its jurisdiction, depending upon various types of businesses and unique conditions involved. For example, the NLRB asserts jurisdiction over gambling casinos when these enterprises are legally operated and their total annual revenue from gambling is at least $500,000.

Section 7. Rights of Employees

This section is perhaps one of the most significant in the Act. It guarantees employees the right to self-organization; to form, join, or assist labor organizations; to bargain collectively through representatives of their own choosing; and to engage in (or refrain from) certain other concerted activities for the purpose of collective bargaining or other mutual aid or protection.

Examples of employee rights protected by Section 7 are:

Forming or attempting to form a union among the employees of a company.

Joining a union.

Assigning a union to organize the employees of any company.

Going out on strike for the purpose of attempting to obtain improved wages, hours, or other conditions of employment.

Refraining from joining a union (in the absence of a valid union shop agreement).

An individual does not have to be a member of a labor union or involved in promoting a labor union in order to be protected by Section 7. Included in Part I are a number of cases in which individual employees claimed that what their employers had prohibited them from doing were "protected concerted activities."

Unfair Labor Practices: Employers

The unfair labor practices of employers are listed in Section 8(a) of the Act; those of labor organizations in Section 8(b). Section 8(e) lists an unfair labor practice that can be committed only by an employer and a labor organization acting together.

Section 8(a) (1). Employers are forbidden from engaging in practices that would interfere with, restrain, or coerce employees in the exercise of rights guaranteed by Section 7.

Section 8(a) (1) constitutes a broad statement against interference by the employer; employers violate this section whenever they commit any unfair labor practices. Thus, a violation of Section 8(a) (2), (3), (4), or (5) also results in a violation of Section 8(a) (1).

Various acts of an employer may independently violate Section 8(a) (1). Examples of such violations are:

Threatening employees with loss of jobs or benefits if they should join or vote for a union.

Threatening to close down the plant if a union should be organized in it.

Questioning employees about their union activities or membership in such circumstances as will tend to restrain or coerce the employees.

Spying on union gatherings, or pretending to spy.

Granting wage increases deliberately timed to discourage employees from forming or joining a union.

Threatening to terminate credit at the company store or to force employees to move out of company housing if the union wins bargaining rights for the employees.

Circulating antiunion petitions among employees.

Section 8(a) (2). Employers may not dominate or interfere with the formation or administration of any labor organization or contribute financial or other support to it.

In this regard, the Board distinguishes between "domination" of a labor organization and conduct that amounts to little more than illegal "interference." When a union is found to be "dominated" by an employer, the Board will normally order the organization completely disestablished as a representative of employees. But if the organization is found only to have been supported by employer assistance amounting to less than domination, the Board usually orders the employer to stop such support and to withhold recognition from the organization until it has been certified by the Board as a bona fide representative of employees.

In recent years, there has been a growth in various types of labor-management cooperative efforts such as quality circles, quality-of-worklife programs, total quality management, employee involvement groups, labor-management participation teams, and the like. In general, these types of efforts do not of themselves violate Section 8(a) (2), unless it leads to a circumvention of the negotiated labor agreement or some other interference with union or employee rights. At the time of writing of this text, a number of NLRB cases were in various stages of litigation. When finally decided, these cases may further clarify the permissible limits of activities of these forms of labor-management cooperation. Also, legislation was pending in Congress to amend the Labor Management Relations Act, which—if passed—would make workplace cooperative arrangements less likely to be considered violations of the Act.

An employer violates Section 8(a) (2) by engaging in activities such as:

Assisting employees in organizing a union or an employee representation plan by providing financial support, legal counsel, or active encouragement.

Conducting a straw vote to determine whether employees favor an inside union, as opposed to one affiliated with one of the national unions.

Signing a union security contract with an inside union to forestall an organizing drive by an outside union.

Exerting pressure on employees to join a particular union.

Permitting a union to solicit dues checkoff authorizations from new employees as they go through the hiring process.

Permitting one union to solicit employees on company premises, while denying a competing union this same privilege.

Section 8(a) (3). This section prohibits discrimination in hiring or tenure of employment or any term or condition of employment that tends to encourage or discourage membership in any labor organization. This provision, together with Section 8(b) (2), prohibits the closed shop, in which only persons who already hold membership in a labor organization may be hired. It also prohibits discriminatory hiring-hall arrangements by which only persons who have "permits" from a union may be hired. However, a proviso of this section permits an employer and labor union to agree to a union shop, where employees may be required to join a union after 30 days of employment (unless a union shop is prohibited by state law as provided for under Section 14[b] of the Act).

Section 8(a) (3) provides that an employee may be discharged for failing to pay the required union initiation fees and dues uniformly required by the exclusive bargaining representative under a lawful union shop contract. The section provides further, however, that no employer can justify any discriminatory action against an employee for nonmembership in a union if the employer has reason to believe that membership in the union was not open to the employee on the same terms and conditions that apply to others, or that the employee was denied membership in the union for some reason other than failure to pay regular dues and initiation fees.[5]

Some examples of types of discrimination in employment prohibited by Section 8(a) (3) include:

Discharging employees because they urged other employees to join a union.

Refusing to reinstate employees when jobs they are qualified for are open because they took part in a union's lawful strike.

Granting of "superseniority" to those hired to replace employees engaged in a lawful strike.

Demoting employees because they circulated a union petition among other employees asking the employer for an increase in pay.

Discontinuing an operation at one plant and discharging the employees involved, followed by opening the same operation at another plant with new employees, because the employees at the first plant joined a union.

Refusing to hire qualified applicants for jobs because they belong to a union. It would also be a violation if the qualified applicants were refused employment because they did not belong to a union, or because they belonged to one union rather than another.

Section 8(a) (4).   Employers may not discharge or otherwise discriminate against employees because they have filed charges or given testimony under this Act. Examples of violations of this section are:

Refusing to reinstate employees when jobs they are otherwise qualified for are open because they filed charges with the NLRB claiming their layoffs were based on union activity.

Demoting employees because they testified at an NLRB hearing.

Section 8(a) (5).   It is an unfair labor practice for an employer to refuse to bargain collectively with the representatives of the employees. The meaning of "bargaining collectively" is more specifically outlined in Section 8(d) of the Act. Section 8(d) has

---

[5]As a result of a case decided by the U.S. Supreme Court (*Communication Workers of America [CWA]* v. *Beck,* June 29, 1988, 128 LRRM 2729), a nonmember of a union in a union shop bargaining unit who objects to paying a dues equivalent may be required to pay only that portion of the dues fee which is used for the actual and legitimate costs of representational activities of the union (e.g., collective bargaining, contract administration, and grievance adjustment).

been applied and interpreted in many cases, and its provisions are among the most significant requirements of the Act.

Examples of employer violations of Section 8(a) (5) are:

Refusing to meet with representatives of a certified union because employees have threatened to go on strike.

Insisting that the union withdraw its demand for a union shop before the company would enter negotiations over a contract.

Insisting that members of the negotiating committee of the union be composed of employees of the company.

Refusing to discuss with union representatives an increase in the price of coffee served in the company cafeteria.

Announcing a wage increase without consulting the union.

Refusing to supply union negotiators with cost and other data concerning a group insurance plan covering the employees.

Subcontracting certain work to another employer without notifying the union that represents the affected employees and without giving the union an opportunity to bargain concerning the change in working conditions of the employees.

Unfair Labor Practices: Labor Organizations

The 1947 and 1959 amendments to the Act made certain activities of labor unions unfair labor practices.

Section 8(b) (1) (A). A labor organization or its agents are forbidden "to restrain or coerce employees in the exercise of the rights guaranteed in section 7." The section also provides that it is not intended to "impair the rights of a labor organization to prescribe its own rules" concerning membership in the labor organization.[6]

Examples of restraint or coercion that violate Section 8(b) (1) (A) when done by a union or its agents include the following:

Mass picketing in such numbers that nonstriking employees are physically barred from entering the plant.

Committing acts of force or violence on the picket line, or in connection with a strike.

Threatening to do bodily injury to nonstriking employees.

Threatening employees that they will lose their jobs unless they support the union's activities.

Stating to employees who oppose the union that those employees will lose their jobs if the union wins a majority in the plant.

---

[6]The regulation of the internal affairs of labor organizations is covered by the Labor-Management Reporting and Disclosure Act (Landrum-Griffin Act) of 1959; this Act is administered by the U.S. Department of Labor.

Entering into an agreement with an employer that recognizes the union as exclusive bargaining representative when it has not been chosen by a majority of the employees.

Fining or expelling members for crossing a picket line that is unlawful under the Act or which violates a no-strike agreement.

Fining employees for conduct in which they engaged after resigning from the union.

Fining or expelling members for filing unfair labor practice charges with the Board or for participating in an investigation conducted by the Board.

Maintaining a seniority arrangement with an employer under which seniority is based on the employee's prior representation by the union elsewhere.

Refusing to process a grievance in retaliation against an employee's criticism of union officers.

Section 8(b) (1) (B).   A labor organization is prohibited from restraining or coercing an employer in the selection of a bargaining representative. The prohibition applies regardless of whether the labor organization is the majority representative of the employees in the bargaining unit. The prohibition extends to coercion applied by a union to a union member who is a representative of the employer in the adjustment of grievances. This section is violated by such conduct as the following:

Insisting on meeting only with a company's owners and refusing to meet with the attorney the company has engaged to represent it in contract negotiations, and threatening to strike to force the company to accept demands.

Striking against several members of an employer association that had bargained with the union as the representative of the employers and secured the signing of individual contracts by the struck employers.

Insisting during contract negotiations that the employer agree to accept working conditions that will be established by a bargaining group to which it does not belong.

Fining or expelling supervisors for the way they apply the bargaining contract while carrying out their supervisory functions.

Section 8(b) (2).   This section bars a union from causing or attempting to cause an employer to discriminate against an employee in violation of Section 8(a) (3). It also prohibits the union from attempting to cause an employer to discriminate against an employee whose membership in the union had been denied or terminated, except where this action was taken by the union because the employee failed to "tender" the regular initiation fees and/or periodic dues uniformly required as a condition of acquiring or retaining membership in the union, where a union shop agreement is in effect.

Contracts or informal arrangements with a union under which an employer gives preferential treatment to union members are violations of Section 8(b) (2). It is not unlawful for an employer and a union to enter into an agreement whereby the employer agrees to hire new employees exclusively through the union hiring hall so long as there is neither a provision in the agreement nor a practice in effect that discriminates against nonunion members in favor of union members or otherwise discriminates on the basis of union membership obligations. Both the agreement and the actual operation of the hiring hall must be nondiscriminatory; referrals must be made without reference to union membership or irrelevant or arbitrary considerations such as race.

Examples of violations of Section 8(b) (2) are:

Causing an employer to discharge employees because they circulated a petition urging a change in the union's method of selecting shop stewards.

Causing an employer to discharge employees because they made speeches against a contract proposed by the union.

Making a contract that requires an employer to hire only members of the union or employees "satisfactory" to the union.

Causing an employer to reduce employees' seniority because they engaged in antiunion acts.

Refusing referral or giving preference on the basis of race or union activities in making job referrals to units represented by the union.

Seeking the discharge of an employee under a union security agreement for failure to pay a fine levied by the union.

Section 8(b) (3).   This section requires a labor organization to bargain in good faith with an employer about wages, hours, and other conditions of employment if it is the representative of that employer's employees. This section imposes on labor organizations the same duty to bargain in good faith that is imposed on employers by Section 8(a) (5). Both the labor organization and the employer are required to follow the procedures within Section 8(d) before terminating or changing an existing contract.

Section 8(b) (3) not only requires that union representatives bargain in good faith with employers but also requires that the union carry out its bargaining duty fairly with respect to the employees it represents. A union, therefore, violates Section 8(b) (3) if it negotiates a contract that conflicts with that duty, or if it refuses to handle grievances under the contract for irrelevant or arbitrary reasons.

Section 8(b) (3) is violated by any of the following:

Insisting on the inclusion of illegal provisions in a contract, such as a closed shop or a discriminatory hiring hall.

Refusing to negotiate on a proposal for a written contract.

Striking against an employer who has bargained, and continues to bargain, on a multiemployer basis to compel it to bargain separately.

Refusing to meet with the attorney designated by the employer as its representative in negotiations.

Terminating an existing contract and striking for a new one without notifying the employer, the Federal Mediation and Conciliation Service (FMCS), and the state mediation service, if any.

Conditioning the execution of an agreement upon inclusion of a nonmandatory provision such as a performance bond.

Refusing to process a grievance because of the race, sex, or union activities of an employee for whom the union is the statutory bargaining representative.

Section 8(b) (4).   This section forbids secondary boycotts and certain types of strikes and picketing; it is a very complicated section. Secondary boycotts; sympathy strikes or boycotts to force recognition of an uncertified union; a strike to substitute another bargaining representative for one certified by the Board; strikes over so-called union jurisdictional disputes or work assignments; and several other types of unfair acts—all are forbidden under this section.

More specifically, Section 8(b) (4) prohibits a labor organization from engaging in strikes or boycotts or taking other specified actions to accomplish certain purposes or "objects" as they are called in the Act. The actions are listed in clauses (i) and (ii); the objects are described in subparagraphs (A) through (D). A union commits an unfair labor practice if it takes any of the kinds of action listed in clauses (i) and (ii) as a means of accomplishing any of the objects listed in the four subparagraphs.

Clause (i) forbids a union to engage in a strike, or to induce or encourage a strike, work stoppage, or a refusal to perform services by "any individual employed by any person engaged in commerce or in an industry affecting commerce" for one of the objects listed in subparagraphs (A) through (D). Clause (ii) makes it an unfair labor practice for a union to "threaten, coerce, or restrain any person engaged in commerce or in an industry affecting commerce" for any of the proscribed objects.

Section 8(b) (4) (A) prohibits unions from engaging in actions specified in clause (i) or (ii) to compel an employer or self-employed person to join any labor or employer organization, or to force an employer to enter a hot cargo agreement prohibited by Section 8(e).

Section 8(b) (4) (B) contains the Act's secondary boycott prohibitions. A secondary boycott occurs if a union has a dispute with Company A and in furtherance of that dispute causes the employees of Company B to stop handling the products of Company A, or otherwise forces Company B to stop doing business with Company A. The dispute is with Company A, called the primary employer; the union's action is against Company B, called the secondary employer; hence, the term *secondary boycott.* Section 8(b) (4) (B) also prohibits secondary action to compel an employer to recognize or bargain with a union that is not the certified representative of its employees.

The prohibitions of Section 8(b) (4) (B) do not protect a secondary employer from the incidental effects of union action that is taken directly against the primary employer. Thus, it is lawful for a union to urge employees of a secondary supplier at the primary employer's plant not to cross a picket line there. Section 8(b) (4) (B) also does not prohibit union efforts to prevent an employer from contracting out work customarily performed by its employees, even though an incidental effect of such conduct might be to compel that employer to cease doing business with the subcontractor.

When employees of a primary employer and those of a secondary employer work on the same premises, a special situation is involved and the usual rules do not apply. A typical example of the shared site or "common situs" situation is where a subcontractor with whom a union has a dispute is engaged at work on a construction site alongside other subcontractors, with whom the union has no dispute. Picketing at a common situs is permissible if directed solely against the primary employer, but it is prohibited if directed against secondary employers regularly engaged at the site. In some situations a company may set aside, or reserve, a certain plant gate, or entrance to its premises, for the exclusive use of a contractor. If a union has a labor dispute with the company and pickets the company's premises, including the gate so reserved, the union may be held to have violated Section 8(b) (4) (B).

Section 8(b) (4) (C) forbids a labor organization to use clause (i) or (ii) conduct to force an employer to recognize or bargain with a labor organization other than the one that is currently certified as the representative of its employees.

Section 8(b) (4) (D) addresses jurisdictional and work assignment disputes. It forbids a labor organization from engaging in actions described in clauses (i) and (ii) for the purpose of forcing any employer to assign certain work to "employees in a particular labor organization or in a particular trade, craft, or class rather than to employees in another labor organization or in another trade, craft, or class." The Act sets up a special procedure for handling disputes over work assignments under Section 10(k).

A proviso to Section 8(b) (4) makes clear that it is not unlawful for a person to refuse to enter the premises of an employer if the employees of that employer are engaged in a lawful strike ratified or approved by a representative of these employees. Another provision permits informational picketing in various circumstances, so long as such publicity and information picketing does not have the effect of inducing any individual employed by any person other than a primary employer to refuse to pick up, deliver, or transfer goods or to refuse to perform services at the establishment of the employer involved in the dispute.

The following union activities are considered to be unfair labor practices under this section:

Picketing a company after three of its four partners refused to comply with the union's demand that they become members (8[b] [4] [A]).

Picketing or threatening to picket a retail store to compel that employer to enter into an agreement whereby that employer will only use a delivery service firm which has an agreement with the union (8[b] [4] [A]).

Picketing the premises of an employer to compel him to cease doing business with another employer who has refused to recognize the union (8[b] [4] [B]).

Threatening an employer by telling her that her business will be picketed if she continues to do business with another employer whom the union has designated as "unfair" (8[b] [4] [B]).

Directing union members not to pick up and deliver products from a plant where the drivers had voted to be represented by a different union, which had received certification from the NLRB (8[b] [4] [C]).

Engaging in a strike to attempt to force the employer to assign to it the job of installing metal doors when the employer had assigned the work to the members of another union (8[b] [4] [D]).

Section 8(b) (5). A union may not require employees under a union shop agreement to pay an initiation fee which the Board finds excessive or discriminatory. The section states that the Board shall consider in determination of these types of fees the practices and customs of labor organizations in the particular industry and the wages currently paid to employees affected. For example, a local union would probably violate this section by raising its initiation fee from $25 to $500, when other locals of the same union charged from $15 to $100 and the starting rate for the job was $240 per week.

Section 8(b) (6).   This section prohibits what is commonly known as featherbedding. Unions may not force an employer to pay or deliver, or to agree to pay or deliver, any money or thing of value for services that are not performed or not to be performed. This section has been narrowly interpreted by the Board and does not include situations in which the work is performed, although it may be "unnecessary."

Section 8(b) (7).   This provision prohibits a union that has not been certified as the bargaining agent from picketing or threatening to picket an employer for the purpose of obtaining recognition by that employer or acceptance by his workers as their bargaining representative. Both recognitional and organizational picketing constitute unfair labor practices when: the employer has recognized a certified union and a new representation election would be barred under the Act (8[b] [7] [A]); a valid NLRB election has been conducted during the previous 12 months (8[b] [7] [B]); or a representation petition has not been filed with the Board "within a reasonable period of time not to exceed 30 days from the commencement of such picketing." (8[b] [7] [C]).

However, this section does not prohibit picketing for the purpose of truthfully advising the public (including consumers) that the company does not employ union members or have a contract with a union unless the effect of the picketing is to interfere with deliveries, pickups, and other services required by the picketed employer.

Section 8(e).   This complicated provision forbids both labor organizations and employers to enter into agreements commonly known as hot cargo agreements. These are defined as agreements where the employer will not handle, use, sell, transport, or deal in any of the products of another employer as required or forced by the labor organization.

Both the construction and garment industries are exempted from the conditions of this section. In the construction industry the parties may agree to a clause that restricts the contracting or subcontracting of work to be performed at the construction site. Typically, the union and the employer agree that subcontracted work will go to an employer who has a contract with the union. A union may strike, picket, or engage in any other lawful activity in order to obtain such an agreement with the employer. A labor organization in the garment (apparel and clothing) industry may not only strike, picket, or engage in other lawful activity to obtain such an agreement, but it may also engage in such activities in order to enforce it.

Section 8(f).   A union and employer in the construction industry may enter into an agreement whereby employees must join the union not later than 7 days after the date of hire, rather than 30 days, as provided in Section 8(a) (3) for all other employers. The parties may enter into such an agreement without having first established the majority status of the union, as required in Section 9.

Free Speech

Section 8(c).   This section of the Act provides that the expression of any views, argument, or opinion shall not constitute or be evidence of an unfair labor practice "if such expression contains no threat of reprisal or force or promise of benefit."

Examples of actions this provision does not protect, and that would be ruled as unfair labor practices, are:

An implied threat by an employer that the organization of a union would result in the loss of certain benefits for employees.

A threat by an employer to close down a plant to move to another location, in the event of a union's winning an election.

A statement by a management official to an employee that the employee will lose her job if the union wins a majority in the plant.

A promise by management that benefits will be improved if a union does not win the representational election.

The Meaning of Collective Bargaining

Section 8(d). This section defines collective bargaining as required of both parties by the Act. This definition imposes a mutual obligation upon the employer and the representative of the employees

to meet at reasonable times and confer in good faith with respect to wages, hours, and other terms and conditions of employment or the negotiation of an agreement or any question arising thereunder and the execution of a written contract incorporating any agreement reached if requested by either party, but such obligation does not compel either party to agree to a proposal or require the making of a concession.

The duty to bargain thus covers all matters concerning rates of pay, hours of employment, or other conditions of employment. These are called mandatory subjects about which the employer, as well as the employees' representative, must bargain in good faith, although the law does not require "either party to agree to a proposal or require the making of a concession." As determined by the NLRB, mandatory subjects of bargaining include but are not limited to such matters as pensions for present and retired employees, bonuses, group insurance, grievance procedure, safety practices, seniority, procedures for discharge, layoff, recall, or discipline, and the union shop. On nonmandatory subjects, that is, matters that are lawful but not related to "wages, hours, and other conditions of employment," the parties are free to bargain and to agree, but neither party may insist on bargaining on such subjects over the objection of the other party.

Section 8(d) also requires that the parties to a collective agreement follow certain steps in terminating or modifying the agreement. Among these requirements are that the party wishing to terminate or modify a labor contract must notify the other party to the contract in writing about the proposed termination or modification 60 days before the date on which the contract is scheduled to expire. This party also must, within 30 days after the notice to the other party, notify the Federal Mediation and Conciliation Service (FMCS) of the existence of a dispute if no agreement has been reached by that time, and further notify at the same time any state or territorial mediation or conciliation agency in the state or territory where the dispute occurred.[7]

---

[7]Procedures of the FMCS are described in Appendix B to this introductory section.

The NLRB has interpreted this section to mean that union employees who go on strike without following the prescribed steps for terminating or modifying the contract lose protection of the law. They may not be reinstated by the Board if the employer discharges them.

Representatives and Elections

Section 9 of the Act is a lengthy section that governs the procedural and legal requirements for the designation of representatives and election of union representatives. It provides for three types of elections among employees:[8]

Representation elections to determine the employees' choice of a collective bargaining agent. These are held upon petition of an individual, employer, employees, or a labor organization. Typically, the NLRB will not hold an election unless the petitioner can show that at least 30 percent of the employees involved have indicated their support for the union, or for an election.

Decertification elections to determine whether or not the employees wish to withdraw the bargaining authority of the union. These are held upon the petition of the employees or a labor organization.

Deauthorization polls to determine whether or not the employees wish to revoke the authority of their union to enter into a union shop contract.

Section 9(a).   This section provides that the union representative designated by a majority of employees appropriate for collective bargaining becomes the exclusive representative of the employees in bargaining. When a union majority representative has been chosen, it becomes unlawful for an employer to bargain with anyone else.

Sections 9(b) and 9(c).   These sections outline in general terms the "rules of the game" for the holding of NLRB elections. Included in 9(b) is the mandate for the Board to decide what group of employees constitutes an appropriate unit for bargaining. The appropriate bargaining unit may extend to one or more employers, to one or more plants of the same employer, or it may be a subdivision of a plantwide unit such as a unit of skilled craftsmen. It is up to the Board to consider similarities of skills, wages, and working conditions; the history of collective bargaining in the company; the wishes of the employees; and any other factors that the Board may consider important in determination of the appropriate unit. Thus, employees who possess common employment interests concerning wages, hours, and conditions of employment usually are grouped together in a bargaining unit. However, Section 9(b) specifically limits the Board in its determination of a bargaining unit in several ways. It may not include professional and nonprofessional employees in the same unit, unless a majority of the professional employees votes to be included in the unit. It also prohibits the Board from including plant guards in the same unit with other employees, and from certifying a

---

[8]The Board also conducts "expedited elections" in connection with Section 8(b) (7) (C) and employer last-offer elections in connection with Section 209 of the Act.

union of guards if it also includes members who are not guards. The Board also may not use "the extent to which employees have organized" as the controlling factor in deciding the appropriate bargaining unit (Section 9[c] [5]).

Section 9(c) (1) authorizes the NLRB to direct an election and certify the results thereof, provided the record shows that a question of representation exists.

An election may be held by agreement between the employer and the individual or labor organization claiming to represent the employees. In such an agreement the parties state the time and place agreed on, the choices to be included on the ballot, and a method to determine who is eligible to vote. They also authorize the NLRB Regional Director to conduct the election.

If the parties are unable to reach an agreement, the Act authorizes the NLRB to order an election after a hearing. The Act also authorizes the Board to delegate to its Regional Directors the determination on matters concerning elections. Under this delegation of authority the Regional Directors can determine the appropriateness of the unit, direct an election, and certify the outcome. Upon the request of an interested party, the Board may review the action of a Regional Director, but such review does not stop the election process unless the Board so orders. The election details are left to the Regional Director. Such matters as who may vote, when the election will be held, and what standards of conduct will be imposed on the parties are decided in accordance with the Board's rules and its decisions.

Section 9(c) (3) prohibits the holding of an election in any collective bargaining unit or subdivision thereof in which a valid election has been held during the preceding 12-month period.

In summary, Section 9 is one of the key sections that constantly confront both unions and management in collective bargaining relationships, particularly in the formative stages of a labor union in its efforts to gain representational status.

Special Provisions for Health Care Institutions

Representation election procedures are the same for health care facilities as for other establishments.[9, 10] Similarly, as to unfair labor practices, the health care area is covered by the same statutory provisions as those that forbid employer or union discrimination

---

[9]In 1975, the NLRB issued its first guidelines for representational units in private health care institutions. In a series of cases—217 NLRB 131–138—these guidelines limited the number of bargaining units to avoid "proliferation" of units in health care organizations. In 1984, the NLRB ruled that it was no longer going to be held to a "community of interest" standard and would begin using a "disparity of interest" standard in health care bargaining unit determination. (See decision of the NLRB, St. Francis Hospital and IBEW Local 474, 271 NLRB No. 160.) However, in 1988, the NLRB developed and proposed new bargaining unit guidelines for acute-care hospitals. Up to eight bargaining units would be considered "appropriate" under the new rules. These are registered nurses; physicians; other professionals; technicians; skilled maintenance employees; office clerical employees; guards; and all other nonprofessional employees. In 1991, the U.S. Supreme Court upheld the NLRB's regulations recognizing up to eight categories of employee bargaining units in hospitals. Further, the Court affirmed the NLRB's authority to "engage in substantive rulemaking."

[10]In a 1994 decision of the U.S. Supreme Court (*NLRB* v. *Health Care and Retirement Corporation of America*), the Court held that one of the NLRB's previous tests for determining whether or not nurses

against employees, failure to bargain in good faith, certain unlawful union picketing, and employer domination or support of a labor organization.

But with a goal of minimizing work stoppages at health care institutions and providing continuity of patient care, Congress in 1974 wrote into the Act another unfair labor practice—*Section 8(g)*. It prohibits a labor organization from striking or picketing a health care institution, or engaging in any other concerted refusal to work, without first giving the employer and FMCS a 10-day notice of such action. The section specifies, "The notice shall state the date and time that such action will commence. The notice, once given, may be extended by the written agreement of both parties."

Additionally, a series of special provisions for the health care industry were added to Section 8(d) of the Act. These health care amendments call for special dispute-settling procedures. A 90-day written notice must be served by employer or union of intent to terminate or modify a collective bargaining contract (30 days more than required by the Act elsewhere). If the dispute continues, the FMCS and similar state agencies must be notified at the 60-day point. If a dispute arises in bargaining for an initial contract, 30 days' notice must be given by the union to the employer, FMCS, and the appropriate agency. In either a contract termination-modification or initial contract dispute, under Section 213 of the Act, the FMCS may, if disagreement continues, invoke a 30-day no-strike, no-lockout period and set up a fact-finding board to make settlement recommendations, while continuing its mediation-conciliation efforts.

All else failing, the 10-day strike or picketing notice must be given as required by Section 8(g).

Prevention of Unfair Labor Practices

Section 10 is very important, in that it outlines the procedural requirements and limitations that are placed upon the Board and interested parties in processing unfair labor practice cases. The LMRA is not a criminal statute. The NLRB's actions are designed to stop unfair labor practices and to restore situations to their "original states"—those that prevailed before the violations occurred—insofar as possible. The orders of the Board serve basically to remedy the situation, not to punish persons who may have violated its provisions. The NLRB is authorized by Section 10(c) not only to issue a cease-and-desist order but "to take such affirmative action, including reinstatement of employees with or without back pay, as will effectuate the policies of this Act."

Sections 10(a), 10(b), 10(c), 10(d). These sections of the Act outline the general procedures by which the NLRB and its regional offices investigate, attempt to prevent, and/or remedy unfair labor practices. Generally, an unfair labor practice charge must be

---

were supervisors was inconsistent with the LMRA. The Court held that concerning nurses, the Board had improperly interpreted and applied the meaning of the phrase "in the interest of the employer" within Section 2(11) of the Act to exclude nurses from supervisory status. Although the ultimate impact of this decision is not clear, at this writing it would appear that the NLRB will be required to adopt case-by-case tests and analyses of nurses' duties in order to determine whether certain nurses are properly classified as "professional employees" or "supervisors."

filed with an office of the NLRB within six months of the date of the occurrence of the alleged unfair labor practice. (As of 1994, about 50 regional and other field offices of the NLRB were located in major cities in various sections of the country.) When a charge is received in the office of the Board, an agent will investigate to see whether formal proceedings are warranted.[11] If the regional office of the NLRB is unable to resolve the issue, and the complaint warrants a full hearing, an Administrative Law Judge (ALJ) from the Board's independent Division of Judges may be assigned to conduct a full, formal hearing to take testimony and examine the evidence. If the opinion of the ALJ is that the evidence presented is not sufficient to justify a finding that an unfair labor practice has been committed, the ALJ will issue an order dismissing the complaint. However, if the ALJ is of the opinion that an unfair labor practice(s) has occurred, he or she will make an appropriate finding and issue a remedial order. In effect, the findings and orders of the ALJ become recommendations to the NLRB. If there is no appeal of the ALJ's decision, the decision and remedial order (if any) of the ALJ become the decision and the order of the Board. If the case is appealed, the NLRB itself will review the determination made by the ALJ and either reverse, modify, or affirm the decision and order of the ALJ.

A remedial order issued by the NLRB usually will require the person, union, or company involved to cease and desist from the unfair labor practice(s) and to take affirmative action designed to remedy the effects of the unfair labor practice(s). Since the LMRA is not intended to designate criminal penalties, these orders will be designed to restore equity to the situation on the assumption that such equity is necessary to guarantee rights protected under the Act. Examples of affirmative actions required of employers are:

Disestablishing a union dominated by the employer.

Offering to hire employees denied employment because of their prounion attitudes or activities.

Offering to reemploy workers who were discharged for union activity; reimburse the employees for all lost wages, including interest; and restore full seniority and all other rights, including promotions, pay increases, pension privileges, and vacation rights that would have been received had the discriminatory discharges not occurred.

Upon request, bargaining collectively with a union as the exclusive representative of the employees in a certain described unit and signing a written agreement if an understanding is reached.

Examples of affirmative actions required of unions are:

Notification to the employee and the employer that the union does not object to the reinstatement or employment of certain persons who were discharged or denied employment as a result of certain discriminatory actions by the union.

---

[11]In the event that the regional office refuses to issue a formal complaint, the person(s) who filed the charge may appeal this decision to the General Counsel of the NLRB, who has final authority to determine whether to issue a formal complaint (Section 3[d]).

Ordering the union to refund dues and fees illegally collected, including interest. Directing the union to bargain collectively with a certain employer and sign a written agreement if an agreement is negotiated.

Sections 10(e) and 10(f).   These sections provide the legal avenues for the enforcement of Board orders and for appeal for relief from Board orders by an employer or union who believes that an order has been issued in error. Normally, the first appeal from an order of the regional office or ALJ will go to the full NLRB itself in Washington, D.C. The NLRB, in order to seek enforcement of its orders, may petition a federal district court or circuit court of appeals for appropriate relief or restraining order. Appeals from a Board or district court order may be made to a federal appeals court, and ultimate appeal can be made to the U.S. Supreme Court. The large majority of cases, however, are not appealed to the federal courts but are decided at Board regional office and/or national NLRB levels.[12]

Section 10(k).   Special procedures for hearing and adjudicating jurisdictional disputes are provided for in this section.

Section 10(l).   This section provides for special priority procedures, including court injunctions, so as to stop quickly certain acts, strikes, and boycotts that may result in "irreparable harm" to the employer. For the most part, these are directed against secondary boycotts and certain types of organizational picketing.

Miscellaneous Provisions

The remainder of the LMRA, although quite extensive in length, is not nearly so important to the duty to bargain collectively as are the provisions discussed to this point. Only brief mention will be made of the more salient miscellaneous provisions covered in the remaining sections that have not been mentioned previously.

Sections 11 and 12—Investigatory Powers and Penalties.   As the title suggests, Sections 11 and 12 outline the legal powers of investigation given the NLRB by the Congress and provide for penalties under the Act.

Sections 13 to 18—Limitations.   Sections 13 through 18 state a series of limitations that the Act is not to be construed as interfering with or diminishing. Except where specifically provided for in the Act, Section 13 guarantees that the right to strike is still a right not to be diminished by the LMRA. Section 14(a) permits supervisors to be

---

[12]Statistically over the years, about 65 percent of the unfair labor practice charges filed with the NLRB are dismissed by the regional offices of the Board or withdrawn by the parties. Of the remainder, over 90 percent usually are settled at the regional office level. Of the cases which are tried by an ALJ, about two thirds are appealed to the full NLRB. Some 20 to 30 percent of Board decisions are appealed to Courts of Appeal; typically the NLRB is sustained in whole or part in over 80 percent of these cases. Only a few cases are reviewed by the Supreme Court, usually some five or fewer annually. Of the unfair labor practice complaints issued by the NLRB's General Counsel, about four-fifths are charges against employers.

members of a labor organization, but states that employers are not required to bargain with supervisors as part of labor organizations. Section 14(b) permits so-called right-to-work laws in states where these laws are enacted. Specifically, Section 14(b) allows states to ban union shop contracts if they so choose. In 1985, Idaho became the 21st state to have a right-to-work law on its statute books. The majority of right-to-work states are located in the southern part of the United States.

Section 19. As amended in legislation passed in 1980, this section provides that any employee who has conscientious objections to joining or financially supporting a labor organization, based on the traditional tenets of a bona fide religion or sect, shall not be required to do so. However, such an employee may be required to make charitable contributions in an amount equal to union dues and initiation fees, and may be required to pay the costs incurred by the union of any requested grievance-arbitration procedure instituted on his/her behalf.[13]

The language in this section defining conscientious objection is not to be construed in such a way as to discriminate among religions or to favor any religious views.

Sections 201 through 205. These sections created and outline the functions of the FMCS and also a National Labor Relations Panel to advise the President on problems of industrial relations. The National Labor Relations Panel, consisting of representatives of management, labor, and the public, has been of limited influence in recent years.

Sections 206 through 210. The national emergency strike provisions, giving the President power to intervene in those types of disputes that the President deems to be a national emergency, are outlined in these sections. These provisions have not been invoked since the late-1970s.

Section 301. This section provides that suits for violation of contracts between an employer and a union may be brought in the federal district courts. Unions are made responsible for the acts of their agents; however, money judgments assessed against a labor organization in a district court are enforceable only against the organization as an entity and not against individual members per se.

Section 303. Strikes and boycotts enumerated in and which violate Section 8(b) (4) are made illegal, as well as being unfair labor practices. Employers may sue to collect damages for injury resulting from such activities.

---

[13]Section 19 was added to the Act in the 1974 amendments for health care institutions, but without the grievance-arbitration proviso. In a case decided in 1990 by the U.S. Court of Appeals for the Sixth Circuit (Cincinnati), that Court held that Section 19 "facially discriminated" among religions in violation of the First Amendment of the U.S. Constitution, "because it exempts from union membership only those employees who are members of bona fide religious organizations having the beliefs described in the statute." Thus Section 19 created "a denominational preference by conferring a benefit on members of the religious organizations described in the statute." According to this Court, when a law differentiates among religions, it "must be invalidated." At the time of writing of this text, it was not clear whether the U.S. Supreme Court would review this case on appeal (or another similar case) to decide upon the constitutional validity of Section 19 of LMRA.

Summary

The remaining provisions of the Act are relatively minor but should be studied by the student of labor relations. Certainly, the complexity of the LMRA will be impressed upon the student by study and application of case situations. Only by extensive analysis of labor-management cases can the student come to understand and appreciate the intent and effectiveness of the Act and its purpose to govern the duty to bargain collectively.

APPENDIX A

EDITED AND UPDATED EXCERPTS FROM THE INFORMATIONAL PAMPHLET, *THE NLRB—WHAT IT IS, WHAT IT DOES**

In recent fiscal years, the NLRB has received annually about 40,000 cases of all kinds. Over three-fourths are unfair labor practice charges. Over the years, charges filed against employers have outnumbered those filed against unions by about 2 to 1. Charges are filed by individual workers, employers, and unions.

What Is the Structure of the NLRB?   The NLRB has five Board Members and a General Counsel, each appointed by the President with Senate consent. The Board Members are appointed to five-year terms, the term of one Member expiring each year. The statute specifies that the President shall designate one Member to serve as Chairman of the Board. The General Counsel is appointed to a four-year term. Reappointments may be made.

Headquartered in Washington, the NLRB has 33 Regional Offices, 2 Subregional Offices, and 17 Resident or smaller field offices throughout the country.

The NLRB's judicial functions are by law separate from its prosecuting functions. The five-member Board acts primarily as a quasi-judicial body in deciding cases upon formal records, generally upon review from Regional Directors' or Administrative Law Judges' decisions. The General Counsel is responsible for the investigation and prosecution of charges of violations of the Act, and he has general supervision of the Regional Offices.

Who Enforces Board Orders?   The NLRB has no statutory independent power of enforcement of its orders, but it may seek enforcement in the U.S. Courts of Appeals. Similarly, parties aggrieved by its orders may seek judicial review in the courts.

Annually, the U.S. Courts of Appeals hand down some 200 decisions related to enforcement and/or review of Board orders in unfair labor practice proceedings. Of these, about 85 percent affirm the Board in whole or in part.

How Do NLRB Procedures Work?   Upon the filing of an unfair labor practice charge with an NLRB Regional Office, members of the professional staff of that office investigate circumstances from which the charge arises, in order to determine whether formal proceedings are

---

*Published by the NLRB, Washington, D.C.

warranted. Approximately one-third of the unfair labor practice allegations are found, after investigation, to require legal disposition. In such a case, the Regional Office works with the parties in an attempt to achieve a voluntary settlement adequate to remedy the alleged violation. A very substantial number of cases are settled at this stage. If a case cannot be settled, then a formal complaint is issued, and the case is heard before an Administrative Law Judge.

NLRB Administrative Law Judges conduct formal hearings and issue decisions, which may be appealed to the five-member Board; if they are not appealed, the Administrative Law Judges' recommended orders become orders of the Board.

The NLRB's traditional emphasis on voluntary disposition of cases at all stages means that less than 5 percent of the unfair labor practice charges and other cases originally filed with the Regional Offices are litigated all the way through to a decision of the Board. Yet, despite the small percentage, the Board is still called to decide on the order of 1,100 unfair labor practice cases and 600 representation cases each year.

In representation election cases, the Regional Directors have the authority to process all petitions, rule on contested issues, and direct elections or dismiss the requests, subject to review by the Board on limited grounds. The NLRB, through its Regional Offices, conducts thousands of representation elections a year, in which hundreds of thousands of employees exercise their free choice by secret ballot.

NATIONAL LABOR RELATIONS BOARD—STATISTICAL INFORMATION FOR FISCAL YEAR 1993†

The following statistics reflect the work of the various NLRB divisions during the 1993 fiscal year and are based on actions taken during that year and previous years.

Fiscal year 1993 saw an intake of 40,281 cases—a number close to that docketed during several previous years, although considerably smaller than the NLRB caseloads during the late 1970s and early 1980s, which were 50,000 or more cases annually. During FY93, the intake of unfair labor practices cases was 33,712, a somewhat lower number than for several previous years. There were 6,132 representation petitions filed in FY93, a figure somewhat higher than for several recent years.

The Board's Regional Offices conducted 3,586 initial representational elections during fiscal year 1993. Some 230,000 employees were eligible to vote in these elections. Unions won 48 percent of these elections, a percentage similar to that during most of the 1980s but considerably lower than the 55 percent or so during most of the 1970s. During FY93, the Board conducted about 530 decertification elections. Unions were decertified in about 70 percent of these elections, about the same percentage as in several previous years.

As remedies, the amount paid to employees as back pay in FY93 was about $46 million; just under 2,000 employees were offered reinstatment. The amount paid to employees in FY1993 as reimbursement for fees, dues, and fines was about $1,280,000.

---

†These statistics were provided in a memorandum from the Office of the General Counsel of the NLRB dated November 18, 1994. These statistics were defined as being "preliminary" and could change very slightly in the final official data report.

APPENDIX B
THE FEDERAL MEDIATION AND CONCILIATION SERVICE (FMCS)*

Federal Mediation and Conciliation Service Mission

Promoting the development of sound and stable labor-management relations.

Preventing or minimizing work stoppages by assisting labor and management to settle their disputes through mediation.

Advocating collective bargaining, mediation, and voluntary arbitration as the preferred processes for settling issues between employers and representatives of employees.

Developing the art, science, and practice of dispute resolution.

And fostering contructive joint relationships of labor and management leaders to increase their mutual understanding and ability to resolve common problems.

The Federal Mediation and Conciliation Service (FMCS) is an independent agency of the Federal Government that uses mediation and other techniques to promote labor-management peace. Since we're a government agency our services are offered without charge.

Our specific mission is to prevent or minimize labor-management disputes having a significant impact on interstate commerce or national defense throughout the nation, both in the private and public sectors of the economy, excepting in the railroad and airline industries.

The Service was created by the Labor-Management Relations Act of 1947 (LMRA—The Taft-Hartley Act). Mediation is an established process for resolving disputes between individuals or groups who sincerely seek a peaceful solution to their differences. It represents a rational alternative to the use of force.

The mediator is a neutral third party whose method and practice may vary. A mediator will listen, review, analyze, reason, explore, and suggest possible solutions to the problems that face representatives of both management and labor.

Collective bargaining is an indispensable ingredient of a free industrial society. Mediation is a time-tested and productive tool that helps preserve and strengthen our collective bargaining system.

What Is the Federal Mediation and Conciliation Service?   The Federal Mediation and Conciliation Service is an independent agency of the Federal Government created by Congress with a director appointed by the President. Its primary duty is to promote labor-management peace.

This responsibility is fulfilled by providing mediation assistance in preventing and settling collective bargaining controversies. For this purpose Federal mediators, known as commissioners, are stationed strategically throughout the country.

The Labor Management Relations Act requires that parties to a labor contract must file a dispute notice if agreement is not reached 30 days—60 days in the health care industry—in advance of a contract termination or reopening date. The notice must be filed with the FMCS and the appropriate state or local mediation agency.

---

*Appendix B consists of adapted excerpts (some updated) from publications of the FMCS, Washington D.C. Appendix C at the end of the Part II introductory section will include additional FMCS material concerning preventive and grievance mediation and alternative dispute resolution.

The notice alerts the service to possible bargaining trouble. If the case falls within the jurisdiction of the service, the regional office then assigns a mediator to check with the employer and union involved to see whether assistance is required.

It is a tribute to the nation's free collective bargaining system that in the overwhelming majority of cases in which notices are filed, the employers and unions reach agreements on their own without requiring mediation aid. Yet in those cases where third-party assistance is needed, it makes good sense to call in the mediator.

Who Are the Mediators?   Mediators are carefully selected and trained. About equal numbers have backgrounds with management and with labor, and many have had some experience with both.

Mediators are picked for the job because of their knowledge and demonstrated skill in collective bargaining. Regardless of background, they are required to maintain strict objectivity as representatives of the public interest.

How Does the Mediator Work?   While methods and circumstances vary, the mediator generally will confer first with one of the parties involved and then with the other to get their versions of the pending difficulties. Then with these problems firmly in mind, the mediator usually will call joint conferences with the employer and union representatives.

Mediators function informally, meeting separately and jointly with the parties to help them find some mutually acceptable solutions.

It is part of the job to listen, review, analyze, suggest, advise, reason, and explore all possible means of reaching an agreement.

The mediator can restart stalled negotiations, improve the bargaining atmosphere, encourage mutual discussions, explore alternative solutions, suggest specific contract clauses that have worked well elsewhere, and provide needed economic data and other information.

A mediator can help bring reason and a fresh viewpoint to the dilemma, and often points the way to a solution. In fact, some 95 percent of disputes receiving active mediation assistance are settled peacefully—without a strike. These are pretty good odds that mediation is a course worth trying.

Even when there is no stalemate or imminent deadline—but mounting difficulties clearly signal real trouble ahead—the mediator can be helpful. The mediator's training and skill often can spot difficulties early and help develop a remedy.

Mediation is a free and voluntary process. It can be requested by either party to a dispute, or the mediator may volunteer to help. There is no cost to either side, and mediation is available not only to private industry but also in public employment and other situations.

The mediator works hard to promote cooperation and understanding between management and labor not only during contract disputes but at other times as well in order to improve day-to-day relations in the workplace.

Through the use of FMCS technical services, unions and employers, with the assistance of the mediator, can improve the labor-management climate. The mediator can give advisory assistance on specific problems and encourage the use of joint labor-management committees. A skilled mediator can provide training and information to improve the knowledge and skill of both parties, can identify trends and developments, can encourage early bargaining to forestall deadline tensions, and will respond to the various needs of labor and management, including government employers and labor organizations, to improve their bargaining relationships.

In addition, the service helps employers and unions in selecting arbitrators to adjudicate labor-management disputes by maintaining a large roster of qualified arbitrators. When an employer and a union need an arbitrator, they need only to notify the service, and the service will provide at no charge a listing of qualified arbitrators in their area who are available to hear the dispute. When the parties have agreed on one name from the list, they notify FMCS and the service notifies the arbitrator.

FEDERAL MEDIATION AND CONCILIATION SERVICE—STATISTICAL INFORMATION FOR FISCAL YEAR 1994

The following statistics reflect the work of the various FMCS offices as summarized in a statistical report of the FMCS for fiscal year 1994.

The FMCS maintained some 75 field offices and 9 District offices throughout the United States. About 205 mediators were on staff. During FY1994, FMCS received 68,268 formal notices of pending bargaining situations. Of these, 22,184 (about 33 percent) were assigned to mediators. Mediators actively participated and gave mediation assistance in 5,993 cases (27 percent of cases assigned). In the negotiation cases where FMCS mediators were monitoring or were active in mediating, there were only 476 work stoppages (2.1 percent of the FMCS cases assigned). This was the lowest number of strikes and lockouts experienced since the end of World War II.

Selected Bibliography

Allen, Robert E., and Timothy J. Keaveny. *Contemporary Labor Relations.* 2nd ed. Reading, Mass.: Addison-Wesley, 1988.

Balfour, Alan. *Union-Management Relations in a Changing Economy.* Englewood Cliffs, N.J.: Prentice Hall, 1987.

Begin, James P., and Edwin F. Beal. *The Practice of Collective Bargaining.* 8th ed. Burr Ridge, Ill.: Richard D. Irwin, 1989.

CCH Guidebook to Labor Relations. Chicago: Commerce Clearing House, 1989.

Cihon, Patrick J., and James O. Castagnera. *Labor and Employment Law.* 2nd ed. Boston: Wadsworth, 1993.

Dunlop, John T. *Industrial Relations Systems. Boston:* Harvard Business School Press, 1993.

The Federal Mediation and Conciliation Service. Washington, D.C.: Federal Mediation and Conciliation Service, U.S. Government Printing Office.

Feldacker, Bruce. *Labor Guide to Labor Law.* 3rd ed. Englewood Cliffs, N.J.: Prentice Hall, 1990.

Flanagan, Robert. *Labor Relations and the Litigation Explosion.* Washington, D.C.: Brookings Institution, 1987.

Fossum, John A. *Labor Relations: Development, Structure, Process.* 6th ed. Burr Ridge, Ill.: Richard D. Irwin, 1995.

Glassman, Alan M.; Naomi Berger Davidson; and Thomas G. Cummings. *Labor Relations: Reports from the Firing Line.* Plano, Tex.: Business Publications, 1988.

A *Guide to Basic Law and Procedures under the National Labor Relations Act.* Washington, D.C.: Office of the General Counsel of the NLRB, U.S. Government Printing Office, 1991.

Hardin, Patrick; James R. LaVaute; and Timothy P. O'Reilly. *The Developing Labor Law: The Boards, the Courts, and the National Labor Relations Act.* Washington, D.C.: Bureau of National Affairs, 1992.

Herman, E. Edward; Joshua L. Schwartz; and Alfred Kuhn. *Collective Bargaining and Labor Relations.* 3rd ed. Englewood Cliffs, N.J.: Prentice Hall, 1992.

Hilgert, Raymond L. *Labor Agreement Negotiations.* 4th ed. Houston: Dame Publications, 1995.

Holley, William H., Jr., and Kenneth M. Jennings. *The Labor Relation Process.* 4th ed. Chicago: Dryden Press, 1991.

Kagel, Sam, and Kathy Kelly. *The Anatomy of Mediation: What Makes It Work.* Washington, D.C.: Bureau of National Affairs, 1989.

Katz, Harry C., and Thomas A. Kochan. *An Introduction to Collective Bargaining and Industrial Relations.* New York: McGraw-Hill, 1992.

Kenney, John J., and Linda G. Kahn. *Primer of Labor Relations.* 24th ed. Washington, D.C.: Bureau of National Affairs, 1989.

Labor Cases. Chicago: Commerce Clearing House.

Labor Relations Reference Manual. Washington, D.C.: Bureau of National Affairs.

Leap, Terry L. *Collective Bargaining and Labor Relations.* New York: Macmillan, 1991.

Leslie, Douglas. *Labor Law in a Nutshell.* 3rd ed. St. Paul, Minn.: West, 1992.

Lewicki, Roy J., and Joseph A. Litterer. *Negotiation.* Burr Ridge, Ill.: Richard D. Irwin, 1985.

————. *Negotiation: Readings, Exercises, and Cases.* Burr Ridge, Ill.: Richard D. Irwin, 1985.

McGuiness, Kenneth C., and Jeffrey A. Norris. *How to Take a Case before the NLRB.* 5th ed. Washington, D.C.: Bureau of National Affairs, 1986.

McKelvey, Jean T., ed. *The Changing Law of Fair Representation.* Ithaca: New York State School of Industrial Relations, Cornell University, 1985.

Mills, Daniel Quinn. *Labor-Management Relations.* 5th ed. New York: McGraw-Hill, 1994.

Mills, Daniel Quinn, and Janice McCormick. *Industrial Relations in Transition.* New York: John Wiley & Sons, 1985.

NLRB Decisions. Chicago: Commerce Clearing House.

Norris, Jeffrey A., and Michael J. Shershin, Jr. *How to Take a Case before the NLRB.* 6th ed. Washington, D.C.: Bureau of National Affairs, 1992.

Robinson, James W., and Roger W. Walker. *Introduction to Labor.* 2nd ed. Englewood Cliffs, N.J.: Prentice Hall, 1985.

Rosenbloom, David H., and Jay M. Shafritz. *Essentials of Labor Relations.* Reston, Va.: Reston, 1985.

Rowan, Richard L., ed. *Readings in Labor Economics and Labor Relations.* 5th ed. Burr Ridge, Ill.: Richard D. Irwin, 1985.

Sandver, Marcus Hart. *Labor Relations: Process and Outcomes.* Boston: Little, Brown, 1987.

Schlossberg, Stephen I., and Judith A. Scott. *Organizing and the Law.* Washington, D.C.: Bureau of National Affairs, 1991.

Simkin, William E., and Nicholas A. Fidlandis. *Mediation and the Dynamics of Collective Bargaining.* 2nd ed. Washington, D.C.: Bureau of National Affairs, 1986.

Sloane, Arthur A., and Fred Witney. *Labor Relations.* 8th ed. Englewood Cliffs, N.J.: Prentice Hall, 1994.

Taylor, Benjamin J., and Fred Witney. *Labor Relations Law.* 6th ed. Englewood Cliffs, N.J.: Prentice Hall, 1992.

Twomey, David. *Labor and Employment Law.* 8th ed. Cincinnati: South-Western, 1989.

Weiler, Paul. *Governing the Workplace: The Future of Labor and Employment Law.* Cambridge, Mass.: Harvard University Press, 1990.

Zack, Arnold M. *Public Sector Mediation.* Washington, D.C.: Bureau of National Affairs, 1985.

Partial Text of the Labor Management Relations Act, 1947[1]

(as amended by the Labor-Management Reporting and Disclosure Act of 1959,[2] by Public Law 93–360, 1974, and by Public Law 96–593, 1980)

[PUBLIC LAW 101—80TH CONGRESS]
[CHAPTER 120—1ST SESSION]
AN ACT

To amend the National Labor Relations Act, to provide additional facilities for the mediation of labor disputes affecting commerce, to equalize legal responsibilities of labor organizations and employers, and for other purposes.

Be it enacted by the Senate and House of Representatives of the United States of America in Congress assembled.

Short Title and Declaration of Policy

Section 1. (a) This Act may be cited as the "Labor Management Relations Act, 1947."

(b) Industrial strife which interferes with the normal flow of commerce and with the full production of articles and commodities for commerce, can be avoided or substantially minimized if employers, employees, and labor organizations each recognize under law one another's legitimate rights in their relations with each other, and above all recognize under law that neither party has any right in its relations with any other to engage in acts or practices which jeopardize the public health, safety, or interest.

It is the purpose and policy of this Act, in order to promote the full flow of commerce, to prescribe the legitimate rights of both employees and employers in their relations affecting commerce, to provide orderly and peaceful procedures for preventing the interference by either with the legitimate rights of the other, to protect the rights of individual employees in their relations with labor organizations whose activities affect commerce, to define and proscribe practices on the part of labor and management which affect commerce and are inimical to the general welfare, and to protect the rights of the public in connection with labor disputes affecting commerce.

---

[1]Also known as the Taft-Hartley Act.
[2]Also known as the Landrum-Griffin Act, Public Law 86–257.

TITLE I—AMENDMENT OF NATIONAL LABOR RELATIONS ACT

Section 101.   The National Labor Relations Act is hereby amended to read as follows:

Findings and Policies

Section 1.   The denial by some employers of the right of employees to organize and the refusal by some employers to accept the procedure of collective bargaining lead to strikes and other forms of industrial strife or unrest, which have the intent or the necessary effect of burdening or obstructing commerce by (a) impairing the efficiency, safety, or operation of the instrumentalities of commerce; (b) occurring in the current of commerce; (c) materially affecting, restraining, or controlling the flow of raw materials or manufactured or processed goods from or into the channels of commerce, or the prices of such materials or goods in commerce; or (d) causing diminution of employment and wages in such volume as substantially to impair or disrupt the market for goods flowing from or into the channels of commerce.

The inequality of bargaining power between employees who do not possess full freedom of association or actual liberty of contract, and employers who are organized in the corporate or other forms of ownership association substantially burdens and affects the flow of commerce, and tends to aggravate recurrent business depressions, by depressing wage rates and the purchasing power of wage earners in industry and by preventing the stabilization of competitive wage rates and working conditions within and between industries.

Experience has proved that protection by law of the right of employees to organize and bargain collectively safeguards commerce from injury, impairment, or interruption, and promotes the flow of commerce by removing certain recognized sources of industrial strife and unrest, by encouraging practices fundamental to the friendly adjustment of industrial disputes arising out of differences as to wages, hours, or other working conditions, and by restoring equality of bargaining power between employers and employees.

Experience has further demonstrated that certain practices by some labor organizations, their officers, and members have the intent or the necessary effect of burdening or obstructing commerce by preventing the free flow of goods in such commerce through strikes and other forms of industrial unrest or through concerted activities which impair the interest of the public in the free flow of such commerce. The elimination of such practices is a necessary condition to the assurance of the rights herein guaranteed.

It is hereby declared to be the policy of the United States to eliminate the causes of certain substantial obstructions to the free flow of commerce and to mitigate and eliminate these obstructions when they have occurred by encouraging the practice and procedure of collective bargaining and by protecting the exercise by workers of full freedom of association, self-organization, and designation of representatives of their own choosing, for the purpose of negotiating the terms and conditions of their employment or other mutual aid or protection.

Definitions

Section 2.   When used in this Act—

(1) The term "person" includes one or more individuals, labor organizations, partnerships, associations, corporations, legal representatives, trustees, trustees in bankruptcy, or receivers.

(2) The term "employer" includes any person acting as an agent of an employer, directly or indirectly, but shall not include the United States or any wholly owned Government corporation, or any Federal Reserve Bank, or any State or political subdivision thereof, or any person subject to the Railway Labor Act, as amended from time to time, or any labor organization (other than when acting as an employer), or anyone acting in the capacity of officer or agent of such labor organization.

(3) The term "employee" shall include any employee, and shall not be limited to the employees of a particular employer, unless the Act explicitly states otherwise, and shall include any individual whose work has ceased as a consequence of, or in connection with, any current labor dispute or because of any unfair labor practice, and who has not obtained any other regular and substantially equivalent employment, but shall not include any individual employed as an agricultural laborer, or in the domestic service of any family or person at his home, or any individual employed by his parent or spouse, or any individual having the status of an independent contractor, or any individual employed as a supervisor, or any individual employed by an employer subject to the Railway Labor Act, as amended from time to time, or by any other person who is not an employer as herein defined.

(4) The term "representatives" includes any individual or labor organization.

(5) The term "labor organization" means any organization of any kind, or any agency or employee representation committee or plan, in which employees participate and which exists for the purpose, in whole or in part, of dealing with employers concerning grievances, labor disputes, wages, rates of pay, hours of employment, or conditions of work.

(6) The term "commerce" means trade, traffic, commerce, transportation, or communication among the several States, or between the District of Columbia or any Territory of the United States and any State or Territory, or between any foreign country and any State, Territory, or the District of Columbia, or within the District of Columbia or any Territory, or between points in the same State but through any other State or any Territory or the District of Columbia or any foreign country.

(7) The term "affecting commerce" means in commerce, or burdening or obstructing commerce or the free flow of commerce, or having led or tending to lead to a labor dispute burdening or obstructing commerce or the free flow of commerce.

(8) The term "unfair labor practice" means any unfair labor practice listed in section 8.

(9) The term "labor dispute" includes any controversy concerning terms, tenure or conditions of employment, or concerning the association or representation of persons in negotiating, fixing, maintaining, changing, or seeking to arrange terms or conditions of employment, regardless of whether the disputants stand in the proximate relation of employer and employee.

(10) The term "National Labor Relations Board" means the National Labor Relations Board provided for in section 3 of this Act.

(11) The term "supervisor" means any individual having authority, in the interest of the employer, to hire, transfer, suspend, lay off, recall, promote, discharge, assign, reward, or discipline other employees, or responsibility to direct them, or to adjust their grievances, or effectively to recommend such action, if in connection with the foregoing the exercise of such authority is not of a merely routine or clerical nature, but requires the use of independent judgment.

(12) The term "professional employee" means

(a) any employee engaged in work (i) predominantly intellectual and varied in character as opposed to routine mental, manual, mechanical, or physical work; (ii) involving the consistent exercise of discretion and judgment in its performance; (iii) of such a character that the output produced or the result accomplished cannot be standardized in relation to a given period of time; (iv) requiring knowledge of an advanced type in a field of science or learning customarily acquired by a prolonged course of specialized intellectual instruction and study in an institution of higher learning or a hospital, as distinguished from a general academic education or from an apprenticeship or from training in the performance of routine mental, manual, or physical process; or

(b) any employee, who (i) has completed the courses of specialized intellectual instruction and study described in clause (iv) of paragraph (a), and (ii) is performing related work under the supervision of a professional person to qualify himself to become a professional employee as defined in paragraph (a).

(13) In determining whether any person is acting as an "agent" of another person so as to make such other person responsible for his acts, the question of whether the specific acts performed were actually authorized or subsequently ratified shall not be controlling.

(14) The term "health care institution" shall include any hospital, convalescent hospital, health maintenance organization, health clinic, nursing home, extended care facility, or other institution devoted to the care of the sick, infirm, or aged person.

National Labor Relations Board

Section 3.   (a) The National Labor Relations Board (hereinafter called the "Board") . . . as an agency of the United States, shall consist of five . . . members, appointed by the President by and with the advice and consent of the Senate . . . for terms of five years each, excepting that any individual chosen to fill a vacancy shall be appointed only for the unexpired term of the member whom he shall succeed. The President shall designate one member to serve as Chairman of the Board. Any member of the Board may be removed by the President, upon notice and hearing, for neglect of duty or malfeasance in office, but for no other cause.

(b) The Board is authorized to delegate to any group of three or more members any or all of the powers which it may itself exercise. The Board is also authorized to delegate to its regional directors its powers under section 9 to determine the unit appropriate for the purpose of collective bargaining, to investigate and provide for hearings, and determine whether a question of representation exists, and to direct an election or take a secret ballot under subsection (c) or (e) of section 9 and certify the results thereof, except that upon the filing of a request therefor with the Board by any interested person, the Board may review any action of a regional director delegated to him under this paragraph, but such a review shall not, unless specifically ordered by the Board, operate as a stay of any action taken by the regional director. A vacancy in the Board shall not impair the right of the remaining members to exercise all of the powers of the Board, and three members of the Board shall, at all times, constitute a quorum of the Board, except that two members shall constitute a quorum of any group designated pursuant to the first sentence hereof. The Board shall have an official seal which shall be judicially noticed.

(c) The Board shall at the close of each fiscal year make a report in writing to Congress and to the President stating in detail the cases it has heard, the decisions it has rendered, and an account of all moneys it has disbursed.

(d) There shall be a General Counsel of the Board who shall be appointed by the President, by and with the advice and consent of the Senate, for a term of four years. The General Counsel of the Board shall exercise general supervision over all attorneys employed by the Board (other than trial examiners and legal assistants to Board members) and over the officers and employees in the regional offices. He shall have final authority, on behalf of the Board, in respect of the investigation of charges and issuance of complaints under section 10, and in respect of the prosecution of such complaints before the Board, and shall have such other duties as the Board may prescribe or as may be provided by law. In case of a vacancy in the office of the General Counsel the President is authorized to designate the officer or employee who shall act as General Counsel during such vacancy, but no person or persons so designated shall so act (1) for more than 40 days when the Congress is in session unless a nomination to fill such vacancy shall have been submitted to the Senate, or (2) after the adjournment *sine die* of the session of the Senate in which such nomination was submitted.

* * * * *

[Omitted: Sections 4 and 5—Compensation and offices of the NLRB.]

Section 6.   The Board shall have authority from time to time to make, amend, and rescind, in the manner prescribed by the Administrative Procedure Act, such rules and regulations as may be necessary to carry out the provisions of this Act.

Rights of Employees

Section 7.   Employees shall have the right to self-organization, to form, join, or assist labor organizations, to bargain collectively through representatives of their own choosing, and to engage in other concerted activities for the purpose of collective bargaining or other mutual aid or protection, and shall also have the right to refrain from any or all of such activities except to the extent that such right may be affected by an agreement requiring membership in a labor organization as a condition of employment as authorized in section 8(a) (3).

Unfair Labor Practices

Section 8.   (a) It shall be an unfair labor practice for an employer—

(1) to interfere with, restrain, or coerce employees in the exercise of the rights guaranteed in section 7;

(2) to dominate or interfere with the formation or administration of any labor organization or contribute financial or other support to it: *Provided,* that subject to rules and regulations made and published by the Board pursuant to section 6, an employer shall not be prohibited from permitting employees to confer with him during working hours without loss of time or pay;

(3) by discrimination in regard to hire or tenure of employment or any term or condition of employment to encourage or discourage membership in any labor organization: *Provided,* that nothing in this Act, or in any other statute of the United States, shall preclude an employer from making an agreement with a labor organization (not established, or assisted by any action defined in section 8(a) of this Act as an unfair labor practice) to require as a condition of employment membership therein on or after the 30th day following the beginning of such employment or the effective date of such agreement, whichever is the later, (i) if such labor organization is the representative of the employees as provided in section 9(a), in the appropriate collective bargaining unit covered by such agreement when made, and (ii) unless following an election held as provided in section 9(e) within one year preceding the effective date of such agreement, the Board shall have certified that at least a majority of the employees eligible to vote in such election have voted to rescind the authority of such labor organization to make such an agreement: *Provided further,* that no employer shall justify any discrimination against an employee for nonmembership in a labor organization (A) if he has reasonable grounds for believing that such membership was not available to the employee on the same terms and conditions generally applicable to other members, or (B) if he has reasonable grounds for believing that membership was denied or terminated for reasons other than the failure of the employee to tender the periodic dues and the initiation fees uniformly required as a condition of acquiring or retaining membership;

(4) to discharge or otherwise discriminate against an employee because he has filed charges or given testimony under this Act;

(5) to refuse to bargain collectively with the representatives of his employees, subject to the provisions of section 9(a).

(b) It shall be an unfair labor practice for a labor organization or its agents—

(1) to restrain or coerce (A) employees in the exercise of the rights guaranteed in section 7: *Provided,* that this paragraph shall not impair the right of a labor organization to prescribe its own rules with respect to the acquisition or retention of membership therein; or (B) an employer in

the selection of his representatives for the purposes of collective bargaining or the adjustment of grievances;

(2) to cause or attempt to cause an employer to discriminate against an employee in violation of subsection (a) (3) or to discriminate against an employee with respect to whom membership in such organization has been denied or terminated on some ground other than his failure to tender the periodic dues and the initiation fees uniformly required as a condition of acquiring or retaining membership;

(3) to refuse to bargain collectively with an employer, provided it is the representative of his employees subject to the provisions of section 9(a);

(4) (i) to engage in, or to induce or encourage any individual employed by any person engaged in commerce or in any industry affecting commerce to engage in, a strike or a refusal in the course of his employment to use, manufacture, process, transport, or otherwise handle or work on any goods, articles, materials, or commodities or to perform any services; or (ii) to threaten, coerce, or restrain any person engaged in commerce or in an industry affecting commerce, where in either case an object thereof is:

(A) forcing or requiring any employer or self-employed person to join any labor or employer organization or to enter into any agreement which is prohibited by section 8(e);

(B) forcing or requiring any person to cease using, selling, handling, transporting, or otherwise dealing in the products of any other producer, processor, or manufacturer, or to cease doing business with any other person, or forcing or requiring any other employer to recognize or bargain with a labor organization as the representative of his employees unless such labor organization has been certified as the representative of such employees under the provisions of section 9: *Provided*, that nothing contained in this clause (B) shall be construed to make unlawful, where not otherwise unlawful, any primary strike or primary picketing;

(C) forcing or requiring any employer to recognize or bargain with a particular labor organization as the representative of his employees if another labor organization has been certified as the representative of such employees under the provisions of section 9;

(D) forcing or requiring any employer to assign particular work to employees in a particular labor organization or in a particular trade, craft, or class rather than to employees in another labor organization or in another trade, craft, or class, unless such employer is failing to conform to an order or certification of the Board determining the bargaining representative for employees performing such work:

Provided, that nothing contained in this subsection (b) shall be construed to make unlawful a refusal by any person to enter upon the premises of any employer (other than his own employer), if the employees of such employer are engaged in a strike ratified or approved by a representative of such employees whom such employer is required to recognize under this Act: *Provided further*, that for the purposes of this paragraph (4) only, nothing contained in such paragraph shall be construed to prohibit publicity, other than picketing, for the purpose of truthfully advising the public, including consumers and members of a labor organization, that a product or products are produced by an employer with whom the labor organization has a primary dispute and are distributed by another employer, as long as such publicity does not have an effect of inducing any individual employed by any person other than the primary employer in the course of his employment to refuse to pick up, deliver, or transport any goods, or not to perform any services, at the establishment of the employer engaged in such distribution;

(5) to require of employees covered by an agreement authorized under subsection (a) (3) the payment, as a condition precedent to becoming a member of such organization, of a fee in an amount which the Board finds excessive or discriminatory under all the circumstances. In making such a finding, the Board shall consider, among other relevant factors, the practices and customs

of labor organizations in the particular industry, and the wages currently paid to the employees affected;

(6) to cause or attempt to cause an employer to pay or deliver or agree to pay or deliver any money or other thing of value, in the nature of an exaction, for services which are not performed or not to be performed; and

(7) to picket or cause to be picketed, or threaten to picket or cause to be picketed, any employer where an object thereof is forcing or requiring an employer to recognize or bargain with a labor organization as the representative of his employees, or forcing or requiring the employees of an employer to accept or select such labor organization as their collective bargaining representative, unless such labor organization is currently certified as the representative of such employees:

(A) where the employer has lawfully recognized in accordance with this Act any other labor organization and a question concerning representation may not appropriately be raised under section 9(c) of this Act;

(B) where within the preceding 12 months a valid election under section 9(c) of this Act has been conducted; or

(C) where such picketing has been conducted without a petition under section 9(c) being filed within a reasonable period of time not to exceed 30 days from the commencement of such picketing: *Provided,* that when such a petition has been filed the Board shall forthwith, without regard to the provisions of section 9(c) (1) or the absence of a showing of a substantial interest on the part of the labor organization, direct an election in such unit as the Board finds to be appropriate and shall certify the results thereof: *Provided further,* that nothing in this subparagraph (C) shall be construed to prohibit any picketing or other publicity for the purpose of truthfully advising the public (including consumers) that an employer does not employ members of, or have a contract with, a labor organization, unless an effect of such picketing is to induce any individual employed by any other person in the course of his employment, not to pick up, deliver or transport any goods or not to perform any services.

Nothing in this paragraph (7) shall be construed to permit any act which would otherwise be an unfair labor practice under this section 8(b).

(c) The expressing of any views, argument, or opinion, or the dissemination thereof, whether in written, printed, graphic, or visual form, shall not constitute or be evidence of an unfair labor practice under any of the provisions of this Act, if such expression contains no threat of reprisal or force or promise of benefit.

(d) For the purposes of this section, to bargain collectively is the performance of the mutual obligation of the employer and the representative of the employees to meet at reasonable times and confer in good faith with respect to wages, hours, and other terms and conditions of employment, or the negotiation of an agreement, or any question arising thereunder, and the execution of a written contract incorporating any agreement reached if requested by either party, but such obligation does not compel either party to agree to a proposal or require the making of a concession:

Provided, that where there is in effect a collective bargaining contract covering employees in an industry affecting commerce, the duty to bargain collectively shall also mean that no party to such contract shall terminate or modify such contract, unless the party desiring such termination or modification—

(1) serves a written notice upon the other party to the contract of the proposed termination or modification 60 days prior to the expiration date thereof, or in the event such contract contains no expiration date, 60 days prior to the time it is proposed to make such termination or modification;

(2) offers to meet and confer with the other party for the purpose of negotiating a new contract or a contract containing the proposed modifications;

(3) notifies the Federal Mediation and Conciliation Service within 30 days after such notice of the existence of a dispute, and simultaneously therewith notifies any State or Territorial agency established to mediate and conciliate disputes within the State or Territory where the dispute occurred, provided no agreement has been reached by that time; and

(4) continues in full force and effect, without resorting to strike or lockout, all the terms and conditions of the existing contract for a period of 60 days after such notice is given or until the expiration date of such contract, whichever occurs later.

The duties imposed upon employers, employees, and labor organizations by paragraphs (2), (3), and (4) shall become inapplicable upon an intervening certification of the Board, under which the labor organization or individual, which is a party to the contract, has been superseded as or ceased to be the representative of the employees subject to the provisions of section 9(a), and the duties so imposed shall not be construed as requiring either party to discuss or agree to any modification of the terms and conditions contained in a contract for a fixed period, if such modification is to become effective before such terms and conditions can be reopened under the provisions of the contract. Any employee who engages in a strike within any notice period specified in this subsection, or who engages in any strike within the appropriate period specified in subsection (g) of this section shall lose his status as an employee of the employer engaged in the particular labor dispute, for the purposes of sections 8, 9, and 10 of this Act, as amended, but such loss of status for such employee shall terminate if and when he is reemployed by such employer. Whenever the collective bargaining involves employees of a health care institution, the provisions of this section 8(d) shall be modified as follows:

(A) The notice of section 8(d) (1) shall be 90 days; the notice of section 8(d) (3) shall be 60 days; and the contract period of section 8(d) (4) shall be 90 days.

(B) Where the bargaining is for an initial agreement following certification or recognition, at least 30 days' notice of the existence of a dispute shall be given by the labor organization to the agencies set forth in section 8(d) (3).

(C) After notice is given to the Federal Mediation and Conciliation Service under either clause (A) or (B) of this sentence, the Service shall promptly communicate with the parties and use its best efforts, by mediation and conciliation, to bring them to agreement. The parties shall participate fully and promptly in such meetings as may be undertaken by the Service for the purpose of aiding in a settlement of the dispute.

(e) It shall be an unfair labor practice for any labor organization and any employer to enter into any contract or agreement, express or implied, whereby such employer ceases or refrains or agrees to cease or refrain from handling, using, selling, transporting, or otherwise dealing in any of the products of any other employer, or to cease doing business with any other person, and any contract or agreement entered into heretofore or hereafter containing such an agreement shall be to such extent unenforceable and void: *Provided,* that nothing in this subsection (e) shall apply to an agreement between a labor organization and an employer in the construction industry relating to the contracting or subcontracting of work to be done at the site of the construction, alteration, painting, or repair of a building, structure, or other work: *Provided further,* that for the purposes of this subsection (e) and section 8(b) (4) (B) the terms "any employer," "any person engaged in commerce or in industry affecting commerce," and "any person" when used in relation to the terms "any other producer, processor, or manufacturer," "any other employer," or "any other person" shall not include persons in the relation of a jobber, manufacturer, contractor, or subcontractor working on the goods or premises of the jobber or manufacturer or performing parts of an integrated process of production in the apparel and clothing industry: *Provided further,* that nothing in this Act shall prohibit the enforcement of any agreement which is within the foregoing exception.

(f) It shall not be an unfair labor practice under subsections (a) and (b) of this section for an employer engaged primarily in the building and construction industry to make an agreement covering employees engaged (or who, upon their employment, will be engaged) in the building and construction industry with a labor organization of which building and construction employees are members (not established, maintained, or assisted by any action defined in section 8(a) of this Act as an unfair labor practice) because (1) the majority status of such labor organization has not been established under the provisions of section 9 of this Act prior to the making of such agreement, or (2) such agreement requires as a condition of employment, membership in such labor organization after the seventh day following the beginning of such employment or the effective date of the agreement, whichever is later, or (3) such agreement requires the employer to notify such labor organization of opportunities for employment with such employer, or gives such labor organization an opportunity to refer qualified applicants for such employment, or (4) such agreement specifies minimum training or experience qualifications for employment or provides for priority in opportunities for employment based upon length of service with such employer, in the industry or in the particular geographical area: *Provided,* that nothing in this subsection shall set aside the final proviso to section 8(a) (3) of this Act: *Provided further,* that any agreement which would be invalid, but for clause (1) of this subsection, shall not be a bar to a petition filed pursuant to section 9(c) or 9(e).

(g) A labor organization before engaging in any strike, picketing, or other concerted refusal to work at any health care institution shall, not less than 10 days prior to such action, notify the institution in writing and the Federal Mediation and Conciliation Service of that intention, except that in the case of bargaining for an initial agreement following certification or recognition the notice required by this subsection shall not be given until the expiration of the period specified in clause (B) of the last sentence of section 8(d) of this Act. The notice shall state the date and time that such action will commence. The notice, once given, may be extended by the written agreement of both parties.

Representatives and Elections

Section 9.   (a) Representatives designated or selected for the purposes of collective bargaining by the majority of the employees in a unit appropriate for such purposes, shall be the exclusive representatives of all the employees in such unit for the purposes of collective bargaining in respect to rates of pay, wages, hours of employment, or other conditions of employment: *Provided,* that any individual employee or a group of employees shall have the right at any time to present grievances to their employer and to have such grievances adjusted, without the intervention of the bargaining representative, as long as the adjustment is not inconsistent with the terms of a collective bargaining contract or agreement then in effect: *Provided further,* that the bargaining representative has been given opportunity to be present at such adjustment.

(b) The Board shall decide in each case whether, in order to assure to employees the fullest freedom in exercising the rights guaranteed by this Act, the unit appropriate for the purposes of collective bargaining shall be the employer unit, craft unit, plant unit, or subdivision thereof: *Provided,* that the Board shall not (1) decide that any unit is appropriate for such purposes if such unit includes both professional employees and employees who are not professional employees unless a majority of such professional employees vote for inclusion in such unit; or (2) decide that any craft unit is inappropriate for such purposes on the ground that a different unit has been established by a prior Board determination, unless a majority of the employees in the proposed craft unit vote against separate representation; or (3) decide that any unit is appropriate for such purposes, if it includes, together with other employees, any individual employed as a guard to enforce against employees and other persons rules to protect property of the employer or to protect the safety of persons on the employers' premises; but no labor organization shall be certified as the representative of employees in a bargaining unit of guards if such organization admits to membership, or is affiliated directly or indirectly with an organization which admits to membership, employees other than guards.

(c) (1) Wherever a petition shall have been filed, in accordance with such regulations as may be prescribed by the Board—

(A) by an employee or group of employees or any individual or labor organization acting in their behalf alleging that a substantial number of employees (i) wish to be represented for collective bargaining and that their employer declines to recognize their representative as the representative defined in section 9(a), or (ii) assert that the individual or labor organization, which has been certified or is being currently recognized by their employer as the bargaining representative, is no longer a representative as defined in section 9(a); or

(B) by an employer, alleging that one or more individuals or labor organizations have presented to him a claim to be recognized as the representative defined in section 9(a),

the Board shall investigate such petition and if it has reasonable cause to believe that a question of representation affecting commerce exists shall provide for an appropriate hearing upon due notice. Such hearing may be conducted by an officer or employee of the regional office, who shall not make any recommendations with respect thereto. If the Board finds upon the record of such hearing that such a question of representation exists, it shall direct an election by secret ballot and shall certify the results thereof.

(2) In determining whether or not a question of representation affecting commerce exists, the same regulations and rules of decision shall apply irrespective of the identity of the persons filing the petition or the kind of relief sought and in no case shall the Board deny a labor organization a place on the ballot by reason of an order with respect to such labor organization or its predecessor not issued in conformity with section 10(c).

(3) No election shall be directed in any bargaining unit or any subdivision within which, in the preceding 12-month period, a valid election shall have been held. Employees engaged in an economic strike who are not entitled to reinstatement shall be eligible to vote under such regulations as the Board shall find are consistent with the purposes and provisions of this Act in any election conducted within 12 months after the commencement of the strike. In any election where none of the choices on the ballot receives a majority, a runoff shall be conducted, the ballot providing for a selection between the two choices receiving the largest and second largest number of valid votes cast in the election.

(4) Nothing in this section shall be construed to prohibit the waiving of hearings by stipulation for the purposes of a consent election in conformity with regulations and rules of decision of the Board.

(5) In determining whether a unit is appropriate for the purposes specified in subsection (b) the extent to which the employees have organized shall not be controlling.

(d) Whenever an order of the Board made pursuant to section 10(c) is based in whole or in part upon facts certified following an investigation pursuant to subsection (c) of this section and there is a petition for the enforcement or review of such order, such certification and the record of such investigation shall be included in the transcript of the entire record required to be filed under section 10(e) or 10(f), and thereupon the decree of the court enforcing, modifying, or setting aside in whole or in part the order of the Board shall be made and entered upon the pleadings, testimony, and proceedings set forth in such transcript.

(e) (1) Upon the filing with the Board, by 30 per centum or more of the employees in a bargaining unit covered by an agreement between their employer and a labor organization made pursuant to section 8(a) (3), of a petition alleging they desire that such authority be rescinded, the Board shall take a secret ballot of the employees in such unit and certify the results thereof to such labor organization and to the employer.

(2) No election shall be conducted pursuant to this subsection in any bargaining unit or any subdivision within which, in the preceding 12-month period, a valid election shall have been held.

Prevention of Unfair Labor Practices

Section 10.   (a) The Board is empowered, as hereinafter provided, to prevent any person from engaging in any unfair labor practice (listed in section 8) affecting commerce. This power shall not be affected by any other means of adjustment or prevention that has been or may be established by agreement, law, or otherwise: *Provided,* that the Board is empowered by agreement with any agency of any State or Territory to cede to such agency jurisdiction over any cases in any industry (other than mining, manufacturing, communications, and transportation except where predominantly local in character) even though such cases may involve labor disputes affecting commerce, unless the provision of the State or Territorial statute applicable to the determination of such cases by such agency is inconsistent with the corresponding provision of this Act or has received a construction inconsistent therewith.

(b) Whenever it is charged that any person has engaged in or is engaging in any such unfair labor practice, the Board, or any agent or agency designated by the Board for such purposes, shall have power to issue and cause to be served upon such person a complaint stating the charges in that respect, and containing a notice of hearing before the Board or a member thereof, or before a designated agent or agency, at a place therein fixed, not less than five days after the serving of said complaint: *Provided,* that no complaint shall issue based upon any unfair labor practice occurring more than six months prior to the filing of the charge with the Board and the service of a copy thereof upon the person against whom such a charge is made, unless the person aggrieved thereby was prevented from filing such charge by reason of service in the armed forces, in which event the six-month period shall be computed from the day of his discharge. Any such complaint may be amended by the member, agent, or agency conducting the hearing or the Board in its discretion at any time prior to the issuance of an order based thereon. The person so complained of shall have the right to file an answer to the original or amended complaint and to appear in person or otherwise and give testimony at the place and time fixed in the complaint. In the discretion of the member, agent, or agency conducting the hearing or the Board, any other person may be allowed to intervene in the said proceeding and to present testimony. Any such proceeding shall, so far as practicable, be conducted in accordance with the rules of evidence applicable in the district courts of the United States under the rules of civil procedure for the district courts of the United States, adopted by the Supreme Court of the United States pursuant to the Act of June 19, 1934 (U.S.C., title 28, secs. 723-B, 723-C).

(c) The testimony taken by such member, agent, or agency or the Board shall be reduced to writing and filed with the Board. Thereafter, in its discretion, the Board upon notice may take further testimony or hear argument. If upon the preponderance of the testimony taken the Board shall be of the opinion that any person named in the complaint has engaged in or is engaging in any such unfair labor practice, then the Board shall state its findings of fact and shall issue and cause to be served on such person an order requiring such person to cease and desist from such unfair labor practice, and to take such affirmative action including reinstatement of employees with or without back pay, as will effectuate the policies of this Act: *Provided,* that where an order directs reinstatement of an employee, back pay may be required of the employer or labor organization, as the case may be, responsible for the discrimination suffered by him: *And provided further,* that in determining whether a complaint shall issue alleging a violation of section 8(a) (1) or section 8(a) (2), and in deciding such cases, the same regulations and rules of decision shall apply irrespective of whether or not the labor organization affected is affiliated with a labor organization national or international in scope. Such order may further require such person to make reports from time to time showing the extent to which it has complied with the order. If upon the preponderance of the testimony taken the Board shall not be of the opinion that the person named in the complaint has engaged in or is engaging in any such unfair labor practice, then the Board shall state its findings of fact and shall issue an order dismissing the said complaint. No order of the Board shall require the reinstatement of any individual as an employee who has been suspended or discharged, or the payment to him of any back pay, if such individual was suspended or discharged for cause. In case the evidence is presented before a member of the Board, or before an examiner or examiners thereof, such member, or such examiner or examiners, as the case may be, shall issue and cause to be served on the parties to the proceeding a proposed report, together with a recommended order, which shall be filed with the Board and if no exceptions are filed within 20 days after service thereof upon such parties, or within such further period as the Board may authorize, such recommended order shall become the order of the Board and become effective as therein prescribed.

(d) Until the record in a case shall have been filed in a court, as hereinafter provided, the Board may at any time, upon reasonable notice and in such manner as it shall deem proper, modify or set aside, in whole or in part, any finding or order made or issued by it.

(e) The Board shall have power to petition any court of appeals of the United States, or if all the courts of appeals to which application may be made are in vacation, any district court of the United States, within any circuit or district, respectively, wherein the unfair labor practice in question occurred or wherein such person resides or transacts business, for the enforcement of such order and for appropriate temporary relief or restraining order, and shall file in the court the record in the proceedings, as provided in section 2112 of title 28, United States Code. Upon the filing of such petition, the court shall cause notice thereof to be served upon such person, and thereupon shall have jurisdiction of the proceeding and of the question determined therein, and shall have power to grant such temporary relief or restraining order as it deems just and proper, and to make and enter a decree enforcing, modifying, and enforcing as so modified, or setting aside in whole or in part the order of the Board. No objection that has not been urged before the Board, its member, agent, or agency, shall be considered by the court, unless the failure or neglect to urge such objection shall be excused because of extraordinary circumstances. The findings of the Board with respect to questions of fact if supported by substantial evidence on the record considered as a whole shall be conclusive. If either party shall apply to the court for leave to adduce additional evidence and shall show to the satisfaction of the court that such additional evidence is material and that there were reasonable grounds for the failure to adduce such evidence in the hearing before the Board, its member, agent, or agency, the court may order such additional evidence to be taken before the Board, its member, agent, or agency, and to be made a part of the record. The Board may modify its findings as to the facts, or make new findings, by reason of additional evidence so taken and filed, and it shall file such modified or new findings, which findings with respect to questions of fact if supported by substantial evidence on the record considered as a whole shall be conclusive, and shall file its recommendations, if any, for the modification or setting aside of its original order. Upon the filing of the record with it the jurisdiction of the court shall be exclusive and its judgment and decree shall be final, except that the same shall be subject to review by the appropriate United States court of appeals if application was made to the district court as hereinabove provided, and by the Supreme Court of the United States upon writ of certiorari or certification as provided in section 1254 of title 28.

(f) Any person aggrieved by a final order of the Board granting or denying in whole or in part the relief sought may obtain a review of such order in any circuit court of appeals of the United States in the circuit wherein the unfair labor practice in question was alleged to have been engaged in or wherein such person resides or transacts business, or in the United States Court of Appeals for the District of Columbia, by filing in such court a written petition praying that the order of the Board be modified or set aside. A copy of such petition shall be forthwith transmitted by the clerk of the court to the Board, and thereupon the aggrieved party shall file in the court the record in the proceeding, certified by the Board, as provided in section 2112 of title 28, United States Code. Upon the filing of such petition, the court shall proceed in the same manner as in the case of an application by the Board under subsection (e) of this section, and shall have the same jurisdiction to grant to the Board such temporary relief or restraining order as it deems just and proper, and in like manner to make and enter a decree enforcing, modifying, and enforcing as so modified, or setting aside in whole or in part the order of the Board; the findings of the Board with respect to questions of fact if supported by substantial evidence on the record considered as a whole shall in like manner be conclusive.

(g) The commencement of proceedings under subsection (e) or (f) of this section shall not, unless specifically ordered by the court, operate as a stay of the Board's order.

(h) When granting appropriate temporary relief or a restraining order, or making and entering a decree enforcing, modifying, and enforcing as so modified, or setting aside in whole or in part an order of the Board, as provided in this section, the jurisdiction of courts sitting in equity shall not be limited by the Act entitled "An Act to amend the Judicial Code and to define and limit the jurisdiction of courts sitting in equity, and for other purposes," approved March 23, 1932 (U.S.C., Supp. VII, title 29, secs. 101–115).

(i) Petitions filed under this Act shall be heard expeditiously, and if possible within 10 days after they have been docketed.

(j) The Board shall have power, upon issuance of a complaint as provided in subsection (b) charging that any person has engaged in or is engaging in an unfair labor practice, to petition any district court of the United States (including the District Court of the United States for the District of Columbia), within any district wherein the unfair labor practice in question is alleged to have occurred or wherein such person resides or transacts business, for appropriate temporary relief or restraining order. Upon the filing of any such petition the court shall cause notice thereof to be served upon such person, and thereupon shall have jurisdiction to grant to the Board such temporary relief or restraining order as it deems just and proper.

(k) Whenever it is charged that any person has engaged in an unfair labor practice within the meaning of paragraph (4) (D) of section 8(b), the Board is empowered and directed to hear and determine the dispute out of which such unfair labor practice shall have arisen, unless, within 10 days after notice that such charge has been filed, the parties to such dispute submit to the Board satisfactory evidence that they have adjusted, or agreed upon methods for the voluntary adjustment of, the dispute. Upon compliance by the parties to the dispute with the decision of the Board or upon such voluntary adjustment of the dispute, such charge shall be dismissed.

(l) Whenever it is charged that any person has engaged in an unfair labor practice within the meaning of paragraph (4) (A), (B), or (C) of section 8(b), or section 8(e) or section 8(b) (7), the preliminary investigation of such charge shall be made forthwith and given priority over all other cases except cases of like character in the office where it is filed or to which it is referred. If, after such investigation, the officer or regional attorney to whom the matter may be referred has reasonable cause to believe such charge is true and that a complaint should issue, he shall, on behalf of the Board, petition any district court of the United States (including the District Court of the United States for the District of Columbia) within any district where the unfair labor practice in question has occurred, is alleged to have occurred, or wherein such person resides or transacts business, for appropriate injunctive relief pending the final adjudication of the Board with respect to such matter. Upon the filing of any such petition the district court shall have jurisdiction to grant such injunctive relief or temporary restraining order as it deems just and proper, notwithstanding any other provision of law: *Provided further,* that no temporary restraining order shall be issued without notice unless a petition alleges that substantial and irreparable injury to the charging party will be unavoidable and such temporary restraining order shall be effective for no longer than five days and will become void at the expiration of such period: *Provided further,* that such officer or regional attorney shall not apply for any restraining order under section 8(b) (7) if a charge against the employer under section 8(a) (2) has been filed and after the preliminary investigation, he has reasonable cause to believe that such charge is true and that a complaint should issue. Upon filing of any such petition the courts shall cause notice thereof to be served upon any person involved in the charge and such person including the charging party, shall be given an opportunity to appear by counsel and present any relevant testimony: *Provided further,* that for the purposes of this subsection district courts shall be deemed to have jurisdiction of a labor organization (1) in the district in which such organization maintains its principal office, or (2) in any district in which its duly authorized officers or agents are engaged in promoting or protecting the interests of employee members. The service of legal process upon such officer or agent shall constitute service upon the labor organization and make such organizations a party to the suit. In situations where such relief is appropriate the procedure specified herein shall apply to charges with respect to section 8(b) (4) (D).

(m) Whenever it is charged that any person has engaged in an unfair labor practice within the meaning of subsection (a) (3) or (b) (2) of section 8, such charge shall be given priority over all other cases except cases of like character in the office where it is filed or to which it is referred and cases given priority under subsection (1).

* * * * *

[Omitted: Sections 11 and 12—Investigatory powers of the NLRB.]

Limitations

Section 13.   Nothing in this Act, except as specifically provided for herein, shall be construed so as either to interfere with or impede or diminish in any way the right to strike, or to affect the limitations or qualifications on that right.

Section 14.   (a) Nothing herein shall prohibit any individual employed as a supervisor from becoming or remaining a member of a labor organization, but no employer subject to this Act shall be compelled to deem individuals defined herein as supervisors as employees for the purpose of any law, either national or local, relating to collective bargaining.

(b) Nothing in this Act shall be construed as authorizing the execution or application of agreements requiring membership in a labor organization as a condition of employment in any State or Territory in which such execution or application is prohibited by State or Territorial law.

(c) (1) The Board, in its discretion, may, by rule of decision or by published rules adopted pursuant to the Administrative Procedure Act, decline to assert jurisdiction over any labor dispute involving any class or category of employers, where, in the opinion of the Board, the effect of such labor dispute on commerce is not sufficiently substantial to warrant the exercise of its jurisdiction: *Provided,* that the Board shall not decline to assert jurisdiction over any labor dispute over which it would assert jurisdiction under the standards prevailing upon August 1, 1959.

(2) Nothing in this Act shall be deemed to prevent or bar any agency or the courts of any State or Territory (including the Commonwealth of Puerto Rico, Guam, and the Virgin Islands), from assuming and asserting jurisdiction over labor disputes over which the Board declines, pursuant to paragraph (1) of this subsection, to assert jurisdiction.

* * * * *

[Omitted: Sections 15, 16, 17, and 18, relating to limitations.]

Individuals with Religious Conviction

Section 19.   Any employee who is a member of and adheres to established and traditional tenets or teachings of a bona fide religion, body, or sect which has historically held conscientious objections to joining or financially supporting labor organizations shall not be required to join or financially support any labor organizations as a condition of employment; except that such employee may be required in a contract between such employees' employer and a labor organization in lieu of periodic dues and initiation fees, to pay sums equal to such dues and initiation fees to a nonreligious, nonlabor organization charitable fund exempt from taxation under section 501(c) (3) of title 26 of the Internal Revenue Code, chosen by such employee from a list of at least three such funds, designated in such contract or if the contract fails to designate such funds, then to any such fund chosen by the employee. If such employee who holds conscientious objections pursuant to this section requests the labor organization to use the grievance-arbitration procedure on the employee's behalf, the labor organization is authorized to charge the employee for the reasonable cost of using such procedure.

* * * * *

[Omitted: Sections 102, 103, and 104, concerning effective dates of certain changes.]

TITLE II—CONCILIATION OF LABOR DISPUTES
IN INDUSTRIES AFFECTING COMMERCE;
NATIONAL EMERGENCIES

Section 201.   That it is the policy of the United States that—

(a) sound and stable industrial peace and the advancement of the general welfare, health, and safety of the Nation and of the best interest of employers and employees can most satisfactorily be secured by the settlement of issues between employers and employees through the processes of conference and collective bargaining between employers and the representatives of their employees;

(b) the settlement of issues between employers and employees through collective bargaining may be advanced by making available full and adequate governmental facilities for conciliation, mediation, and voluntary arbitration to aid and encourage employers and the representatives of their employees to reach and maintain agreements concerning rates of pay, hours, and working conditions, and to make all reasonable efforts to settle their differences by mutual agreement reached through conferences and collective bargaining or by such methods as may be provided for in any applicable agreement for the settlement of disputes; and

(c) certain controversies which arise between parties to collective bargaining agreements may be avoided or minimized by making available full and adequate governmental facilities for furnishing assistance to employers and the representatives of their employees in formulating for inclusion within such agreements provision for adequate notice of any proposed changes in the terms of such agreements, for the final adjustment of grievances or questions regarding the application or interpretation of such agreements, and other provisions designed to prevent the subsequent arising of such controversies.

Section 202.   (a) There is hereby created an independent agency to be known as the Federal Mediation and Conciliation Service (herein referred to as the "Service") . . . The Service shall be under the direction of a Federal Mediation and Conciliation Director (hereinafter referred to as the "Director"), who shall be appointed by the President by and with the advice and consent of the Senate . . .

(b) The Director is authorized, subject to the civil-service laws, to appoint such clerical and other personnel as may be necessary for the execution of the functions of the Service . . .

(c) The principal office of the Service shall be in the District of Columbia, but the Director may establish regional offices convenient to localities in which labor controversies are likely to arise. The Director may by order, subject to revocation at any time, delegate any authority and discretion conferred upon him by this Act to any regional director, or other officer or employee of the Service. The Director may establish suitable procedures for cooperation with State and local mediation agencies. The Director shall make an annual report in writing to Congress at the end of the fiscal year.

* * * * *

[Omitted: Section 202(d), which relates to the original creation of the FMCS.]

Functions of the Service

Section 203.   (a) It shall be the duty of the Service, in order to prevent or minimize interruptions of the free flow of commerce growing out of labor disputes, to assist parties to labor disputes in industries affecting commerce to settle such disputes through conciliation and mediation.

(b) The Service may proffer its services in any labor dispute in any industry affecting commerce, either upon its own motion or upon the request of one or more of the parties to the dispute, whenever in its judgment such dispute threatens to cause a substantial interruption of commerce. The Director and the Service are directed to avoid attempting to mediate disputes which would have only a minor effect on interstate commerce if State or other conciliation services are available to the parties. Whenever the Service does proffer its services in any dispute, it shall be the duty of the Service promptly to put itself in communication with the parties and to use its best efforts, by mediation and conciliation, to bring them to agreement.

(c) If the Director is not able to bring the parties to agreement by conciliation within a reasonable time, he shall seek to induce the parties voluntarily to seek other means of settling the dispute without resort to strike, lockout, or other coercion, including submission to the employees in the bargaining unit of the employer's last offer of settlement for approval or rejection in a secret ballot. The failure or refusal of either party to agree to any procedure suggested by the Director shall not be deemed a violation of any duty or obligation imposed by this Act.

(d) Final adjustment by a method agreed upon by the parties is hereby declared to be the desirable method for settlement of grievance disputes arising over the application or interpretation of an existing collective bargaining agreement. The Service is directed to make its conciliation and mediation services available in the settlement of such grievance disputes only as a last resort and in exceptional cases.

Section 204.   (a) In order to prevent or minimize interruptions of the free flow of commerce growing out of labor disputes, employers and employees and their representatives, in any industry affecting commerce, shall—

(1) exert every reasonable effort to make and maintain agreements concerning rates of pay, hours, and working conditions, including provision for adequate notice of any proposed change in the terms of such agreements;

(2) whenever a dispute arises over the terms or application of a collective bargaining agreement and a conference is requested by a party or prospective party thereto, arrange promptly for such a conference to be held and endeavor in such conference to settle such dispute expeditiously; and

(3) in case such dispute is not settled by conference, participate fully and promptly in such meetings as may be undertaken by the Service under this Act for the purpose of aiding in a settlement of the dispute.

* * * * *

[Omitted: Section 205, which creates a national labor-management panel to advise the Director of FMCS.]

National Emergencies

Section 206.   Whenever in the opinion of the President of the United States, a threatened or actual strike or lockout affecting an entire industry or a substantial part thereof engaged in trade, commerce, transportation, transmission, or communication among the several States or with foreign nations, or engaged in the production of goods for commerce, will, if permitted to occur or to continue, imperil the national health or safety, he may appoint a board of inquiry to inquire into the issues involved in the dispute and to make a written report to him within such time as he shall prescribe. Such report shall include a statement of the facts with respect to the dispute, including each party's statement of its position but shall not contain any recommendations. The President shall file a copy of such report with the Service and shall make its contents available to the public.

Section 207.   (a) A board of inquiry shall be composed of a chairman and such other members as the President shall determine, and shall have power to sit and act in any place within the United States and to conduct such hearings either in public or in private, as it may deem necessary or proper, to ascertain the facts with respect to the causes and circumstances of the dispute.

* * * * *

Section 208.   (a) Upon receiving a report from a board of inquiry the President may direct the Attorney General to petition any district court of the United States having jurisdiction of the parties to enjoin such strike or lockout or the continuing thereof, and if the court finds that such threatened or actual strike or lockout—

(i) affects an entire industry or a substantial part thereof engaged in trade, commerce, transportation, transmission, or communication among the several States or with foreign nations, or engaged in the production of goods for commerce; and

(ii) if permitted to occur or to continue, will imperil the national health or safety, it shall have jurisdiction to enjoin any such strike or lockout, or the continuing thereof, and to make such other orders as may be appropriate.

* * * * *

Section 209.   (a) Whenever a district court has issued an order under section 208 enjoining acts or practices which imperil or threaten to imperil the national health or safety, it shall be the duty of the parties to the labor dispute giving rise to such order to make every effort to adjust and settle their differences, with the assistance of the Service created by this Act. Neither party shall be under any duty to accept, in whole or in part, any proposal of settlement made by the Service.

(b) Upon the issuance of such order, the President shall reconvene the board of inquiry which has previously reported with respect to the dispute. At the end of a 60-day period (unless the dispute has been settled by that time), the board of inquiry shall report to the President the current position of the parties and the efforts which have been made for settlement, and shall include a statement by each party of its position and a statement of the employer's last offer of settlement. The President shall make such report available to the public. The National Labor Relations Board, within the succeeding 15 days, shall take a secret ballot of the employees of each employer involved in the dispute on the question of whether they wish to accept the final offer of settlement made by their employer as stated by him and shall certify the results thereof to the Attorney General within 5 days thereafter.

Section 210.   Upon the certification of the results of such a ballot or upon a settlement being reached, whichever happens sooner, the Attorney General shall move the court to discharge the injunction, which motion shall then be granted and the injunction discharged. When such motion is granted, the President shall submit to the Congress a full and comprehensive report of the proceedings, including the findings of the board of inquiry and the ballot taken by the National Labor Relations Board, together with such recommendations as he may see fit to make for consideration and appropriate action.

* * * * *

[Omitted: Section 211, which covers authorization for collection and dissemination of collective bargaining information by federal agencies, and Section 212, which exempts persons covered by provisions of the Railway Labor Act from the provisions of the LMRA.]

Conciliation of Labor Disputes in the Health Care Industry

Section 213.   (a) If, in the opinion of the Director of the Federal Mediation and Conciliation Service, a threatened or actual strike or lockout affecting a health care institution will, if permitted to occur or to continue, substantially interrupt the delivery of health care in the locality concerned, the Director may further assist in the resolution of the impasse by establishing within 30 days after the notice to the Federal Mediation and Conciliation Service under clause (A) of the last sentence of section 8(d), which is required by clause (3) of such section 8(d), or within 10 days after the notice under clause (B), an impartial Board of Inquiry to investigate the issues involved in the dispute and to make a written report thereon to the parties within 15 days after the establishment of such a Board. The written report shall contain the findings of fact together with the Board's recommendations for settling the dispute, with the objective of achieving a prompt, peaceful and just settlement of the dispute. Each such Board shall be composed of such number of individuals as the Director may deem desirable. No member appointed under this section shall have any interest or involvement in the health care institutions or the employee organizations involved in the dispute.

* * * * *

[Omitted: Section 213(b), which provides for compensation for members appointed to a Board formed under Section 213(a).]

(c) After the establishment of a board under subsection (a) of this section and for 15 days after any such board has issued its report, no change in the status quo in effect prior to the expiration of the contract in the case of negotiations for a contract renewal, or in effect prior to the time of the impasse in the case of an initial bargaining negotiation, except by agreement, shall be made by the parties to the controversy.

(d) There are authorized to be appropriated such sums as may be necessary to carry out the provisions of this section.

Title III

Suits by and against Labor Organizations

Section 301.   (a) Suits for violation of contracts between an employer and a labor organization representing employees in an industry affecting commerce as defined in this Act, or between any such labor organizations, may be brought in any district court of the United States having jurisdiction of the parties, without respect to the amount in controversy or without regard to the citizenship of the parties.

(b) Any labor organization which represents employees in an industry affecting commerce as defined in this Act and any employer whose activities affect commerce as defined in this Act shall be bound by the acts of its agents. Any such labor organization may sue or be sued as an entity and in behalf of the employees whom it represents in the courts of the United States. Any money judgment against a labor organization in a district court of the United States shall be enforceable only against the organization as an entity and against its assets, and shall not be enforceable against any individual member or his assets.

(c) For the purposes of actions and proceedings by or against labor organizations in the district courts of the United States, district courts shall be deemed to have jurisdiction of a labor organization (1) in the district in which such organization maintains its principal offices, or (2) in any district in which its duly authorized officers or agents are engaged in representing or acting for employee members.

(d) The service of summons, subpoena, or other legal process of any court of the United States upon an officer or agent of a labor organization, in his capacity as such, shall constitute service upon the labor organization.

(e) For the purposes of this action, in determining whether any person is acting as an "agent" of another person so as to make such other person responsible for his acts, the question of whether the specific acts performed were actually authorized or subsequently ratified shall not be controlling.

* * * * *

[Omitted: Section 302—Restrictions on payments to employee representatives.]

Boycotts and Other Unlawful Combinations

Section 303.   (a) It shall be unlawful, for the purpose of this section only, in an industry or activity affecting commerce, for any labor organization to engage in any activity or conduct defined as an unfair labor practice in section 8(b) (4) of the National Labor Relations Act, as amended.

(b) Whoever shall be injured in his business or property by reason of any violation of subsection (a) may sue therefor in any district court of the United States subject to the limitations and provisions of Section 301 hereof without respect to the amount of the controversy, or in any other court having jurisdiction of the parties, and shall recover the damages sustained by him and the cost of the suit.

* * * * *

[Omitted are the following sections: Section 304—Restrictions on political contributions; Title IV—Creation of a joint committee to study and report on basic problems affecting labor relations and productivity.]

Title V

Definitions

Section 501.   When used in this Act—

(1) The term "industry affecting commerce" means any industry or activity in commerce or in which a labor dispute would burden or obstruct commerce or tend to burden or obstruct commerce or the free flow of commerce.

(2) The term "strike" includes any strike or other concerted stoppage of work by employees (including a stoppage by reason of the expiration of a collective bargaining agreement) and any concerted slowdown or other concerted interruption of operations by employees.

(3) The terms "commerce," "labor disputes," "employer," "employee," "labor organization," "representative," "person," and "supervisor" shall have the same meaning as when used in the National Labor Relations Act as amended by this Act.

Saving Provision

Section 502.   Nothing in this Act shall be construed to require an individual employee to render labor or service without his consent, nor shall anything in this Act be construed to make the quitting of his labor by an individual employee an illegal act; nor shall any court issue any process to compel the performance by an individual employee of such labor or service, without his consent; nor shall the quitting of labor by an employee or employees in good faith because of abnormally dangerous conditions for work at the place of employment of such employee or employees be deemed a strike under this Act.

Separability

Section 503.   If any provision of this Act, or the application of such provision to any person or circumstance, shall be held invalid, the remainder of this Act, or the application of such provision to persons or circumstances other than those as to which it is held invalid, shall not be affected thereby.

Index to Cases for Part I

Case Number and Title	Principal Issues of Case	Principal LMRA Provisions Involved
1. Discharge of a New Employee for a "Bad Attitude"	Discharge of employee who made prounion comments in presence of company executive.	8(a) (1), 8(a) (3)
2. Were the LPNs Agents of the Employer?	Union's charges that certain employees acted on behalf of management to interfere with union-organizing effort.	2(2), 2(13), 8(a) (1), 8(c)
3. A Dispute over Employees to Be Included in the Bargaining Unit	Appropriate status of certain personnel concerning their inclusion in a bargaining unit.	9(c)
4. Jurisdiction of the NLRB over a Government Contractor	Company's contention that it was not an employer under LMRA because it was subject to requirements of another federal statute.	2(2), 2(6), 2(7), Sec. 6, Sec. 9, 8(a) (5), 8(d)
5. Was the Company's Posted Notice an Unlawful Threat?	Company's posted notice during union representational election campaign that union claimed was unlawful.	Sec. 7, 8(a) (1), 8(c)
6. Were the Employees Laid Off in a Discriminatory Manner?	Layoff of certain employees following union representational election.	8(a) (1), 8(a) (3)
7. Discharge for Lying, or a Pretext for Terminating a Union Organizer?	Discharge of union organizer for allegedly untruthful statements.	8(a) (1), (8)(a) (3)
8. Discharge for Gross Negligence, or for Union Activities?	Discharge of three employees for a costly production error; two of three employees were union adherents.	8(a) (1), 8(a) (3)
9. Termination of the Nurse for a "Threat of Retaliation"	Termination of union supporter who engaged in a verbal confrontation with her supervisor.	8(a) (1), 8(a) (3)
10. The Sample NLRB Ballot Marked with an "X" in the "No" Box	Contested representational election due to alleged employer misconduct.	9(c)
11. Racial/Ethnic Prejudice during a Union Representational Election	Union distribution of controversial magazine letter to bargaining unit employees that employer claimed improperly prejudiced election outcome.	9(c)

51

Index to Cases for Part I (*continued*)

Index to Cases for Part I (*continued*)

53

Index to Cases for Part I (*concluded*)

Case Number and Title	Principal Issues of Case	Principal LMRA Provisions Involved
30. The Union's Letter to Nonmember Employees Who Crossed the Picket Line	Union letter to nonmember bargaining unit employees who crossed picket line to work during strike.	2(13), Sec. 7, 8(b) (1) (A)
31. Should the NLRB Twice Defer to the Arbitrator's Award?	Discharge of elected union president under terms of an arbitrator's award banning him from holding union office.	Sec. 7, 8(a) (1), 8(a) (3)
32. Religious Objections to Paying Union Dues	Issue of whether employee was entitled to exemption from union financial obligations on religious grounds.	8(a) (3), 8(b) (2), Sec. 19
33. Was the Union Contract Proposal a "Hot Cargo" Clause?	Union effort to have owner-drivers of trucks become employees and union members.	8(b) (4) (A), 8(b) (4) (B), 8(e), 10(I)
34. Who Should Install the Fiber Optic Cable System?	Jurisdictional issue involving claims of two unions to perform disputed work.	8(b) (4) (i) and (ii), 8(b) (4) (D), 10(k), 10(I)
35. A "Work Preservation" or "Cease Doing Business" Issue?	Union's effort to require funeral home to comply with arbitrator's decision interpreting contractual provision that required hiring drivers from an industry "extra board."	8(b) (4) (i), 8(b) (4) (ii), 8(e), 10(I), Sec. 301
36. Was the Attempted Consumer Boycott Legal?	Union handbilling of customers at a shopping center to urge them not to patronize stores.	8(b) (4), 8(b) (4) (ii) (B), 10(I)

CASE 1
DISCHARGE OF A NEW EMPLOYEE FOR A "BAD ATTITUDE"

Company:
  Salem Leasing Corporation, Hickory, North Carolina

Employee and Union:
  Sam Hanson[1] and the International Union of Electrical, Radio, and Machine Workers

Background

Salem was a truck leasing company with eight locations in North Carolina. Sam Hanson, who was hired by Salem in June 1982, worked at its facility in Hickory, North Carolina. Hanson was hired as a "tire man"; his responsibilities included changing tires on trucks, maintaining a tire inventory, and filling out the required paperwork. Hanson was also given additional duties as a "fuel man" when the fuel man quit. Hanson successfully completed Salem's 90-day probationary period for new employees. He was fired on October 26, 1982, one month after his probationary period had ended.

Hanson had previously worked from 1973 to 1981 for General Electric at its unionized plant near Hickory, but he had been laid off because of economic conditions. While employed at General Electric, Hanson was a member of the International Union of Electrical, Radio, and Machine Workers, AFL-CIO, a membership that he maintained while working for Salem. None of Salem's employees were represented by a labor organization.

Hanson was fired one week after a company-sponsored and -financed fishing trip to a campground in South Carolina, which took place on October 17 and 18, 1982. On the evening of October 17, during a poker game in Hanson's room, Hanson responded to questions from fellow employees regarding his employment at G.E. and his union membership. He described his pay and benefits at G.E. and the amount of his union dues. He expressed a desire to return to G.E., because his pension there would vest in six months. He stated, however, that given current economic conditions, he probably would not be rehired for a couple of years. At one point during the game, Hanson commented on a pot won by another player, saying, "Take that little bit of change; it's just chicken feed, like what I'm making."

Also in the poker game was a Salem vice president, George Scalia. A day or two after the fishing trip, Scalia called Marcus Newman, president of Salem, and told him that Hanson had a "bad attitude." Newman then called Arnie Donner, operations manager at the Hickory facility, and told him that Hanson had a "bad attitude." Donner fired Hanson a few days later.

On October 29, 1982, Hanson, with the assistance of Larry Kitchen, business representative of the union, filed charges with the NLRB alleging that Hanson's discharge

---

[1]The names of all individuals are disguised.

was in violation of Sections 8(a) (1) and 8(a) (3) of LMRA. Hanson and the union urged that Hanson be reinstated and made whole for all lost pay and benefits, and that the company be ordered to cease and desist in any and all activities designed to discriminate against employees and discourage membership in a labor union.

Position of the Employee and the Union

Counsel for Sam Hanson and the union argued that there was no credible evidence that Hanson was an inadequate employee. Hanson had successfully completed the 90-day probationary period and had even been assigned additional responsibilities. Thus, the firing of Hanson shortly after he had made favorable comments about General Electric, a unionized employer, in front of a Salem vice president was quite indicative that the real motive for discharging Hanson was his prounion remarks, to which the company management objected.

In this regard, an office employee named Melanie Smith testified that in late September 1982, Arnie Donner had told several employees including herself that they "ought to be thankful that there wasn't any union organization because all the union places were going broke . . . "

Another employee, Willie Carol, submitted a notarized affidavit claiming that on the same day that Hanson was fired, he heard Arnie Donner tell another supervisor, Timothy Bunges, that the company "should not have hired a union man." Carol acknowledged that he didn't know whether Donner was referring to Sam Hanson.

In summary, counsel for Sam Hanson and the union claimed that Hanson's discharge was motivated primarily by the company's desire to "thwart and chill" any prounion organizing efforts and prounion sentiments among Salem's employees. The company had clearly violated Sections 8(a) (1) and 8(a) (3) of the Act, and the NLRB should order the requested remedy accordingly.

Position of the Company

Several company managers testified vigorously that Sam Hanson's discharge in October 1982 would have occurred irrespective of any prounion comments that Hanson had made. Even though Hanson had completed his probationary period, his work performance was marginal at best, and it was poorer than most of his fellow employees. Economic conditions during fall 1982 had necessitated terminating several employees, and Hanson was one of those who was terminated. Arnie Donner testified that he had chosen to terminate those employees with the least job tenure and the poorest work performance. In his view, Hanson was "among the worst of the lot." The company felt that Hanson's comments in front of Vice President Scalia showed that Hanson was very disloyal to the company, and this was what Scalia had meant when he reported to the company president that Hanson had a "bad attitude" that could not be tolerated. The company's motives in discharging Hanson had nothing to do with discriminating against Hanson because of his prounion sentiments. Hanson was an "at-will" employee who could be terminated at any time by the company, and the company had chosen to discharge him for his poor work performance and bad attitudes.

Concerning alleged "antiunion" comments that union witnesses ascribed to Arnie Donner, the company claimed that these were isolated statements of just one manager that were taken out of context. None of Donner's statements nor the discharge of Hanson were intended to interfere with any employee's protected legal rights to attempt to join a labor union if this was his or her desire.

In summary, the company claimed that the unfair labor practice charges were without foundation; they were a misguided attempt by Hanson and the union to embarrass the company and to regain employment for Hanson, who was an unsatisfactory employee. The company urged that the unfair labor practice charges be dismissed in their entirety.

Questions

1. Why is this type of case difficult for the NLRB to decide?
2. Did Sam Hanson's comments reflect disloyalty and a "bad attitude" toward the company? Why, or why not?
3. Does the fact that several other employees were terminated at about the same time as Hanson for economic and other reasons prove that Hanson's discharge would have happened irrespective of any of his prounion sentiments? Discuss.
4. Why should any manager be careful to avoid making statements such as those attributed to Arnie Donner in this case?

CASE 2
WERE THE LPNS AGENTS OF THE EMPLOYER?

Employer:
St. Paul's Church Home, St. Paul, Minnesota

Union:
Local No. 113, Service Employees Union

Background

In 1981, the union was engaged in an intensive organizing campaign to gain representational rights for certain employees of St. Paul's Church Home. On August 27, 1981, the union sent a letter to James Hammer,[1] administrator of the nursing home, which claimed that the union had secured signed authorization cards from a majority of employees, and that the employer should recognize the union as the employees' bargaining representative.

At approximately noon the same day, a group of employees who were opposed to the union met with Administrator Hammer on the back porch of the main building. These employees were Vickie Shear, Elizabeth Dore, Brian Paul, and Magda Krantz. Shear and Dore were Licensed Practical Nurses (LPNs); Paul and Krantz were employees who served as orderlies in the care of residents and patients. The four discussed the union organizing campaign with Hammer and told him that they opposed having a union in a health care facility. They requested permission from Hammer to hold meetings with the employees, and they asked Hammer if he would speak at these meetings. Elizabeth Dore said that such meetings were needed to find out why so many of the employees wanted a union to represent them. Hammer gave them permission to proceed. A number of prounion employees had observed the group on the back porch, but at this time they did not know what was being discussed.

Shortly after, Elizabeth Dore announced over the intercom system that there would be two employee meetings in the chapel, the first at 1 P.M. and the second at 2 P.M. She urged all employees who could be spared from their regular duties to attend. When the first meeting began, Administrator Hammer, Elizabeth Dore, and Vickie Shear were in the front part of the chapel. Vickie Shear opened the meeting and did most of the talking.

After her opening remarks, Shear expressed her concerns about the union organizing effort, and then asked the assembled employees why they wanted a union when they were not willing to discuss their complaints with supervisors and management. At this point, a prounion employee, Betsy Conrad, stood up and said, "What gives you the right to call us here and ask us about the union? We don't have to listen to you!" Administrator Hammer then stood up and said that Conrad was right, and that the employees did not have to listen to Shear or him if they didn't want to do so. A large

---

[1]The names of all individuals are disguised.

group of employees then left the chapel, and the meeting soon adjourned. A second group of employees assembled in the chapel at 2 P.M. Some of them had been present at the first meeting.

Vickie Shear was again at the front of the chapel with Administrator Hammer. After Hammer made several general remarks concerning the union organizing campaign, a number of prounion employees indicated their objections to having Hammer at a meeting where employees wanted to express their views; they felt Hammer should leave. Hammer acquiesced to this request and left the chapel. Vickie Shear then assumed the role of chairperson of the meeting, and there ensued a discussion concerning the pros and cons of the employees' voting for the union to represent them. Near the end of the meeting, Vickie Shear expressed her opposition to the union: "If you vote for the union and the union gets in, all of the benefits that you now have will be gone, and this place will be run with a lot more rules than before."

Also at this meeting was Elizabeth Dore, who was seated near the front of the chapel. Immediately after Vickie Shear's statement, Dore stood up and said, "Vickie's right! If the union gets in, you can kiss all of your benefits good-bye!"

Shortly after, the union filed unfair labor practice charges alleging that St. Paul's Church Home had illegally interfered with the union's organizing efforts in violation of Section 8(a) (1) of the Labor Management Relations Act.[2] The union requested that the NLRB order the employer to cease and desist its interference with the protected activities of its employees.

Position of the Union

The union claimed that the actions and statements of the two LPNs, Vickie Shear and Elizabeth Dore, constituted unfair labor practices, because they had served as agents of management at St. Paul's Church Home within the meaning of Sections 2(2) and 2(13) of LMRA. The union pointed out that Shear and Dore and two other antiunion employees had met with Administrator Hammer, who had expressly authorized a meeting to ascertain why employees wanted union representation. At the initial meeting—which was announced over the intercom system, held on company time, and attended by Hammer—Shear asked employees why they wanted a union. This query, in the union's view, was a direct violation of Section 8(a) (1) of LMRA. At the second meeting, convened shortly after the first meeting ended, Shear and Dore both stated to the employees that they would lose their benefits if they chose the union. This, in the union's view, was an even more blatant violation of Section 8(a) (1) of the Act, since it was a threat of reprisal as prohibited under Section 8(c).

The union claimed that even though Shear and Dore were not supervisors or managers, they had acted on behalf of the employer, and the employer was accountable for what they did and said. Hammer had expressly authorized the LPNs to hold a meeting to find out why the employees wanted the union. Although Hammer may not have

---

[2]During the ongoing union organizing campaign in 1981, the union also filed a number of other unfair labor practice charges involving claims of interference, improper surveillance, and discrimination. These involved other incidents at the employer's facility and other personnel.

specifically authorized their loss-of-benefits threats, these statements furthered the employer's position in opposing the union. The meetings were held under circumstances leading employees reasonably to believe that they reflected the management's position, rather than individual employee sentiment. It was only logical to conclude that Shear and Dore were agents of the employer, and as such, the employer had violated the Act by interrogating employees and threatening them with loss of their benefits if they selected the union.

Position of the Employer

The employer strongly denied that the LPNs had spoken and acted on behalf of the management of St. Paul's Church Home. Administrator Hammer acknowledged that he had agreed to permit the antiunion employees to announce and hold two meetings in the chapel. At the first meeting, he told the employees that they did not have to stay and listen if they did not want to. At the second meeting, he left the chapel because of the sentiment of prounion employees that he should do so. When Shear and Dore made their statements about the possible loss of benefits if the union gained representational rights, Hammer had not been present. Hammer testified that he had never given Shear and Dore any instructions or authority concerning what they should or would say at these meetings. Shear and Dore had expressed their own personal viewpoints; what they said had not been authorized by Hammer. Further, they were LPNs, who were not supervisors or managers.

Counsel for the Church Home argued that under Section 2(13) of the Act, the responsibility of an employer for the actions of others who are alleged to be its agents has been held by the NLRB to be controlled by the application of the common law rules of agency.[3] The establishment of an agency relationship requires proof of an employer's specific bestowal of authority on the asserted agent, whether actual or apparent, either in advance or by later agreement.

The employer in this case did not give authority to Shear or Dore, or give them specific approval to do and say what they did. In no way were Shear and Dore acting as agents of management. Therefore, the unfair labor practice charges filed by the union were devoid of any substance and should be dismissed.

Questions

1. Were the LPNs acting as agents of the employer? Why, or why not?
2. In connection with the first question above, what inferences—if any—should be drawn from the facts that: (a) Administrator Hammer was seen with a group of antiunion employees shortly before the meetings were called and held; (b) the Home's intercom system and chapel were used; (c) Hammer was present at some time during both meetings?

---

[3]The primary case citation here was *Electric Motors & Specialties*, 149 NLRB 1432, 57 LRRM 1513 (1964).

3. Could the unfair labor practice charges involved in this situation be of sufficient consequence to move the NLRB to order the employer to recognize the union, or at least for the Board to direct a representational election? Discuss.

4. Why should both employers and labor organizations be careful in regard to the interpretation and application of Sections 2(2), 2(5), and 2(13) of LMRA? Discuss.

CASE 3
A DISPUTE OVER EMPLOYEES TO BE INCLUDED IN THE BARGAINING UNIT

Company:
   S&S Parts Distributors Warehouse, Inc., Nashville, Tennessee

Union:
   Local No. 150, Retail, Wholesale & Department Store Union

Background

The company was engaged in the wholesale distribution of auto parts from its Nashville, Tennessee, facility. The company sold parts to customers located in the Nashville metropolitan area and within a 120 to 150 mile radius of Nashville.

In early 1984, the union filed a petition with the NLRB to conduct an election to determine whether the union would represent certain employees at the company. The regional director of the NLRB had determined that the unit appropriate for collective bargaining within the meaning of Section 9(c) of LMRA should include the following:

> All order pullers, packers, truck loaders, shipping department employees, customer order takers, core department (return goods) employees, local truck drivers, and the will-call employee and the receiving employee employed at the Employer's Nashville, Tennessee, warehouse facility; excluding office clerical employees, outside salespersons, guards, and supervisors as defined in the Act.

However, a dispute arose concerning whether five additional employees (who held four different job classification positions) should be included in the bargaining unit. Pursuant to Section 9(b) of LMRA, the NLRB took additional testimony and evidence in order to determine which, if any, of these employees should be included in the bargaining unit and vote in the representational election.

Company Operations.   Customers ordered parts from the company over the telephone by calling a special "sales" number, or by coming in person to the "will-call" desk in the Nashville facility. The company arranged for delivery of ordered parts to customers, or customers could pick up the parts themselves at the will-call desk.

Customer orders were designated "regular" or "special." Regular orders were filled from an inventory of parts maintained at the Nashville facility. Special orders were those the company did not have in stock; these were filled by obtaining parts from other local facilities that did have them in stock, or by ordering them directly from the manufacturer.

The entire wholesale operation was performed in a single building divided into a warehouse area and an office area. The warehouse was two stories high and occupied two-thirds of the building, stretching in front and to the right of the front entrance. The center of the warehouse was filled with shelves on which the regular inventory of parts was stored. The will-call desk was located in the left front corner of the warehouse area inside the front entrance to the building, and the "core" or returned goods department was located in the right front corner.

The office area occupied the remaining one-third of the building and was divided into two floors. The first floor contained the offices of the president, vice president, and plant manager, as well as the only restrooms in the facility. The second floor contained the employee breakroom and one other large room in which catalogs listing auto parts were stored. The shipping department, where customer orders were staged and loaded on trucks, was located at the rear of the warehouse area.

The company recorded parts received, ordered, shipped, and returned on computer terminals (or CRTs) consisting of a video screen and a keyboard. Information entered on the terminals was processed by a computer in Memphis, Tennessee, which was owned by another company and shared by other businesses.

Six employees took "regular" customer orders over the telephone. These customer order takers shared an office in the first floor office area with the receptionist/switchboard operator. (The parties had agreed that the receptionist/switchboard operator should be excluded from the collective bargaining unit.)

Each of the regular customer order takers sat in front of a CRT. When ordering a part, the customer provided the order taker with his customer number and the part number. The order taker entered this information on the CRT, but the customer was not invoiced at this time. The computer generated a typed copy of the order called a "pick ticket" on a printer located in the warehouse area.

Four shipping desk employees sorted the pick tickets as they emerged from the printer; they then placed them in metal carts and put the carts on a moving track that made a circuit of the warehouse floor. Thirteen order pullers removed the carts from the track and read the accompanying pick tickets. They put the ordered merchandise in the carts and replaced them on the track. The track conveyed the carts to the staging area, where the orders were checked and packed.

The order takers communicated to employees on the warehouse floor via an intercom or by calling through a window between their office and the warehouse area. An order taker could call an order back up on the CRT to verify a part number if an order puller became confused. The order taker could also use the CRT to check the balance in inventory of a particular part if the order puller was unable to find it.

In the mornings, order pullers were given "lost sales" forms listing parts that the computer showed had been reduced to a zero balance in inventory. The order pullers checked to see if they had a supply of these parts. If the parts were on hand, the order pullers wrote this information on the forms. One will-call employee passed merchandise to customers across the will-call desk, secured customer signatures on the pick tickets accompanying the merchandise, and placed the tickets in a basket from which they were taken and used for billing the customers.

The company's merchandise was staged on racks in the shipping department before being loaded on trucks. Each customer's order was placed in a space on the racks labeled with the customer's name.

Five truck loaders unloaded incoming trucks and loaded orders on outgoing trucks. The company employed three local truck drivers to make two scheduled delivery runs a day to customers in the city of Nashville. The company also employed four packers and one receiving employee.

The company sometimes would be unable to ship as many parts as ordered. To ensure that customers were billed only for merchandise received, orders were retrieved on a CRT each evening and corrected to reflect goods actually shipped. This processing was known as "entering the pick results for the day." One of the six regular order takers received customer calls only in the morning and entered the pick results for the day in the afternoon.

Two employees received returned goods in the core or returned goods department. Returned goods arrived in plastic boxes accompanied by packing slips, also called credit memos. The returned goods employees unloaded the merchandise and verified that the packing slips correctly reflected the parts returned. They then stored returned parts on shelves in the core department until it was determined if the parts should be replaced in inventory, sent back to the manufacturer, or returned to the customer.

The Disputed Employees

The company contended that five employees, who held four different job classification positions, should be included in the proposed bargaining unit and be permitted to vote in the representational election. They were:

1. Jane Schiller,[1] customer credit clerk.
2. Debra Martin and Connie Karlton, special-order takers.
3. Carla Delsing, catalog employee.
4. Betty Mullins, bookkeeper/substitute order taker.

Each of the disputed employees was paid an hourly wage, as were all the other employees to be included in the bargaining unit. They punched the same time clock, received the same fringe benefits, used the same breakroom, and were scheduled to take the same breaks as the other included employees.[2]

Jane Schiller, Customer Credit Clerk.   Jane Schiller handled the paperwork for the core department. She shared an office in the first-floor office area with Connie Karlton. The office contained a CRT.

After the two core employees checked the credit memo listing parts returned against the accompanying merchandise, the credit memo was given to Schiller who entered it on the CRT, and the computer automatically issued a credit to the customer.

If there was no price in the system for a returned part, Schiller looked up the price on the price sheets in her office, the warehouse area, or the purchasing department. Schiller would return this paperwork to the returned goods manager in the core department, Charles Sen, who supervised the two core employees. Sen checked the paperwork to ensure that it was in order before the credit was issued to the customer.

---

[1]The names of all individuals are disguised.

[2]Most employees worked from approximately 8 A.M. to 5 P.M. Some warehouse employees stayed until 7 or 8 P.M. to load trucks, and the "pick results" employee worked until 7 or 8 P.M. to finish reconciling the day's orders.

If a returned part was not in the system and no longer on the price sheet, Schiller took the corresponding packing slip back to the core department. The part was pulled from the shelf and sent back to the customer because the company could not issue a credit.

Schiller spent 85 to 90 percent of her time in her office, 50 percent on the CRT. Company management had indicated that Schiller was not physically located in the core department only because it would be prohibitively expensive to run a CRT cable out there, and a CRT in the core department would not be secured against unauthorized use.

Although Charles Sen supervised Schiller in the completion of her core department paperwork, her supervisor in regard to performance evaluation, pay, and discipline was the coordinator of the advertising program, Art Woods.

Debra Martin and Connie Karlton, Special-Order Takers.[3]   Debra Martin worked with Shelby Malone in the purchasing department, an office located in the first-floor office area. Malone was a member of management who performed supervisory duties including setting up price sheets, handling outside salespersons, and inventory buying and feasibility studies on new lines.

Martin placed special orders for parts obtained directly from out-of-town manufacturers. She received these orders from customers over the telephone. On a given day, she could spend a great deal of time on the telephone, or very little.

Merchandise ordered for a customer by Martin was either drop shipped by the supplier to the customer, or delivered to the company and routed through the Nashville warehouse. Martin received the invoices for drop shipments. When the company was billed for a special order, Martin wrote a pick ticket that was punched into the computer by the pick results employee so that the customer in turn was billed for the merchandise.

Martin was expected to follow up on all special orders. She routinely went into the warehouse area to check on special orders that were being delivered to the warehouse for shipment to customers. Martin might ask the warehouse manager for information about an order. Or she might go out on the warehouse floor to ask the receiving employee if an order had come into the warehouse, or ask the shipping desk employees how an order was being handled.

Martin kept records of the special orders she placed for customers and of merchandise the company sent back to its suppliers. She spent a few minutes every day filing, and she also kept track of merchandise coming into the warehouse to replenish the regular inventory. She used a calculator and worked on the CRT in the purchasing office daily.

Connie Karlton, whose desk was in a corner section of the office with Jane Schiller, placed special orders for parts that were not stocked by the company but which were

---

[3] All the regular order takers and the two special-order takers had transferred from warehouse positions. All order takers and CRT operators were trained by the company; training included typing skills if needed. All the regular order takers and both Jane Schiller and Debra Martin could substitute for the so-called pick employees.

available from other local suppliers. Throughout each day, she took customer requests for parts over the telephone and wrote the corresponding pick tickets. She also ordered parts listed on computerized pick tickets that were sent in to her, called "musts."

Company truck drivers picked up local special orders. The shipping desk employees sorted and staged the special orders brought in by the drivers throughout the day. Karlton went into the warehouse area to check on special orders even more frequently than Martin, because all orders placed for customers with local suppliers were routed through the warehouse.

Martin did not share an office with Karlton, because the manufacturers with whom Martin dealt were also the suppliers of the company's regular inventory. Karlton did not use a CRT.

Both Martin and Karlton were under the supervision of the company's warehouse manager, Henry Milburn, although Milburn's desk was located in the warehouse.

Carla Delsing, Catalog Employee.   Carla Delsing shared the catalog room in the second-floor area with the company's clerk/typist. The parties had agreed that the clerk/typist should be excluded from the collective bargaining unit. Delsing's office was reached by passing through the employee breakroom. She, too, was supervised by the warehouse manager, Henry Milburn.

Manufacturers periodically issued new lines of replacement parts with new part numbers and constantly revised the prices of parts. Catalogs listing new part numbers and revised price sheets were mailed to the company by manufacturers and routed to Delsing. The 30-by-40-foot room in which Delsing worked was lined with 8-foot-high bins like those used on the warehouse floor to store auto parts. Delsing filed new catalogs in the bins in alphabetical order by manufacturer. She also removed and replaced superseded price sheets according to the manufacturers' instructions.

The company routinely shipped updated catalogs to customers with their orders of auto parts. Delsing placed catalogs to be shipped in the spaces allotted to customers on the rack in the staging area. She would go down to the shipping department 10 to 12 times a day to stage catalogs.

Sometimes a customer would call and request that a catalog be delivered on other than a regularly scheduled delivery day. It was not part of Delsing's job to talk on the telephone, but she might take a customer's order for a catalog if she was available. Otherwise, such orders were taken by the regular customer order takers and passed on to Delsing.

Betty Mullins, Bookkeeper/Substitute Order Taker.   Betty Mullins had worked as a regular customer order taker for nine months. Several weeks before the hearing in this case, Mullins was assigned new duties in the bookkeeping department. She shared an office in the first-floor office area with the head bookkeeper and the cashier and accounts payable bookkeeper. The parties had agreed that the head bookkeeper and the cashier and accounts payable bookkeeper lacked sufficient community of interest with other warehouse employees to be included in the proposed bargaining unit.

Mullins' principal classification was bookkeeper. The head bookkeeper supervised Mullins in her bookkeeping functions. Mullins kept small sets of books for customers who requested this service. She did not keep the company's books or have access to payroll or personnel records. Occasionally, the head bookkeeper would ask her to add time cards. Mullins kept a check journal, a general ledger, and a record of the daily receipts at the company's store location. She used a typewriter and an adding machine.

Ellen Cornelius, the company's vice president, testified that Mullins had not worked as an order taker since she had been assigned to the bookkeeping department. But as soon as Mullins had learned her new duties, she was to be designated as a regular fill-in order taker and be called upon to substitute for full-time order takers who were ill or on vacation. Cornelius added, however, that any prediction as to how much time Mullins would spend as an order taker in the future would be pure speculation, and that "it could be a lot of time, very little, or none at all."

Positions of the Parties

In essence, the company claimed that all five of the disputed employees should be in the proposed collective bargaining unit, because their work was closely aligned and integrated with the other employees who were to be in the warehouse bargaining unit. Citing a number of prior NLRB decisions,[4] the company further claimed that the work of these employees brought them into considerable contact with the warehouse employees; that their jobs did not require special skills or training as a prerequisite for their transfer to these jobs from the warehouse; and that all their work duties were necessary for the smooth functioning of the company's warehouse operations and dealings with customers.

The union contended, however, that the job positions of the five employees were all essentially clerical positions. These employees had been "promoted" from warehouse positions, and they no longer shared a direct community of interest or similar job duties with other employees who were to be in the bargaining unit. In particular, the union contended that Carla Delsing and Betty Mullins were office clericals who had responsibilities and duties that were quite different from those of warehouse employees. The union urged that all five of the disputed employees be excluded from the proposed bargaining unit and not be permitted to vote in the representational election.

Questions

1. Over the years, the NLRB has used various considerations to determine appropriate collective bargaining units and who should be included in a bargaining unit. Among the most important has been the "community of duties and interests of employees involved." In this regard, the NLRB will consider the following factors: (1) the degree of functional integration in the plant or office; (2) common supervision; (3) the nature of employee skills and functions; (4) the interchangeability and contact among employees; (5) the work site and general

---

[4]Among these were: *American Parts Systems,* 254 NLRB 901, 106 LRRM 1193 (1981); *Birdsall, Inc.,* 268 NLRB 186, 114 LRRM 1257 (1983); and *Napa Columbus Distribution Co.,* 269 NLRB 1052, 116 LRRM 1001 (1984).

working conditions; and (6) wages and benefits paid. With these types of considerations in mind, which of the disputed employees should or should not be included in the proposed collective bargaining unit in this case?

2. Why would the company be in favor of all of the five employees being in the bargaining unit and the union opposed?

3. Why are bargaining unit determinations of crucial significance in representational election outcomes and the longer-term relationships between the parties? Discuss.

CASE 4
JURISDICTION OF THE NLRB OVER A GOVERNMENT CONTRACTOR

Company:
  Dynaelectron Corporation, Aerospace Operations Division, Meridian, Mississippi
Union:
  United Automobile and Aerospace Workers

Background

In July 1987, the company was engaged in performing organizational-level maintenance on T-2 aircraft for the U.S. Navy at the Naval Air Station (NAS) in Meridian,
Mississippi. Organizational maintenance was performed at the site where an aircraft
was located, whether shore- or aircraft carrier–based. Such services included inspection, service, lubrication, adjustment or replacement of parts, and flight line services.
The existing contract between the company and the Navy was a one-year fixed-price
contract, with an option to renew annually for a total duration not to exceed five years.
   The union had filed a petition with the NLRB to conduct a representational election
to determine whether the union should represent the production and maintenance
employees at NAS Meridian. The company objected and contended that the petition
should be dismissed, because the company was a contractor subject to the terms of the
Service Contract Act and thus did not possess the ability to bargain meaningfully with
a labor organization. The Service Contract Act, originally passed in 1965 and amended
by Congress in 1972, applies to every contract in excess of $2,500 entered into by the
federal government where the primary purpose of the contract is to provide services to
the federal government. Under the Service Contract Act, the Department of Labor
(DOL) issues area wage determinations that set forth the minimum wages and fringe
benefits to be provided to service employees in a locality. The DOL wage determination
for the Meridian area in 1985 had established the minimum hourly wage rates for 23
job classifications. In addition, the wage determination required that the company must
provide fringe benefits with an average contribution of $1.08 an hour. These benefits
included life, accident, and health insurance; sick leave; pension and saving plans;
personal leave; severance pay; a specified amount of vacation based on length of
service; and nine paid holidays each year. As long as it maintained benefits valued at
at least the minimum rate, the company could provide these benefits in any form it
chose, and the company did not need the approval of the DOL or the Navy to change
the benefit package.

Position of the Company

The company contended that, because it was subject to the requirements of the Service
Contract Act, it was not an employer within the meaning of Section 2(2) of LMRA, and
that it was not engaged in commerce within the meaning of Sections 2(6) and 2(7) of

the Act. Therefore, the NLRB should decline jurisdiction in this case and not hold any representational election pursuant to Section 6 and Section 9 of LMRA.

The company made a number of major arguments in support of its position. First, the company asserted that when the Department of Labor (DOL) established a wage/benefit determination for an area (i.e., Meridian, Mississippi), this in effect had removed the company's control over terms and conditions of employment for its employees. The company's contract with the Navy was based on a compensation package for employees mandated by and consistent with the DOL's determination.

In this context, the company next contended that if the union should gain representational rights for the employees, the company's ability to bargain would be extremely limited and unrealistic. For example, if the company entered into negotiations with a labor organization during the period of the government contract, and a collective bargaining agreement resulted in costs and a contract price higher than that for which the company had bid, the company would not be able to recoup the difference until the next fiscal year, if at all. Therefore, the company would be unlikely to offer the union any additional wages/benefits beyond those specified in the DOL determination. This, in turn, would probably mean that the union would file unfair labor practices alleging that the company was not bargaining in good faith as required under Section 8(a) (5) and 8(d) of the Act.

Finally, the company asserted that it was the U.S. Navy Department which really was the employer, because the Navy exercised control over labor-management relations and the employees. Employees of the company had to adhere to Navy standards of dress and appearance and wear uniforms that identified them as the contractor's employees. The company's employees were subject to Navy regulations and directives, and the Navy's contracting officer could request that the company remove employees from contract work for unethical conduct, violation of Navy regulations, breach of security, or misconduct. Since the Navy really controlled employee relations, it (the Navy) was the true employer, and this, too, meant that the company could not realistically be expected to bargain with a union about wages, hours, and other terms and conditions of employment.

The company urged that the NLRB decline jurisdiction in this case matter and thus refuse to hold a union representational election.

Position of the Union

The union argued that the company was using a collection of invalid claims as a pretext for avoiding holding a representational election and eventually having to bargain with the union.

First, the union contended that the legislative history of the Service Contract Act supported the conclusion that Congress did not intend to exclude employees fulfilling federal government service contracts from the NLRB's jurisdiction. The Service Contract Act was enacted in 1965 to ensure that employees of service contractors received the prevailing wages and fringe benefits paid other employees performing similar work in the same locality. The statute was amended in 1972 to protect employees of successor contractors. These amendments established procedures to permit the Department of Labor to base the prevailing rates on collectively bargained rates, thereby preventing replacement contractors from underbidding incumbent contractors that have collective bargaining relationships with labor organizations.

Nothing in the Service Contract Act excluded an employer from an obligation to enter into a collective bargaining agreement where a union had gained representational rights for the employees. In fact, the Service Contract Act contemplated collective bargaining, since this law expressly provided that collectively bargained wages and benefits could be substituted for the prevailing compensation rates as determined by the DOL.[1] The statute, as amended, requires that every contract to furnish services for the federal government must contain minimum compensation standards based on either *(a)* prevailing wages and benefits; or *(b)* where a collective bargaining agreement exists, on the wages and benefits provided in the collective bargaining agreement.

The union further argued that the company, not the U.S. Navy or the Department of Labor, was indeed the employer and thus subject to the requirements of the Labor Management Relations Act (LMRA). The company was not prohibited from bargaining with a union concerning higher wages or higher fringe benefits. The company also had the ultimate authority to determine the primary terms and conditions of employment, including responsibility for hiring, discipline, and terminations.

In summary, since the company otherwise met the NLRB's standards for asserting jurisdiction under the LMRA, the mere fact that the employer also had to comply with requirements of the Service Contract Act should not bar the NLRB's assertion of jurisdiction over the Dynaelectron company. The union urged that the NLRB should direct that a representational election be held to determine whether the union would represent employees at the company.

Questions

1. Evaluate the company's contentions in this case. Which are the most persuasive? Least persuasive? Discuss.
2. Evaluate the union's contentions to the effect that the Service Contract Act did not exclude contract employers from also being covered by requirements of the LMRA.

---

[1]With respect to employee wage rates, the Service Contract Act provides that each service contract must contain: "A provision specifying the minimum monetary wages to be paid the various classes of service employees . . . as determined by the Secretary . . . in accordance with prevailing rates for such employees in the locality, or, where a collective bargaining agreement covers any such service employees, in accordance with the rates for such employees provided for in such agreement, including prospective wage increases provided for in such agreement as a result of arm's-length negotiations." 41 U.S.C. §351(a)(1).

With respect to employee fringe benefit levels, the Service Contract Act provides that each contract must contain: "A provision specifying the fringe benefits to be furnished . . . as determined by the Secretary . . . to be prevailing for such employees, in the locality, or where a collective bargaining agreement covers any such service employees, to be provided for in such agreement, including prospective fringe benefit increases provided for in such agreement as a result of arm's-length negotiations." 41 U.S.C. §351(a) (2).

3. The Fair Labor Standards Act (FLSA) as amended requires most employers in the private sector of the economy to pay at least a minimum hourly wage (as of 1991, $4.25) and to pay time and one-half for hours worked beyond 40 hours a week. For a private sector contractor, are these FLSA requirements similar to, or different from, the requirements with which a contractor with the federal government must comply under the Service Contract Act? Discuss.

4. Should the NLRB exert jurisdiction in this case? Why, or why not?

CASE 5
WAS THE COMPANY'S POSTED NOTICE AN UNLAWFUL THREAT?

Company:
   Milford Plains Limited Partnership, operators of Hamilton Inn, Milford, Connecticut

Union:
   Local Union No. 371, United Food and Commercial Workers (UFCW)

Background

The company operated a motel and restaurant in Milford, Connecticut. In early 1991, several employees contacted the local union office to inquire concerning union representation. The employees were provided with union authorization cards for them and other employees to sign. Subsequently, the cards were distributed to virtually all the wage-grade employees, and the union sent a staff representative to assist the employees in union organizational efforts.

The union representational campaign became known to the company's owners. Shortly after learning about it, the owners posted a notice on several bulletin boards used for employee communication purposes. The notice stated:

WHAT CAN THE UFCW GIVE YOU?

1. The <u>right</u> to <u>walk</u> a picket line.
2. The <u>right</u> to <u>go</u> out on strike.
3. The <u>right</u> to <u>pay</u> dues to the United Food and Commercial Workers Union.
4. The <u>right</u> to <u>throw</u> brickbats at cards of nonstrikers—even if they are your friends.
5. The <u>right</u> to <u>fear</u> for your safety and the safety of your loved ones if you oppose United Food and Commercial Workers Union strikes.
6. The <u>right</u> to <u>worry</u> over whether the United Food and Commercial Workers Union will let you work!

The union immediately filed unfair labor practice charges against the company contending that this notice was unlawful interference in violation of Section 8(a) (1) of LMRA.

Position of the Union

The union claimed that the company's posted notice went far beyond the permissible limits for employer communication as protected by Section 8(c) of LMRA. The company's notice referred to various consequences that would befall employees if they chose to have the union represent them. The company was predicting that employees would suffer violence and experience fear if they exercised their Section 7 right to vote for union representation. The notice even implied that the union would control whether or not unionized employees would be allowed to work. All these assertions by the company were threats that were unlawful and that constituted significant interference in the protected rights of employees to choose a union if they wished to do so.

The union urged the NLRB to find that the company had violated Section 8(a) (1) of the Act. The union requested the Board to direct the company to remove the posted notice, disavow its assertions, and post a new notice stating that it would not unlawfully interfere with the employees' protected rights.

Position of the Company

The company contended that the posted notice was nothing more than a statement of opinion concerning the possibilities of what might occur if the employees chose to join the union. An employer may discuss "in the abstract" various types of possible consequences of employees' joining a union, such as strikes, dues payments, and even the violence that can accompany union/management confrontations. Further, unions do attempt through negotiation of a labor agreement to control work assignments in certain situations.

The company argued that its notice was neither a threat of reprisal or force, nor promise of benefit, such as prohibited by Section 8(c) of LMRA. The company contended that the unfair labor practice charges were without merit and should be dismissed by the Board.

Questions

1. Did the posted notice of the company constitute a threat in violation of Section 8(c) and Section 8(a) (1) of LMRA? Why, or why not?

2. The company's posted notice was obviously designed to plant fears in the minds of the employees. Does a message that invokes fear constitute a threat that is unlawful interference?

3. Examine each of the six assertions in the company's posted notice. Which of these standing alone would appear to be lawful (if any)? Which of these standing alone would be appear unlawful (if any)? Taken collectively as a whole, was the company's posted notice lawful or unlawful?

4. Compare the issues in this case with those in Case 11, "Racial/Ethnic Prejudice during a Union Representational Election." Are there limits to free speech in a representational campaign? If so, what should these be?

CASE 6
WERE THE EMPLOYEES LAID OFF IN A DISCRIMINATORY MANNER?

Company:
Webb Furniture Enterprises, Inc., Galax, Virginia

Union:
Furniture Workers, AFL-CIO

Background

In 1981, the union waged a vigorous representational campaign that culminated in an NLRB-conducted election on October 14, 1981. The election result was 188 votes for and 204 votes against the union, with 20 challenged ballots. After resolution of the challenged ballots, the union still had lost the election.

Immediately thereafter, the union filed certain charges and objections with the NLRB concerning the election.[1] The union also distributed leaflets after the election announcing that the union would continue its efforts to organize the company's workers. On February 5, 1982, while the union's election objections were still pending, the company laid off 24 employees, allegedly for economic reasons.

On February 23, 1982, the union filed additional unfair labor practice charges against the company claiming that the layoff of at least eight of the employees was precipitated by discriminatory antiunion motivations of the company in violation of Sections 8(a) (3) and 8(a) (1) of LMRA.

Eventually these charges focused on the layoffs of four employees, Scott Hahn, Ed Pelayo, Laura Valli, and Steve Mortimer.[2] The union claimed that each of these employees had been laid off in a disparate, discriminatory manner; that the company was guilty of unfair labor practices; and that the company should be ordered to reinstate these employees and make them whole for all lost pay and benefits for the periods that they were discriminatorily laid off.

The company denied that its layoffs were motivated by antiunion considerations. The company claimed that: (1) all of the layoffs were economically necessary because of severely reduced business; and (2) that the criteria used in laying off the employees were related to business performance and were applied in a uniform, nondiscriminatory manner. In this regard, the company claimed that it considered job performance, versatility, physical condition, and attendance in deciding which employees would be laid off. If these factors resulted in a tie, then management claimed that it relied on seniority as the deciding factor.

---

[1] Among these were unfair labor practice charges concerning the company's no-solicitation rule and the interrogation of an employee concerning his union activities. The union was upheld on these charges, but the NLRB did not direct that a new election be held as part of its remedial order.

[2] The names of all individuals are disguised.

Scott Hahn.   Scott Hahn was employed in the machine room at the time he was laid off. Before the October 14, 1981, election, Hahn had signed union literature on several occasions, signed a union card, attended union meetings, worn union T-shirts and buttons daily, and passed out union literature before work on numerous occasions. Plant Superintendent Artis Reinhold acknowledged in testimony that Hahn was an "experienced machinist and a good man." Hahn testified on his own behalf that he had received "a lot of compliments" on the quality of his work before the layoff.

Nearly all the company's supervisors had observed Hahn passing out union literature. Plant Superintendent Reinhold admitted that he had examined union literature that was posted on a bulletin board to determine which employees had signed it. Reinhold also stated that he was in frequent contact with supervisors to determine the strength of the union's support in the various departments.

At the same time, Plant Superintendent Reinhold strongly maintained in his testimony that Scott Hahn was laid off because Hahn had originally been hired as a "spare hand," and because the department's assistant foreman could readily assume Hahn's job duties. Hahn's job function was to fill in for absentees in the department. Other employees were assigned to a specific machine eight hours a day. Reinhold testified that he could do without Hahn more easily than any of the other employees in the machine room, because the assistant foreman could take Hahn's place. Further, a primary basis for Hahn's being laid off was that he had been the least senior employee in this department.

The union maintained that Hahn had been singled out for layoff because of his strong and highly visible activities on behalf of the union. The company's reasons for laying off Hahn were merely a pretext designed to disguise the antiunion motivation of the company.

Ed Pelayo.   Ed Pelayo was employed as a ripsaw operator in the rough-end department when he was laid off. He had signed certain posted union literature and worn a union T-shirt and buttons several days a week before the election. He had also solicited for the union and distributed union cards. Several of the company's supervisors acknowledged that they had observed Pelayo wearing a union T-shirt and soliciting on behalf of the union.

Company managers claimed that Pelayo had been laid off principally because of his attendance record, which was "among the worst in the department." Moreover, the company claimed that Pelayo was "not versatile," that is, he could handle only one machine, and the company needed to retain those employees who could be assigned to different machines in the interests of efficiency and economy, particularly during a severe business decline such as was occurring in early 1982.

The union introduced attendance records that showed that two other employees in the same department who were not laid off had poorer attendance records than did Pelayo. Kaye O'Keefe and Adam Nolan had been absent 45½ days and 26½ days, respectively, in 1981; Pelayo had been absent 25 days during this same period. Neither O'Keefe nor Nolan had ever signed union literature or worn union buttons on the company's premises. The union claimed that there was no evidence to indicate that either O'Keefe or Nolan was more versatile than Pelayo, since both O'Keefe and Nolan normally operated only one machine in this department.

Laura Valli.   Laura Valli was employed in the company's cabinet room at the time she was laid off. She had signed union literature on several occasions, and her name had appeared in a union advertisement in a local newspaper on September 21, 1981. This advertisement had listed employees who supported an ongoing strike by one of the union's locals at another facility. Valli also had worn union buttons at work.

Plant Superintendent Artis Reinhold conceded that he had not only read posted union literature to determine who had signed it, but also read the newspaper in which the union advertisement had appeared with Laura Valli's name in it. But Reinhold maintained that Valli's layoff had had nothing whatsoever to do with her support of the union. Rather, Valli was laid off primarily because (1) her absenteeism record was among the worst in the cabinet department and (2) her job could easily be divided up among other employees who were retained. The company stressed its need to be more efficient in a time of economic duress.

The union again introduced attendance records showing that two other employees in the same department who were not laid off had poorer attendance records than did Laura Valli. Hadley Perkins and Margaret Hunter had been absent 56½ days and 37½ days, respectively, in 1981; Valli had been absent 34 days during this same period. The union acknowledged that Perkins' job could not be divided up readily among remaining employees, but the union claimed that Margaret Hunter's job was essentially the same as Laura Valli's and could have been divided up just as easily if Valli had been retained and Hunter had been laid off. The union pointed out that neither Perkins nor Hunter had ever signed union literature or worn union buttons on the job.

Steve Mortimer.   Steve Mortimer was employed in Department 3 of the company's facility before being laid off. He had signed union literature on two occasions, but had not worn union buttons to work at any time. Plant Superintendent Reinhold testified that Mortimer was laid off solely because of his high absenteeism rate. Although Reinhold acknowledged that he probably was aware that Mortimer had signed some union literature, this had had nothing to do with Mortimer's layoff. The union's claim of a discriminatory layoff of Mortimer was just an effort to have Mortimer reinstated from layoff and was a claim totally devoid of any merit.

The union once again introduced attendance records to show that another employee in the same department who had not been laid off had a worse attendance record than did Steve Mortimer. Wes Pritzell had been absent 29 days in 1981, while Mortimer had been absent 20 days during that year. The union further pointed out that Wes Pritzell had never signed any union literature or worn union buttons on the job.

Questions

1. Under settled NLRB case law, if there is sufficient (i.e., prima facie) evidence to suggest that an employer's actions were motivated in part by antiunion (i.e., discriminatory) considerations, the employer then has the primary burden of showing that its actions would have occurred irrespective of any antiunion motivation or interference with the protected activities of the employees. With this in mind, evaluate the layoffs of each of the employees in this case to

determine whether or not the layoffs were or were not discriminatory in violation of LMRA.

2. Why are these so-called dual motivation cases often difficult for the NLRB to resolve? Discuss.

3. Why should employers be very careful if they use absenteeism of an employee as a major justification for some type of adverse personnel action (e.g., layoff, discharge)? Discuss.

CASE 7
DISCHARGE FOR LYING, OR A PRETEXT FOR TERMINATING A UNION ORGANIZER?

Company:
   Industrial Label Corporation, Omaha, Nebraska

Union:
   Local No. 520, Graphic Arts Union

Background

Martin Dalton[1] worked as a press operator on the company's day shift. The company operated eight presses; 18 employees worked on the day shift, and 6 employees at night. Dalton was sometimes required to complete press runs on jobs that a night-shift operator had started. On June 19, 1980, a night-shift operator, Alice Higgins, had left a job for Dalton to run. Dalton ran the job, but it was discovered that a significant error had been made, and the run had to be repeated. On the same day, Dalton saw Higgins when she reported for the night shift. She told Dalton that she had heard that the morning job had had to be rerun. She then asked Dalton whether he had obtained supervisory approval to run the job. He responded that he had done so. On the following day, June 20, Dalton was called to President Robert Fishman's office and was asked in the presence of Vice President Carl Neilson and an office secretary whether he had obtained supervisory approval for the previous day's press run. Dalton acknowledged to Fishman that he had not received supervisory approval. Fishman then asked Dalton whether he had told Higgins that he had received approval. Dalton then admitted that he had lied to Higgins, explaining his action as being prompted by Neilson's earlier caution to avoid arguing with night-shift employees. Fishman then discharged Dalton, stating that his dishonesty violated a company policy and that Dalton had been warned earlier that if he lied again he would be discharged.

Shortly thereafter, the union filed unfair labor practice charges on behalf of Martin Dalton against the company. The union claimed that Dalton's discharge was motivated primarily by Dalton's union organizing efforts, and his discharge thus violated Sections 8(a) (3) and 8(a) (1) of the Labor Management Relations Act.

Position of the Union

The union pointed out that in March 1980, Martin Dalton had openly undertaken a one-person organizing campaign for the union among company employees. Dalton had distributed union literature, carried a notebook bearing the union's logo, left the notebook in plain view at his workstation, and placed union decals prominently on his automobile. In May 1980, the union had formally notified company management that

---

[1]The names of all individuals are disguised.

an organizing campaign was under way.

Martin Dalton testified that during his morning break on June 18, 1980, he had telephoned the union's president, Otis Strong, from company Vice President Carl Neilson's office to report on the status of the campaign. Dalton told Strong that the number of signed authorization cards indicated the union would win an election. Carl Neilson had come to the doorway of the office and overheard Dalton's part of this conversation. On being observed by Dalton, Neilson had shaken his head and walked away. Later that day, Neilson told Dalton to keep the "damn union crap" for his own personal time.

Concerning the incident that the company claimed had precipitated his discharge, Martin Dalton testified that his so-called lying to Alice Higgins had been a response to a direct order by the company vice president, Carl Neilson. Dalton worked as a day-shift press operator, and Higgins operated the same press during the night shift. In February 1980, they had had a very heated argument regarding the cleanliness of their shared work area. Shortly thereafter, Carl Neilson had told Dalton to "take any steps necessary" to avoid arguments with Higgins. Dalton did not deny that he told Higgins on June 19, 1980, that he had obtained supervisory approval to run the job in question. But he said that he had just been trying to avoid an argument with Higgins, as he had been told to do.

The union contended the real reason the company had discharged Martin Dalton was Dalton's union activities. Company management was aware of Dalton's conspicuous union activities and had discovered on June 19 that Dalton thought the union could win an election. Dalton was discharged the very next day after the company learned the union campaign had apparently been successful.

In the union's view, the company chose to magnify an insignificant event into one of major proportions in order to justify discharge. The so-called lying incident was not the actual reason for the discharge of Dalton. The company had not been harmed by Dalton's lie to Higgins. But by claiming that Dalton's lie was a violation of the company's dishonesty policy—despite Neilson's previous warning to avoid arguing with Higgins—the company seized on this opportunity to discharge Dalton. This exaggeration of a minor event cast serious doubt on the company's asserted motivations for the discharge.

In summary, the union claimed that the company had seized on Dalton's lie to Higgins as a pretext for terminating the chief union organizer among its employees, and thereby had violated Sections 8(a) (3) and 8(a) (1) of LMRA.

The union requested that the company be ordered to reinstate Martin Dalton with full back pay and restoration of all benefits, and be ordered to cease and desist in its discriminatory actions and interference with the union organizing efforts.

Position of the Company

The company maintained that it had discharged Martin Dalton for lying to a fellow employee about a work-related matter, and that this was the third such incident involving dishonesty on Dalton's part.

The company first introduced its employee policy manual—which Dalton acknowledged having received—which specifically included a statement to the effect that dishonesty in company matters would be considered grounds for automatic dismissal.

Company president Robert Fishman testified that he had had two prior confrontations with Dalton involving dishonest statements. In July 1976, Dalton was accused of lying about the nature of certain work instructions previously given to him by a supervisor. Since the company could not definitely determine who was lying, Fishman had only warned Dalton that he would be disciplined if the company later determined that he had lied.

In December 1979, Dalton suffered a back injury and was hospitalized. The attending physician recommended that Dalton rest for 8 to 10 weeks before returning to work. Fishman requested that Dalton seek a second opinion from his own personal physician. Dalton consulted a local clinic physician, who confirmed the original diagnosis. Dalton then reported this information to Fishman but presented it as the opinion of his own doctor. Fishman, however, spoke to Dalton's personal physician and determined that Dalton had been lying. He confronted Dalton with this knowledge. After some discussion, Fishman told Dalton that he would be terminated if he ever lied about a company matter again.

The incident of lying by Dalton on June 19, 1980, was in the company's view sufficient grounds in itself for terminating Dalton. But when he terminated Dalton on June 20, Fishman reminded Dalton that he had been warned twice before about lying, and was being discharged for his cumulative acts of dishonesty, which represented direct violations of company policy.

The company maintained that it had the right to discharge Dalton for his repeated dishonesty, which could no longer be tolerated, and that this discharge action had had nothing to do with Dalton's union-organizing activities. The company urged that the unfair labor practice charges filed by the union be dismissed in their entirety.

Questions

1. Was the company's discharge of Martin Dalton justified, or was it a pretext to terminate a union organizer in violation of LMRA? Discuss.
2. Was Martin Dalton's past record relevant in concluding that his pattern of "dishonesty" justified his termination? Discuss.
3. Why is it difficult for the NLRB to determine the employer's true motive in a situation of this sort?
4. Compare the issues in this case with those in Case 20, "Discharge for Using the Photocopier in a Hazardous Waste Dispute."

CASE 8
DISCHARGE FOR GROSS NEGLIGENCE, OR FOR UNION ACTIVITIES?

Company:
Bay Corrugated Container, Inc., Monroe, Michigan

Union:
Clothing and Textile Workers, Chicago and Central States Board

Background

In early September 1990, employee Rudy Buckle[1] met with a union representative to discuss the representation of the company's employees. Between that time and October 24, 1990, Buckle held several employee meetings at his home and visited the homes of about 50 employees to solicit their support for the union. Buckle also passed out union literature at the gate of the company's plant, in full view of management, approximately five times prior to October 24.

Employee Doak Mayhew was also active in the union organizing drive. He visited employees' homes to discuss the union, passed out union cards, handbilled at the front gate, and placed union literature on tables in the cafeteria. After handbilling at the front gate on October 15, Mayhew was met by Vice President of Data Processing Jeanine Randolph, Human Resources Director Ruth Walpole, and Executive Vice President Derek Thames. As Mayhew entered the plant, Randolph asked Mayhew, "How's the union thing going at the gate?"

On October 10, Executive V. P. Derek Thames met with press department employees to discuss the union-organizing drive. During this meeting, Thames stated that he had heard rumors that there was to be a union meeting that day at 4:30 P.M. and that he knew where it was to be. Thames stared at Rudy Buckle while making this statement. (In fact, a union meeting was held that evening at Buckle's home.)

On October 19, Assistant Plant Manager Raymond Milburn approached Rudy Buckle and Doak Mayhew at the ward press machine. Mayhew asked Milburn what kind of guarantees existed that Mayhew would keep his job if he signed a union card. Milburn replied, "You guys do what you gotta do; we'll do what we gotta do. But we'll get you guys."

About a week prior to October 24, employee Andrea Garceo met with Plant Manager Carl Rutherford to discuss a production problem that involved Garceo and Rudy Buckle. During this meeting, Rutherford told Garceo that Buckle was the one heading the union-organizing drive. Rutherford commented that he could not understand why Buckle was doing this because the company had done so much for him. Rutherford added, "Rudy is kind of walking a thin line with his job, starting all this union stuff."

On October 23, 1990, Rudy Buckle, Doak Mayhew, and Andrea Garceo were assigned as a work crew to run an order for Digitron Packaging on the ward press

---

[1]The names of all individuals are disguised.

machine. The order was to print the Ford logo and a legal phrase on about 5,500 boxes. Carl Rutherford had directed Garceo to rush the order and told her he would be monitoring how fast the crew finished this order.

In preparing the press to run the order, Buckle and Mayhew followed instructions contained on a factory card and print code. The print code set forth the printing specifications for the box to be manufactured, including the size and placement of any printing on the panels. Once the order was set up, Buckle and Mayhew ran a test sheet and checked it against the information on the factory card and print code. They apparently concluded that the test sheet conformed to the specifications. Andrea Garceo also checked the order; believing it was correct, she concurred in running the order.

With approximately 1,000 pieces remaining to print, Quality Control Manager Karen Eastman notified Buckle and Garceo that the order had been printed with the legal phrase in the wrong place. Later that day, all three employees were called in to a meeting with Plant Manager Carl Rutherford, Human Resources Director Ruth Walpole, and Quality Control Manager Karen Eastman. Rutherford showed the employees the erroneously printed box with the legal phrase to the side of the logo, when the print code specified the placement of the legal phrase below the logo. Rutherford asked the employees what was wrong with the finished box when compared with the print code he was holding. Doak Mayhew acknowledged that the printed box did not conform to the print code, but he stated that the dies would not fit in the panel in accordance with the print code. Rutherford replied that the print code for this order had been made up erroneously by the sales department and left at the press for the employees to run. Rutherford said he could not comprehend how all three employees had missed the error in the print code when they had checked the test sheet against the printing specifications.

The following day, Andrea Garceo, Rudy Buckle, and Doak Mayhew were discharged. Carl Rutherford accused them of gross negligence and misconduct, and he told them he failed to understand how they could have made such an incredible mistake, which had cost the company some $5,700. Mayhew responded that he could not understand how Rutherford could discharge him after five and one-half years of good service, and that it was no wonder the employees wanted a union. Rutherford said that the discharges had nothing to do with a union.

Shortly thereafter, the union filed unfair labor practice charges against the company claiming that the company's discharges of the three employees violated Sections 8(a) (3) and 8(a) (1) of the Labor Management Relations Act.

Position of the Union

The union argued that the prounion activity of Doak Mayhew and Rudy Buckle was the primary motivating factor in the company's decision to discharge them on October 24, 1990. Immediately prior to October 24, Buckle and Mayhew had openly supported the union and had handbilled at the front gate of the company plant. Management had full knowledge of their union activities. Further, management persons had exhibited their antiunion hostility by threatening Mayhew and Buckle with loss of their jobs for supporting the union, by creating the impression among employees that their union activities were under surveillance, and by stating that Buckle was "walking a thin line with his job" because he had started the "union stuff."[2]

In the union's view, the company had decided to discharge Andrea Garceo, who had not openly supported the union, in an effort to cover up its discriminatory discharges of Buckle and Mayhew. The union claimed that the production mistake was not solely attributable to the three employees who were discharged. The boxes involved had never been manufactured before by the company and had required the use of a new print code. Although new orders generally had a white slip attached to the factory card to alert the workers that it was a new order, the Digitron print code had not had a white slip attached. Indeed, the print code given to the employees had been incorrect and it was this that had resulted in the misprinted cartons. Although the employees may have erred in their belief that the test sheet sufficiently conformed to the print-code specifications, this did not mean that the employees' error was intentional or that they were grossly negligent.

The company's sales department was responsible for making up factory cards and print codes in accordance with factory specifications. The person in the sales department who had drawn up the print code in question admitted that she had not been aware that it would not fit on the panel of the carton ordered. She said that it had been an unusual oversight on the part of the sales department. Despite the sales department's admitting an error, and despite the company's alleged concern over the magnitude of this error, no one in the sales department had been investigated or disciplined.

The union claimed that heretofore the company had issued only written warnings to employees who committed production errors for the first time. Mayhew, Buckle, and Garceo had never before been warned or disciplined by the company for any infraction.

The union urged that the company had discriminatorily discharged Mayhew and Buckle because of their union activities and had discharged Garceo to posture itself in its pretext of seizing on the production mistake to discharge these employees. By so doing, the company had violated Sections 8(a) (3) and 8(a) (1) of LMRA. The employees should be reinstated and made appropriately whole for all lost wages and benefits, and the company should be directed to cease in its interference with the employees' protected rights.

Position of the Company

The company claimed that the discharges of Rudy Buckle, Doak Mayhew, and Andrea Garceo had nothing to do with any union activities that any of them might have been pursuing. Each of them deserved discharge because of intentional and gross negligence and misconduct in failing to detect an erroneous print code, not consulting higher management for directions, and running the erroneous print on an order of 5,500 cartons. The company claimed that, from time to time, the sales department might

---

[2]The union had also filed unfair labor practice charges against the company concerning these matters. In a separate decision, the NLRB held that the company had violated Section 8(a) (1) of LMRA by creating an impression of surveillance of employees' union activities and by threatening employees with job loss because of such activities.

prepare a print code that could not be printed properly once it reached a machine. The burden and responsibility for catching these problems was the work crew machine operators'. Buckle, Mayhew, and Garceo knew that the proper procedure for any problems with a new item was that they should first consult their supervisor, and that they were responsible for double checking when they encountered any such problems. They failed to do so, and in the company's view not to have double checked with a supervisor was an intentional act on their part, probably motivated by their hostile attitudes toward the company. The October 23 printing error had cost $5,700, and the company had never before sustained a manufacturing error of this magnitude. Such an act of gross negligence and misconduct on their part deserved the penalty of termination, irrespective of any other factors associated with their employment.

In support of its assertion that the employees intentionally failed to detect and report the erroneous print code, the company pointed out that Garceo, Mayhew, and Buckle subsequently admitted in their applications for unemployment compensation that the reason for their discharge was that they had "missed the error" when they set up the press. By their own words, therefore, they acknowledged that they had deliberately decided to run the order when they should have first checked out the order with their supervisor, instead choosing not to do so. Since it was their responsibility to prevent such a gross error from occurring, their discharges were fully justified in view of the magnitude of the cost of their misconduct.

The company asserted that the union's unfair labor practice charges on behalf of Buckle, Mayhew, and Garceo were without merit and simply an effort to have them reinstated in their jobs. The company urged the NLRB to dismiss the charges.

Questions

1. Evaluate each of the contentions of the union and the company. Which do you find the most and which the least persuasive?

2. Does an employer have a right to discharge employees who make costly mistakes because of negligence that may have been unintentional? Discuss.

3. To what degree should the company's other unfair labor practices (see footnote 2) weigh upon the NLRB's determination of this case?

4. Did the company violate LMRA by discharging the employees for alleged gross negligence and misconduct? Why, or why not?

CASE 9
TERMINATION OF THE NURSE FOR A "THREAT OF RETALIATION"

Employer:
   Fairfax Hospital, Division of Inova Health Systems and Fairfax Health System, Inc.,
   Fairfax, Virginia

Union:
   Fairfax Professional Nurses Association, Affiliated with the American Nurses Association
   (ANA)

Background

On March 7, 1990, nurse Karla Reynolds,[1] while in an employee lounge during her morning break, engaged in a verbal confrontation with her supervisor, Teresa Barth. Nurse Laura Engert heard the entire conversation and nurse John Stewart heard part of the conversation, which all parties involved later described as "a heated discussion." Reynolds strongly protested the hospital's posting and distributing antiunion literature while prohibiting union supporters' posting and distributing union materials.[2]

A management-posted memorandum, which was the immediate cause of the dispute, described an incident in which a hospital patient on his way to surgery allegedly was told that he would not receive good medical treatment because his wife had refused to support the union. During the "heated" conversation, Reynolds challenged the truthfulness of this memorandum, stating that in all her years of nursing she had never seen conduct such as that. She said that the incident had been fabricated by hospital management, and she questioned how Barth could believe such a thing. Supervisor Barth commented that the hospital's posting was unpleasant, and then stated, "You better get used to it because there will be a lot more of these things coming!" Reynolds replied, "If that is so, you can expect retaliation!" With that comment, Karla Reynolds ended the conversation and left the room.

Supervisor Teresa Barth reported the conversation to her supervisor, Martha Masters, assistant administrator for nursing services. After consultation with several hospital officials, including the chief administrative officer, the human resources director, and legal counsel, a decision was reached to terminate Karla Reynolds. When Reynolds reported to work the morning of March 8, 1990, Masters discharged Reynolds for "gross insubordinate conduct."

Shortly thereafter, the union filed unfair labor practice charges against the hospital contending that the hospital's discharge of Karla Reynolds had violated Sections 8(a) (3) and 8(a) (1) of the Labor Management Relations Act.

---

[1] The names of all individuals are disguised.

[2] The union had filed Section 8(a) (1) unfair labor practice charges concerning these actions by hospital management, which were to be resolved by the NLRB in separate cases.

Position of the Union

The union first pointed out that hospital management had known Karla Reynolds was a leading union advocate. She was a member of the Fairfax Professional Nurses Association steering committee, and she had been observed handing out union leaflets in front of the hospital to members of management as well as to fellow employees. Reynolds had been one of several nurses whose pictures and interviews had appeared in a union brochure identifying various individuals who were promoting a union for the hospital. In the union's view, the discharge of Karla Reynolds was primarily a result of Reynolds' being a leader in the union's organizing campaign.

In the union's view, the hospital seized on Reynolds' statement about "retaliation" as a pretext for discharging her because of her union activities. Reynolds had simply been using the word "retaliation" in the sense that the union would be disseminating its own prounion information to counteract or retaliate against information the hospital was disseminating that the union considered untruthful. The discussion between Reynolds and her supervisor, Teresa Barth, was acknowledged by all to have been a heated one in which strong opinions were exchanged. Reynolds' statement about "retaliation" was hardly a threat to Barth personally or to the hospital that deserved disciplinary response, much less termination.

The union pointed out that the hospital had showed its strong opposition to the union by interfering with the union's attempts to post its own literature and to distribute various materials. The union had filed other unfair labor practice charges protesting these actions by hospital management.

In summary, the union claimed that the hospital's discharge of Karla Reynolds because of her so-called retaliation statement was a pretext for terminating her for her protected union activity in violation of Sections 8(a) (3) and 8(a) (1) of the Act. The union urged the NLRB to direct that Karla Reynolds be reinstated and made whole for all lost income and benefits, and urged that the hospital be ordered to post a notice that it would abide by provisions of the Labor Management Relations Act.

Position of the Employer

The hospital maintained that the use of the word "retaliation" in the context of the conversation between Karla Reynolds and Teresa Barth was clearly a threat deserving of the ultimate penalty of discharge. Supervisor Teresa Barth had been frightened, and sincerely felt the word "retaliation" meant Reynolds was threatening her and others in supervision with physical harm. Reynolds' statement was so threatening as to amount to an assault on her supervisor, thus justifying an immediate dismissal.

Reynolds' strongly worded statement was grossly insubordinate. She was placing her supervisor and employer on notice that retaliation would take place that might include physical and verbal abuse of the hospital and its supervisors. If such insubordinate conduct were condoned in any way by the hospital, the proper discipline necessary for maintaining decorum and patient care in the hospital could not be maintained.

The hospital acknowledged that Karla Reynolds had been a nurse satisfactorily employed in the hospital for some 15 years, and that hospital management was aware of her prounion sentiments. But these factors did not weigh in the decision to terminate Karla Reynolds. The hospital maintained that her threat of retaliation was a serious breach of discipline and was totally unacceptable conduct. Her termination was fully justified irrespective of any other factors. The hospital urged that the unfair labor practice charges filed by the union be dismissed.

Questions

1. Was the statement promising "retaliation" a threat that was extremely insubordinate conduct, or was it merely an exchange in a heated conversation not deserving of hospital response? Discuss.
2. Does it make any difference in this case that the employer had been opposed to union organizing efforts and had other unfair labor practice charges filed against it by the union? Why, or why not?
3. Did her "retaliation" statement justify the discharge of Karla Reynolds, or was it a pretext for terminating her for her prounion sentiments and activities? Discuss.
4. Why is it difficult for the NLRB to determine the motivation for an employer's actions in cases of this nature?

CASE 10
THE SAMPLE NLRB BALLOT MARKED WITH AN "X" IN THE "NO" BOX

Company:
    Baptist Home for Senior Citizens, Cook Springs, Alabama
Union:
    United Steelworkers of America

Background

In early 1988, the union had filed a petition with the NLRB to conduct a representational election for a proposed bargaining unit consisting primarily of housekeeping, dietary, and laundry employees. Two days before the scheduled date for the election, management distributed a two-page document to the great majority—perhaps all—of the employees. The first page of the document was a memorandum on the company's stationery and was signed by John Morgan,[1] administrator of the facility. In question and answer format, the memorandum explained certain mechanics of the election; it concluded by stating, "I urge you to exercise your right to vote and to protect your own best interest and what you now have by *Voting No!!* on Thursday."

The second page was stapled to Morgan's memorandum. It was a photocopy of the NLRB's sample ballot for the election; there was an "X" in the "No" box on the ballot.

The election resulted in 33 votes for and 46 against the union, with 4 challenged ballots. The union immediately filed objections to the election outcome under Section 9(c) of LMRA.

Position of the Union

The union acknowledged that the two-page document had been distributed and discussed by management with a substantial number of the employees. However, two employees, Phyllis Roosevelt and Sharon Jensen, testified that they had received copies of the two-page document without any explanation that management personnel had marked the sample NLRB ballot with an "X" in the "No" box. Roosevelt and Jensen claimed that other employees had similarly received the two-page document without any explanation from company managers.

Roosevelt and another employee, Richard Hamp, also testified that shortly before the election they had seen copies of the marked sample NLRB ballots, not attached to Morgan's memorandum, lying on the table in the employees' breakroom. They did not know who had placed the unattached ballots on the breakroom table.

Roosevelt testified that she saw a stack of the marked ballots, again not attached to the memorandum, lying on John Morgan's desk in his office the day before the election.

The union claimed that the election results had been seriously tainted, because (1) not every employee had been clearly informed that the sample NLRB ballots had been

---

[1] The names of all individuals are disguised.

marked "No" by the company managers; and (2) this lack of information along with unattached marked ballots in the employees' breakroom undoubtedly had led some employees to believe that the NLRB endorsed a "No" vote against the union. A number of employees probably had voted against the union because of this misrepresentation.

The union contended that, by these actions, management had seriously and improperly influenced the outcome of the election. The union urged that the results of the representational election be set aside, and the NLRB order a new representational election free of this type of employer electioneering.

Position of the Company

Jeremy Trushold, as assistant administrator at the facility, testified that copies of the two-page document were distributed to employees at group meetings held two days before the election. Trushold testified that he explained to those in attendance that he had marked the sample NLRB ballot "No," and that he encouraged them to do the same. John Morgan, the chief administrator, testified that at group meetings that he held with employees on the night shift, he also had explained that "we" had marked the sample ballot "No," in the hope that the employees would support the company in the election. Morgan further testified that because not all employees had attended the group meetings, other management personnel attempted to contact individually those employees who had not attended the meetings. Morgan believed that all or virtually all employees were informed about the information contained in his memorandum and that company management had marked the "No" box on the sample NLRB ballots.

Concerning the so-called unattached sample NLRB ballots allegedly on the employees' breakroom table, company witnesses claimed no knowledge whatsoever. The company claimed it was highly possible that certain employees—both those for and against the union—could have unstapled or torn apart the two-page document and left copies of the marked sample ballots on the table. Company management should not be held accountable in any way for such employee behavior, assuming that this did in fact occur.

The company claimed that employee Phyllis Roosevelt's testimony that she saw a stack of marked ballots, not attached to the memorandum and on the desk in John Morgan's office, was inconsequential. Morgan's office was not readily accessible to employees, and the company had not left the unattached ballots in that office intending that employees should come in and observe them in that condition.

In summary, the company claimed that all—or virtually all—of the employees had received the two-page document, and that the employees were informed and understood that it was the company's position—not the NLRB's—that they should vote "No" in the representational election. The company had a right to express its view in this fashion, and the company did not in any way restrain, interfere with, or coerce the employees in their voting choice. The union's objections were without merit, and the NLRB should certify the results of the election.

Questions

1. Should an employer be permitted to mark a sample NLRB ballot as the company did in this case, even if the company clearly explains to all employees that the marking is only the company's position and preference? Why, or why not?
2. Evaluate the union's contention that some employees were led to believe that the NLRB had endorsed a "no" vote against the union.
3. Evaluate the company's contention that it should not be held accountable if certain employees had separated the two-page document and left the marked sample ballots on the breakroom table.
4. Should the election outcome be set aside by the NLRB? Why, or why not?

CASE 11
RACIAL/ETHNIC PREJUDICE DURING A UNION
REPRESENTATIONAL ELECTION

Company:
  KI (USA) Corporation, Berea, Kentucky

Union:
  United Automobile Workers of America (UAW)

Background

The company was a subsidiary of a Japanese corporation, adhered to certain Japanese management programs, and provided training in Japan for its American managers. The company employed both Japanese nationals and Americans in its management ranks, with Japanese nationals predominant in the higher ranks. At the Berea, Kentucky, manufacturing facility, on-site supervisory management was composed mainly of Americans, whose assigned role was to use a blend of American and Japanese management concepts. The Berea facility was the focus of a union-organizing campaign in 1991 and early 1992.

In March 1992, on the day before the representational election, the union held a meeting attended by a number of employees and several union (UAW) representatives. At the end of the meeting, one of the union representatives made available to the employees various printed materials, including a copy of a letter that had first appeared as a "letter to the editor" in the January 1991 issue of *Easy Rider* magazine, a publication directed to Harley-Davidson owners, operators, and fans:

You Should Know

Voice from Japan

In regard to your article "Bubba's 5th Annual Honda Drop" in the October issue, if you want to destroy Japanese products, you should start with your Harley-Davidson motorcycles. I recently toured a Harley-Davidson dealership and was given the opportunity to examine the 1991 models and "genuine" parts. I saw more made-in-Japan, -Korea, and -Taiwan labels than you could even find in a Japanese company. Perhaps that is why Harley-Davidsons are finally being praised as quality products—because of the excellent Japanese parts on them.

As a Japanese businessman and investor, I am appalled at the typical lazy, uneducated American worker I have had to deal with in your country. The Japanese work force and management philosophy are proven superior, and your half-witted American managers are constantly studying our techniques. In America it is your political leaders who are doing you the most harm, not the Japanese. The fact that Americans believe in such false patriotism and political lies shows how ignorant and weak you have become.

I suggest the Americans start developing a healthy respect for Japan because one of my colleagues will eventually become your boss and/or own your company. In Japan we have a very rich tradition and long history of patience, but we will not show patience with your disrespect and racism toward our proud and growing empire.

Toshito Nakamura
Osaka, Japan

The contents of the letter clearly indicated that it was written in response to an article in the *Easy Rider* publication. The union's sole addition to the letter was the "You Should Know" banner, and underlining some of the text of the letter. The union did not refer to the letter in any of its other campaign materials. The letter was reproduced and widely disseminated among the proposed bargaining unit employees, a majority of whom voted in favor of having the United Automobile Workers Union represent them. Shortly after the election, the company filed exceptions to the representational election under Section 9(c) of LMRA, urging that the results be set aside.

Position of the Company

The company position relied heavily on a previous NLRB decision[1] in which the Board held that it would set aside elections "when a party engages in a campaign which seeks to overstress and exacerbate racial feeling by irrelevant, inflammatory appeals." The company pointed out that apparently some employees did believe that Japanese employers had very negative attitudes about American workers. These employees were concerned that their own employer shared these views. The union had sought to appeal to these concerns by distributing copies of the letter written by a Japanese businessman, Toshito Nakamura, who had written that American workers were lazy and uneducated, and that Americans were ignorant and weak. However, there was no evidence whatsoever that Mr. Nakamura had any relationship to the company, nor was there any evidence that the company in any way shared his views.

By distributing the letter to the employees the day before the election, the union had sought to capitalize on the employees' concerns that all Japanese, including company management, held negative views of American workers. Thus, the union had sought to lump top company management together with Mr. Nakamura solely on the basis that they were both Japanese, and to ascribe to the company the offensive, biased views of Mr. Nakamura. This was a gross distortion and untruthful, and had no place in a representational election conducted by the NLRB. In the company's view, the high Board standards and "laboratory conditions" required for conducting a representational election had been seriously compromised by the union's appeal to racial and ethnic prejudice. It was logical to conclude that numerous employees had been influenced to vote according to their prejudices rather than according to their real preferences about

---

[1]This case was *Sewell Manufacturing Company,* 138 NLRB 66, 50 LRRM 1532 (1962).

the UAW's representing them. The company urged the NLRB to set aside the results of the election and to order that another representational election be held that would be untainted by this improper union conduct.

Position of the Union

The union position relied to some extent on the same NLRB decision that was cited by the company. In that decision, the Board had distinguished unacceptable racial, inflammatory appeals from "isolated, casual, prejudicial remarks." The Board had stated in this case that it would not set aside a representational election or "condemn relevant campaign statements merely because they may have racial overtones."

The union noted that before the election campaign employees had expressed concern among themselves about the company's Japanese owners and managers not appreciating the American employees and the American supervisors, and although the employees had expressed such concerns during the election campaign, there was no evidence that the union had created or directly contributed to these concerns. The union had not provided any commentary to the employees about how the letter written by a Japanese businessman and investor might relate to the company's attitudes toward its employees. By making available a copy of Mr. Nakamura's letter to the employees without comment, the union was not making an inflammatory, emotional appeal to prejudice. Rather, the union was merely urging the employees to vote for the union to prevent the discrimination or lack of appreciation they perceived might or did exist. Providing the employees with the text of the offensive letter did not lower or dilute the election standards to such a degree that employees could not make up their own minds about union representation.

In the union's view, the company was grossly exaggerating the importance of the letter merely in order to overturn the election outcome. The union urged the NLRB to dismiss the company's complaint, to certify the union as the representative of bargaining unit employees, and to direct the company to recognize and engage in collective bargaining with the union.

Questions

1. Both the company and the union utilized aspects of the NLRB's *Sewell Manufacturing Company* case decision in support of their respective positions. Why is this type of case precedent one that can be manipulated to justify either side's position?

2. What inferences, if any, can be drawn from the facts that (*a*) the American employees had previously expressed concerns about their company's Japanese owners; (*b*) the union provided the employees with a copy of the Nakamura letter without commentary?

3. Should the NLRB set aside the results of the representational election because its standards for proper election atmosphere/conduct had been compromised? Why, or why not?

CASE 12
THE SUPERVISORS WHO WANTED A LABOR UNION

Employer:
Wright Memorial Hospital, Trenton, Missouri

Union:
Service Employees International Union, Local No. 50

Background

At the time of this case, Wright Memorial Hospital was a 78-bed facility in Trenton, Missouri, located in a one-story building with a basement. The main floor was divided into three wings with a nursing station in each wing. Each nursing station had a registered nurse in charge on each of three shifts. Fifteen registered nurses so assigned were called charge nurses.

On October 8, 1980, the union filed a petition to be certified as the bargaining representative of certain employees, including the charge nurses at the hospital. On October 22, 1980, the NLRB's Region 17 office (Kansas City) conducted a hearing on the representation petition. At the hearing, the hospital contended that the charge nurses were supervisors within the meaning of Section 2(11) of LMRA, and thus they could not be part of the bargaining unit [Section 2(3) of LMRA]. The union urged the inclusion of the charge nurses. The Regional Director for the NLRB rejected the hospital's arguments and decided that the charge nurses were professional employees rather than supervisors. Under Sections 2(12) and 9(b) of the Act, professional employees may be included in a bargaining unit with nonprofessionals, if the majority of the professionals vote for inclusion in that unit.

On November 17, 1980, the hospital, pursuant to Section 9(c) of the Act, filed a timely request for review of the Regional Director's decision. The hospital, however, did not request a stay of the election. While the hospital's request for review was pending before the NLRB, the election campaign proceeded. A number of charge nurses campaigned actively on behalf of the union. The nurses wore union buttons to work, attended union meetings, handed out union buttons, passed out authorization cards, and responded to questions at union meetings.

On December 4, 1980, the Board conducted a secret-ballot election. The ballots were subsequently impounded, and the ballots of the charge nurses were segregated from the others pending disposition of the hospital's request for review. Five months after the election, on May 5, 1981, the NLRB overruled the Regional Director and held that the charge nurses were supervisors. While acknowledging that the charge nurses did not hire, fire, or interview potential employees, the Board held that the charge nurses were supervisors because they had the authority to "hold employees over to work overtime, release employees from work, assign work and set priorities for employees, call in off-duty employees to work, resolve complaints or grievances, evaluate employees in writing, give written reprimands, send employees home on disciplinary suspension without pay, and recommend harsher discipline up to and including discharge." The Board remanded the case to the Regional Director for the purpose of opening and counting the ballots of the eligible voters.

On June 11, 1981, the ballots of the eligible voters were opened and counted. Of the 147 ballots cast, 87 were in favor of the union, 55 were against representation by the union, and 5 were challenged.

On June 18, 1981, the hospital filed objections to the election. The hospital argued that (1) the union had recruited a large number of the hospital's charge nurse supervisors, and those supervisors had solicited support and campaigned on behalf of the union throughout the election campaign; (2) a number of the union's organizational and strategy meetings, which were attended by employees, were held in the homes of supervisors; (3) charge nurse supervisors actively solicited employees to sign authorization cards on behalf of the union and to vote in favor of the union; and (4) three supervisors served as principal organizers on behalf of the union. On July 9, 1981, a hearing was held on those objections, and the hearing officer subsequently recommended that the objections be overruled in their entirety and that the union be certified. On March 10, 1982, the NLRB adopted the hearing officer's recommendations and certified the union.

On July 16, 1982, the union requested that the hospital bargain with it. By letter dated July 22, 1982, the hospital refused to bargain with the union. On August 11, 1982, the union filed unfair labor practice charges against the hospital, alleging that the hospital had violated Sections 8(a) (5) and 8(a) (1) of the Act by refusing to recognize and bargain with the union. The hospital admitted its refusal to bargain but argued that the union was improperly certified.

Position of the Union

The union argued primarily that there was no evidence whatsoever to show that the charge nurse supervisors' activities on behalf of the union had been coercive upon the employees, nor had the supervisors caused any employees to vote for the union because they feared future retaliation by the supervisors if they did not support the union. The union acknowledged that most of the charge nurses (12 or 13 of 15) signed authorization cards and wore union buttons. But such activity in itself was not coercive, nor did it imply retaliation against employees who did not want a union to represent them.

Several of the charge nurses acknowledged in testimony that they had spoken to other employees about benefits of the union, but they maintained that nothing was stated by any charge nurse that was threatening or coercive.

The union admitted that three charge nurses actively participated in the union campaign. But, contrary to the hospital's assertion, the union claimed that they did not hold leadership positions in the campaign. Two of the three charge nurses were members of an 18-member union campaign committee,[1] but they had no more influence

---

[1]The union campaign committee was composed of two charge nurses, two licensed practical nurses, two paramedics, and representatives of the aids, lab technicians, and medical records, dietary, and housekeeping staff. The members of the committee were selected by the union business agent and employees.

than any other committee members. The union business agent controlled and directed the campaign, chaired all meetings of the committee, and acquired the majority of the 140 authorization cards signed by hospital employees. Further, the meetings attended by the three charge nurses were informal discussions in which all individuals in attendance could and did participate. The charge nurses' participation was limited to answering a number of questions directed to them.

In summary, the union argued that there was nothing in the record to indicate that the employees did not exercise their free choice in the union representational election. There was no evidence whatsoever that the charge nurse supervisors ever threatened or in any way implied retaliation against employees who did not support the union. Nor was the active union campaigning of a number of the charge nurses of such a magnitude as to significantly taint the outcome of the election. The union had won a clear majority without counting any of the charge nurses' ballots. In the union's view, the hospital was raising objections primarily in an effort to avoid its statutory obligation to recognize and bargain with the union. The union urged that the hospital be found in violation of Sections 8(a) (1) and 8(a) (5) of the Act and be ordered to recognize the union and bargain with it accordingly.

Position of the Hospital

The hospital relied primarily upon its continuing objections to certification of the union because of the charge nurses' active participation in the union organizing effort when they were actually supervisors. In the hospital's view, the charge nurses (the overwhelming majority of whom supported the union) had immediate and virtually complete control over their employees' working lives.

The cumulative effect of the prounion activities of the supervisors should require that the election be overturned. The supervisors engaged in almost every type of prounion activity, and the evidence should support a finding that the supervisors' actions interfered with the employees' free choice to such an extent that the supervisors' actions materially affected the results of the election.

The hospital also argued that the hospital was unfairly deprived of its right to utilize its charge nurse supervisors against the union in the campaign. The hospital engaged in an aggressive antiunion campaign. The hospital organized an antiunion committee, distributed handouts two to three times a week, and held mandatory meetings at which the hospital's antiunion position was clearly stated. But the charge nurse supervisors were not part of this antiunion campaign, although the hospital had a right to expect them to be agents of management.

In summary, the hospital contended that the representational election was so tainted that the NLRB was in error when it certified the union as bargaining agent for the employees. Because of this error and the serious questions that the hospital had concerning whether the majority of the employees really wanted the union to represent them, the hospital rightfully refused to recognize and bargain with the union until its appeal concerning the representational election was decided. In the hospital's view, the results of the first election should be set aside, and the Board should conduct a second election that would be free of the taint and coercive actions and influence of the charge nurse supervisors. Therefore, the unfair labor practice charges were without merit and should be dismissed.

Questions

1. Evaluate: *(a)* the hospital's position that the charge nurse supervisors' prounion activities were coercive in nature; and *(b)* the union's position that these activities were not coercive and did not taint the outcome of the election.
2. What inferences—if any—should be placed on the fact that the charge nurses wanted a union to represent them?
3. Should the NLRB have ordered a new representational election in May or June 1981 when the Board decided that the charge nurses were supervisors and not professional employees under LMRA? Why, or why not?
4. Why would the hospital refuse to recognize and bargain with the union while its objections to the certification of the union were still pending? Discuss.

CASE 13
BOISTEROUS PROUNION CONDUCT DURING A REPRESENTATIONAL ELECTION

Company:
   Pepsi-Cola Bottling Company of Petersburg, Inc., Petersburg, Virginia

Union:
   Local Lodge No. 10, International Association of Machinists and Aerospace Workers

Background

On June 7, 1988, the regional office of the NLRB conducted a representational election at the company plant to determine whether the union would gain collective bargaining rights to represent a unit of the plant's production and maintenance employees. The essential facts of what occurred, and which became an issue, were not disputed by the parties.

The election booths were located in the lunchroom and were open from 6:15 to 7:45 A.M. and from 3:30 to 5 P.M. Approximately 15 minutes before the morning voting period began, a group of about 15 to 20 employees entered the plant. Some of them proceeded to the restroom area inside the locker room; the others assembled near the time clock located outside the locker room. Most of the employees wore shirts and caps bearing the union's logo, and the shirts also bore the caption, "Geared For Action." While walking through the plant, the group chanted slogans, cheered, and clapped. Between 6:05 and 6:10 A.M., the group proceeded to the aisleway outside the lunchroom and formed lines on both sides of the aisleway, which came within 10 to 15 feet of the lunchroom door. While waiting for the election booths to open, the employees engaged in further cheering, clapping, and talking among themselves and with other employees passing by. The employees made remarks such as, "We're going to take over," "We're counting on you," "Welcome to our house," "This is the day we've been waiting for," "Here comes one of our boys," and other similar comments. Several employees walked between the lines of the union supporters and were greeted by name or patted on the back as they walked by.

When the election booths opened at 6:15 A.M., a group of approximately 10 employees were already in line to vote. After the voting began, the voting line extended into the aisleway outside the lunchroom perpendicular to the lines of union supporters. Employees continued to filter through the lines of the union supporters after the election booths opened. The union supporters left their formation, one or two at a time, to enter the other line of employees waiting to vote. After these individuals cast their ballots, they returned to the lines of union supporters. The group continued to clap, chant, cheer, and to make remarks to employees passing between their lines until sometime between 6:30 and 6:40 A.M. At this time, two members of management asked the group to leave the area if they had voted. The group then left the plant.

At the end of the day when the voting was completed, the tally showed that the union had won the representational election by one vote, 36 to 35. The company immediately filed objections to the election outcome under Section 9(c) of LMRA.

Position of the Company

The company claimed that the cheering, clapping, and comments made by the prounion employees had occurred in "no-electioneering" areas outside the lunchroom. The prounion supporters composed at least one-fifth of the eligible voters, and their boisterous conduct continued unabated throughout the first 25 minutes or so of the election in front of employees in line to vote. Further, their line formation forced employees walking down the aisleway, including those going to vote, to walk between lines of union supporters and be subjected to their chants, cheers, and other antics.

The company claimed that this electioneering behavior violated the NLRB's standards for election conduct. The employees who had to walk between the lines of union supporters were forced to endure disruptive and coercive comments that could have influenced their votes. In an election decided by only one vote, this improper behavior determined the outcome of the election if just one employee was pressured into voting for the union because of the union supporters' conduct. Therefore, a new representational election should be ordered and held by the Board, free of any taint of improper electioneering on the part of union supporters.

Position of the Union

The union argued strongly that the behavior of the group of union supporters was not electioneering or objectionable conduct. The supporters were not union agents. The noise level inside the voting room was not so loud or obstructive as to impair a voter's ability to understand the Board agent's instructions and cast a ballot. The union supporters' remarks made outside the lunchroom could not be heard by voters inside the room; further, the union supporters' remarks were not "specific overtures" to individuals to vote for the union and thus did not constitute electioneering. But even if such statements were held to be electioneering, the remarks were brief and were not made to potential voters within the Board's described no-electioneering zone.

In summary, the union claimed that the company was just using a trivial incident to have the results of the election overturned and avoid union representation. The majority of the employees had voted for the union, and it was preposterous to conclude that a brief period of enthusiastic, boisterous behavior by union supporters was crucial to the outcome of the election. The union urged that the election results be certified by the NLRB, and that the company be directed to recognize and commence collective bargaining with the union.

Questions

1. Was the behavior of the union supporters improper electioneering, or was it just boisterous enthusiasm of little consequence? Discuss.
2. Should it make any difference in the NLRB's decision that the election was decided by a single vote? Why, or why not?
3. Evaluate the union's contention that the behavior of the union supporters was not crucial to the outcome of the election.

4. Political candidates and their supporters typically engage in "last-minute electioneering" as voters arrive at their polling places to vote. Does such electioneering sway voters, or have most voters made up their minds beforehand? Discuss.

5. NLRB election rules prohibit an employer from "making campaign speeches to assembled groups of employees on company time within the 24-hour period before the election." No such rule exists in regard to labor organizations. Would such a rule for labor organizations be realistic, or helpful in preventing incidents such as occurred in this case?

CASE 14
PAYMENT OF A SIGNING BONUS TO NONSTRIKING EMPLOYEES

Company:
   Kimtruss Corporation, Madera, California

Union:
   Woodworkers, Local Union No. 3-533

Background

The company was engaged in the manufacture and nonretail sale of wooden trusses, with an office and place of business in Madera, California. About two and one-half years earlier, the company had purchased the business, recognized the union, and adopted the existing collective bargaining agreement that would expire on May 31, 1990. The parties had agreed to meet and negotiate a new collective bargaining agreement on May 23, 24, and 25, 1990. The union's negotiating team was headed by Business Representative Adam Bullock, assisted by Business Agent Tony Bailey. The company's chief negotiator was attorney Celia Parsons, aided by Plant Manager Arthur Jerome.[1]

On May 25, 1990, the parties reached a tentative agreement for a new three-year labor-management contract that would expire on May 31, 1993. Wage rates during the first year of the new agreement would not change; however, all employees who were working the week ending June 8, 1990, would receive a bonus based on their length of service with the company as follows:

   30 days to six months—$125 bonus

   Over six months—$300 bonus

Effective June 1, 1991, all employees would receive an across-the-board increase of 15 cents/hour. A similar across-the-board increase of 15 cents/hour would become effective on June 1, 1992.

The bonus was referred to as a "signing bonus" to be paid in lieu of an hourly wage rate increase during the first year of the contract. On May 25, 1990, Bullock and Bailey and other members of the union bargaining committee said that they would recommend the agreement subject to ratification by union members.

However, on May 25, too many employees were absent and could not vote; consequently the union ratification vote was rescheduled for May 31. On that date, business agent Tony Bailey, discussing the tentative agreement with union employees prior to the vote, stated that those employees who voted "no" on the tentative agreement would be voting to strike. A majority of the employees voted to reject the tentative agreement.

Bailey reported the contract rejection to the union's chief negotiator, Adam Bullock. Bullock then telephoned Plant Manager Jerome; upon hearing that the employees had

---

[1]The names of all individuals are disguised.

rejected the contract, Jerome expressed surprise. Bullock indicated that he, too, was surprised. Next, Bullock reported the contract rejection to the company's attorney, Celia Parsons. Parsons stated that the company would implement its last offer the next day. Bullock responded, "Okay, and we know what we have to do." Both the company and the union spent the remainder of the day preparing for a strike, which was to begin the next day, June 1.

Parsons, after learning about the employees' vote to reject the contract, advised Plant Manager Jerome:

> We ought to put up a notice to the employees telling them that we are going to implement our last offer and get it out to them this afternoon if at all possible.

After talking with attorney Parsons, Jerome called the plant and dictated a statement to his secretary, Karen Hardy. After Hardy typed the statement, she faxed it to Jerome for his review. Jerome reviewed it, made no changes, and telephoned Hardy with instructions to mail a copy to every bargaining unit employee and to post the notice at various places around the plant. The notice stated, in relevant part:

> Kimtruss Corporation will implement its last contract offer as of June 1, 1990. Current wages, hours, and conditions plus bargaining agreements . . .
>
> All employees not working June 1, 1990, through June 8, 1990, will not be paid the signing bonus.

By late afternoon of May 31, the notice had been posted at the plant. It was seen by swing-shift employees who reported the notice to business agent Tony Bailey who had come to the plant to begin strike preparations for the next day. Bailey telephoned Howard Mackey, a vice president of the International Union, and informed Mackey of the exact wording of the notice. Mackey told Bailey that the notice did not reflect the company's final offer and, in his opinion, the company had committed an unfair labor practice. Following Mackey's instructions, Bailey wrote "Unfair Labor Practice" on the union's picket signs and informed the employees of the alleged unfair labor practice.

On June 1, the employees began the strike. On June 8, the company paid the bonuses only to nonstriking employees who had crossed the picket lines to report to work. On June 14, the company began to hire permanent replacements to fill the jobs left open by striking employees.[2]

The union immediately filed unfair labor practice charges against the company, claiming that by its actions the company had violated Sections 8(a) (1), 8(a) (3), and 8(a) (5) of the Labor Management Relations Act.

Position of the Union

The union contended that the company had violated Section 8(a) (1) of the Act, when on May 31, 1990, in anticipation of a strike by employees to begin the next day, management announced that a bonus would not be paid to employees who were not

---

[2]The bargaining unit consisted of some 40 employees; about a third of these employees did not strike and were paid the bonuses.

working June 1 through 8, 1990. The company further violated Section 8(a) (3) by paying the bonuses to otherwise eligible nonstriking employees and denying the bonuses to otherwise eligible striking employees.

After committing these unfair labor practices, the company subsequently fired striking employees. What had begun as an economic strike then became an unfair labor practice strike in violation of Section 8(a) (5).

The union argued that the company notice concerning the bonus payments as written by Plant Manager Arthur Jerome was blatant interference intended to deter the employees from their protected right to strike. The notice requiring employees to be working June 1–8, 1990, was not consistent with what the parties had agreed upon, namely, a signing bonus in lieu of a wage increase during the first year of the contract. Further, the timing of the company notice was obviously an inducement to discourage employees from striking. By paying the bonuses only to nonstriking employees and subsequently replacing striking employees, the company was discriminating against employees who had exercised their protected right to strike. Thus, what began as an economic strike became an unfair labor practice strike, and the company had engaged in bad faith bargaining prohibited by Section 8(a) (5) of the Act.

The union urged that the company be held in multiple violations of the Act. The union requested that all permanently replaced employees be reinstated to their job positions and be made whole in every way, including payment of the bonus and all lost wages and benefits.

Position of the Company

The company claimed that there was no evidence whatsoever that it had timed the contested notice in order to deter the employees from a strike. The ratification vote took place on the afternoon of May 31, 1990, the day the collective bargaining agreement expired. It was necessary for the company, once it learned that the employees had rejected the tentative agreement, to issue a notice of its decision to implement its final offer and to inform employees of the terms and conditions under which employees would be working on June 1. That the union had planned a strike for June 1 should not in any way warrant a conclusion that the notice was a response to the planned strike. Nor by posting the notice on May 31 had the company interfered with the employees' protected rights or violated the LMRA.

The company reiterated its position that its May 31 notice that the signing bonus contained in its last contract offer would be withheld from employees not working between June 1 and 8 was proper and lawful. When the company paid the bonuses only to employees who worked after the strike began, this payment constituted an implementation of a wage increase bargained in good faith. The bonuses were based on employee service and were in lieu of a wage increase; thus, each bonus was an accelerated wage increase and compensation for services to be performed during the coming year.

The company pointed out that the NLRB had long established that an employer who had bargained in good faith to impasse with a union could implement its final offer and pay wage increases contained within the final offer to nonstriking employees and any replacements. The company claimed that it had not committed any unfair labor practices. The union strike was clearly an economic one. The company had bargained in good faith with the union. The employees rejected the tentative agreement and some of them went out on strike. Thus it was an economic strike, since it was neither caused nor prolonged by any unfair labor practices on the part of the company. Those employees who continued to be on strike after June 14, 1990, were replaced; this, too, was lawful. The company contended that all the unfair labor practice charges were without merit and should be dismissed by the NLRB.

Questions

1. Evaluate the major contentions of both parties. Which of these do you find to be the most and which the least persuasive?
2. Was the company notice issued by Plant Manager Jerome consistent with the parties' contractual agreement? Why, or why not?
3. Did the company commit unfair labor practices by: *(a)* making the contested announcement? *(b)* paying the signing bonuses to nonstriking employees? *(c)* hiring replacements for striking employees? If so, what should be the remedy ordered by the NLRB?
4. Why is it difficult at times for the Board to determine whether a strike of this nature is economic, or is the result of an employer's (alleged) unfair labor practices?

CASE 15
A PRESUMPTION OF UNION INTERFERENCE DURING A
DECERTIFICATION ELECTION

Company:
   Burkart Foam, Inc., Cairo, Illinois

Union:
   Local Lodge No. 1076, International Association of Machinists and Aerospace Workers

Background

The union was certified as the collective bargaining representative of the company's production and maintenance employees in December 1969. Inspection employees were later added to the unit. The parties' most recent collective bargaining agreement had expired on September 4, 1984. When the parties had been unable to reach agreement on a new contract, the employees commenced a strike on September 5, 1984.

In February 1985, enough employees filed a petition with the NLRB to conduct a decertification election to determine whether the union would continue as the bargaining representative for the employees.

On April 11, 1985, the regional office of the NLRB conducted an election among the bargaining unit employees. The tally of ballots showed 211 votes for and 197 against the union with 20 challenged ballots. Both parties filed timely objections to the election under Section 9(c) of the Act.

On May 14, 1985, the Board office concluded its rulings on the challenged ballots. The revised tally showed 229 votes for and 197 against the union. However, as part of its objections to the conduct of the decertification election, the company had filed unfair labor practice charges against the union. The company alleged that the union had violated Section 8(b) (1) (A) of LMRA by maintaining in its constitution a provision restricting resignation from union membership. This provision was in the union's constitution throughout the period of the strike and at the time of the decertification election. The provision at issue was identified as Article L, Section 3, of the international union's constitution, which stated:

> Improper Conduct of Member . . .
>   Accepting employment in any capacity in an establishment where a strike or lockout exists as recognized under this Constitution, without permission. Resignation shall not relieve a member of his obligation to refrain from accepting employment at the establishment for the duration of the strike or lockout if the resignation occurs during the period of the strike or lockout or within 14 days preceding its commencement. Where observance of a primary picket line is required, any resignation tendered during the period that the picket line is maintained, or within 14 days preceding its establishment, shall not become effective as a resignation during the period the picket line is maintained, nor shall it relieve a member of his or her obligation to observe the primary picket line for its duration.

Position of the Company

Citing a number of prior NLRB decisions,[1] the company contended that any restrictions placed by a union on its members' right to resign were unlawful. The company argued that the NLRB had consistently held that a union may not lawfully restrict the right of its members to resign or otherwise refrain from protected Section 7 activities. Thus, the union's maintenance of the constitutional provision restricting resignations restrained and coerced employees from exercising their Section 7 rights, which is a violation of Section 8(b) (1) (A) of LMRA.

The company further contended that the maintenance of the constitutional provision tainted the election. A presumption of interference was warranted because the unlawful union constitutional provision was inherently destructive of Section 7 rights, and tended to force the strikers to vote for the union and the nonstrikers to vote against it. This interference was particularly objectionable in cases such as this where the margin of the union's victory was slight.

Since the election was conducted in the midst of a strike, the maintenance of the union's constitutional provision necessarily had a coercive impact on every employee who was a member of the union. The company urged that the results of the decertification election be set aside because the union's unfair labor practice had tainted the decertification election. The company urged that the union be ordered to remove and disavow the constitutional provision at issue, and a new decertification election be conducted by the NLRB.

Position of the Union

The union contended, first of all, that its constitutional provision restricting resignation from the union during strike periods was lawful. The proviso included within Section 8(b) (1) (A) of LMRA permits a union "to prescribe its own rules with respect to the acquisition or retention of membership." Any union needs to maintain discipline and solidarity during a strike, and the union's constitutional restriction was necessary to protect the ability of the union to represent its members engaged in a lawful strike.

The union further contended that the company's unfair labor practice charges were primarily an effort to set aside the results of the election won by the union. Even if the constitutional provision at issue was held by the Board to be a technical violation of LMRA, this should not be sufficient grounds to set aside the election outcome. No real violation of Section 8(b) (1) (A) had occurred, because the union did not enforce the constitutional provision at issue. The union never threatened to enforce the provision against any bargaining unit employee, and therefore did not restrain or coerce any employee.

The union argued that any conclusions about how employees might have voted because of the union's constitutional provision would be speculative and contradictory.

---

[1]These included: *Machinists Local 1414 (Neufeld Porsche-Audi)*, 270 NLRB 1330, 116 LRRM 1257 (1984); and *Machinists Local 1769 (Dorsey Trailers)*, 271 NLRB 911, 117 LRRM 1004 (1984).

The provision did not impair the employees' ability to vote or campaign for their preferred position during the election period. And even if the provision might have caused some employees to remain on strike when they were faced with the possibility of replacement, it is equally possible that employees who remained on strike because they thought the union's provision prevented them from resigning would resent the union and vote against it.

The union urged that the unfair labor practice charges be dismissed, and that the results of the election be certified with the union remaining as the collective bargaining representative for the company employees.

Questions

1. Was the union's constitutional provision lawful, or did it violate the Act? Discuss.
2. Evaluate the union's contention that if the NLRB found the constitutional provision to be a technical violation of LMRA, it was not serious enough to set aside the outcome of the election.
3. Why would a labor organization want to maintain such a constitutional restriction on member resignations during a strike?
4. Should the NLRB order a new election? Why, or why not?

CASE 16
WAS THE EMPLOYEE INVOLVEMENT COMMITTEE A VIOLATION OF LABOR LAW?

Company:
Research Federal Credit Union, Warren, Milford, and Detroit, Michigan

Union:
Food and Commercial Workers, Local Union No. 876

Background

The Union Organizing Campaign.   The employer was a credit union with its main office in Warren, Michigan, and branches located in Milford and Detroit, Michigan. In early March 1990, several employees met with representatives of the union. The union then actively began an organizational campaign and solicited signed union authorization cards from a number of employees. Shortly thereafter, the union filed a petition with the regional office of the National Labor Relations Board requesting that a representational election be held. The union claimed that it had obtained signed representation authorization cards from a majority of the some 20 to 25 employees in a proposed bargaining unit. The NLRB subsequently directed that a representational election take place on May 21, 1990.

The Employment Involvement Committee (EIC)—Preelection.   On April 4, 1990, company management advised all its employees that it had retained a management consultant, Walter Meckfuss.[1] On April 30, management called for all employees from its several locations to attend an employee meeting. Walter Meckfuss, the company's new management consultant, was present at this meeting.

Meckfuss announced at the April 30 meeting that the company had decided to form an "employee involvement committee," or EIC, to consist of an employee and a supervisory representative from each of the three offices. Supervisory representatives were to be appointed by management, and employee representatives were to be elected by employees in their respective offices. Meckfuss stated that the purpose of the EIC was to improve communication and morale in the firm and to enable the employees to have an important say in improving work operations and other aspects of their jobs.

Because the first EIC meeting was scheduled for the next day, May 1, representatives and their alternates were selected almost immediately. For example, the Milford branch employees elected Carla Lee and Teresa Coleman as their representative and alternate, respectively, in a restaurant on the way home from the meeting. The Milford branch supervisor, Martin Post, was present during this election process.

---

[1]The names of all individuals and certain data are disguised.

EIC meetings were held on May 1, 7, and 16, 1990. All meetings were held at the Warren facility or elsewhere in Warren. The meeting of May 16 was held in the evening; the other meetings were held during working hours. The May 16 meeting was for all representatives and alternates; the other meetings were just for representatives, although an alternate could attend in the absence of the representative. In her representative capacity, Carla Lee received her normal pay for the daytime meetings she attended as well as mileage between her branch in Milford and the meeting site in Warren. Dinner was supplied by the company at the May 16 evening meeting.

The May 1 meeting was attended by the three employee representatives, and Jane Havis, branch manager at Warren, Martin Post, branch manager at Milford, and Walter Meckfuss. Meckfuss explained what the EIC was supposed to do, saying that the employee members were to be the "unbiased eyes and ears" of the employees they represented. They should try to get the employees in their respective departments to talk with them regarding any problems they felt needed attention. The representatives were then to bring these problems and suggestions to the EIC meetings. At the meetings, if solutions to such problems were found, they would be presented to top management or the Board of Directors. Some possible topics for action by the EIC discussed at the May 1 meeting were smoking policies, part-time benefits, and annual reviews. The meeting lasted about an hour and a half, during which an EIC chairperson and secretary were selected.

At the May 7 meeting, a smoking policy was discussed; Meckfuss suggested that the EIC might come up with ideas to solve the smoking problem if representatives would discuss the matter with the employees they represented and ask for their opinions. The question of a constantly changing sick-time policy was also brought up. Meckfuss responded that it was a difficult subject, and that management had been studying the benefit package and comparing it with similar businesses in the area. On the subject of educational reimbursement, Meckfuss advised the representatives to ask their fellow employees how they wanted it handled, and then a written policy would be developed. Personal leave days, employee reviews, and Christmas bonuses were also discussed.

The May 16 evening meeting of all representatives and alternates took place in Warren at a local restaurant. Two members of the Board of Directors were also present, Nepah Rentul and Sam Barrow. An outline for discussion was presented, which included such topics as a smoking policy, wage and salary review, and sick-time benefits. Carla Lee asked whether employees were to get an ample pay raise. Meckfuss responded that management was checking with similar-sized credit unions within the area to determine an appropriate salary scale. With respect to sick time, Meckfuss said that he felt the employees would again be allowed seven sick days annually (the number of days of annual paid sick leave had been reduced from seven to five in 1989). However, Meckfuss stated that nothing could be done in these areas until after the union representational election. With respect to the matter of vacation benefits for part-time employees, Meckfuss suggested that the representatives solicit input from the employees and come up with a formula. There was also a discussion about credibility between the employees and the Board of Directors. Sam Barrow stated that he would meet with the EIC members occasionally, and that he wanted to have more open communication between the Board and all of the staff. Walter Meckfuss stated that he knew that annual reviews were a problem and something had to be done about them. He added that it was possible that a special committee could be established to conduct annual reviews for employees.

The Representational Election.   On May 21, 1990, the NLRB conducted a union representational election for the employees in the proposed bargaining unit. By a vote of 12 to 9, a majority voted against having the union certified as their bargaining representative.

The Employee Involvement Committee (EIC)—Postelection.   Two EIC meetings were held on May 30 and June 20, 1990, after the election. The May 30 meeting was a predinner meeting at a local restaurant. At this meeting, the EIC developed a memo for employees listing and describing six issues that the EIC would be presenting at the next Board of Directors meeting, scheduled for June 21. Those issues were wage and salary pay scales, including the area wage survey and part-time employee benefits; cleaning out the ventilation system at Warren; smoking areas; sick time; employee transactions; and memos. The latter two issues involved setting a specific time during the day to see supervisors for access to money and slowing down the number of memos that were being issued. By memo to the EIC dated May 31, Sam Barrow responded to some of the issues raised in the EIC's May 30 memo, informing the EIC that the firm was getting bids regarding ventilation system maintenance; that sick-time policy and cash incentive awards would be announced at the June Board meeting; and that new procedures were in place to ensure more consistency in policies.

At the June 20 meeting of the EIC, Meckfuss stated with respect to sick-time policy proposals that he did not think there would be any problem with them, and that the employees should have gotten what they had asked for a long time ago. He commented that proposals dealing with part-time benefits would be more difficult because of the costs. With respect to smoking areas, the Warren EIC employee representative had a suggestion for a location in the Warren offices where a smoking area might be designated. Meckfuss said that he would ask management to check with the fire marshal for approval. During the meeting, Meckfuss stated that wages would not be discussed because the wage survey was not complete.

The Union's Unfair Labor Practice Charges.   Shortly after the representational election, the union filed unfair labor practice charges against the company claiming that the company had violated Sections 8(a) (1), 8(a) (2), and 8(a) (5) of the Labor Management Relations Act. The union claimed that the employee involvement committee (EIC) was a labor organization within the meaning of Section 2(5) of LMRA, and that it had been created by management to deny the employees their own union representation.

Position of the Union

The union claimed that the purpose of the employee involvement committee was to undercut the employees' desire for a union. The EIC had been created by the company without any employee request for such an entity shortly after the union had begun its representational campaign. The nature of the EIC had been determined by management, and employees had been directed to select representatives and alternates.

Meetings were called by management, some on company time with the employee representatives paid for attendance. Although the meetings were led by a management consultant, it was clear that Meckfuss was serving as an agent of management and the Board of Directors. Virtually every topic discussed at the EIC meetings dealt in some way with wages, hours of employment, and working conditions. In the union's view, the EIC was designed to create in the employees' minds the sentiment that there was no need for a labor union. This was particularly evident in the efforts of Meckfuss and members of the Board of Directors to solicit employee grievances and promise to remedy them.

The union argued that the EIC was a labor organization created and dominated by the company in violation of Sections 8(a) (2) and 8(a) (1) of the Labor Management Relations Act. By soliciting employee grievances and promising to improve various working conditions, the employer further violated Section 8(a) (1) since these matters were contingent upon the outcome of the union election.

Finally, the union argued that it had attained a valid majority of employees who had signed union authorization cards. The company had refused to recognize these cards and had insisted on a formal NLRB election. By refusing to recognize and bargain with the union when it had obtained signed authorization cards from a majority of employees, and by having unlawfully interfered with the union, the employer had violated Section 8(a) (5) of LMRA. The union requested as a remedy that the NLRB under Section 10(c) of the Act direct that the EIC be disestablished and that the company recognize and bargain with the union because of the company's significant unfair labor practices that destroyed a valid union majority.

Position of the Company

The company claimed that it had not violated any provisions of the Labor Management Relations Act by organizing an employee involvement committee (EIC). The purpose of the EIC was to provide a means for employees to address various concerns and to present recommendations for solutions to management and/or the Board of Directors. The company had contemplated the formation of the EIC for several months prior to the union representational election. No employees were forced to participate in the EIC. The employees and their representatives had found the EIC to be an appropriate forum in which to express their concerns. The EIC was not dominated by management; the management consultant, Mr. Meckfuss, was merely a conduit between management and the employee representatives. No employee was disciplined or reprimanded for anything that was said or brought up within the EIC.

The company strongly contested the allegation that the EIC was a labor organization within the meaning of Section 2(5) of LMRA. The EIC was a venue for presenting employees' concerns to management, such as is widespread in American industry. Quality circles, quality-of-work-life programs, and the like provide a cooperative means by which employees and management can discuss and solve mutual problems. These nonadversarial programs should be fostered and not condemned by labor laws. The fact that the employees rejected the union was an indication that they considered the EIC to be a viable mechanism for addressing their concerns.

Although the company denied that the EIC violated Sections 8(a) (1) and 8(a) (2), it argued that in the event the NLRB should rule that some technical violation had occurred, an order to recognize and bargain with the union would be totally improper. A majority of employees had voted against the union. If the NLRB should find that the company had inadvertently violated the Act, the appropriate remedy would be to direct that a new representational election be held to determine the employees' wishes concerning union representation.

Questions

1. Does it make a difference in this case that the employee involvement committee (EIC) was organized during the union representational campaign?
2. Even though employee representatives were not forced to serve on the EIC, did the employees have any real alternative to agreeing to participate? Discuss.
3. Was the EIC a labor organization within the meaning of LMRA, or was it rather a means by which employees and management could communicate about employee concerns? Discuss why various types of participative management efforts throughout business and industry often operate in a "gray area" of labor law.
4. If the NLRB finds a violation of the Act because of the EIC, what should be the appropriate remedy directed by the Board?

CASE 17
DISCHARGE FOR FAILURE TO PAY UNION DUES

Company:
R. H. Macy & Co., Inc., Bronx, New York

Union:
Local No. 3, International Brotherhood of Electrical Workers

Individual:
Alan Gomez[1]

Background

From 1978 until his discharge on January 8, 1981, Alan Gomez had been employed by Macy's as an electrician. In that capacity, Gomez was covered by a collective bargaining agreement containing a union security clause. This clause required that, as a condition of employment, all bargaining unit employees become and remain members of the union after 30 days of employment. As the contract did not contain a dues-checkoff provision, unit employees submitted their dues directly to the union. From April 1978 to September 1979, Gomez paid his dues on a quarterly basis. However, because of personal financial difficulties, Gomez did not remit any dues for the last quarter of 1979, and until December 17, 1980, he had remitted no dues for any quarter period in 1980.

In late December 1980, Gomez feared that he might be discharged pursuant to the terms of the union security agreement if he did not catch up on his dues. On December 17, 1980, Gomez forwarded a check to the union for $252.80 covering dues owed for the four quarters of 1980; he believed that this amount was all he owed the union. However, Gomez had not paid dues for the last quarter of 1979, and he was therefore still in arrears for that quarter.

On December 22, 1980, the union's executive board met to discuss the dues status of various members, including that of Gomez. A form letter dated December 30, 1980, was thereafter mailed out to Gomez advising him that he had been listed as a "ceased" member,[2] and that if he wished to remain a member he would have to pay the sum of $66.70, which represented dues owed for the last quarter of 1979, plus a reinstatement fee of $30. According to the letter, such payments would assure him "good standing in the union until December 31, 1980." Gomez did not receive the letter until several days after the December 30 date. Upon receipt of the letter, Gomez (believing that his dues had been brought up to date by his December 17 check) phoned the union office. After he had questioned the contents of the union's letter, Gomez was told that if he paid the amount stated in the letter, he would no longer be a "ceased" member but would be reinstated.

---

[1]The names of all individuals are disguised.

[2]A member was classified as "ceased" when his dues were in arrears for six months or more. A "lapsed" member was one whose dues were in arrears for only three months. Although a lapsed member was still considered a union member, a ceased member was not.

However, prior to this, on December 22, 1980, George Hulser, a Macy's manager, had informed Macy's vice president for labor relations Bernice Wambles that union business representative Tony Mataya had requested that Gomez be discharged for failing to pay union dues for a long period of time. Wambles had advised Hulser that such a request must be made in writing. Thereafter, a letter dated December 26, 1980, and signed by Mataya was mailed to Wambles stating that according to the union's records Gomez was not a member in good standing, having failed to pay his dues since September 1979; the union requested that Gomez be discharged from his position as of the date of this letter. Wambles did not receive this letter until January 5, 1981.

Upon receipt of the union's letter, Wambles reviewed the collective bargaining agreement to verify that the union's request for Gomez' discharge was proper. After doing so, she notified Macy's personnel manager, Alice Kelso, of Gomez' apparent dues delinquency and instructed that, in accordance with the union security agreement, Gomez be discharged. On January 8, 1981, Kelso summoned Gomez to her office, and informed him that at the union's request, he was being terminated for failing to pay dues as required under the union contract. Although Gomez protested that a mistake had been made, he was advised by Kelso that he would have to take the matter up with the union. Gomez responded that the union was out to get him because of an earlier discrimination suit he had filed against the union concerning job assignments.

Immediately after leaving Kelso's office, Gomez went to the union's office, where he tendered a $225 check postdated for the following day, January 9, 1981, covering the amount requested by the union in the December 30 letter plus an advance payment for two additional quarters. Gomez returned to Kelso's office later that afternoon but was denied reinstatement because of his failure to produce a receipt indicating his union dues had been paid.

Subsequently, Alan Gomez filed charges with the NLRB against the company alleging a discriminatory discharge in violation of Sections 8(a) (3) and 8(a) (1) of the Labor Management Relations Act. Gomez filed similar charges against the union alleging violations of Sections 8(b) (1) (A) and 8(b) (2) of the Act.

While these charges were still being litigated, Gomez was reinstated to his former position in late May 1981.

Position of the Individual

Although Alan Gomez acknowledged he had fallen behind some 15 months in his dues to the union, his failure to make payments was not a willful and deliberate attempt to avoid his financial obligations but resulted from his personal financial difficulties and the union's own inattention to the matter. On his own initiative, Gomez had mailed a check to the union before any request for his discharge had been made in an amount that he in good faith, but erroneously, believed was sufficient to cover all his dues obligations. He claimed that his failure to include his dues for the last quarter of 1979 in his December 17, 1980, check did not result from an intentional act, but from a lack of knowledge of the extent of his dues delinquency, which primarily was the fault of the union.

Alan Gomez claimed that by failing to inform him specifically of his 1979 dues obligations and by failing to give him an opportunity to clear up his dues account prior to seeking his discharge, the union had discriminated against him in violation of Sections 8(b) (1) (A) and 8(b) (2) of the LMRA. In part, Gomez felt that the union was retaliating against him for his having filed an employment discrimination suit against the union a year or so before, a suit that he subsequently dropped. And since the company had unlawfully discharged him upon the request of the union, the company too had violated Sections 8(a) (3) and 8(a) (1) of the Act. Alan Gomez requested that his discharge of January 8, 1981, be rescinded, and that he be made whole by the union and/or the company for the period between his termination and his reinstatement.

Position of the Company

The company claimed that it simply acted on the request of the union to terminate Alan Gomez for his failure to pay dues, as required by the collective bargaining agreement. The company had no reasonable basis whatsoever to believe that the union's request was either improper or unlawful. The union's dues problem with Alan Gomez was an internal union matter. If there was anything unlawful about what happened, it was the union's total responsibility, not the company's. The company requested that the unfair labor practice charges filed against the company by Alan Gomez be dismissed.

Position of the Union

The union argued that it had the right both under its collective bargaining agreement with the company and under Section 8(b) (2) of the LMRA to request the company to terminate Alan Gomez for his failure to pay all his delinquent union dues. Although Gomez had made an effort to pay most of his delinquent dues at the end of 1980, he still owed dues for the last quarter of 1979 when the union made its request to the company to have Gomez terminated. Gomez had been a "free rider" for a long period of time, and the union could not overlook his dues delinquency any longer. The union requested that the unfair labor practice charges filed against the union by Alan Gomez be dismissed.

Questions

1. Evaluate the company's position that it simply acted on the union's request to discharge Alan Gomez for his failure to pay union dues. Does a valid union shop clause in a negotiated labor agreement absolve the company of any responsibility in this matter?
2. Evaluate the union's position that it had the right to request Alan Gomez' discharge both under the labor contract and within the provisions of LMRA, even though Gomez had paid most of the dues he owed.
3. Was Alan Gomez discriminated against in violation of the Act? If so, by the company, the union, or both?
4. Regardless of the NLRB's findings concerning the discrimination charges, why is a case such as this "embarrassing" to both the company and the union?

CASE 18
THE UNION'S REFUSAL TO FURNISH ITS MEMBERSHIP LISTS

Employers:
  Apple City Electric, Inc.; J&M Electric, Inc.; and Valley Electric Service of Wenatchee, Inc.; all of Wenatchee, Washington

Union:
  Local Union No. 497, International Brotherhood of Electrical Workers

Background

The three employers in this case had been signatories, as part of their membership in the National Electrical Contractors Association (NECA), to a two-year areawide contract with the union that was to expire in June 1984. In early 1984, the employers decided that they no longer would be part of the NECA areawide contract. The three employers each informed NECA and the union that they would bargain for a new contract on a separate basis. On March 31, 1984, the employers notified the union of their intent to amend or terminate the expiring contract. Between April 25 and July 17, 1984, the parties met six times in efforts to negotiate a successor agreement. An attorney, Allen Rich,[1] jointly represented the three employers during the negotiations.

At the first bargaining session on April 25, Rich informed the union that the employers wanted a number of changes in the employee referral system. The expiring NECA contract contained provisions that required the employers to use the union's hiring hall as the exclusive source of applicants for employment. Rich said that the employers had experienced problems with the qualifications of certain employees referred by the union; the employers also were dissatisfied with a 48-hour provision for filling referral requests, which had caused delays in meeting their employment needs. The parties discussed a number of possible alternatives, but did not reach any agreement on these issues.

During a bargaining session held on May 19, 1984, attorney Allen Rich made an oral request for a list of the names and addresses of all the union members who were subject to the referral system under the then-existing NECA contract. The union refused to furnish this information. The chief spokesman for the union, Business Representative Carl Georgio, told Rich that the union's referral books could be provided for visual inspection, but could not be copied by any of the employers. Georgio also told Rich that he (Rich) would not be permitted to see the referral books. On May 24, 1984, Rich made a written request for this information; the union again rejected this request. In his response, Georgio stated that the union had a policy of refusing to release any information about a member unless the particular member signed a release, or unless there was a court order directing the union to furnish such information. Further, the union

---

[1]The names of all individuals are disguised.

allowed only its own members to inspect the lists of known members and their addresses, but it did not allow any members to copy the membership lists.

Shortly thereafter, the employers jointly filed charges with the NLRB, claiming that by refusing to provide the requested information, the union was not bargaining collectively in good faith as required by Section 8(b) (3) of the Labor Management Relations Act and as is further defined within Section 8(d) of the Act.

Position of the Employers

Counsel for the employers argued that the membership lists sought by the employers were clearly relevant to collective bargaining and should be furnished by the union at the request of the employers. The employers needed to have this information regarding the referral system for contract negotiations, since it was very relevant to the employers' concerns about union applicants' qualifications and was also related to problems with the previous contract's 48-hour provision for filling employment needs, which the employers wished to change.

Two previous NLRB cases were cited in support of the employers' position. In both these cases, the NLRB had found that the unions had violated Section 8(b) (3) of LMRA by refusing to provide lists of their members who were covered under union hiring hall contractual provisions.[2] In both these cases, the Board concluded that such information was "relevant and necessary to the collective bargaining process."

Concerning the union's claim that the requested information was "confidential" and would invade the union members' right to privacy, counsel for the employers argued that this claim was without any merit. There was nothing in the employers' request or in the past conduct of the employers to suggest that the employers would use the referral lists to harass or discriminate against any union members.

Finally, it was not a sufficient response for the union just to offer the employers an opportunity to view the referral lists while denying their chief negotiator, Mr. Rich, any such opportunity. Rather, it was necessary for the employers' chief negotiator to have a copy of the referral lists in order to have time and sufficient information at hand for carrying out his role on behalf of the employer group.

The employers urged that the union be found in violation of the Act, and be ordered to provide the requested information, which was germane to the collective bargaining process.

Position of the Union

The union argued that any compelled disclosure of its membership lists would infringe on the members' First Amendment rights under the Constitution. The union contended that release of such information was precluded by the Landrum-Griffin Act,[3] which was

---

[2]These cases were *Asbestos Workers Local 80 (West Virginia Insulators)*, 248 NLRB 143, 103 LRRM 1370 (1980); and *Printing & Graphic Communications Local 13 (Oakland Press Co.)*, 233 NLRB 994, 97 LRRM 1047 (1977).

[3]This is also known as the Labor-Management Reporting and Disclosure Act of 1959.

carefully drafted to preserve the confidentiality of union membership lists by giving members themselves only a limited right to inspect such lists.

In this regard, the union cited a prior court case in which the court had been reluctant to allow even the U.S. Secretary of Labor to possess a copy of the union's membership lists in the absence of assurances that the lists would not be available to outsiders.[4]

The union claimed that the two previous NLRB cases cited by the employers had not considered the confidentiality and First Amendment issues, and therefore were not applicable to this case.

Finally, the union contended that its offer to supply the requested information by allowing the employers to see the referral books was sufficient to meet its bargaining obligations under LMRA. There is nothing in the Act or in NLRB case law that requires either party to provide information in exactly the manner requested or demanded by the other side. The union offered to permit the employers to see the union's referral lists, and this inspection should have satisfied whatever needs the employers had for collective bargaining purposes. The employers' unfair labor practice charges of "bad faith" bargaining were groundless, and should be dismissed by the Board.

Questions

1. Evaluate the employers' reasons for requesting the union's membership lists.
2. Evaluate the union's reasons for refusing to permit the employers' chief negotiator to see the membership lists and also for refusing any copying of the lists by the employers themselves.
3. Should the union's First Amendment and Landrum-Griffin law arguments be considered by the NLRB in this case? Why, or why not?
4. Was the union in violation of Sections 8(b) (3) and 8(d) of the Labor Management Relations Act? Why, or why not?

---

[4]*Teamsters* v. *Goldberg,* 303 F.2d 402, 49 LRRM 2968 (D.C. Cir. 1962).

CASE 19
THE EMPLOYER'S REFUSAL TO FURNISH HOSPITALIZATION
INSURANCE INFORMATION

Company:
Ideal Corrugated Box Corporation, Parkersburg, West Virginia

Union:
Local No. 124, Paperworkers Union

Background

For many years the union had been the exclusive representative for a unit of the company's employees. This unit was defined in the parties' collective bargaining agreement to include "all production and maintenance employees employed by Ideal Corrugated Box Corporation at its Parkersburg, West Virginia, facility, excluding all time keepers, clerks, office clerical employees, guards, and supervisors as defined in the Labor Management Relations Act, as amended." The parties' collective bargaining agreement at the time of this case was effective from September 29, 1986, to May 31, 1989.

On November 9, 1987, company management posted a notice to all employees that it was changing its hospitalization insurance carrier. A second notice dated January 1988 stated that the employees' hospitalization coverage would remain the same, but that certain surgical operations and hospital confinements would require a second opinion, to be paid for by the carrier. The January notice also stated that the company's method of payment had changed, which might result in a paperwork change for employees.

On November 27, 1987, the union requested in writing that the company furnish the union with the following information:

1. A complete copy of the previous medical and accident hospitalization insurance policy in effect prior to December 1, 1987, including all amendments thereto.
2. A complete copy of the new medical and accident hospitalization insurance policy, which went into effect on or about December 1, 1987, including all amendments thereto.
3. All claims experienced under the previous medical and accident hospitalization insurance policy for the past two years.
4. The percentage and dollar amount of premium increases in the previous medical and accident hospitalization insurance policy over the past two years and the effective dates of such increases.
5. The premium cost for the previous medical and accident hospitalization insurance policy in effect prior to December 1, 1987.
6. The premium cost for the new medical and accident hospitalization insurance policy, which took effect on or about December 1, 1987.
7. A list of all changes in coverage, if any, under the new medical and accident hospitalization insurance policy versus the coverage contained in the previous policy.

8. The name and address of the agent handling the new medical and accident hospitalization insurance policy, which went into effect December 1, 1987.
9. Information as to whether the employer contacted the new insurance carrier to discuss the possibility of developing new insurance coverage or whether the carrier contacted the employer.

In a written letter and also at a meeting, company management informed union representatives that the company would not furnish the union with the requested information. Shortly thereafter, the union filed unfair labor practice charges with the NLRB alleging that the company's refusal constituted a violation of Sections 8(a) (5) and 8(a) (1) of LMRA.

Position of the Union

The union asserted that the information requested was necessary for and relevant to the union's performance and function as exclusive collective bargaining representative for employees in the unit. The union pointed out that there had been some changes in the hospitalization insurance policy, such as the requirement of a second opinion when surgery was indicated for treatment. Therefore, the requested information was necessary to determine whether there were any changes in actual coverage that would serve as a basis for filing a grievance or for presenting new bargaining proposals at the next round of contract negotiations.

In essence, the union asserted that it was well-established from prior NLRB and court decisions that employers have a duty to furnish relevant information to a labor organization during the term of a labor-management agreement.[1] The company's refusal to furnish the requested relevant information constituted a violation of Sections 8(a) (5) and 8(a) (1) of LMRA. The company should be ordered by the NLRB to furnish the requested information to the union and to cease and desist in its unfair labor practices.

Position of the Company

The company basically contended: (1) that it had no legal obligation to the union to furnish the information during the mid-term of the parties' collective bargaining agreement; and (2) that there had been no actual change in the company's hospitalization insurance policy that justified complying with the union's unnecessary and burdensome request.

The company contended that changing insurance carriers from Blue Cross/Blue Shield of Parkersburg to Blue Cross/Blue Shield of Charleston did not violate the LMRA, because the company's collective bargaining agreement with the union did not specify that hospitalization insurance benefits must be provided by any particular insurance carrier. The company pointed out that no employees had been denied their contractual benefits as a result of the change in insurance carriers. The minor changes

---

[1]For example, see *NLRB* v. *Acme Industrial Co.*, 385 U.S. 432, 436, 64 LRRM 2069 (1967).

placed in effect were only procedural and administrative, not substantive. Further, the company argued that the union's request for insurance information was premature, because the parties were not engaged in contract negotiations. This was especially so at this time, since the information requested was excessive and would require many hours of work to provide.

In support of its position, the company cited a prior NLRB decision in which the Board deferred to an arbitrator's award that a change in insurance carriers was permitted by the parties' collective bargaining agreement.[2] In the company's view, this case was analogous in that the only basis for a dispute was whether the company could change hospitalization insurance carriers during the life of the collective bargaining agreement; such a dispute should be decided by an arbitrator, not by the NLRB.

The company claimed the unfair labor practice charges were without merit and should be dismissed.

Questions

1. Was the union's request for information relevant to its responsibility as the collective bargaining representative for the employees, or was it primarily a "fishing expedition" of little consequence? Discuss.
2. Evaluate the company's contention that it had no obligation to furnish the requested information to the union.
3. Should the dispute in this case be decided by the NLRB, or should it be referred to an arbitrator under the parties' collective bargaining agreement? Discuss.
4. Compare the issues in this case with those in Case 23, "The Union's Request for Access to an Employee's Confidential Personnel File."

---

[2]*Bay Shipbuilding Corp.,* 251 NLRB 809, 105 LRRM 1376, (1980).

CASE 20
DISCHARGE FOR USING THE PHOTOCOPIER IN A HAZARDOUS WASTE DISPUTE

Company:
  Blue Circle Cement Company, Tulsa, Oklahoma

Union:
  Local Union D421, United Cement, Lime, Gypsum & Allied Workers (Division Affiliated with the Boilermakers Union)

Background

Early in 1991, officers of Local D421 of the union, the recognized collective bargaining representative of the plant employees, became aware that the company, a cement manufacturer, was making plans to burn hazardous waste as a fuel to heat its cement kilns. The union decided to actively oppose the company's plans because of health and safety concerns. In a local union meeting, employee members voted that the union should attempt to enlist community support for its position. Union President Ralph Truppel,[1] with the approval of the union membership, appointed Sam Suiters as the union's environmental officer and spokesperson to lead the fight because of Suiters' background, interests, and contacts in the field of environmental issues. Suiters was a founder and member of a nonprofit volunteer local environmental organization called Earth Concerns of Oklahoma (ECO). Like the union, ECO opposed the company's plans to burn hazardous waste. Suiters, therefore, would be ECO's spokesperson as well as the union's. Suiters told his fellow union members that he would be "wearing two hats."

Suiters' activities in opposition to the company's hazardous waste burning plans were numerous and various. He researched the issue of burning hazardous waste at other cement plants and the nature of the hazardous materials. He solicited ideas from other company employees, raised the issue at union meetings, led community opposition, and organized and participated in rallies near the company plant that were attended by employees and nearby residents. To publicize one such rally held on June 3, 1991, Suiters distributed a leaflet on behalf of the union, ECO, and other environmental groups that asked citizens "to join us in a demonstration in solidarity with workers and residents threatened by hazardous waste burning." Suiters acted as press spokesman and explained the dangers of the company's plans to the local media covering the rallies. On frequent occasions, he discussed the issue with the company's plant operations manager, Don Pernell. In his public speeches, he often referred to a chart entitled "Toxic and Hazardous Chemicals in Industry," which had been provided to him by Don Pernell.

Suiters participated in ongoing union picketing outside the company plant that protested not only the company's hazardous waste plans but several other issues that were on the union's agenda at the time. The union was attempting to achieve a successor bargaining agreement with the company, which recently had undergone a

---

[1]The names of all individuals are disguised.

change in corporate ownership. The prior collective bargaining agreement with the previous owners had expired. The union's rallies and picketing combined the hazardous waste issue with contractual economic issues.

On July 27, 1991, Plant Operations Manager Don Pernell observed Sam Suiters using the company's photocopier in the production office during worktime. Suiters admitted to Pernell that he was photocopying five copies of a seven-page section of a Greenpeace publication. On closer inspection, Pernell saw that Suiters was photocopying a piece from a publication of the environmental organization Greenpeace on the topic of toxicological properties of heavy metals, which criticized "sham recycling" and stated that heavy metals in hazardous waste could be released by burning.

Pernell at this point said to Suiters, "This must be the biggest joke for ECO that you can sit here and copy their materials on my machine and distribute it against us."

Pernell immediately suspended Suiters, and on August 5, Pernell discharged Suiters. Consistent with his initial reaction that Suiters intended to distribute the photocopied materials in opposition to the company's plans to burn hazardous waste, Pernell's discharge letter to Suiters stated that the company "cannot condone an employee working against the company's legitimate business interests by using its equipment and materials on paid time."

Shortly thereafter, the union filed unfair labor practice charges protesting that Sam Suiters' discharge was unlawful interference in violation of Section 8(a) (1) of the Labor Management Relations Act.

Position of the Union

The union claimed that the suspension and discharge of Sam Suiters for using the company's photocopier was a pretext for terminating him for pursuing his legitimate union activities that the company found objectionable. The union presented a series of witnesses who testified that the company routinely permitted employees to use its photocopiers during worktime to copy a variety of materials, both personal and work-related. It was evident, therefore, that the discharge of Suiters for using the photocopier during worktime to photocopy materials pertaining to hazardous waste, while permitting others to use the photocopiers with impunity, amounted to gross disparate treatment.

The union noted that the company had refused to process a union grievance on behalf of Sam Suiters since, in consequence of the recent change in corporate ownership, no collective bargaining agreement was currently in place. In the union's view, Suiter's discharge would not meet the just cause standard for discipline required in virtually all labor agreements. At the same time, the company's discharge of Suiters in this situation was unlawful.

The union claimed that Suiters' discharge violated Section 8(a) (1) of LMRA, since Suiters was engaged in activities protected by Section 7 of the Act. The union pointed out that Sam Suiters had participated in union activities in opposition to the company's hazardous waste burning plans, and the company knew he was the union's environmental officer. The union's efforts to oppose the company's plans were broad in scope and were supported by environmental organizations. The union, a local environmental organization (ECO), and Suiters all shared the same goal of maintaining a healthy and safe workplace at the company. In the union's view, the company had seized on the photocopier incident to find a reason to terminate Suiters, since the company considered Suiters a "union rabble-rouser" who was causing difficulties for the company, both inside the firm and in the nearby community.

The union urged the NLRB to find that the company had violated Section 8(a) (1) of LMRA, and urged that Suiters be reinstated and made appropriately whole for all lost pay and benefits.

Position of the Company

According to operations manager Don Pernell, when he discovered Sam Suiters at the photocopier copying the Greenpeace article and suggested to Suiters, "It must be the biggest joke for ECO that you can sit here and copy their materials on my machine and distribute it against us," Suiters made no reply. More to the point, Suiters did not claim that he was copying the article for the union or that he was engaged in union business. When Pernell was in the process of suspending Suiters about an hour later for unauthorized use of the copier to copy documents that weren't of a company nature, Suiters simply claimed that he had permission from two office managers to make personal copies. Suiters again did not claim to have been engaged in union business.

After Pernell suspended Suiters, Pernell discussed the matter in separate conversations with union grievance committee chairperson Nellie Azella and union President Ralph Truppel. Neither of these union officials said anything about Suiters having been engaged in union activity when he was copying the article.

During Suiters' discharge interview a few days later, he once again did not claim that he was copying the article for the union, or that he was engaged in union business. His only defense was that everyone else used the copier to make personal copies, and this was the sole defense for his unauthorized, unethical, dishonest behavior.

In the company's view, the union's 8(a) (1) unfair labor practice charges against the company were a desperate effort on the part of the union and Sam Suiters to have his job restored. There was no basis for the claim that Suiters' unauthorized personal use of the photocopier was protected union activity. He was doing the photocopying on his own and for a local environmental organization, ECO. Suiters was a disloyal employee who had associated himself with an extremist environmental cause to the detriment of his company. The company was fully justified in terminating Sam Suiters, since he was not engaged in protected union activity when he was caught in a personal act of dishonesty.

The company urged the NLRB to dismiss the unfair labor practice charges in their entirety.

Questions

1. Does it make any difference in this case that Sam Suiters was wearing "multiple hats" (i.e., had different areas of special interest) when he was observed copying the materials in the company's production office during worktime? Discuss.

2. *(a)* Why would the company refuse to accept a grievance on Suiters' behalf even though there was no collective bargaining agreement in place at the time of this case? *(b)* If there had been a collective bargaining agreement in place, is it likely that the union would have filed unfair labor practice charges on Suiters' behalf in addition to filing a grievance under a grievance/arbitration procedure? Discuss.

3. Should the company have overlooked the unauthorized (perhaps dishonest) act by Suiters because he was the union's chief environmental spokesperson in the hazardous waste issue? Why, or why not?

4. Does an employer have the right to expect a certain amount of loyalty from its employees, for instance, a right to expect that an employee will not publicly attack the firm's policies? Discuss.

5. Was the company's discharge of Sam Suiters lawful, or was it in violation of LMRA? Discuss.

CASE 21
JUDICIAL REVIEW OF THE NLRB'S "PUNITIVE" REMEDY CONCERNING THE HEALTH CARE PLAN

Company:
   North Star Steel Company, St. Paul, Minnesota

Union:
   United Steelworkers of America

Background

On July 30, 1987, the United Steelworkers of America was certified by the NLRB as the recognized bargaining agent for 24 clerical employees of North Star. The company refused to acknowledge this certification; the company would not bargain with the union and filed an exception to the unit certification with the Board. On July 27, 1988, the Board found that the union's certification was valid, and that North Star had violated Sections 8(a) (5) and 8(a) (1) of the LMRA by refusing to recognize and bargain with the union. This ruling was affirmed by the District of Columbia Circuit in December 1989. The company then began bargaining with the union.

Before the union's certification, North Star had maintained a health care insurance plan for its employees. Historically, this plan had required employees to contribute to the payment of premiums. The plan covered the majority of employees at the North Star plant, including the clerical workers, and allowed North Star to make unilateral changes in the amount of money the employees needed to contribute to maintain their coverage. This system was continued after the union was certified to represent the clerical employees, even though North Star was challenging that certification and refusing to bargain.

In early 1990, the union and the company began bargaining. They started with noneconomic issues and moved on, after making no headway, to economic issues. In May 1990, the parties reached a tentative agreement on many of the issues. Included in this agreement was a union proposal for continuation of the employer's health care plan in its current form, allowing the company to continue making unilateral changes in the contribution amounts paid by employees each year. The tentative agreement had as a condition, however, that the parties reach a final, total collective bargaining agreement. The union maintained that its agreement to continue the health care plan represented an effort to stimulate negotiations on other, more pressing issues. Despite this concession, however, no final overall agreement was reached.

After the parties failed to reach a final agreement, the union filed an amended complaint with the NLRB, alleging that North Star had violated Sections 8(a) (5) and 8(a) (1) of the Act by unilaterally raising the employees' contribution amounts to the health care plan during 1988, 1989, and 1990. The case was submitted to an Administrative Law Judge (ALJ) on stipulated facts. North Star conceded that it had committed a technical violation of Section 8(a) (5), but the company argued that imposing a monetary make-whole remedy was inappropriate because the employees were in the same position that they would have been in had the company bargained with the union when it was originally certified. The ALJ concluded otherwise, however. The ALJ ordered North Star to return the employees to the status quo that had existed in 1987 and to reimburse them for all the incremental health care premium costs they had paid from January 1988 to July 18, 1990, when the negotiations, according to the ALJ, had reached an impasse.

On appeal to the NLRB, the ALJ's decision was affirmed, with the exception of the ALJ's finding that negotiations had reached an impasse in 1990. The Board determined that no impasse had occurred, and that the monetary make-whole remedy should continue to accrue until an agreement was reached or until a negotiating impasse did occur. The Board stated:

> Consequently, we shall order that the status quo ante be restored. That is, the terms and conditions of the unit employees' health insurance program shall be returned to the level in existence before January 1988, the date of the Respondent's initial illegal unilateral action. The Respondent's monetary liability shall also continue until the status quo ante is restored.[1]

The company decided to appeal the NLRB's decision insofar as the Board's make-whole remedy order was concerned. The company claimed that this remedy was "punitive" and beyond the Board's authority as provided in Sections 6 and 10(c) of LMRA.

Reasoning of the NLRB

In its decision, the NLRB disagreed with the Administrative Law Judge's conclusion that a bargaining impasse had occurred between the parties as of July 18, 1990. The ALJ had concluded that because of the bargaining impasse, the company had lawfully implemented changes in its health care plan as of July 18, 1990. Therefore, the ALJ had only ordered the company to make the employees whole for "any losses they had incurred" as a result of the company's Section 8(a) (5) violation prior to that date, that is, from January 1988 to July 18, 1990.

However, the NLRB determined that a collective bargaining impasse had not occurred as of July 18, 1990. The Board reviewed the history of the parties' attempts beginning January 19, 1990, to negotiate an initial collective bargaining agreement. The first and subsequent sessions during January and February had focused on non-economic matters. After failing to reach agreement on noneconomic items, the parties had begun, in March 1990, to discuss economic issues.

On March 7, 1990, the union presented its economic proposals. One union proposal was that the company continue its current health care insurance program. The parties met several times between March 7 and May 2, 1990, when they reached tentative agreement on some issues, including the proposal that the clerical bargaining-unit employees should be covered by the health insurance program then in effect. However, all agreed-upon provisions were tentative and conditioned on the terms of a final

---

[1]*North Star Steel Company and United Steelworkers,* 305 NLRB No. 7, September 30, 1991, 139 LRRM 1090. The "Respondent" is the company.

collective bargaining agreement. The parties subsequently met on May 16 and July 18, 1990. No further collective bargaining sessions were scheduled after July 18, 1990, and no collective bargaining agreement was concluded.

The NLRB cited a previous case decision, where it had held:[2]

> Whether a bargaining impasse exists is a matter of judgment. The bargaining history, the good faith of the parties in negotiations, the length of the negotiations, the importance of the issue or issues as to which there is disagreement, the contemporaneous understanding of the parties as to the state of negotiations, are all relevant factors.

In the instant case, the NLRB determined that the company's claim that a bargaining impasse had been reached on July 18, 1990, was not conclusive, and therefore the effect of the company's prior Section 8(a) (5) violation continued beyond that date. The NLRB ordered the company to restore the employees' health care plan to the status quo of January 1988, and to make the clerical employees whole for all the incremental premium costs and losses they had incurred from January 1988 until such time as the parties would reach a binding agreement on the health care plan stipulations, or until a lawful bargaining impasse between the parties on the health care plan had occurred.

Position of the Company

The North Star Company filed an appeal of the National Labor Relations Board's make-whole remedy arguing that the Board's order was "punitive" and excessive and exceeded the Board's statutory authority under Section 10(c) of the LMRA. The company acknowledged that it technically had violated Section 8(a)(5) of the Act when it did not bargain with the union while it was filing exceptions to the certification of the union in 1987. The company was within its legal right to file exceptions to the NLRB's determination of the election outcome and the company's judicial appeal of that decision. When the court affirmed the certification of the union in December 1989, the company began bargaining for an initial contract with the union.

In the company's view, it had bargained in good faith with the union and attempted to reach an initial collective bargaining agreement. Section 8(d) of the Act does not require the parties to agree on every proposal that may be forthcoming. In 1990 the union itself had proposed a continuation of the health care insurance program for clerical employees then in effect. This program included a provision that the company could make the necessary changes in the employees' contributions to premium costs of the health care plan, and this was reasonable, especially in view of the incredibly rising costs of health care coverage.

The company had implemented various changes in this health care plan during the period of the company's challenge to the certification of the union. The union in fact had agreed to what the company had done, when during the negotiations in early 1990 it proposed the old plan's continuation. Nevertheless, the National Labor Relations Board had ordered that the status quo of January 1988 be returned. This was an

---

[2]*Taft Broadcasting Co.*, 163 NLRB 475, 478, 64 LRRM 1386 (1967), enfd. 395 F.2d 622 (67 LRRM 3032) (D.C. Cir. 1968).

excessive and punitive determination by the NLRB because the employees really had suffered no financial loss. The employees would have been subject to the same premium rate changes even if a collective bargaining agreement had been reached as early as 1988. This was apparent because the union had reached the same conclusion during negotiations in 1990.

In summary, the company contended that its minor technical violation of LMRA did not deserve the punitive remedy ordered by the National Labor Relations Board. The company claimed that the employees had not suffered any financial loss during the period in question, and therefore the NLRB's remedy was beyond its statutory authority, which only permitted make-whole remedies involving real financial loss. The company urged that the Court of Appeals overturn the National Labor Relations Board's order.

Questions

1. In a whole line of prior decisions concerning this issue, the courts have generally deferred to the National Labor Relations Board's judgment unless there is a finding that the NLRB exceeded its statutory authority granted under Section 10(c) of the Act. Why is this a "slippery" area of determination, especially for a Court of Appeals?

2. Evaluate the conclusions reached by the Administrative Law Judge and the National Labor Relations Board concerning whether a bargaining impasse between the parties had occurred as of July 18, 1990. Why is this determination critical in regard to the remedial orders?

3. Is the company position valid that the employees had suffered no monetary loss during the period that the company was challenging the union certification and beyond?

4. Should the Court of Appeals sustain or set aside the NLRB's remedial order? Discuss.

CASE 22

THE REFUSAL TO SIGN AND ABIDE BY A LABOR CONTRACT

Company:
    Maintenance Service Corporation, West Allis, Wisconsin

Union:
    International Association of Machinists and Aerospace Workers, District No. 10

Background

The company and the union had been parties to a series of collective bargaining agreements since 1973. The bargaining unit consisted of the company's production and maintenance employees and truck drivers.

On February 28, 1980, the parties signed a labor agreement that was to expire on December 31, 1982. Also on February 28, 1980, the parties signed a separate "side-bar" letter,[1] which provided:

> The Company will not employ an additional number of foremen, so as to increase the number of foremen in the work force, through December 31, 1982. In the event of layoff of any bargaining unit employee, no foreman shall perform bargaining unit work. In the event that the shop is not working overtime, foremen shall not perform bargaining unit work.

The 1980–82 collective bargaining agreement was extended until noon on February 25, 1983. On that date, the employees went on strike; during the strike, seven supervisors performed bargaining unit work. On June 16, 1983, the company sent a letter to the employees threatening to hire permanent replacements on June 27 if the employees failed to return to work by that date.

On June 22, 1982, Colin Moore,[2] the company president, and Duane Ling, the union's assistant director, met for the purpose of negotiating a new collective bargaining agreement and a strike settlement agreement. Moore commented that foremen had been performing bargaining unit work during the strike, and he indicated that the company intended that foremen would continue to do so afterwards. Ling said that he hoped the problem would disappear, since the practice violated the union's constitution. Neither man mentioned the "side-bar" letter.

On June 25, 1983, the parties met again and reached a tentative contract and strike settlement agreement. Neither agreement referred to the issue of foremen performing bargaining unit work or to the "side-bar" letter. On June 28, 1983, the union membership ratified the tentative contract.

On July 6, 1983, Colin Moore mailed the text of the tentative agreement to the union for review and signature. Upon receipt, Duane Ling called Moore and told him that the contract looked fine except that the "side-bar" letter was not included. Moore

---

[1]This type of letter is sometimes referred to as a "memorandum of understanding," and it may or may not be included as an appendix to a labor agreement.

[2]The names of all individuals are disguised.

responded that he knew nothing about a "side-bar" agreement. Ling offered to send Moore a copy of the letter, which Moore claimed he had never seen before.

When Colin Moore received the copy of the "side-bar" letter, he discovered that it had been negotiated and signed by his father, Elton T. Moore, on February 28, 1980. The senior Mr. Moore had been president of the company at that time; in June 1981 Elton Moore had retired and Colin Moore had become company president.

After reviewing the "side-bar" letter, Colin Moore decided not to agree to it, and he informed the union by letter of this decision. The union, in a telephone call from Duane Ling, informed the company that it would not sign the tentative contract reached June 25, 1983, because there was no agreement with respect to supervisors' not performing bargaining unit work.

In mid-July, Ling called Moore in an attempt to resolve the problem. Ling suggested that the union would sign the contract without the "side-bar" if the company would pay medical insurance for six months for employees who were still on layoff after the strike. No agreement was reached.

Because of vacation and other commitments, it was not until September 7, 1983, that Moore and Ling again met to discuss the unresolved contract. At this meeting, Moore stated that the company's position was that the parties had negotiated a contract with no restrictions on the amount of bargaining unit work that foremen might perform. Ling then proposed changing the dates in the "side-bar" agreement to make it effective September 30, 1983. Moore did not agree to this proposal.

On September 21, the parties met again, and Moore reiterated that he had no intention of signing the "side-bar" agreement, but he was prepared to sign the contract as negotiated with no restrictions. The parties discussed alternatives, such as restricting the amount of work a foreman could do to two or four hours a day. Moore asked if the foremen could join the union, but the union representative responded that they could not. The meeting ended with no resolution.

Shortly thereafter, each party filed unfair labor practice charges against the other alleging "refusal-to-bargain" violations of the Labor Management Relations Act. The union claimed that the company had violated Sections 8(a) (1) and 8(a) (5), as related to Section 8(d) of the Act; the company claimed that the union had violated Section 8(b) (3), also as related to Section 8(d).

After investigation, on October 19, 1983, the Regional Director of the NLRB dismissed all these unfair labor practice charges. The Regional Director found that there had been "no meeting of the minds" on the "side-bar" letter or on the subject of foremen doing bargaining unit work. The Regional Director observed that although there was no reference to the "side-bar" letter during the negotiations leading to the June 25, 1983, tentative agreement, the union had contended that language in the strike settlement stating that "all of the items in the tentative agreement, as well as the expired labor agreement as modified, shall constitute the new agreement," was intended to include the "side-bar" letter. On the other hand, the Regional Director also noted the company's position that the "side-bar" letter was a separate document that did not modify the prior contract. The Regional Director therefore concluded he was unable to find that a collective bargaining agreement had existed between the company and union. He further directed that the parties should resume bargaining in order to resolve their dispute.

On January 3, 1984, the parties met again. Colin Moore and Andrew Burback, the company's attorney, represented the company. Charles Pickett, the union's director; Travis Unger, the union's business representative; and Alan Grier, the union's local attorney, represented the union. Colin Moore asserted that the parties had a past practice of foremen working, and the company would be willing to sign the contract with that understanding. Alan Grier replied that when the "side-bar" letter was signed, the past practice was broken. Grier then said, however, that the union would sign the contract "as is" and "take it on a case-by-case basis if a foreman did any great amount of work." Colin Moore eventually stated that he wanted a written agreement on how working foremen would be treated, because he was puzzled by the union's position regarding past practice. The company representatives stated at the end of the meeting that they would respond further by letter.

On January 4, 1984, Andrew Burback, the company attorney, wrote a letter to the union, which included the following:

> At the conclusion of our meeting yesterday, I stated that the Company would attempt to develop language concerning the issue of foremen performing bargaining unit work. As I understand the Union's position, it does not object to foremen performing bargaining unit work unless the Company uses foremen to prevent laid-off bargaining unit employees from being recalled on a regular full-time basis. Based on our discussion, it appears that the Union has no objection to the work which is presently being performed by the foremen; this matter became an issue only after the strike, and, then, only for a short period of time.
>
> Accordingly, in order to settle this issue and the parties' collective bargaining agreement, the Company proposes that the following be added to the contract as Article II, Section 2:
>
> "Foremen may perform work normally performed by bargaining unit employees except that, in the event of a layoff of a bargaining unit employee from a seniority list, each foreman may perform work normally performed by employees within that seniority list if such work performed by each individual foreman is less than 40 hours per week."

In a letter dated January 11, 1984, Travis Unger replied for the union:

> Please be advised that the Union is in complete disagreement with your letter and language, dated January 4, 1984. The Union is willing to sit down and sign the contract as soon as the Company is ready.
>
> It is the Union's understanding, as explained to the Company, that supervisors working doing bargaining unit work will not be tolerated while employees are on layoff. With that understanding the Union will sign the contract. Any cases of supervisors working will be taken on a one-to-one basis in the grievance procedure.

In a letter dated January 13, 1984, Andrew Burback replied for the company:

> Maintenance Service Corporation cannot sign the agreement under the conditions you have suggested in your letter of January 11, 1984, particularly in view of your comment that you are in "complete disagreement" with our letter of January 4, 1984. In view of the comments made by the Union during our meeting of January 3, which comments I attempted to summarize in my letter, I am at a loss to explain why you are in "complete disagreement." It would be helpful to the progress of our negotiations if you would provide an explanation.

Burback also proposed scheduling another bargaining session and suggested that a Federal mediator be appointed.

In a letter dated January 16, 1984, Travis Unger replied for the union:

> In response to your most recent January 13, 1984, letter, it is the Union's position that they are willing to sign the contract without language pertaining to supervisors doing bargaining unit work. If there is no one laid off from that seniority list, or to deprive any employee of any overtime, that might be a different situation.
>
> If this meets your approval, please contact my office and set up a date for signing.

On February 6, 1984, the union filed new refusal-to-bargain charges with the NLRB against the company, alleging that since on or about January 3, 1984, the company had refused to sign the June 25, 1983, agreement, and had made unilateral changes by ceasing dues deductions, refusing to put a wage increase into effect, and eliminating the grievance procedure. The union claimed that these actions constituted violations of Sections 8(a) (5) and 8(a) (1) of the Act, and the union urged a cease and desist order be directed at the company.

On February 28, 1984, Colin Moore wrote a letter to the union, requesting a meeting and stating that the "working foreman language of our letter of January 4, 1984, is negotiable within the general framework."

On March 6, 1984, Travis Unger sent the following letter to Colin Moore:

> Be advised that the Union will sign the contract as negotiated and ratified, without any conditions.
>
> Please contact my office at your very earliest convenience to set up a date to sign the agreement.

In response to the union's latest letter, Colin Moore wrote a letter to the union dated March 9, 1984, requesting a meeting and asking the following questions:

1. If the contract is signed, what is the Union's position as to foremen performing bargaining unit work?
2. If the contract is signed, will it be retroactive, particularly with respect to working foremen?
3. If the contract is signed, will the Union dispute or file a grievance concerning the work presently being performed by the foremen?
4. If the contract is signed, will the Union dispute or file a grievance concerning the work performed by the foremen after the strike?

The union did not respond to this March 9, 1984, letter, which led Colin Moore to write another letter dated March 28, 1984, which included the following:

> In your letter of March 6, 1984, you stated that the Union will sign the agreement "without any conditions." While I would much rather discuss face to face what "without any conditions" means, in the absence of a meeting or a written response from the Union to my March 9 letter, and based upon your representation that the Union will sign "without any conditions," the Company proposes that the parties sign the agreement with the understanding that (1) the agreement does not cover the issue of foremen performing bargaining unit work and (2) there are no other conditions which restrict the Company's right to assign foremen to bargaining unit work.

On April 6, 1984, Travis Unger sent copies of the June 25, 1983, negotiated agreement to Colin Moore and requested in an attached letter that Moore sign the agreement copies.

However, on April 12, 1984, Colin Moore replied by letter to Unger that he would not sign the June 25, 1983, agreement because of the unresolved issues. In his letter, Moore again raised essentially the same questions about the union's position that he had posed in his March 9 letter. Moore inquired whether the union agreed that the tentative contract, if signed, did not cover foremen performing bargaining unit work and that there were no other restrictions on the company's right to assign foremen such work.

In a letter dated April 30, 1984, Duane Ling responded, "The Union's answer is no."

On May 15, 1984, Moore called Ling in response to the union's April 30 letter. Moore asked Ling, "Assuming I sign the contract today or tomorrow, what would happen regarding the working foremen issue?" Ling responded that he did not know, and he could not give him an answer one way or another.

The labor agreement remained unsigned as the NLRB investigated the unfair labor practice charges that had been filed by the union.

Position of the Union

The union primarily claimed that as of January 3, 1984, the union had accepted the company's contract offer, which previously had been agreed on by the parties as of June 25, 1983. This contract offer had never been withdrawn by the company. At the meeting of January 3, 1984, the union had indicated that it would accept the terms of the contract "as is," and without the "side-bar" letter. However, the company refused to agree to this and abide by the new contract; further, the company continued to insist on additional contract language or commitments from the union to the effect that the union would never raise the issue of foremen doing bargaining unit work under the new contract. This the union refused to do.

The union argued that there had been a standing, viable contract offer since June 25, 1983, which the union had agreed to accept as of January 3, 1984. The company's refusal at that time and thereafter to agree and abide by it was clearly bad-faith bargaining that violated Sections 8(a) (5) and 8(a) (1) of the Act as these are related to Section 8(d). The union urged that the company be directed to sign and implement the terms and conditions of the new contract, and that employees be made whole as appropriate for any lost wages and benefits that might have been denied them since January 3, 1984, because of the company's violations of the Act.

Alternatively, the union argued, if there was some question concerning whether the January 3, 1984, meeting constituted a firm understanding of the union's acceptance of the contractual offer, then March 6, 1984, and thereafter should be considered as the period of the company's unfair labor practices. On March 6, 1984, the union, by letter, had accepted the contract offer without conditions. All the union's arguments were applicable in regard to this date and in regard to the union's requested remedies.

Position of the Company

The company asserted that throughout the periods in contention, the company had bargained in good faith with the union and had not violated the LMRA. According to the company, there was no agreement at any time between the company and the union over the issue of foremen performing bargaining unit work. The company pointed out that the union first raised the issue of the "side-bar" letter on July 6, 1983, after the June 25, 1983, tentative agreement had been reached; the union had declined to sign the contract because there was no agreement regarding supervisors' performing bargaining unit work. Subsequent negotiations between the parties in September produced no common understanding on the issue. The Regional Director of the NLRB dismissed each party's unfair labor practice charges in October 1983, recognizing the parties' failure to agree.

Similarly, the company maintained that there was no agreement between the parties over this same issue during the January 3, 1984, meeting, or during any of the subsequent communications and correspondence between the parties including the union's March 6, 1984, letter. Just because the union offered at these times to sign a contract did not mean that the company had to sign such a contract when there was still a substantive issue over which there was no agreement. The company was not obligated to sign a contract that contained only the matters upon which the company and union had agreed, while a major issue remained unresolved.

The company urged that the unfair labor practice charges filed by the union should be dismissed.

Questions

1. Was the company in violation of LMRA after the meeting of January 3, 1984? Why, or why not?
2. Was the company in violation of LMRA following the union's offer by letter of March 6, 1984? Why, or why not?
3. Does the dismissal by the NLRB, in October 1983, of the previous unfair labor practice charges filed by both parties have any bearing upon the positions of the parties in 1984? Discuss.
4. Discuss why "side-bar" letters and other such agreements that are not included in the labor contract can become difficult obstacles in the ongoing relationships between a company and a union.

CASE 23
THE UNION'S REQUEST FOR ACCESS TO AN EMPLOYEE'S CONFIDENTIAL PERSONNEL FILE

Employer:
   Salt River Valley Water Users' Association, Phoenix, Arizona

Union:
   International Brotherhood of Electrical Workers, Local Union No. 266

Background

The Association and the union were parties to a collective bargaining agreement that included procedures for grievance processing and arbitration of grievances arising under the agreement. In early 1984, a dispute arose when two bargaining unit employees, Charley Dennis and Julio Garza,[1] were caught sleeping on the job. The Association fired Garza but only suspended Dennis. The union filed a grievance on behalf of Garza, requesting that he be reinstated with back pay. The union notified the Association that it was prepared to arbitrate the grievance, if necessary, to resolve the dispute.

In order to determine whether Garza had been the victim of disparate treatment, the union sought access to Charley Dennis' personnel file. The union filed a request to obtain three categories of information in Dennis' file: performance reviews, disciplinary records, and any other record on which the company might rely in the grievance and arbitration proceedings. The Association responded by letter that in accordance with its established personnel policy, the requested information would not be released without Dennis' consent.

The relevant portion of the Association's personnel policy (identified as "HR 305"), which management cited in denying the union's request, included the following:

1. Accessibility of employee records is as follows:
   a. SRV employee—has a right to review or correct his/her personal records.
   b. SRV management—has the right to review employee record information for job-related reasons.
   c. Outside agencies—accessible with employee consent.
   d. Instances covered by law—accessible with legal documents.

The union then filed unfair labor practice charges against the Association, alleging violations of Sections 8(a) (1) and 8(a) (5) of the Labor Management Relations Act. The union urged that the Association be compelled to release the requested information to the union.

Position of the Union

The union pointed out that the NLRB has often held that under Sections 8(a) (1) and 8(a) (5) and as further defined under Section 8(d), the failure of an employer to provide a union with the information necessary to intelligently evaluate grievances may

---

[1]The names of all individuals are disguised.

constitute an unfair labor practice.[2] The union in this case needed to examine Charley Dennis' personnel file in order to determine whether another employee who was grieving his discharge had been singled out by management in a disparate or discriminatory fashion. The Association's confidentiality policy permitted its managers to have access to the records of a nongrieving employee in connection with grievance proceedings. In letters to the union and in meetings, the Association had relied on Dennis' employment history in responding to Garza's grievance. To explain the less severe punishment given to Dennis, management representatives had claimed that Dennis had an "unblemished record," and that his file showed him to be an "exceptionally reliable employee who rarely took days off or used sick leave."

The union argued that it was not appropriate or equitable that management should be permitted to refer to such information in its own defense, while at the same time denying the grievant's bargaining representative access to this and other relevant information.

The union pointed out that arbitrators routinely consider employee work records in deciding grievance cases and in determining whether employers have applied disciplinary actions in a consistent, evenhanded, and nondiscriminatory manner. Without access to Charley Dennis' personnel file in this case, the union would be unable to determine whether or not Julio Garza—a Hispanic employee—had been discharged in a manner that was arbitrary or discriminatory.

The union emphasized that its sole objective in requesting access to Dennis' personnel file was to carry out its statutory responsibility (under Section 8(b) (1) (A) of LMRA) to represent Garza in processing his grievance. The union would not use any of this information to harass or embarrass Dennis, or publicize it in any forum other than in weighing the merits of and processing Garza's grievance.

In summary, the union argued that the Association's concern about the confidentiality of Dennis' personnel file was misplaced, and that the Association had a statutory obligation to provide the requested information to the union.

Position of the Employer

The Association argued that it had an across-the-board, uniform policy to protect confidential employee records, which contained sensitive information. Included in an employee's personnel file were disciplinary records, which described infractions and the discipline imposed; performance reviews; and evaluations by the employee's supervisors.

Release of such information to any outside party, without an employee's consent, could result in significant invasions of an individual's privacy, and possibly lead to abusive consequences.

The Association argued that some NLRB and court decisions have ruled that in certain situations it is not necessary to provide confidential information to the union if there is no evidence that the employer is attempting to interfere with the union's

---

[2]Among the cases cited were: *NLRB* v. *Truck Drivers Local Union No. 449,* 353 U.S. 87, 96, 39 LRRM 2603 (1957); and *Pfizer, Inc.,* 268 NLRB 916, 115 LRRM 1105 (1984).

obligations and rights in representing its members.[3] In this situation, the Association had informed the union concerning the general nature of Charley Dennis' work record and the reasons for discharging Garza but not Dennis. The union could also obtain information about Dennis' performance record by other procedures, such as by interviewing his supervisors. Therefore, the Association was not withholding relevant information from the union; the Association was only preserving its uniform policy of protecting confidential information about employees and protecting their privacy.

In the Association's view, the unfair labor practice charges of the union were without merit and should be dismissed.

Questions

1. Why have the NLRB and the courts interpreted Sections 8(a) (5) and 8(d) of LMRA to include the obligation of an employer to furnish certain types of relevant information to a labor organization?
2. Compare this case with Case 18, in which an employer representative was seeking certain information from a union and filed unfair labor practice charges under Section 8(b) (3) of the Act.
3. Why is it often difficult for the NLRB to weigh statutory rights of the parties under LMRA against concerns of parties for maintaining confidentiality of sensitive information, including the privacy rights of individuals?
4. Does it make any difference in this case that the employer informed the union concerning Dennis' work record without permitting the union to inspect his personnel file? Why, or why not?

---

[3]The case primarily cited here was *Detroit Edison Co. v. NLRB,* 440 U.S. 301, 100 LRRM 2728 (1979).

CASE 24
DISCHARGE FOR DISRUPTIVE CONDUCT, OR FOR PROTECTED UNION ACTIVITY?

Company:
  Cincinnati Suburban Press, Inc., a Subsidiary of Suburban Communications Corporation, Cincinnati, Ohio

Union:
  The Newspaper Guild

Individual:
  George Fuller[1]

Background

The company was an Ohio corporation with an office and place of business in Cincinnati, Ohio. The company published and distributed a chain of weekly newspapers in the Cincinnati metropolitan area. The individual who filed charges in this case, George Fuller, was employed as a reporter in the editorial department from November 1984 until his discharge on February 2, 1987.

In October 1985, Fuller helped to initiate a union organizing campaign among employees in the editorial department. The Newspaper Guild union organizing campaign culminated in an NLRB election in April 1986, in which the editorial department employees voted against union representation by a vote of 24 to 19. Efforts to organize the editorial department employees, however, did not end with the April 1986 election. Fuller and other employees formed a committee called "The April 87 Committee," which immediately began efforts to organize the employees, with a view to an April 1987 election. In June 1986 Fuller and others mailed an "opinion survey" to the employees. In July 1986 the results of this survey were mailed to employees and certain members of management. Fuller also passed out prounion "business cards" at the July company picnic, which was attended by both employees and management personnel.

Management was well aware of Fuller's continuing efforts to organize its employees. In August 1986, when some literature that had been posted on the employee bulletin board was taken down, Derrick Collins, the company's vice president, spoke with Fuller and asked him how long the union "agitating" was going to continue. Fuller responded that it would continue until April 1987, when another election could be held.[2]

In October 1986, Fuller posted on the employee bulletin board a handwritten "Six Month Update," which urged employees to vote for union representation in April 1987. On October 16, 1986, Duane Silverman, the company's executive editor, asked Fuller if he had posted the document. Fuller admitted to Silverman that he had. In December

---

[1]The names of all individuals are disguised.
[2]This response was consistent with Section 9(e) (2) of LMRA.

1986, an article that Fuller wrote entitled, "Dirty Tricks in the Newsroom," was published in *The Cincinnati Review of Politics and the Arts.* This publication was available for purchase at bookstores throughout the metropolitan area, as well as being a subscription publication that was mailed to regular subscribers. Fuller's article reviewed the April 1986 union campaign and the opposition encountered during the drive. As an analytical and historical review of the union's organizing efforts, the article discussed the antiunion acts of certain of the company's managers, supervisors, and employees. Fuller gave copies of the published article to fellow employees, and he talked about using the article as part of the continuing union campaign.

Management first became aware of the article in January 1987. Managing Editor Oscar Willow telephoned Silverman on January 9, 1987, and told him about the article. Although he personally had not yet read the article, Willow told Silverman that he considered it libelous. Willow later obtained a copy of the article and gave it to Silverman. In turn, Silverman contacted Mildred Hawthorne, the vice president of personnel for Suburban Communications Corporation. On January 12, 1987, Hawthorne began an investigation into the circumstances surrounding the article; on January 22, 1987, she suspended Fuller without pay pending completion of the investigation. Although Hawthorne interviewed some of the employees named in the article and others during her investigation, neither she nor Silverman interviewed or questioned Fuller about the article. Acting on Hawthorne's recommendation, management decided to discharge Fuller. On February 2, 1987, Fuller was given a discharge letter signed by Hawthorne, the relevant portions of which follow:

> The Company has completed its investigation of your violation of Company Rules 18 and 29:
>
> 18. Making false, vicious, or malicious statements concerning any employee, supervisor, the Company, or its product.
>
> 29. Unlawful, improper, or unseemly conduct on or off the Company premises or during nonworking hours which affects the employee's relationship to his/her job, to his/her fellow employees, or to his/her supervisors, or affecting the Company's product, reputation, or goodwill in the community.
>
> Our investigation has revealed that you did, indeed, violate these rules. The seriousness of these violations warrants your immediate discharge. Your suspension of January 22, 1987, is converted to an immediate discharge. Your discharge under Rules 18 and 29 is based on the following: Your conduct and the article you authored in the *Cincinnati Review* injured the reputation, image, integrity, and truthfulness of Cincinnati Suburban Press newspapers and its management, and has embarrassed, humiliated, and ridiculed your fellow employees.
>
> Your disruptive conduct has impaired employee relationships with fellow employees and our supervisors.

Shortly thereafter, George Fuller filed unfair labor practice charges with the NLRB claiming that he had been discriminatorily interfered with, suspended, and discharged in violation of Sections 7, 8(a) (1), and 8(a) (3) of the LMRA.[3]

---

[3]Fuller's unfair labor practice charges were filed on an individual basis. Fuller received financial support from the union in retaining legal counsel to assist him in pursuing these charges.

Position of the Individual

Counsel for George Fuller claimed, first of all, that the two company rules Fuller was accused of violating were themselves in violation of Section 8(a) (1) of LMRA. These company rules had been included in Mildred Hawthorne's termination letter to Fuller, and were Company Rules 18 and 29, respectively.

Counsel for Fuller argued that these rules were so overly broad and coercive that, in and of themselves, they would restrict almost any activity or statements by an employee the company considered offensive. The company used these rules as pretext for discharging Fuller, who had been suspended and terminated because of his continual efforts to organize the editorial department employees. Company management was well aware of Fuller's prounion sympathies and efforts. The article Fuller wrote for another publication contained facts and opinions about what had occurred at the company during the union organizing campaign. Even though management found it to be offensive, this does not mean that the article was slanderous or libelous.

Finally, counsel for Fuller claimed that even though Fuller had acted alone when he wrote the article in question, the writing and publication of the article were "inextricably intertwined" with his ongoing union organizing efforts. Such activity is protected by Section 7 of LMRA, and thus the company violated Sections 8(a) (3) and 8(a) (1) by suspending and discharging him. The company should be ordered to reinstate Fuller to his former position and to make him whole for all lost earnings and benefits to which he would be entitled. Further, the company should be directed to cease and desist in its unlawful maintenance of those rules that violated employees' protected rights under the LMRA.

Position of the Company

The company claimed that its rules No. 18 and 29 were both proper and lawful. These rules were absolutely necessary for maintenance of internal discipline, and were applicable to all company personnel, including certain managers and supervisors. It was essential for the company to have public confidence in its integrity, and these company rules had nothing to do with external employment laws, such as the LMRA.

George Fuller, acting on his own, had chosen to violate these company rules when he wrote the article which was published in another journal. Fuller's article contained exaggerations, misrepresentations, insults, and distortions of facts. For example, Fuller had reported inaccurately the number and purpose of "merit pay increases" that were granted to company employees during 1985. Most serious, however, was that Fuller had publicly damaged the integrity of executive editor Duane Silverman by writing, "One effort at persuasion by executive editor Duane Silverman would have been laughable had it not indicated an insidious disregard for the truth." This sentence alone showed that Fuller had publicly damaged the integrity of Silverman and the truthfulness of the newspapers Silverman published.

The company claimed that Fuller's behavior was not "protected concerted activity" under Section 7 of LMRA. Rather, Fuller had acted on his own in violation of longstanding and appropriate company rules. As an "at-will" employee, Fuller was properly discharged by the company. All the unfair labor practice charges should be dismissed.

Questions

1. Were company rules No. 18 and 29 in violation of LMRA? Why, or why not?
2. Employees at times write articles or letters for newspapers openly critical of their employers. Should it make any difference in this case that Fuller himself was an editorial employee of a newspaper? Discuss.
3. Although Fuller wrote and published the "offensive" article on his own volition, was his conduct protected under Section 7 of LMRA? Discuss.
4. Was Fuller's discharge for rules' violations a pretext for terminating him because of his prounion activities? Discuss.

CASE 25
WAS THE ESOP LEVERAGED BUYOUT PROPOSAL PROTECTED CONCERTED ACTIVITY?

Company:
  Harrah's Lake Tahoe Resort Casino, Stateline, Nevada

Individual:
  Leroy Gastoni[1]

Background

At the time of this case in early 1991, the company was a nonunionized employer. The company had a savings and retirement plan for its employees that consisted of a qualified 401(k) plan and an Employee Stock Ownership Plan, or ESOP.[2] Under the existing ESOP, qualified employees on an annual basis received one share of stock in the firm's parent company, the Promus Corporation. Promus stock was publicly traded, and 1 percent of the stock was dedicated to the company's ESOP. The company's 401(k) plan allowed employees to make their fund contributions from several sources, including Promus stock.

Employee Leroy Gastoni had studied financial analysis at a university business school, and he was convinced that a leveraged buyout of the Promus Corporation by the ESOP would be in the employees' best interests. In essence, Gastoni's idea was that the ESOP borrow $335 million to purchase 50 percent of the outstanding Promus stock and assume $450 million of Promus' corporate debt. Gastoni's plan envisioned that the debt would be serviced by operating income. He prepared and sent to the chairman of the board of the Promus Corporation a written proposal outlining his ideas for a leveraged buyout of Promus Corporation by the ESOP, and distributed copies of this proposal to company employees.

Gastoni also prepared a three-page summary of his proposal, as well as a petition for employees to sign, which he used to solicit employee support. After receiving some complaints from employees that his proposal was still too technical, he wrote a leaflet

---

[1]Name is disguised.

[2]A 401(k) plan derives its name from Section 401(k) of the Internal Revenue Code that enables employers to establish retirement savings plans in which employees can contribute through a payroll deduction program. An employee's contribution reduces that employee's taxable income, meaning that the employee does not pay income taxes on the contribution amounts until he or she begins drawing from the plan fund after retiring. Many companies match employee contributions in some way, and employees may be permitted to choose in which types of investments they wish to have their money placed, including company stock purchase plans. An employee stock ownership plan, or ESOP, typically is one in which employees purchase company stock through some type of payroll deduction or installment plan. Here, too, employees usually can sell the stock or withdraw dividends only upon retirement or termination of their employment at which time the proceeds become taxable income. See Arthur W. Sherman, Jr., and George W. Bohlander, *Managing Human Resources,* 9th ed. (Cincinnati: South-Western, 1992), pp. 372–73 and 417; or Wendell L. French, *Human Resources Management,* 3rd ed. (Boston: Houghton Mifflin, 1994), pp. 427–28.

entitled "Money for Nothin" for distribution among the employees. The "Money for Nothin" leaflet stated in pertinent part:

> Our ESOP Trust borrows money from a commercial bank to buy 50% of Promus stock for the employees.
>
> Since the employees then own 50% of the stock, we get 50% of the operating income ("profits").
>
> For the following 10 to 15 years, we use our share of the profits to pay off the bank loan.
>
> At the end of 10 years, each employee owns stock which could be worth as much as 3 times his annual earnings (salary plus tips). If we leave sooner, we get less. If we stay longer, we get more.

The remainder of the leaflet explained, in Gastoni's words, why "the stock costs us nothin!" The leaflet suggested that by implementing this proposal, the employees could promise to management and the company as a whole "one of the most dynamic and profitable service companies in America." Gastoni claimed in the leaflet that current employees would benefit from his proposal through increased job stability, pay, and pension funding, and from enhanced morale, productivity, and profitability through "participative management." Gastoni distributed the leaflet primarily to employees in the company cafeteria.

Gastoni's leaflet, petition, and proposal became known in due course to company managers, who discussed them at a staff meeting. The managers concluded that Gastoni's activities were an embarrassment to company management, and they were disturbed that Gastoni had perhaps even implied that current management was sympathetic to and even endorsing the leveraged buyout proposal. Leroy Gastoni was summoned to his supervisor's office and terminated.

Subsequently, Leroy Gastoni through his personal attorney filed unfair labor practice charges against the company. Specifically, Gastoni charged that the company had violated Section 8(a) (1) of the Labor Management Relations Act by unlawfully interfering with his Section 7 rights to pursue "concerted activities for the purpose of . . . mutual aid or protection." Although later he was reinstated, and his termination was converted to a month's suspension without pay, nevertheless Gastoni through his attorney persisted in his unfair labor practice charges against the company.

Position of the Company

The company contended that employee Leroy Gastoni had operated on his own in an improper manner that deserved summary termination. His proposal and the accompanying literature were his own ideas and creations. Section 7 of the LMRA protects concerted activities, not individual actions by an employee acting on his own volition. Gastoni was an at-will employee; therefore, the company had the right to terminate him for his proposals and leaflets that were embarrassing to corporate management and that even implied that management had in some way approved or endorsed the leveraged buyout proposal.

Alternatively, the company argued, if the NLRB should determine that Gastoni's actions were concerted in nature, nevertheless these were not protected by Section 7 of the Act. Counsel for the company pointed to a previous NLRB and court decision, which found that individual actions such as those of Leroy Gastoni were protected by Section 7 of the Act only if the action or proposals related "to employees' interests as employees."[3]

In the company's view, Gastoni's proposal aimed primarily at having employees assume the role of owners with ultimate corporate control, that is, the proposal sought fundamentally to change how and by whom the corporation would be managed. Thus, Gastoni's proposal favoring a leveraged buyout by the ESOP had little or nothing to do with improving the employees' interests as employees, the necessary precondition for protection by Section 7 of LMRA. Counsel for the company pointed out that Gastoni's proposal contemplated the employees themselves controlling the corporation. Gastoni had even used the term "participative management" in a way that anticipated changes by which the employees would take over the running of the corporation.

In summary, the company argued that Gastoni had operated on his own, and that his proposal and related handouts and materials were not directed toward improving the employees' situation as employees but rather toward their taking over ownership and control. This was beyond any construction as "concerted activities for . . . mutual aid or protection" as in Section 7 had been constituted and interpreted. The company urged that the unfair labor practice charges be dismissed.

Position of the Individual

Gastoni maintained that his activities fell within the interpretation of "concerted activities" under Section 7 of the Act. His proposal and the accompanying literature he'd handed out were designed not just for his own benefit, but for the benefit of his fellow employees. If activities such as his were not concerted in nature, even if initiated by an individual, how could anyone acting on his own do anything in a nonunion setting without fear of being disciplined or terminated?

Through his counsel, Gastoni argued that his proposal and his accompanying leaflet were not aimed at changing corporate management control, but rather at accruing benefits to the employees as employees. His ESOP proposal was not really designed to produce changes in management. At the time of his proposal, employees were able to own Promus stock through the existing ESOP and the 401(k) plan, economic benefits granted and maintained by the company and clearly terms and conditions of employment. It was evident from the language of his proposal and leaflet that his primary object was to increase employee monetary benefits by enhancing the existing retirement benefit programs. Significantly, his leaflet had not referred to any major increased managerial role by the employees who might become part owners of the company. Rather, the message had focused on the profits that would accrue to employees if they were to own 50 percent of the stock. Although his leaflet mentioned "participative management" in terms of "enhanced morale, productivity, and profitability," this was just a tangential reference to a more cooperative and profitable enterprise that could result, thus improving the savings and retirement benefits of employees.

---

[3]*Eastex, Inc.* v. *NLRB*, 437 U.S. 556, 567, 98 LRRM 2717 (1978).

In summary, Gastoni through his attorney contended that the focus of his ESOP activities was on the improvement of an existing benefit of employment, a matter of immediate concern to employees. Therefore, his activities on behalf of the ESOP proposal were concerted activities protected by the mutual aid or protection clause of Section 7 of the Act. The NLRB should find that the company violated Section 8(a) (1) of the Act by suspending (after first discharging) Gastoni for his activities and by interfering with his right to engage in protected activities. Gastoni should be made whole for all lost pay and benefits.

Questions

1. Were Leroy Gastoni's essentially individual activities pursued on his own as an at-will employee, or could they be considered "concerted" and thus within the protection of Section 7 of the Act? Discuss.

2. Assuming Gastoni's actions could be considered concerted, were they primarily related to the employees' interests as employees, or were they aimed primarily at changing the management and gaining managerial control of the company? Discuss.

3. Evaluate the primary contentions of Gastoni and of the company. Which do you find the most and which the least persuasive?

4. Compare the issues in this case with those in Case 24, "Discharge for Disruptive Conduct, or for Protected Union Activity?"

CASE 26
THE DISTASTEFUL AND OFFENSIVE DEFINITION OF A "SCAB"

Company:
Southwestern Bell Telephone Company, Houston, Texas

Union:
Communications Workers of America, Local No. 12222

Background

On a Monday morning in early September 1984, Jan Betheda,[1] an equipment technician, reported to two of her supervisors that there was a "distasteful and offensive" memorandum on two union bulletin boards in the plant and office complex of the company. The supervisors, Art Laclede and Debbie Lynkirk, investigated and discovered on both union bulletin boards a printed memorandum entitled, "Jack London's Definition of a Scab."[2] In pertinent part, the memorandum included the following:

JACK LONDON'S DEFINITION OF A SCAB

After God had finished the rattlesnake, the toad, and the vampire, he had some awful substance left with which he made a SCAB. A SCAB is a two-legged animal with a corkscrew soul, a water-logged brain, and a combination backbone made of jelly and glue. Where others have hearts, he carries a tumor of rotten principles.

When a SCAB comes down the street, men turn their backs and angels weep in Heaven, and the devil shuts the gates of Hell to keep him out. No man has the right to SCAB, so long as there is a pool of water deep enough to drown his body in, or a rope long enough to hang his carcass with. Judas Iscariot was a gentleman . . . compared with a SCAB; for betraying his master, he had the character to hang himself—a SCAB hasn't.

Esau sold his birthright for a mess of pottage. Judas Iscariot sold his Savior for thirty pieces of silver. Benedict Arnold sold his country for a promise of a commission in the British Army. The modern strikebreaker sells his birthright, his country, his wife, his children and his fellow men for an unfulfilled promise from his employer, trust, or corporation.

Esau was a traitor to himself. Judas Iscariot was a traitor to his God. Benedict Arnold was a traitor to his country.

A strikebreaker is a traitor to himself, a traitor to his God, a traitor to his country, a traitor to his family, and a traitor to his class.

THERE IS NOTHING LOWER THAN A SCAB.

After discussing their finding with the company's Director of Human Resources Management, Laclede and Lynkirk removed the two identical memoranda from the union's bulletin boards. They then informed all employees in several meetings of their

---

[1]The names of all individuals are disguised.

[2]Jack London (1876–1916) was an American writer and adventurer. He wrote a number of novels and adventure books and also wrote several books that dealt with poverty and social injustice. The source of the "Definition of a Scab" attributed to Jack London was not identified on the posted memoranda.

actions. They further told employees that any reposting of this "Definition of a Scab" memorandum was prohibited, and that any individuals found doing so would be subject to discipline, including suspension.

Shortly thereafter, the union filed unfair labor practice charges with the NLRB, alleging that the company had violated Section 7 and Section 8(a) (1) of the LMRA by removing the memorandum from the union's bulletin boards and by threatening disciplinary action against the employees.

Position of the Union

The union claimed that there had never been any company rules concerning what could or could not be posted on union bulletin boards located on company premises. The union had negotiated with the company for the right to have these bulletin boards, and there were no specific negotiated restrictions placed on this privilege.

In the union's view, the "Definition of a Scab" memorandum was an expression of opinion that was not disruptive to employee work performance or discipline. Just because someone considered it distasteful or offensive did not justify the company's actions and threats to discipline employees. There had been no work disruption; even though employees were observed in groups discussing the memorandum, this was not unusual or threatening to anyone. Therefore, the company had violated Sections 7 and 8(a) (1) of the Act by interfering with the union's protected rights and by attempting to coerce and restrain the union and the employees in their expression of those rights. The union requested that the company be ordered to cease and desist in this and any other actions that would tend to interfere with the union's statutory rights and negotiated privileges.

Position of the Company

The company pointed out that the posting of the "Definition of a Scab" memorandum had occurred only several days following the end of a several weeks' strike during which some one-third to one-half of the employees had crossed the union's picket lines in order to work. In the company's view, the memorandum was aimed primarily at these employees, who had exercised their personal freedom of choice in a difficult situation. Not only was the memorandum offensive to them, but it was likely to contribute to further animosity, internal dissension, and strife that could lead to wholesale disruptions in employee discipline and work performance. An employer cannot afford simply to wait until a breakdown in discipline occurs. In this situation, company management had decided that, for the sake of avoiding further deterioration in workplace harmony and employee morale, the "provocative and inflammatory" memorandum should be removed. The company did not interfere with any of the union's protected rights in this matter when it removed this offensive and "sacrilegious" memorandum.

In support of its position, the company cited a Supreme Court decision that employers have an "undisputed right . . . to maintain discipline in their establishments," which under some circumstances may limit the exercise of employee rights guaranteed by Section 7 (*Republic Aviation Corp.* v. *NLRB,* 324 U.S. 793, 797–798, 16 LRRM 620 [1945]).

Similarly, the NLRB has found "special circumstances" can exist that would justify an employer's ban on otherwise protected activity in the workplace if "objective evidence supports the employer's belief that the ban was necessary to maintain decorum and discipline among its employees" [*Midstate Telephone Corp.,* 262 NLRB 1291–1292, 110 LRRM 1533 (1982)]. In the company's view, this was a "special circumstance" that fully justified the company's position. The unfair labor practice charges should be dismissed.

Questions

1. Was the "Definition of a Scab" memorandum a real threat to maintenance of employee decorum and discipline? Why, or why not?
2. Does it make any difference in this case that the company and union had not negotiated any specific limits or rules concerning what could be posted on the union bulletin boards? Discuss.
3. Why does a situation of this type pose a major dilemma for company management? Were there other alternatives that the company might have pursued? Discuss.
4. Was this situation a "special circumstance" under the NLRB's rulings that would justify the company's position? Why, or why not?

CASE 27
THE CONTESTED IMPLEMENTATION OF A DRUG-TESTING POLICY

Company:
   Kysor/Cadillac, an Operating Division of Kysor Industrial Corporation, Cadillac, Michigan
Union:
   Local Union No. 545, United Automobile Workers

Background

On January 10, 1990, employee Kent LaBelle[1] was involved in a worksite accident. The supervisor in the plant, Marvin Zurwith, required LaBelle to go to the plant's medical/first aid station to submit to a drug test administered by the nurse (R.N.) in charge. LaBelle did so and was found drug free. However, Kent LaBelle reported the incident to his union shop steward, Mickey Giraldi, who later questioned Plant Manager LaRue Pendleton about LaBelle's drug test. Pendleton told Giraldi, "It is company policy as of January 1st, 1990." Shortly afterward, on February 12, Giraldi attended a forum on drug testing with the company's managers and supervisors and several other union shop stewards. At this meeting, Giraldi asked how the company could impose a drug policy without first negotiating with the union. Pendleton was asked by another shop steward if he had posted the so-called drug-free workplace policy; Pendleton admitted that he had not. The next day, on February 13, the company posted a notice dated February 8, 1990, at several places in the plant and offices announcing its "drug-free workplace policy." This policy prohibited possession or consumption of drugs or alcohol in the workplace and/or working under their influence. The notice stated in part:

> The Company reserves the right to require any employee who it believes to be in violation of the foregoing policy during working hours to undergo at Company expense appropriate urinalysis, breath, or other testing procedures, to assist the Company in determining whether violation of the foregoing policy has occurred. Any employee who refuses a Company request to submit, or who fails to submit, to such testing procedures will be subject to discipline up to and including discharge.

On February 26, 1990, the company discharged employee Martha Seiko because she refused to submit to a drug test in conjunction with medical treatment for a workplace accident. The next day Giraldi and union Business Representative Herman Hilton met with Pendleton and Laura Jensen, the company's human resources manager. Hilton protested the company's right to fire Martha Seiko for refusing to take a drug test. Laura Jensen showed Hilton and Giraldi signed "consent forms," which were part of employment application papers that all new employees since 1986 had been required to sign as a condition of accepting employment. Both Kent LaBelle and Martha Seiko had signed these forms when they were hired in 1986 and 1987, respectively. In effect,

---

[1]The names of all individuals are disguised.

these forms stated that they recognized the company's right to test them for substance abuse under certain circumstances, including workplace accidents. Giraldi and Hilton protested that this was the first time that they had heard of such signed "consent forms." Further, they accused the company of telling the union for almost two months that its new drug policy applied to all employees, without making any distinction between those employees who had not signed the "consent forms" (prior to 1986) and those employees who had done so (1986 and beyond). Jensen and Pendleton responded that in 1986 they had met with several union shop stewards to show them and discuss the "consent forms" that were to become part of the employment application process. At that time, no one from the union had objected.

Shortly thereafter, the union filed unfair labor practice charges against the company alleging that by its actions the company had violated Sections 8(a) (5) and 8(a) (1) of the Labor Management Relations Act.

Position of the Union

The union contended that by unilaterally implementing its drug-testing policy without first having negotiated its terms with the union, the company had violated Sections 8(a) (5) and 8(a) (1) of the Act. The union cited a previous NLRB decision in which the NLRB had found that any post-accident drug testing of employees was a mandatory subject of collective bargaining.[2] The company had forced employee Kent LaBelle to subject himself to a drug-testing policy against his will. Similarly, the company had discharged employee Martha Seiko who refused to submit to a drug test under the company's unilaterally imposed policy. These were violations of Section 8(a) (1) of the Act.

The union contended that even if the company managers had discussed the so-called consent forms with selected union shop stewards in 1986, there was no evidence whatsoever that the union had waived its right to negotiate about drug testing for all bargaining unit employees. The company on its own had announced and imposed a substance abuse policy which was to apply to all employees. Yet the company sought to justify its actions regarding employees LaBelle and Seiko on the basis of so-called consent forms that they had signed in 1986 and 1987. In the union's view, the company was attempting to "have it both ways" to avoid its obligation to negotiate a drug-testing policy with the union.

The union urged the NLRB to find that the company had violated Section 8(a) (5) by implementing a drug-testing policy without first negotiating it with the union, and that the company had violated Section 8(a) (1) by its actions toward employees Kent La-Belle and Martha Seiko. As a remedy, the company should be required to negotiate any substance abuse/drug-testing policy with the union, and employee Martha Seiko should be reinstated to her former position and made whole for all lost wages and benefits.

Position of the Company

The company contended that it had not violated the Labor Management Relations Act. In 1986, company management had provided union representatives with copies of the

---

[2]This case was *Johnson-Bateman Company,* 295 NLRB 180, 131 LRRM 1393 (1989).

proposed employee consent forms which were to become part of the employment application process. This form required new employees to consent to a drug test in the event of a workplace accident. Union representatives had not objected to the implementation of these consent forms. Both employees Kent LaBelle and Martha Seiko, along with other new employees since 1986, had signed these forms. Therefore, the company had every right to take the actions it had regarding LaBelle and Seiko, since they had agreed to these conditions of their employment. The company had the right to discipline employees who had signed the consent forms, and who then refused to honor their commitments, and this is what the company had done in the Seiko situation.

The company said the issuance of the new policy in 1990 was necessitated to some degree by the requirements of the 1988 Federal Drug-Free Workplace Act.[3] The company did not believe that it was necessary to negotiate with the union concerning these stipulations, since the company was mandated by federal law to have a policy to insure a drug-free workplace. Nevertheless, the company subsequently did negotiate in 1991 with the union, and the union agreed to a uniform drug-testing policy for all employees. This occurred after the instant case, and therefore the unfair labor practice charges against the company had become moot. The agreement on the drug-testing policy was virtually identical to that first announced and implemented by the company in 1990.

The company urged that all the unfair labor practice charges be dismissed by the NLRB.

Questions

1. Does it make any difference in this case that employees Kent LaBelle and Martha Seiko signed consent forms giving the company the right to test them for substance abuse and presumably to discipline them for a refusal to submit to a test? Why, or why not?

2. Did the fact that some union representatives knew about and had not objected to the so-called consent forms in 1986 mean that the company was not obligated to negotiate with the union about the drug-testing policy that was implemented in 1990? Why, or why not?

---

[3]The Drug-Free Workplace Act of 1988 applies to employers who have contracts with the federal government of $25,000 or more. This law requires such federal contractors to implement policies and procedures to enable their organizations to be free of drug abuse and to make reasonable "good faith" efforts to maintain a drug-free working environment. Included within provisions of this law are requirements that a firm must develop a drug-free awareness program, and it must administer discipline and/or require participation in a rehabilitation program for employees who violate a criminal drug statute in the employment setting. The Drug-Free Workplace Act does not specifically require or mention drug testing. However, many employers have developed and implemented various types of drug-testing programs as a means of facilitating compliance with the law. See Robert J. Nobile, "The Drug-Free Workplace: Act on It!" *Personnel* 67, no. 2 (February 1990), pp. 21–23; Janet Deming, "Drug-Free Workplace Is Good Business," *HRMagazine* 35, no. 4 (April 1990), pp. 61–62; Carl Weissburg and Dorothy Stephens, "Feds War on Drugs in the Workplace," *Health Systems Review* 24, no. 2 (March–April 1991), pp. 65–67; and Patricia S. Wall, "Drug Testing in the Workplace: An Update," *Journal of Applied Business Research* 8, no. 2 (Spring 1992), pp. 127–32.

3. To what degree, if any, does the company's argument concerning the need for a policy consistent with the 1988 Drug-Free Workplace Act support the company's position in regard to announcing its policy in 1990? Discuss.

4. The company and the union agreed to a drug-testing policy subsequent to the filing of the union's charges in this case. This policy apparently was nearly identical to the policy the company had announced in 1990. Does this render the unfair labor practice charges moot? Why, or why not?

CASE 28
DID THE EMPLOYEE HAVE THE RIGHT TO HAVE A UNION
REPRESENTATIVE PRESENT?

Company:
Eagle Discount Supermarkets, Midwestern Food Division of Lucky Stores, Inc., Glen Ellyn, Illinois

Union:
Food and Commercial Workers, Local No. 1540

Background

On May 1, 1982, the company acquired several grocery stores from another retail chain, Kohl's. The employees working at Kohl's were represented by the Food and Commercial Workers Union. As part of the transfer-of-ownership agreement, the company and the union agreed to continue in effect most terms of the collective bargaining agreement. One major change, however, was the elimination of a provision concerning "just cause" for discharge during a 30-day probationary period for store personnel. Under the transfer-of-ownership agreement, an employee could be terminated during the 30-day probationary period at the sole discretion of the company. Of approximately 450 employees affected by this transfer of ownership, about 40 were terminated under the new probationary provision.

Pamela Golden[1] first began working for Kohl's in 1977. By March 1979 she had attained the position of deli manager of the Hanover Park store. Despite the title of "deli manager," this was a bargaining unit position and Golden was included within the unit represented by the union. She held this position until the Hanover Park store closed late in 1981. Following the closing of that store, her next job placement became the subject of dispute. Her permanent assignment remained unsettled until February 1982, when certain grievances were resolved on her behalf. Golden was on maternity leave from mid-February until August 1982. During her leave, Eagle Discount Stores had acquired ownership of the stores in which Golden had worked, and her assignment upon her return to work again became the subject of controversy. She once more grieved the issue. On August 11, 1982, Golden began working at the Glen Ellyn store under Manager Elmer Ellis. Golden was subject to a 30-day probationary period at this time.

A scheduling problem arose almost immediately. Golden told Ellis that her child-care responsibilities made it inconvenient for her to have to open the deli in the mornings. Ellis agreed to keep her situation in mind when arranging the schedule. Golden was not scheduled to work on August 12, and she was out sick on both August 13 and 14. When she returned to work and saw the posted schedule, she objected to the number of successive workdays she had been given. The schedule was then revised. On

---

[1]The names of all individuals are disguised.

August 19, she again raised objections to the following week's schedule. This led Ellis to respond that she would have to abide by the schedule. Golden in turn responded that she probably would have to "take my problem to the union."

On August 20, 1982, Pamela Golden worked until 9:30 P.M., one-half hour past her scheduled quitting time, because she had to serve a late customer. She did not put the deli in good order before she left. When Elmer Ellis arrived the next morning, he discovered that the deli case was in disarray, some unwrapped cheese had been left out on the counter, and the refrigerator door was ajar. When Golden came in to work, Ellis gave her a written reprimand about the condition of the deli. The writeup contained admonishments about Golden's "poor attitude and work habits."

On August 24, Golden was scheduled to begin work at 1 P.M. At noon she called Ellis and told him that she had been unable to get a babysitter. She asked if it would be all right not to report as scheduled. Ellis replied that it was not all right in view of the difficulty he would have trying to find a replacement, but he also said, "If you cannot come in, you cannot come in."

Midway through her shift on August 26, Golden was called to Ellis' office. He told her he wanted to discuss her attendance with her. Assistant Manager Christine Kuroski was present in Ellis' office. When Golden arrived, she asked that she be permitted to have a union representative present as her witness. Ellis, however, handed her a written warning concerning her absences on August 13 and 14 and her having called off work on short notice on August 24. Golden looked at the writeup and said that she refused to sign it. Ellis stated he would read the warning to her, whereupon Golden began to leave the room, stating that she wanted her union representative present. At that point Ellis pointed to the telephone on his desk and said, "Here, call and we can set up a meeting whenever you want to talk." Golden did nothing. Ellis then attempted to read the warning aloud, and Golden left the office and walked down the hall. Ellis followed her, reminding her that he was her boss and that it was important that they talk. He told her she could either return to his office or punch out and leave. Golden followed Ellis back into his office. Ellis again attempted unsuccessfully to have her read the warning or to listen to him read it to her. At that point Ellis told her to punch out and that she was suspended. Ellis then called District Manager Tony Carbo to inform him what had happened. Upon Carbo's instructions, Ellis telephoned Golden later that day and told her she was fired.

Shortly thereafter, the union filed unfair labor practice charges against the company, claiming that the company had violated Sections 7, 8(a) (1), and 8(a) (3) of LMRA by denying Pamela Golden her right to have a union representative present at the meeting of August 26, 1982, and by discriminatorily reprimanding and later discharging her in retaliation for asserting her protected rights. The union requested that Pamela Golden should be reinstated to her job position and made whole for all lost pay and benefits.

Position of the Union

The union claimed that the first written reprimand given to Pamela Golden on August 20 was in major part a retaliation for her statement that she would probably seek the union's assistance in her scheduling dispute with Manager Elmer Ellis.

The union's primary charges, however, focused on the incidents of August 26, 1982, during which Pamela Golden requested that a union representative be present during her meeting with two company managers. The union claimed that the company had clearly violated Golden's statutory right under the well-known NLRB *Weingarten*[2] decision, which was upheld by the U.S. Supreme Court. This right, which is well-established law, required the company to permit Golden to have a union representative present at an investigatory interview that she reasonably believed could result in disciplinary action.

The company's illegal refusal to permit her to have her union representative present was the primary cause for the subsequent behavior of Pamela Golden in her refusal to listen to Ellis read a warning to her. Golden was not being insubordinate to Ellis; rather, she was asserting her rights under LMRA to have a representative present in a meeting that she believed was disciplinary in nature. The union concluded that Golden was suspended and discharged because she insisted upon her right to a representative and also because she had filed grievances during the summer of 1982 concerning her assignment dispute. The union urged that the unfair labor practice charges be upheld, and that the company be ordered to comply with the reinstatement remedy requested by the union.

Position of the Company

Concerning the first written reprimand issued by Manager Ellis on August 20, the company argued that this reprimand had nothing to do whatsoever with any retaliation against Golden for her seeking help from the union with her work schedule. Ellis issued the reprimand solely because of the unsatisfactory condition in which Golden had left the deli area the evening before.

The company contended strongly that it had not violated Golden's statutory (i.e., *Weingarten*) rights. Elmer Ellis had called Pamela Golden into his office on August 26 for the purpose of delivering to her a disciplinary writeup concerning her poor attendance and of advising her orally of the necessity of improving her attendance. He was taking a firm disciplinary step based on what he had concluded was an unacceptable record. In this type of meeting, an employee does not have a statutory right to have a union representative present. The company stressed that the NLRB had held that when an employer has reached a decision to levy certain discipline upon an employee, no Section 7 right to union representation arises if the meeting is held simply to inform or to impose that discipline upon the employee.[3]

Pamela Golden refused in this meeting to permit her manager to administer that discipline to her. She became totally insubordinate and therefore was suspended. After review of her entire work and attendance record, she then was discharged as an unsatisfactory probationary employee, as the company contractually had the right to do.

---

[2]*NLRB* v. *J. Weingarten,* 420 U.S. 251, 88 LRRM 2689 (1975).
[3]The key NLRB case cited here was *Baton Rouge Water Works,* 246 NLRB 995, 103 LRRM 1056 (1979).

In summary, the company claimed that the unfair labor practice charges should be dismissed, since they primarily were an effort by Golden and the union to obtain reinstatement for her to which she was not entitled under either LMRA or the labor agreement.

Questions

1. Why is a decision in this type of case a "close call," which causes difficulties for all parties concerned?
2. Distinguish between the *Weingarten* case cited by the union and the *Baton Rouge Water Works* case cited by the company. Is there a clear demarcation between the major considerations in these cases? Discuss.
3. Should an employer permit an employee to have a union representative present in a meeting whenever an employee requests this? Why, or why not?
4. Under Section 7 of LMRA, which speaks of protected "concerted activities" and "mutual aid or protection," the NLRB in 1982 held that an unrepresented employee had the right to have a co-worker present during an investigatory interview that the employee reasonably believed could lead to disciplinary action. In 1985, however, the NLRB reversed itself and held that only employees represented by a labor union had the *(Weingarten)* right to representation during an investigatory interview. Why is this area of "unsettled" labor law apt to become a major judicial issue at some time in the future? Discuss.

Case 29
The Grievance-Processing Fee for Nonmembers in a Right-to-Work State

Company:
Davis Company, Memphis, Tennessee

Union:
Local No. 282, International Union of Electronic, Electrical, Salaried, Machine, and Furniture Workers

Background

The union represented the production and maintenance employees at the company's plant located in Memphis, Tennessee. Tennessee is a so-called right-to-work state. Under Tennessee state law, union shop contracts cannot be negotiated; this type of state law is authorized by Section 14(b) of the LMRA.[1]

The parties negotiated a collective bargaining agreement, effective September 12, 1986, through September 11, 1989, which contained a grievance and arbitration procedure. However, this collective bargaining agreement did not contain either a union security or agency shop clause.

On or about September 10, 1987, the union sent or hand-delivered a memorandum to all the bargaining unit employees who were not members of the union. This memorandum included the following statement:

ATTENTION ALL NONMEMBERS

Effective immediately, all nonmembers will be charged a fee for handling grievances, an equal amount to the cost of representation, or the dues left to be paid under the contract, whichever is less.

Subsequently, on November 20, 1987, the union posted the following notice on the employee bulletin board:

ATTENTION ALL NONMEMBERS

Effective immediately, all nonmembers will be charged a fee for handling grievances, an equal amount to the cost of representation, or the dues left to be paid under the contract, whichever is less.

The Union will not refuse to process your grievances because of this policy. Should you wish to file a grievance, please follow the normal contract procedures.

---

[1]Section 14(b), the so-called right-to-work provision, reads as follows: "Nothing in this subchapter shall be construed as authorizing the execution or application of agreements requiring membership in a labor organization as a condition of employment in any State or Territory in which such execution or application is prohibited by State or Territorial Law."

Shortly thereafter, the company on behalf of Alexandria Yowell,[2] an employee, filed unfair labor practice charges against the union. These charges alleged that the union's action was in violation of Section 8(b) (1) (A) and Section 7 of the LMRA as amended.

Position of the Company

The company contended that in the absence of a valid union security clause, a labor organization breaches its duty of fair representation by charging or threatening to charge nonmembers the costs of processing grievances. The LMRA requires that an exclusive bargaining representative must act fairly and impartially on behalf of all bargaining unit employees, particularly in right-to-work states where union security clauses are prohibited. Both the September 10 and November 20, 1987, notices represented discriminatory treatment of nonmembers, because they indicated that the union would attempt to collect future payments for grievance processing.

The company argued that the union was attempting to coerce nonmember employees to join the union, which was violative of their protected rights under Section 7 of the Act to refrain from joining the union. The company urged that the union's proposed grievance-processing fee be held in violation of the LMRA, and that the union be ordered to cease and desist in any efforts to impose such a discriminatory fee.

Position of the Union

The union contended that it had not breached its duty of fair representation, because the proposed grievance-processing fee was reasonable and for services rendered. Failure to charge nonmembers any fee would treat nonmembers and members unequally. The union argued that the November 20, 1987, notice stated that implementation of the grievance-processing charge would not interfere with employees' rights under the collective bargaining agreement. The union further claimed that it had acted in accord with the notice by not refusing to process nonmembers' grievances or threatening to institute suits to compel payment for such services. However, the union asserted that the LMRA did not mandate that unions must provide grievance-processing services free of charge. A union should not be required to provide totally free representation and services to those employees who decided not to be members even though they received all rights and benefits of union membership. This principle is established in Section 19 of LMRA, which provides that even where a union shop is present, a union may charge a grievance-processing fee for an employee who is not in the union because of valid religious conscientious reasons.

Common sense and fundamental fairness should support the concept that a labor organization be able to collect reasonable expenses it incurs on behalf of nonmembers (called free-riders) the union by law must represent. In a right-to-work state, nonmember employees in a bargaining unit benefit directly from union efforts on their behalf. Letting unions recoup the costs of grievance processing does not constitute coerced "membership" within the meaning of Section 14(b) of LMRA.

---

[2]Name is disguised.

For all these reasons, the union claimed that it was well within its rights in its effort to charge a grievance-processing fee for nonmembers. The union requested that the unfair labor practice charges filed by the company be dismissed.

Questions

1. Evaluate the union's arguments concerning the need for grievance-processing fees to cover the union's expenses incurred representing nonmembers in the bargaining unit. Why is this problem at the core of any union's efforts to attain a union shop in those states where union shops are not prohibited by state law?
2. Why would the company be interested in pursuing these unfair labor practice charges when the issue is largely an internal union problem? Discuss.
3. Why was this case an important one in the continuing controversy over union representation and rights in right-to-work states? Compare the issues in this case with those in Case 49, "Revocation of Dues Checkoff in a Right-to-Work State."
4. Discuss the pros and cons of Section 14(b) of LMRA from the standpoint both of this case and of labor relations in general. Why will the application of Section 14(b) likely continue to be a controversial issue?

CASE 30
THE UNION'S LETTER TO NONMEMBER EMPLOYEES WHO CROSSED THE PICKET LINE

Company:
Unit Distribution of Bloomington, Inc., Normal, Illinois

Union:
Chicago Truck Drivers, Helpers and Warehouse Workers (Independent) Union

Background

In mid-1990, an election was conducted in which a majority of voting employees in the bargaining unit selected the union as their collective bargaining representative. The bargaining unit had been defined by the NLRB regional office as follows:

> All full-time and regular part-time production, maintenance, shipping and receiving employees, including all fork lift operators, material handling associates, and material expeditors (inventory control specialists) employed by the Employer at its Inbound Logistics Center located in Normal, Illinois, serving the Caterpillar, Inc., customer; but excluding all office clerical employees, guards, professional employees, and supervisors as defined in the Act.

The company filed certain objections to the election. However, the NLRB overruled these objections and certified the union as the exclusive representative of unit employees.

In late 1990, the union called a strike against the company as part of its efforts to secure a favorable collective bargaining agreement. This strike lasted from November 3 through December 12, 1990. However, during the strike, a number of employees who had not joined the union and who had voted against having the union represent them crossed the union picket lines and continued to work.

On November 20, 1990, the union's vice president, Peter Gorman,[1] authored, signed, and distributed a letter to those bargaining unit employees who had crossed the picket line to work for the company. This letter stated in part:

> Once the National Labor Relations Board certifies the Union as the collective bargaining representative, all employees who are members of the bargaining unit—those that were eligible to vote in the election—will be required to become members of the Union under the Union security provision that will be contained in the contract, or seek employment elsewhere. A member of the Union is bound by the Constitution of the Union (Article VI, Section 5.1) and is subject to <u>fines</u> if he/she violates the Constitution of the Union (Article VIII). Violation of a lawfully called strike by crossing an authorized picket line is a violation of the Union's Constitution (Article VI, Section 8; Article VIII). Those unit employees who continue to cross the picket line and work will become members of the Union and will be subject to charges, trial, and fines under the Union's Constitution.
>
> We ask you to reconsider your decision to continue to work and instead <u>Join Us on the Picket Line</u>. Those employees who have crossed the picket line but at this time choose to stop

---

[1]Name is disguised.

working and join their fellow workers will not be subject to any fines or other disciplinary action by the Union.

The bargaining unit employees to whom the November 20 letter was distributed were not members and had paid no dues to the union. Further, there was no signed collective bargaining agreement between the parties covering bargaining unit employees, nor had any union security clause (such as a union shop) been negotiated. The company filed unfair labor practice charges against the union alleging that the union's letter to the nonmember, nonstriking employees had violated Section 8(b) (1) (A) and Section 7 of the LMRA.

Position of the Company

The company contended that the union's November 20 letter was unlawful because it was distributed to nonmembers at a time when there was no collective bargaining agreement and no union security clause in effect. Thus, the union violated Section 8(b) (1) (A) by threatening to fine or otherwise discipline the nonmember employees, since these threats were coercive and calculated to deter them from exercising their statutory rights protected by Section 7 of LMRA.

The company claimed that the union was trying to subject the nonmember employees to the requirements of its constitution prior to the existence of a contract between the company and the union. The union was suggesting that fines would be imposed retroactively after the employees were required to become members of the union, assuming that an agreement was reached containing a union shop provision. Allowing a union to discipline members retroactively for premembership conduct would undermine the statutory right of nonmember employees to cross picket lines and to engage in other protected activities without penalty.

The company urged the NLRB to find that the union by the actions of its officer Peter Gorman[2] had violated the Act. The company requested that the union be required to rescind the unlawful letter, and that the union be required to notify all the employees in the bargaining unit accordingly.

Position of the Union

The union contended that the unfair labor practice charges filed by the company were nonmeritorious and simply an effort to interfere with the union's right to impose discipline on the nonmember employees it was required by the Act to represent. The union pointed to the proviso within Section 8(b) (1) (A) that enables a union to "prescribe its own rules with respect to the acquisition or retention of membership therein." The NLRB and the courts have long maintained that a union may lawfully fine member employees for crossing a picket line during an authorized strike. Without the right to impose this collective self-discipline, a union would be impotent to exert a unified effort to achieve a better contract. In the instant case, the nonmember employees who

---

[2]There was no dispute that the union vice president who wrote and sent the letter was an agent of the union under Section 2(13) of LMRA.

crossed the picket line were nevertheless represented by the union. Once a collective bargaining agreement was negotiated with the company, it would have a union shop provision. During negotiations prior to the strike, company management had not expressed objections to the inclusion of a union security provision in the agreement. The union letter of November 20, 1990, was only an effort by the union to maintain the same standards for all the employees it represented, members and nonmembers. It was only a matter of time before all employees would become members of the union.

In summary, the union contended that its November 20 letter was lawful and permitted by LMRA; that the company unfair labor practice charges were without merit and an intrusion into union affairs; and that the NLRB should dismiss the unfair labor practice charges accordingly.

Questions

1. Section 8(b) (1) (A) of LMRA has long been a controversial section. Why is it difficult to differentiate between protected Section 7 rights and the union's right to prescribe its own rules and regulations?

2. What was the primary purpose of the November 20 letter sent by the union to the nonstriking nonmembers? Was the letter essentially a threat to nonmembers who had crossed the picket line, or was it a realistic notification of a likely outcome of negotiations with the company?

3. Is there a difference between a nonmember who crosses a picket line and an employee who previously was a union member but who resigns from the union during a strike and crosses a picket line? Discuss.

4. Contrast the issues in this case with those in Case 15, "A Presumption of Union Interference during a Decertification Election."

CASE 31
SHOULD THE NLRB TWICE DEFER TO THE ARBITRATOR'S AWARD?

Company:
Barton Brands, Inc., Bardstown, Kentucky

Union:
Local No. 23, Distillery, Wine, and Allied Workers International Union

Background

The company, a Delaware corporation with an office and place of business in Bardstown, Kentucky, was engaged in the manufacture and nonretail sale and distribution of alcoholic beverages and related products. Local No. 23 of the Distillery, Wine, and Allied Workers International Union represented most of the company's production employees at Bardstown. At the time of this case, the parties had a collective bargaining agreement that was in effect from July 1984 through June 1987.

On July 10, 1986, company management discharged Jerry Ogden[1] for an allegedly insubordinate act. At the time of his discharge, Ogden was plant chairman for the local union, a position equivalent to chief steward. Ogden had been elected by the union to hold the position of plant chairman from January to December 31, 1986. Ogden was a production worker who had been employed by the company since 1980.

On July 11, 1986, Ogden filed a grievance concerning his discharge. On July 23, 1986, Ogden also filed a charge with the NLRB alleging that the company had discharged him for attempting to process a grievance, which was a violation of Sections 8(a) (3) and 8(a) (1) of LMRA. On August 25, 1986, the Regional Director of the NLRB deferred this charge to the contractual grievance procedure pursuant to established Board policy in cases of this type.[2]

Ogden's grievance was processed to arbitration. On January 16, 1987, after a hearing, the arbitrator issued an award in which he found that Ogden was "clearly insubordinate on the day of his discharge" and there was "no evidence to suggest that Ogden was discriminated against because of his union activities." The arbitrator found, however, that there were "slight mitigating circumstances" that warranted a lesser penalty than discharge. Acknowledging that Ogden had been plant chairman for only seven months at the time of his discharge, the arbitrator found some validity in the union's contention that, in the "heat of the moment," Ogden believed that he was entitled to

---

[1]Name is disguised.

[2]In cases of this nature where an individual has filed a grievance under a contractual grievance procedure and also has filed unfair labor practice charges with the NLRB, the Board often will defer (delay) its handling of the unfair labor practice charges until the contractual remedies have been exhausted. See *United Technologies Corp.*, 268 NLRB 557 (1984).

The NLRB normally will defer to an arbitrator's decision when: (1) the unfair labor practice issue was presented to and considered by the arbitrator; (2) the arbitral proceedings were fair and regular; (3) all parties agreed to be bound; and (4) the decision is "not repugnant to the purposes and policies of the Act." See *Spielberg Mfg. Co.*, 112 NLRB 1080 (1955); *Olin Corp.*, 268 NLRB 573 (1984).

have his grievance problem considered immediately. The arbitrator, therefore, converted Ogden's discharge to a disciplinary suspension from the date of his discharge through the date of the award, and directed Ogden's reinstatement but with a forfeiture of back pay and other benefits during the time of the suspension. Further, relying on "the possibility of continued friction if Ogden was to remain as a union steward," the arbitrator held that as a condition of reinstatement Ogden should resign his position as plant chairman and "refrain from serving as steward or in any other official capacity" in the union's dealings with the company for three years following reinstatement. The arbitrator further ruled that violation of this condition would "result in revocation of the reinstatement and immediate termination." By the time the arbitrator's award was issued, Ogden's term of office as plant chairman had expired.

On March 4, 1987, the regional director of the NLRB dismissed the pending unfair labor practice charges Ogden had filed on the grounds that the underlying contractual issue was factually parallel to the unfair labor practice issue; the arbitration proceeding was fair and regular; and the arbitrator was presented generally with all the facts underlying the parallel grievance and unfair labor practice issues. Ogden appealed this decision, and his appeal was denied by the General Counsel of the NLRB by letter dated March 27, 1987.

This letter stated in pertinent part:

> The appeal is denied. Apart from other considerations, it was concluded that the evidence was insufficient to establish that you were discharged in violation of the National Labor Relations Act. While your appeal contends that the arbitrator "exceeded his authority" and that the Union failed to properly present your case to the arbitrator, these contentions are not relevant to our decision which rests on the prearbitration evidence which was presented during the investigation of the unfair labor practice charge. According to that evidence, your conduct was unprotected under the Act and thus your discharge for such conduct was not unlawful under the Act.

The company had reinstated Ogden to layoff status in January 1987, following the issuance of the arbitrator's award. There were a number of employees on layoff, and Ogden's employee seniority was too low to entitle him to be actively employed at this time.

However, on May 20, 1987, while still on layoff, Ogden was elected president of the local union. By letter dated May 28, 1987, the union notified the company that Ogden would take office as president on June 1, 1987. The company, by letter dated June 1, 1987, notified Ogden that he was terminated, effective immediately, pursuant to the terms of the arbitrator's award.

Shortly thereafter, the union filed unfair labor practice charges with the NLRB claiming that the company had violated Sections 8(a) (3) and 8(a) (1) of the Act by discharging Ogden. The union requested that the Board order that Ogden be reinstated and made whole for monetary and other losses as a result of this discharge.

Position of the Union

The union contended that the company had unlawfully discharged Ogden for being elected union president. Under Section 7 of the LMRA, Ogden did not lose his right to hold union office as a result of his July 1986 misconduct while serving as plant chairman. Further, Section 7 of the Act protects the right of the union to choose its own representatives to process grievances and lead a union for the union's mutual aid and protection.

The union argued that there had been no waiver of Section 7 rights by either Ogden or the union. Even though there had been no immediate appeal to the NLRB contesting the terms of the arbitrator's award, this did not constitute a clear and unequivocal waiver. No arbitrator has the authority to require employees to abandon their Section 7 rights. Because the arbitrator's award could not be reconciled with the policies of the Act, deferral to or enforcement of the arbitrator's award was not appropriate. The union contended that it was not improper for the Board to defer to the arbitrator's decision regarding Ogden's July 1986 discharge. But the NLRB should find that Ogden's July 1987 discharge was unlawful, because the two situations were not factually parallel, and the second discharge was not presented to the arbitrator.

In summary, the union urged that the NLRB find that Ogden's second discharge violated Sections 8(a) (3) and 8(a) (1) of LMRA, and that Ogden be reinstated and made whole as deemed appropriate by the Board.[3]

Position of the Company

The company contended that Jerry Ogden had lost his right to hold union office because he had abused his position in July 1986, and because the arbitrator conditioned his reinstatement with the company to ensure that he would not abuse a union office again. The relevant contractual provision from the parties' collective bargaining agreement on which Ogden's first discharge was arbitrated contained the following provision:

> The decision of the arbitrator . . . shall be final and binding on all parties involved in such controversy or grievance and shall conclusively determine same.

Thus, when Ogden was elected union president in May 1987, the company was well within its contractual rights to terminate Ogden for his and the union's violation of the terms of the arbitrator's award.

The company maintained that the arbitrator had the authority to formulate the conditional remedy concerning Ogden, because the union had agreed to arbitrate Ogden's grievance and to be bound by the arbitrator's decision. When the company reinstated Ogden pursuant to the arbitrator's award, it also was upheld by the NLRB's deferral and dismissal of the unfair labor practice charges filed by Ogden in 1986.

In summary, the company contended that this "second round" of unfair labor practice charges was without merit and should be dismissed, because Ogden's second discharge was based on an arbitrator's award to which the NLRB had previously deferred.

Questions

1. Does the fact that the NLRB deferred to the arbitrator's award in 1987 mean that the NLRB should again defer to the arbitrator's award and dismiss the unfair

---

[3]In this regard, the union claimed that, as union president, Ogden could and would have appointed himself as plant chairman with "superseniority" that would have entitled him to be reinstated from layoff status on or about June 1, 1987.

labor practice charges surrounding Jerry Ogden's second discharge? Why, or why not?

2. Examine the NLRB's criteria for deferral to an arbitrator's decision as cited in footnote 2. How should these be applied to the factual circumstances of this case?

3. Since both parties had agreed contractually to be bound by an arbitrator's decision, was the company justified in terminating Ogden when he became president of the local union? Discuss.

CASE 32
RELIGIOUS OBJECTIONS TO PAYING UNION DUES

Company:
   Grand Rapids City Coach Lines, Inc., Grand Rapids, Michigan

Union:
   Local No. 836, Amalgamated Transit Union

Background

The company was in the business of providing bus operators and maintenance employees to the Grand Rapids Area Transit Authority for the operation and maintenance of public transportation. During the year preceding this case, the company had gross revenues in excess of $500,000 and provided services valued in excess of $50,000 to the Grand Rapids Area Transit Authority, which in turn purchased and received goods and services valued in excess of $50,000 from out-of-state sources. There was no dispute that the company was an employer within the meaning of the LMRA.

Local No. 836 of the Amalgamated Transit Union represented a unit of bus operators and maintenance employees. During 1986, the company and the union were parties to a collective bargaining agreement, which required employees covered by the contract to become members of the union after 30 days of employment. Martin Walsh[1] had worked for the company for over a year, but he had not become a union member. On October 20, 1986, the union asked Walsh to sign an authorization card for the company to deduct from his pay an initiation fee and union dues and to forward the money to the union. Walsh refused to sign such an authorization. On November 11, 1986, the union again asked Walsh to sign such an initiation fee and dues checkoff, and he again refused.[2] By letter dated November 18, 1986, the union then requested the company to discharge Walsh for failure to pay his union initiation fee and dues. When the company refused to discharge Walsh, the union on December 16, 1986, filed a grievance to compel the company to live up to the collective bargaining agreement in effect. No action was taken on that grievance. Instead, on February 9, 1987, the company filed unfair labor practice charges against the union claiming that the union had unlawfully demanded that the company discharge an employee and filed a grievance to achieve that objective, which violated Section 8(b) (2) and Section 19 of the LMRA as amended.

Position of the Company

The company claimed that it had refused to discharge Martin Walsh because the company believed that Walsh was entitled to a religious exemption from membership in the union. Walsh had told both company and union officials that his reason for

---

[1]The names of all individuals are disguised.

[2]At about this time, Martin Walsh offered to pay an amount equal to union dues to a charitable organization. The union refused to accept this offer.

refusing to pay union dues and an initiation fee was because to do so would be "against my Christian convictions to join the union or pay its dues." Walsh claimed that he was a member of a church called "The Body of Jesus Christ."

The company's 8(b) (2) charges against the union were based on its understanding of Section 19 of the 1980 amendment to the Labor Management Relations Act. In pertinent part this section says:

> Any employee who is a member of and adheres to established and traditional tenets or teachings of a bona fide religion, body, or sect which has historically held conscientious objections to joining or financially supporting labor organizations shall not be required to join or financially support any labor organization as a condition of employment.

Company witnesses testified that Walsh had convinced them that his religious views were deep and sincere, and that Walsh was not using his religious convictions simply as a device to escape the union's initiation fee and dues in a union shop. The company, therefore, had refused to discharge Walsh as requested by the union. When the union submitted its grievance, the company decided to file unfair labor practice charges against the union in order to determine whether or not Walsh was entitled to an exemption from union obligations as a condition of his continued employment. The parties had agreed to place the union grievance on hold pending the NLRB's decision in the case.

The company urged that the unfair labor practice charges be upheld, and that the union be directed to withdraw its request and grievance that Martin Walsh be discharged.

Position of the Union

The union claimed that it had been extremely patient with Martin Walsh. The union had offered Walsh the option of paying an initiation fee and dues' equivalent as paid by all members without actually requiring Walsh to join the union. Walsh adamantly refused this option.

Bill Tidwell, the union's financial secretary, testified that when Walsh first claimed a religious privilege as the basis for his refusal to pay union dues, he asked Walsh to identify the church or religious organization to which he belonged. In a written reply to the union, Walsh said, "The assembly which I attend is not a denomination or religious organization established by a constitution, or man." Walsh did mention the phrase "faith assembly," saying it had been located in Warsaw, Indiana, although he did not have the address of that group. Walsh later gave Tidwell the name of the "minister" of that group, although he thought that this man had been dead for three years. When Tidwell looked into the matter and inquired at Warsaw, he could not locate any such person or organization. Tidwell said that he had checked with the police department there, but they could not help him either.

Tidwell stated that he and other union officers had pressed Walsh concerning his religious views. Walsh consistently relied on quotations from the Bible. In letters to the union, Walsh explained his religious objections about joining the union primarily by citing numerous biblical passages from the New Testament. When Walsh was asked to explain his generalizations that his "church" was based on these quotations from the Bible, Walsh had responded, "I, personally, have objections, based upon Scripture, to joining the union. These beliefs came to me by my own personal consideration."

When Walsh was asked why he did not or could not identify his "church" or "organization"—if in reality there existed such a religious group—he only replied that he "did not want to involve that organization, because I did not want to involve the leadership in the church with this union squabble, and because I personally have objections to joining a union and paying the dues as set forth from the Word of God."

The union eventually had concluded that Walsh was not a "member" of any "bona fide religion, body, or sect" as contemplated under Section 19 of LMRA. In the union's view, Walsh did not qualify for a religious exemption that would excuse him from paying the union's initiation fee and dues in a union shop as is permitted under Section 8(a) (3) of LMRA. The union consequently did not violate Section 8(b) (2) of LMRA by requesting and filing a grievance with the company to discharge Walsh for his refusal to meet his union obligations. The unfair labor practice charges were without merit and should be dismissed.

Questions

1. Why does a case of this nature place both the company and the union in an awkward position? Discuss.

2. Does it matter in this case that Walsh may or may not have been a member of an "organized" religious body or group?

3. Did the union violate LMRA in requesting and filing a grievance with the company to the effect that Walsh should be discharged? Why, or why not?

4. What are the precedent implications of this type of case in regard to religious exemptions under Section 19 of LMRA as amended? Discuss.

CASE 33
WAS THE UNION CONTRACT PROPOSAL A "HOT CARGO" CLAUSE?

Company:
   Helmkamp Construction Company, Wood River, Illinois

Union:
   Chauffeurs, Teamsters, Warehousemen, and Helpers, Teamsters Local Union No. 525

Background

Helmkamp Construction Company, a general contractor, had maintained a fleet of trucks to fulfill its hauling needs and occasionally perform contract hauling for others. Truck drivers employed by Helmkamp were covered under a collective bargaining agreement with Teamsters Union Local No. 525, due to expire April 30, 1983.

Late in 1982, Helmkamp decided to close down its trucking division and sell its trucks, because the trucking operation was no longer profitable. Future trucking needs would be satisfied by independent owner-contractors.

In January 1983, Helmkamp's president, Farley Duncan,[1] met with the union business representative, Milton Murphy, and disclosed Helmkamp's plans. Murphy neither protested the decision nor requested bargaining over the effects of closing the trucking division. Murphy did express his regrets and noted the growing nationwide problem of owner-operators replacing union drivers.

Helmkamp's attorney wrote an official letter about this matter, which was delivered to Murphy on February 28. The letter confirmed the plan to close the trucking operation, terminate the existing collective bargaining agreement at its expiration on April 30, 1983, and thereafter utilize lease agreements with independent owner-operators to satisfy Helmkamp's trucking needs. Subsequently, Duncan agreed to a request from Murphy to meet with Barclay Jones, president of the Illinois Conference of Teamsters.

In early March, Duncan, Jones, and Murphy met at a local hotel. Duncan reiterated Helmkamp's intentions and offered to bargain over the effects of the impending closure of its trucking operation. In April, however, Jones wrote Duncan to request negotiations to continue or replace the existing collective bargaining agreement. Duncan responded by letter on April 18, 1983, that Helmkamp still intended to eliminate its trucking division and saw no need to enter into a new collective bargaining agreement since the company no longer would employ any truck drivers. Duncan again indicated his willingness to bargain over the effects of the termination. He received no response from the union.

Duncan called Murphy again in May to remind him that liquidation of Helmkamp's trucks was nearing completion. Murphy requested that Helmkamp postpone sale of the last few trucks pending a later meeting.

---

[1]The names of all individuals are disguised.

Duncan and Murphy next met on August 18, 1983. Murphy presented Duncan with two contracts and demanded that Helmkamp sign one. Both contained contractual clauses that would require Helmkamp to carry owner-drivers on the company's payroll and further require these owner-drivers to join the union as a condition of being employed by Helmkamp.[2] Duncan refused to sign, because Helmkamp would no longer own any trucks nor have need for its own drivers. Murphy said it made no difference, and they would "both have to get [their] best hold and see what would happen."

On August 19, Duncan received a telegram from Barclay Jones, stating that Helmkamp had the union's last and best offer, and if Helmkamp refused to sign, the union would "take all legal economic recourse that was deemed necessary."

Helmkamp sold or leased its remaining trucks and laid off the last of its drivers on August 23. Helmkamp thereafter began to utilize independent owner-contractors for its trucking needs. On August 26, the union struck Helmkamp and began to picket. The picketing expanded to various construction sites.

Shortly thereafter, the company filed unfair labor practice charges with the NLRB, claiming that the union had violated Sections 8(b) (4) (A) and 8(b) (4) (B) of LMRA, by picketing and threatening to picket Helmkamp to force self-employed owner-drivers to join the union and force Helmkamp to enter into an agreement prohibited by Section 8(e) of the Act.

Responding to this complaint and as required under Section 10(l) of the Act, the Regional Office of the NLRB petitioned the district court for the Southern District of Illinois to issue an injunction to stop the strike and picketing. Accordingly, the court on September 7 issued a temporary restraining order on the union to stop the strike and picketing; the union complied with this order.

Subsequently, Helmkamp signed a new collective bargaining agreement with the union on September 21, 1983, containing the disputed union membership clause requirements. In return, the union agreed not to enforce the disputed clauses pending determination of their legality.

Position of the Company

The company cited Section 8(e) of LMRA—the so-called hot cargo provision—which prohibits

> any contract or agreement . . . whereby [an] employer ceases or refrains or agrees to cease or refrain from handling, using, selling, transporting, or otherwise dealing in any of the products of any other employer or to cease doing business with any other person.

The company attorney noted that the Board and the courts have held that agreements that limit an employer to subcontracting only with businesses that recognize a union or have a union contract violate Section 8(e).[3]

---

[2]The contractual provisions in dispute are included at the end of the case.

[3]See *Local 814, International Brotherhood of Teamsters* v. *NLRB*, 546 F.2d 989, 93 LRRM 2800 (D.C. Cir. 1976), cert. denied, 434 U.S. 818, 96 LRRM 2512 (1977).

The clauses at issue here, which would force independent owner-operators to join the union by requiring them to be carried on the company payroll as employees, were union signatory clauses that focused on the union affiliation of a subcontractor or subcontractor's employees. That is to say, they restricted subcontracting work solely to those who had union membership. In the company's view, such clauses were a blatant violation of Section 8(e).

Further, Section 8(b) (4) (A) of the Act prohibits strikes by labor organizations designed either to force a self-employed person to join a labor organization or to force an employer to enter into an agreement prohibited by Section 8(e).

Similarly, Section 8(b) (4) (B) of the Act prohibits a labor organization from engaging in secondary strikes and other forms of coercive action for the purpose of "forcing or requiring any person to cease using, selling, handling, transporting, or otherwise dealing in the products of any other producer, processor, or manufacturer, or to cease doing business with any other person . . ." It was apparent that the union's strike and picketing were aimed at forcing the independent owner-drivers to join the union and to force Helmkamp to enter into an agreement that, in the company's view, violated Section 8(e). Since the union's objectives were in violation of the Act, the union's actions also violated Sections 8(b) (4) (A) and 8(b) (4) (B) of the Act. The company urged that the union be found guilty of the unfair labor practices as charged, that the disputed contractual provisions be permanently voided, and that the union be ordered to cease and desist from any efforts to obtain such contractual provisions in the future.

Position of the Union

The union claimed that its objectives and actions were all taken in an effort to preserve jobs and work for its members. The company had long recognized the union as the collective bargaining agent for the truck drivers employed by Helmkamp. In early 1983, the company had unilaterally decided to sell its fleet of trucks and use independent contractors for its trucking needs. Therefore, the union had acted in an effort to preserve jobs and work for the displaced truck drivers. The proposed new union contracts, which contained the "owner-driver" provisions (see end of the case), would enable some of the displaced truck drivers who could afford to own their own trucks to retain their jobs with Helmkamp and also retain their collective bargaining rights under a union contract. Other owner-drivers to be utilized by the company would have similar contractual protection and rights that long had been afforded to drivers employed by Helmkamp.

The union claimed that the only real change would be that the truck drivers to be employed by the company would have to own their own trucks.

In summary, the union reiterated its position that the disputed contractual clauses were legitimately designed to preserve work for its members. The NLRB previously had held that if a union's primary objective is to preserve work for its members, such actions as are necessary to achieve this objective are not necessarily violative of LMRA.[4] The union urged that the unfair labor practice charges be dismissed, and that the collective bargaining agreement that had been negotiated between the company and union become valid and placed into effect.

---

[4]See *National Woodwork Manufacturers Ass'n.* v. *NLRB,* 386 U.S. 612, 634, 64 LRRM 2801 (1967).

The Disputed Contractual Provisions

The two contracts, one a multiemployer agreement between the Illinois Conference of Teamsters and the Associated General Contractors of Illinois, the other between the Teamsters and individual employers covering three local union jurisdictions, contained the following pertinent clauses:

Article XXIV—Owner-Driver

24.1 The Term "Owner-Driver" means an individual, who, in addition to being employed to perform services covered by this Agreement is also the owner and operator of the equipment. Legal or equitable title must be in the name of the driver. The following provisions shall apply to all Owner-Drivers engaged to perform work.

24.2 The Owner-Driver shall be carried on the payroll of the Employer as an employee and as such, all the terms and conditions of the Agreement, including Article IV, Procurement of Labor, shall be applicable to him. A separate referral list will be kept for Owners-Drivers.

Article III—Union Security

3.1 It is understood and agreed by and between the parties hereto that as a condition of continued employment and effective after the seventh day following the beginning employment on the execution date of this Agreement, whichever is the later, all persons hereafter employed to work within the bargaining unit which is the subject of the Agreement, as well as all persons presently so working but who are not members of one of the Local Unions referred to herein, shall become members of the particular Local Union having jurisdiction for representation purposes over the geographical area within which such persons then work. It is further understood and agreed that as a condition of continued employment all persons who are presently members in good standing of one of the Local Unions referred to herein or who hereafter become such shall be required to pay the periodic dues of the Local Union having jurisdiction for representation purposes over the geographical area within which such persons work a majority of the time figured on a month by month basis.

3.3. The failure of any person to become a member of a Local Union in the manner and within the time above provided for shall obligate his Employer, upon written notice from the Union to such effect and to the further effect that Union membership was available to such person on the same terms and conditions generally available to other members, to forthwith discharge such person. Further, the failure of any person to pay the monthly periodic dues required shall, upon written notice from the Union to his Employer to such effect, obligate his Employer to discharge him forthwith.

Questions

1. Does it make any difference in this case that this company is in the construction industry? (Suggestion: Closely scrutinize the entire text of Section 8(e) of LMRA.)

2. Why is a determination of the primary objective of the union in this type of case crucial to the question of unfair labor practice charges? Discuss.

3. Why have the NLRB and the courts often had difficulty in defining union and employer actions that may violate the so-called secondary boycott and hot cargo provisions of LMRA? Discuss.

CASE 34
WHO SHOULD INSTALL THE FIBER OPTIC CABLE SYSTEM?

Companies:
   State Street Bank, Quincy, Massachusetts; American Telephone & Telegraph (AT&T), and
   its Subcontractor, Comm-Tract Corporation

Unions:
   Local Union No. 103, International Brotherhood of Electrical Workers (IBEW); Local
   Union No. 4340, Communications Workers of America (CWA)

Background

This case involved a jurisdictional dispute the NLRB heard and decided pursuant to the
requirements of Section 10(k) of the Labor Management Relations Act.

In 1991, State Street Bank had contracted with AT&T to install a fiber optic communications system in its buildings in Quincy, Massachusetts. AT&T subsequently
subcontracted with Comm-Tract Corporation, a local electric firm, to install fiber optic
cable between several buildings at the State Street Bank complex. The job included
bringing the cable into the Palmer Building, the main building; terminating the cable
at a switch panel there; and completing the necessary splicing, testing, and documentation. Comm-Tract began work on the project in early November 1991. The employees
performing the work were covered by a collective bargaining agreement between
Comm-Tract and Local 4340 of the Communications Workers of America (CWA),
effective November 1990 through November 1993.

State Street Bank had also contracted with Massachusetts Electric Construction
Company (Mass Electric) to perform certain other electrical wiring installation work
inside the Palmer Building. Mass Electric's employees were represented by Local 103
of the International Brotherhood of Electrical Workers (IBEW). Mass Electric had no
contract with AT&T covering the work subcontracted to Comm-Tract.

On November 15, 1991, Comm-Tract's President, Joseph Pitts,[1] received a telephone call from a Comm-Tract employee, Roger Blodsoe. Blodsoe said that a problem
had arisen at the job site with Local 103, and he asked that a union shop steward come
to the site. The following Monday, November 18, Pitts met at the job site with Blodsoe.
Also present were CWA Local 4340 Shop Steward Vernon Ternhula who also was an
employee of Comm-Tract, and IBEW Local 103 Business Agent Bill Hogarty. Hogarty
said that although he did not have a problem with Comm-Tract being on the job site,
he felt that Local 103 Shop Steward Dirk Kaminski "might have a problem." Kaminski
was not at the job site at the time.

On November 21, Comm-Tract employee Doris Schoenberg met Kaminski as she
was picking up panels that had been left by AT&T to be installed by Comm-Tract.
Kaminski told Schoenberg that he "had a big problem" with the employees represented
by the CWA being on the job; that the CWA "was not supposed to be there," and if the

---

[1]The names of all individuals are disguised.

CWA employees remained, it was possible that the IBEW employees "would walk off the job."

Schoenberg reported this confrontation to her CWA shop steward, Vernon Ternhula. Ternhula, in turn, called Joseph Pitts and asked Pitts to speak with Kaminski. Pitts did so, and in a telephone conversation with Kaminski, Kaminski told Pitts that the CWA "did not live up to community standards;" that "this work had to be performed by Local 103;" and, "if Comm-Tract employees continued to perform the work, employees represented by Local 103 would walk off the job." Pitts asked Kaminski if IBEW Local 103 was claiming this work and if that meant that Comm-Tract and the CWA could not perform it. Kaminski responded, "Yes!"

On the same day, Pitts met with Burt Lewin, a State Street Bank vice president. After conferring, they contacted Jeremy Wolf, a general foreman with Mass Electric whose IBEW Local 103–represented employees were also working in the Palmer Building. Burt Lewin asked Wolf whether the Mass Electric employees could "supervise" the Comm-Tract employees in their duties. Wolf called his manager, who told Wolf that this would be "featherbedding," and "Local 103 would not permit it." After getting this report from Wolf, Lewin asked Wolf if Mass Electric employees could complete the work under the "supervision" of Comm-Tract employees. Wolf again consulted his manager, and was told this arrangement would be permissible. When this solution was proposed to Comm-Tract's president, Joseph Pitts, Pitts soundly rejected the idea.

On November 22, Pitts and CWA Local 4340 District Director Paul Merchette went to the job site and met with Dirk Kaminski and Bill Hogarty of IBEW Local 103. Hogarty said that the dispute concerned "community standards," but he added that it was more involved because Local 103 had $200 million in pension fund money in the State Street Bank, and in turn, Local 103 should get the work at the State Street Bank. Kaminski stated, "It's our work, we want it, and that's the direction from the Local and all of our members!"

Before leaving, Merchette noticed that several AT&T employees represented by IBEW Local 2222 were working on a major switch in the Palmer Building. He asked why they were there. Kaminski replied, "They belong to IBEW; that's okay."

To prevent any disruption on the project, Burt Lewin, VP of State Street Bank, requested AT&T to remove the Comm-Tract employees from the job site. AT&T informed Joseph Pitts of this request, and the Comm-Tract employees were told to stop work at the site. It was generally agreed that the remaining work would take the IBEW workers about one and one-half days to complete.

Shortly thereafter, Comm-Tract and Local 4340 of the CWA jointly filed unfair labor practice charges against Local 103 of the IBEW claiming that IBEW Local 103 had violated Section 8(b) (4) (D) of the Labor Management Relations Act.

General Contentions of the Parties

It was agreed that the disputed work primarily involved the installation of fiber optic cable between the buildings of the State Street Bank complex in Quincy, Massachusetts, through the existing manhole system, including splicing, terminations, testing, documentation, and the installation of voice and data systems.

IBEW Local 103 contended that State Street Bank, the owner of the job site, should be a party to the jurisdictional issue, because State Street Bank and not Comm-Tract had the "ultimate control" over assignment of the work in dispute. Local 103 had long maintained an ongoing relationship with State Street Bank. State Street Bank held all of the Local 103's pension and trust funds. In the past, employees represented by Local 103 had performed virtually all of State Street's electrical and related work, or it had been performed by other IBEW members. The AT&T company had been informed by Local 103's Business Agent Bill Hogarty that any State Street Bank electrical work belonged to the IBEW. Untimately, the decision to remove the Comm-Tract employees from the job site was purely a business decision made by AT&T at the request of State Street Bank. Local 103 contended that the unfair labor practice charges were instigated by Comm-Tract solely for the purpose of getting a broad order against Local 103. The NLRB should dismiss the unfair labor practice charges, and limit its determination of work jurisdiction only to the disputed work at State Street Bank.

However, Local 4340 of the CWA and Comm-Tract contended that AT&T had subcontracted with Comm-Tract to perform the work in dispute. AT&T had received a "Request for Proposal" (RFP) from State Street Bank specifying only that the work done on the project be performed by "union labor." The RFP did not specify any particular union or local union. Therefore, as a subcontractor, Comm-Tract had the discretion to assign the disputed work to whichever group of employees it desired. Comm-Tract decided to assign the work to employees represented by the CWA and its Local 4340. CWA Local 4340 and Comm-Tract claimed that there had been a number of prior jurisdictional confrontations of this nature with the IBEW. They cited several instances in which Local 103 had threatened that IBEW employees would walk off the job if Comm-Tract refused to assign certain electrical and telecommunications work to employees represented by the IBEW rather than to employees represented by the CWA. They urged that IBEW Local 103 had violated Section 8(b) (4) (D) of LMRA; that the NLRB should award the disputed work to the CWA; and that the Board should issue a broad order awarding this type of work to Comm-Tract employees represented by the CWA Local 1430 to cover any future disputes that might arise between all the parties.

Stipulations and Contentions Regarding the Disputed Work

1. *Certification and collective bargaining agreements.* Neither of the unions had been certified as the exclusive collective bargaining representative of Comm-Tract's own employees. However, since 1980 Comm-Tract had been party to a series of collective bargaining agreements with Local 4340 covering the installation of voice and data communications systems. The current collective bargaining agreement was effective November 1990 through November 1993. Comm-Tract sometimes used a hiring-hall arrangement with CWA Local 4340 to meet its employment/project needs. Comm-Tract had no contract or similar arrangement with IBEW Local 103.

2. *Employer preference and past practice.* Comm-Tract's president, Joseph Pitts, testified that his company preferred to use employees represented by Local 4340 to perform the disputed work, and that this had been its practice since 1980. Employees represented by Local 103 of the IBEW had never performed this

work for Comm-Tract. Comm-Tract's preference in this regard was uniform over all its projects. IBEW Local 103 contended that State Street Bank, owner of the site and the firm with the "ultimate control" over the assignment of the work, preferred that employees represented by Local 103 perform the work, because they had been doing similar work on the site for six years. Further, State Street Bank held all Local 103's pension and trust funds, and this represented a continuing relationship that both the bank and the union had fostered. State Street Bank, therefore, had properly preferred and requested AT&T and Comm-Tract to remove the CWA employees from the job site in favor of IBEW Local 103.

3. *Area and industry practice.* Both the CWA and IBEW concurred that they had contracts with various employers in eastern Massachusetts engaged in the installation and servicing of voice and data transmission systems, which was similar to the work in dispute.

4. *Relative skills.* Joseph Pitts testified that Comm-Tract employees were trained by his company in the use of its equipment, were highly skilled, and were performing work of acceptable quality to the satisfaction of the contractor in this dispute, AT&T, both at this site and at other sites. He further testified that in one instance, Comm-Tract had subcontracted five cable terminations to be performed by employees represented by IBEW Local 103. The employees represented by Local 103 were unable to perform these cable terminations, and the work ultimately had to be performed by Comm-Tract employees. Consequently, Comm-Tract's cost on the project had gone up drastically.

   IBEW Local 103's assistant training director, Jason Gallone, testified that Local 103 had a four-year telecommunication apprenticeship program in Massachusetts that had been registered at both the state and Federal levels. In addition to on-the-job training, IBEW apprentices received 150 hours of in-class training per year. In his view, IBEW-trained employees were more skilled and better trained than employees represented by the CWA.

5. *Economy and efficiency of operation.* Joseph Pitts testified that it was more efficient and economical for his company to assign the work in dispute to its own employees represented by CWA Local 4340, because they were specifically trained in the operation and use of his company's own equipment. Representatives of IBEW Local 103 asserted that employees represented by it had been performing voice and data installation at the State Street Bank site for six years, and that they had a general knowledge of the job especially important when performing post-installation warranty work.

6. *Prior jurisdictional awards or agreements.* The NLRB had previously decided a jurisdictional dispute involving Comm-Tract, the CWA, and IBEW Local 103. In this case,[2] the Board had awarded the installation of telephone and data systems equipment, including associated cabling and connections, to the Comm-Tract employees represented by the CWA rather than to the employees represented by Local 103. The Board had made this determination relying on the employer's

---

[2] *Electrical Workers IBEW Local 103 and Comm-Tract,* 289 NLRB 281, 128 LRRM 1285 (1988).

collective bargaining agreement, the employer's preference, area practice, relative skills, and the economy and efficiency of operations.

Comm-Tract President Joseph Pitts testified that on at least two other jobs in eastern Massachusetts in 1989 and 1990, the IBEW had directed threats at Comm-Tract similar to those made in this case, which had resulted in downtime on the projects and lost work for Comm-Tract employees.

Questions

1. Study carefully the provisions of Sections 8(b) (4) (i) and (ii), 8(b) (4) (D), 10(k), and 10(1) of LMRA. Discuss why the NLRB was directed by these parts of the Act to give priority handling and determination of disputes involving Section 8(b) (4) violations.

2. Did IBEW Local 103 violate Section 8(b) (4) (D) in this case? Why, or why not?

3. When required to make a jurisdictional determination, the NLRB typically will consider the following factors in deciding which union to award jurisdiction over disputed work: (1) certification and collective bargaining agreements; (2) company preference and past practice; (3) area and industry practice; (4) relative skills; (5) economy and efficiency of operation; and (6) any prior jurisdictional awards or agreements concerning the type of work in dispute. Weigh each of these in this case concerning the IBEW and CWA and make an overall determination to award the cable system work to which union.

4. Should the NLRB limit its jurisdictional award to this case, or should the Board make a broad determination to cover possible future disputes? Discuss.

CASE 35
A "WORK PRESERVATION" OR "CEASE DOING BUSINESS" ISSUE?

Company:
   Kutis Funeral Home, Inc., St. Louis, Missouri

Union:
   Miscellaneous Drivers, Helpers, Healthcare, and Public Employees Union, Teamsters
   Local Union No. 610

The Unfair Labor Practice Charges

The company was a funeral establishment in the St. Louis, Missouri, area. The union had represented a bargaining unit of the firm's limousine and hearse drivers for over 40 years. The parties' most recent collective bargaining agreement was effective from July 1, 1989, to June 30, 1992.

In early 1991, the company filed unfair labor practice charges against the union alleging that the union had violated Sections 8(b) (4) (i), 8(b) (4) (ii) (A), and 8(e) of the Labor Management Relations Act by entering into an agreement, maintaining a grievance, and seeking to enforce through arbitration and judicial action a provision (Article XVI, Section 18) in the parties' bargaining agreement that provided:

> Any funeral establishment hiring full-time chauffeurs may make first-call body removals for all other Employers who also hire full-time chauffeurs, and may do the same for other nonhiring firms. In all other respects, the previous practice of renting and trading livery equipment between all signatories to the contract shall prevail.

This same provision was included in a number of collective bargaining agreements the union had negotiated with several funeral service and other establishments in the St. Louis metropolitan area.

Background

The company normally employed three drivers. Because it had more limousines and hearses than it had drivers, it was not uncommon for the company to require additional drivers and sometimes vehicles (livery) on busy days. When it required an additional driver for a vehicle it owned, the company used a driver from a permanent board of extra drivers known as the "extra board" administered by a joint committee of the union's representatives and representatives of funeral service establishments signatory to bargaining agreements with the union, including the Kutis company. The extra board was composed of approximately five or six drivers who were available to employers, like the company, whose need for drivers and vehicles might fluctuate.

The 1989–92 bargaining agreement between the company and union included terms and conditions of employment covering extra board drivers. This agreement, as well as other similar collective bargaining agreements with other firms referred to as union signatories, required signatory employers either to call an extra board driver directly when seeking an additional driver, or to use a referral service operated by the union. All these agreements gave referral preference to extra board drivers. The company participated, along with other signatory firms, in making monthly fringe benefit contributions on behalf of extra board drivers and in administering the board. In the event of layoff, the company's drivers had the contractual right to go on the extra board.

In previous years when the Kutis company needed both extra drivers and vehicles, it had sometimes initially attempted to borrow manned equipment by trade from other firms that had contracts with the union. The usual understanding was that the favor would be returned by trade, if possible, when the trading partner so requested. When equipment was not available by trade, however, the company would have to secure equipment and drivers elsewhere. Prior to April 1990, the company had generally met its needs in such circumstances by renting drivers and equipment from Hoppe Livery Company, with whom the union also had a collective bargaining relationship. However, if employees represented by the union at Hoppe were unavailable, Hoppe management then assisted the company in obtaining drivers and equipment from nonunion sources, or the Kutis company did so directly. In April 1990, Hoppe went out of business. Thereafter, if the Kutis company was unable to secure drivers and equipment from its usual trading partners, it simply used nonunion personnel as it had in the past.

After Hoppe's demise, the union insisted that before using nonunion drivers, the company must first attempt to trade with Hoffmeister Mortuaries, Inc., a signatory to a similar collective bargaining agreement with the union. The union insisted that this was consistent with Article XVI, Section 18, the so-called trading provision of the company's collective bargaining agreement with the union. When the company declined to trade with Hoffmeister because it had not done so in the past and because Hoffmeister was its major business competitor, the union filed a grievance against the company. The union pursued the grievance to arbitration, seeking an award that the company must obtain, as needed, "equipment and drivers from other signatories to the labor agreement." The union claimed in the arbitration hearing that its agreement with Kutis meant that the company could not use livery and drivers from nonunion firms before first seeking to trade with Hoffmeister.

On April 10, 1991, the arbitrator found that the trading provision in the parties' collective bargaining agreement "prohibits all signatory establishments from hiring nonunion livery without first resorting to trading." The arbitrator ordered that the company "is required to attempt to trade with Hoffmeister prior to resorting to hire of nonunion livery." When the company refused to comply with the arbitrator's award, the union filed suit under Section 301 of the LMRA seeking enforcement of the award in the United States District Court for the Eastern District of Missouri. That action was stayed by the District Court pending disposition of the unfair labor practice charges filed by the company against the union, which the NLRB heard on a priority basis as required under Section 10(1) of LMRA.

Position of the Union

The union acknowledged that as interpreted by the arbitrator in his award, Article XVI, Section 18, in the parties' collective bargaining agreement could be viewed as interfering with the company's preference of hiring extra chauffeurs from nonunion firms.

The arbitrator's decision upheld the negotiated provision that required the company to trade with and give preference to union signatories, such as Hoffmeister, before obtaining livery and drivers elsewhere. Stating this another way, the provision required the company not to do business with nonunion livery firms without first attempting to trade with union signatory Hoffmeister. Thus, the provision could be seen as falling within the proscription of Section 8(e) making it an unfair labor practice "to enter into any contract or agreement, express or implied, whereby such employer ceases or refrains or agrees . . . to cease doing business with any other person."

However, Section 8(e) applies only to contracts or agreements that have secondary objectives. An agreement with primary objectives, such as the preservation of existing bargaining unit work, does not violate Section 8(e). The union pointed to a U.S. Supreme Court decision[1] in which the court ruled that contractual provisions such as the one in dispute were lawful if the objective was a primary one, such as work preservation for an employer's union members. The Supreme Court had held:

> The touchstone is whether the agreement or its maintenance is addressed to the labor relations of the contracting employer vis-à-vis his own employees, or is intended to benefit union members generally.

The union asserted that in this case, the contractual provision and the arbitrator's award were primarily addressed to the labor relations and employees of the company, and were therefore lawful. The thrust of the Article XVI, Section 18 provisions was to preserve work opportunities for drivers on the extra board, because these drivers had contractual rights to drive vehicles traded or rented between employers who had contracts with the union. The extra board drivers became employees of the company when the company used their services, and they would be covered by negotiated wage rates contained in the bargaining agreement. The preservation of job opportunities for extra board drivers benefited the company's regular employees because these regular employees had the contractual right to be placed on the extra board during periods of layoff. Therefore, the extra board drivers were part of the "relevant work unit" for work-preservation purposes, which the NLRB had previously designated appropriate and necessary in cases of this nature.

The union maintained that the negotiated provision thus had a lawful primary objective of preserving work for the company's employees. When the arbitrator ruled in the union's favor and the company refused to comply with the arbitrator's decision, the union had properly sought enforcement of the arbitrator's award. The union urged that the company's unfair labor practice charges be dismissed by the NLRB, and the company be directed to comply with the collective bargaining agreement and the decision of the arbitrator.

Position of the Company

The company urged that the contractual provision in dispute was basically designed to benefit union employees of other firms and the union generally, rather than to preserve work for the company's own employees. As interpreted by the arbitrator, the provision

---

[1]*National Woodwork Mfrs. Assn.* v. *NLRB*, 386 U.S. 612, 645, 64 LRRM 2801 (1967)

had no direct bearing on the company's use of the extra board. The union had not sought an award pertaining to the company's decision to use, or refusal to use, the extra board. Rather, the arbitrator's award was directed at the company's refusal to trade vehicles and drivers with Hoffmeister, its chief competitor. In the company's view, the role of the extra board was peripheral to the contractual provision at issue in the award. Use of the extra board by Hoffmeister in the trading process would arise only if Hoffmeister's own employees were unavailable and Hoffmeister placed extra board employees on its payroll. As a result, the effect of the trading provision, as determined by the arbitrator and the union, was to benefit Hoffmeister's regular employees and not the employees of Kutis Funeral Home.

Further, the provision attempted to benefit and serve union interests generally, and this was its overriding objective. In the union's own written post-hearing brief to the arbitrator, the union had contended that the company's failure to trade with Hoffmeister eventually could lead to the following scenario:

> If a signatory employer has available equipment which sits idle while nonsignatory equipment and drivers are used, eventually the equipment which sits idle will be eliminated. Ultimately full-time drivers whose employers are unable to support a full-time driver with its own business will have to eliminate such positions, unless by trading with other signatories a sufficient level of combined business exists to justify the continued employment of the driver and maintenance of the equipment.

Thus, by its own words, the union's objective was to maintain job opportunities for union employees throughout the St. Louis area, not just for Kutis company employees.

In the company's view, therefore, the union's actions constituted a secondary boycott since the union was attempting to prohibit the company from using extra chauffeurs and vehicles from nonunion firms before attempting to obtain them from its unionized chief competitor. Article XVI, Section 18, as interpreted and applied by the arbitrator, was clearly a "cease doing business" provision in violation of Sections 8(b) (4) (i), 8(b) (4) (ii) (A), and 8(e) of LMRA.

The company urged that the NLRB sustain its unfair labor practice charges, and that the union be directed to withdraw its grievance and course of action aimed at enforcing the arbitrator's award.

Questions

1. The contested contractual provision had been negotiated between the parties and between the union and other firms, apparently without serious dispute until this case. The company had complied with the provision until the Hoppe firm went out of business. Should the fact that the company had complied with the provision for a considerable period of time make any difference in the NLRB determination? Discuss.

2. The arbitrator interpreted and applied the disputed provision in favor of the union's position. The union sought enforcement of the arbitrator's award through court action, and the court stayed its decision pending the ruling of the NLRB. Should the NLRB and/or the court defer to the arbitrator's award in this matter?

3. Evaluate the arguments of the union and of the company concerning the union's objectives, which the union asserted were work preservation for company employees, and which the company asserted were "cease doing business" with a nonunion employer. Which of these arguments do you find to be the most and which the least persuasive?

4. If the NLRB should decide in the company's favor, would this mean that the contested contractual provision was totally unlawful, or only unlawful as applied to the circumstances of this case? Discuss.

CASE 36
WAS THE ATTEMPTED CONSUMER BOYCOTT LEGAL?

Company:
   The Edward J. DeBartolo Corporation, Tampa, Florida

Labor Organization:
   Florida Gulf Coast Building Trades Council, AFL-CIO

Background

At the time of this case in 1980, the DeBartolo Corporation owned and operated East Lake Square Mall, a shopping center in Tampa, Florida. Approximately 85 tenant-merchants occupied the shopping center under conditions set forth in a standard lease with DeBartolo. Under this lease agreement, each tenant paid DeBartolo a set minimum rent. The standard lease further provided that each tenant's minimum rent would automatically increase 10 percent on the date each additional department store of a certain size or larger opened for business. In addition to the minimum rent, each tenant paid DeBartolo a percentage rent based on a percentage of the tenant's adjusted gross sales in excess of a set yearly figure.

The standard lease also provided that all tenants would pay a proportionate share of the costs of operating, maintaining, and repairing the common areas of the shopping center. Arrival of a new tenant in the shopping center would reduce each tenant's proportionate share. Additionally, tenants had to join and pay dues to a merchants' association, the purpose of which included joint advertising projects. DeBartolo, through the standard lease, exercised control over its tenants' construction work, business hours, signs, and equipment. Each tenant agreed not to use its premises in any way that might injure the reputation of the shopping center or interfere with the operations of the other tenants.

Wilson's Department Store was to become a tenant of DeBartolo's when it agreed to construct a department store that would connect to and become part of East Lake Square Mall. Wilson's contracted with the High Construction Company to build its store. High Construction Company was a nonunion general contractor that paid wages considerably lower than those paid to union building tradesmen in the area. The Florida Gulf Coast Building Trades Council was an association of AFL-CIO building trades unions in the area that had a continuing dispute with the High Company—as well as with several other nonunion contractors—concerning what the unions claimed were substandard wages and benefits paid by the nonunion contractors.

In early January 1980, several individuals hired by the Building Trades Council appeared at all four entrances of East Lake Square Mall to distribute handbills to everyone who was willing to accept them. The following was the message contained on each handbill:

PLEASE DON'T SHOP AT EAST LAKE SQUARE MALL. PLEASE.

The FLORIDA GULF COAST BUILDING TRADES COUNCIL, AFL-CIO, is requesting that you do not shop at the stores in the East Lake Square Mall because of the Mall ownership's contribution to substandard wages.

The Wilson's Department Store under construction on these premises is being built by contractors who pay substandard wages and fringe benefits. In the past, the Mall's owner, The Edward J. DeBartolo Corporation, has supported labor and our local economy by insuring that the Mall and its stores be built by contractors who pay fair wages and fringe benefits. Now, however, and for no apparent reason, the Mall owners have taken a giant step backwards by permitting our standards to be torn down. The payment of substandard wages not only diminishes the working person's ability to purchase with earned, rather than borrowed, dollars, but it also undercuts the wage standard of the entire community. Since low construction wages at this time of inflation mean decreased purchasing power, do the owners of East Lake Mall intend to compensate for the decreased purchasing power of workers of the community by encouraging the stores in East Lake Mall to cut their prices and lower their profits?

CUT-RATE WAGES ARE NOT FAIR UNLESS MERCHANDISE PRICES ARE ALSO CUT-RATE.

We ask for your support in our protest against substandard wages. Please do not patronize the stores in the East Lake Square Mall until the Mall's owner publicly promises that all construction at the Mall will be done using contractors who pay their employees fair wages and fringe benefits.

IF YOU MUST ENTER THE MALL TO DO BUSINESS, please express to the store managers your concern over substandard wages and your support of our efforts.

We are appealing only to the public—the consumer. We are not seeking to induce any person to cease work or to refuse to make deliveries.

FLORIDA GULF COAST BUILDING TRADES COUNCIL, AFL-CIO.

The DeBartolo Corporation filed unfair labor practice charges with the NLRB, claiming that the labor organization's handbilling, which requested that consumers cease doing business with all tenants of DeBartolo in its East Lake Square Mall, violated Section 8(b) (4) (ii) (B) of the LMRA. Pursuant to Section 10(l) of the Act, the Regional Office of the NLRB shortly thereafter petitioned the federal district court to issue an injunction to stop the handbilling pending final adjudication of the Board with respect to the matter. An injunction was issued by the Thirteenth Judicial Circuit, Hillsborough County, Florida, and the handbilling ended at that time.

Position of the Company

The DeBartolo Corporation first noted that Section 8(b) (4) (ii) (B) of LMRA makes it an unfair labor practice for a labor organization to threaten, coerce, or restrain any person with the object of forcing or requiring any person to cease doing business with any other person. In the company's view, the Building Trades Council violated Section 8(b) (4) (ii) (B) of the Act when, in furtherance of its primary dispute with the High Construction Company, it distributed handbills calling for a total consumer boycott of DeBartolo and the tenant employers leasing space at East Lake Square Mall. The DeBartolo company acknowledged that as a result of High's construction of a department store for Wilson's, the union could urge a total consumer boycott of Wilson's as well as High. This was true because the labor organization had a primary labor dispute with High involving the payment to its employees of alleged substandard wages and fringe benefits. But High was not a tenant of DeBartolo, did not operate department stores, and had no contract or business relationship with DeBartolo or any tenant other than Wilson's. Therefore, DeBartolo and the tenant employers other than Wilson's had no relationship to High and, as neutral persons, were protected by Section 8(b) (4) (ii) (B) from any secondary activity by the AFL-CIO labor organization.

The company then addressed that provision of Section 8(b) (4) of the Act that exempts from the secondary boycott prohibitions

> publicity, other than picketing, for the purpose of truthfully advising the public, including consumers and members of a labor organization, that a product or products are produced by an employer with whom the labor organization has a primary dispute and are distributed by another employer, as long as such publicity does not have an effect of inducing any individual employed by any person other than the primary employer in the course of his employment to refuse to pick up, deliver, or transport any goods, or not to perform any services, at the establishment of the employer engaged in such distribution.

The company claimed that this so-called publicity proviso—which allows a union to request consumers of secondary employers who in some way have a relationship to the primary employer in a labor dispute to bring pressure on the secondary employer to cease doing business with the primary employer—does not encompass activity against secondary employers who have no relationship with the primary employer. There was no "producer-distributor" relationship between High and DeBartolo or between High and the tenant employers other than Wilson's. In a previous NLRB case,[1] the Board held that unless there was a producer-distributor relationship, the publicity proviso of Section 8(b) (4) did not apply.

In summary, the DeBartolo company maintained that the AFL-CIO labor organization's handbilling constituted a secondary boycott that was not protected by the publicity proviso within the Act. The union should be found guilty of an unfair labor practice and ordered to cease and desist permanently from this type of activity.

Position of the Labor Organization

The Building Trades Council pointed out that the handbilling was conducted in an orderly manner without any picketing or patrolling. The handbilling did not have the effect of inducing any individual employed by any person other than the High Company to refuse, in the course of employment, to pick up, deliver, or transport any goods, or to perform any services. Since the labor organization had a continuing primary dispute with the High Construction Company, any effect of the handbilling was of a primary, not secondary, nature with the High Company.

The major argument of the Building Trades Council was that the handbilling was publicity (e.g., informational in nature) that was protected activity under the proviso to Section 8(b) (4) of the Act. The labor organization, citing the same precedent NLRB case as did DeBartolo, asserted that the mall tenants were connected with the "product" produced by the High Company for Wilson's store, because the tenants (including Wilson's) derived substantial benefit from each other's presence, and that this benefit

---

[1]The case cited was *United Steelworkers of America, AFL-CIO-CLC (Pet, Incorporated)*, 244 NLRB No. 6, 102 LRRM 1046 (1979).

was enhanced by the existence of the Wilson's store. DeBartolo, in turn, was related to its tenants, because DeBartolo was dependent upon their commercial success, which it attempted to secure by exercising certain controls over its tenants through leases. The labor organization contended that distribution of handbills directed at DeBartolo as owner of the mall was consistent with the Section 8(b) (4) proviso, and that including the tenants was legal because the mall and the tenants were perceived as one and the same by the public.

The labor organization urged that the Board construe the Section 8(b) (4) proviso to protect this type of handbilling in order to avoid generation of a substantial First Amendment issue under the U.S. Constitution. The Building Trades Council argued that the unfair labor practice charges filed by DeBartolo Corporation were without merit and should be dismissed.

Questions

1. Why is the question of a producer-distributor relationship crucial to the NLRB's decision in this case? Discuss.
2. Evaluate the labor organization's assertion that the case could involve a First Amendment issue under the U.S. Constitution. Should this be a consideration of the NLRB in deciding this type of case? Why, or why not?
3. Study the provision within Section 8(b) (7) (C) of LMRA that protects certain types of union informational picketing and publicity. What are the similarities and differences in this provision compared with the publicity proviso within Section 8(b) (4)? Discuss.

PART II

Case Problems in Union-Management Relations: Cases from Grievance Arbitration

Conflict Resolution, Grievance Procedures, and Arbitration*

The potential for conflict exists within every organization. This is true of families, business organizations, social groups, or government agencies. Conflicts may range from minor differences of opinion to open hostility resulting in physical violence. Yet, humane democratic institutions attempt to resolve intraorganizational and interpersonal conflicts in an orderly manner. While conflict can be destructive, and often is, it need not be. Differences of opinion, when openly confronted and fully aired, often lead to new understandings and subsequent improved relationships.

The resolution of conflict is critical to personal, group, and organizational viability. Conflict creates in both individuals and organizations tensions and diversions that hinder or prevent attainment of goals. Further, striving to attain goals in itself creates tension and conflict. It is imperative that conflicts be resolved in such a manner that attainment of goals of the organization will not be thwarted. It may be hoped that resolution of conflict will produce new understanding and harmony, which will help move the organization toward its goals at an increased pace.

While an organization is concerned with the attainment of its goals and objectives, individuals in the organization are also concerned about the attainment of their own goals and objectives. Hence, the potential for conflict between an organization and the individuals in it arises. A company's need for higher productivity may conflict with an individual's need for security in advancing years. Differences may develop over the relative importance of productivity and of length of service in determining layoffs. Not all individuals in an organization share the same objectives. Young employees place less importance on length of service in determining promotions than do older

---

*This section provides a brief introductory overview of major considerations and issues inherent in the grievance-arbitration process. It does not include, however, a discussion of the sizable body of law that has developed on the subject of labor arbitration. This topic usually is covered fully in major texts with which these cases are normally used. A selected bibliography is included at the end of this section.

employees. Interpersonal and intergroup conflict in the work force may develop from such differences.

Ours is a democratic society that places a high value on justice and the protection of individual rights. Democratic ideals are consistent with the concept of participation in organizations. Values attached to protection of human rights have stimulated the development of various mechanisms that aim to promote the administration of laws, policies, rules, and procedures in a humane and equitable manner, giving full consideration to human dignity and welfare.[1]

Approaches to Conflict Resolution

Concern for human rights in our society has resulted in the development of various means whereby injured parties may appeal decisions made by those exercising power over them. Almost every type of organization has developed one or more appeal procedures.

Most government agencies have appeal procedures that enable employees to seek redress from acts of agency administrators. Labor unions have internal procedures for the protection of members from harassment within their own ranks. For example, the International Union of United Automobile, Aerospace, and Agricultural Implement Workers of America has expended unusual effort to provide its members a fair opportunity for defense against union decisions concerning them, and has provided well-defined and speedy avenues of recourse in the event of alleged unjust acts by officers and administrators. Religious institutions have developed appeal procedures that provide members with avenues of recourse against the clergy or governing boards. For example, the Roman Catholic Church has formulated internal procedures that members may employ to seek redress.

Many business organizations also have appeal procedures, which exist in both union and nonunion companies. Many nonunion organizations have developed formalized problem-solving or complaint procedures that provide employees the right to appeal decisions made concerning them by their supervisors. In most instances, recourse may be sought all the way up through the organization to the president. Some nonunion employers are even offering opportunities for "juries" of employees to render final decisions in complaints that have gone through a number of steps without resolution.

Formalized appeal procedures seem to become more necessary as organizations become larger and more institutionalized. Further, the more demanding and urgent the goals and objectives of the organization, and the more they press on individuals, the less freedom an individual is able to exercise. The hierarchical and authoritarian nature of some organizations tends to produce dependency of the subordinate on the superior. Dependency, in turn, tends to create frustration in the individual seeking freedom of

---

[1] For an excellent discussion of the historical and legal background of the grievance-arbitration mechanism in labor relations, see Daniel Quinn Mills, *Labor-Management Relations,* 5th ed. (New York: McGraw-Hill, 1994), pp. 582–98.

self-expression on the job. Inability to exercise freedom of self-expression, in turn, may block the individual's search for satisfaction through work.

Thus, appeal procedures provide opportunity for individuals to exercise greater control over their environment and expand the opportunities to achieve personal goals through work. Such procedures give individuals a chance to contest those decisions or actions of management that employees feel are unfair and that violate their rights and the obligations of the employer.

Grievance Procedures

Appeal opportunities are generally formalized in unionized organizations in grievance procedures that are included in the collective bargaining agreement. These procedures vary considerably from organization to organization. Typically, however, they provide that, at the first step, the employee take the grievance to either the immediate supervisor or the union steward.[2] The supervisor, the steward, and the employee discuss the issue and, in many circumstances, arrive at an amicable settlement. Most grievances are settled on an informal basis at this first step. If the parties are unable to agree, either because the supervisor disagrees with the request of the employee or because the supervisor lacks authority to make a decision, the grievance is appealed to the second step of the grievance procedure. Typically, the grievance committee of the union and the plant superintendent or office manager attempt to reach a settlement. However, grievances that are not settled at the first step of the grievance procedure may not be settled at the second step either; they are then usually appealed to the third step of the grievance procedure. At this level, the handling of the grievance is quite formalized; the parties involved may include members of top management of the company and members of the national office of the union. An estimated 97 percent of all collective agreements in the private sector provide that, if the parties are unable to arrive at a decision at the third (or fourth) step of the grievance procedure, either party may petition for arbitration of the dispute by a third party.

The following is a typical grievance procedure that shows the various steps to be followed in processing a grievance to final resolution.[3]

Article III—Grievance Procedure and Arbitration
Section 1. An employee shall first question the immediate supervisor concerning a difference in the interpretation or application of particular clauses or provisions of this Agreement or any of its supplementals before it shall be subject to the grievance procedure herein defined.

---

[2]A distinction customarily is drawn in labor relations between a *complaint* and a *grievance*. A complaint refers to any feeling of injury or injustice, real or imagined, expressed or unexpressed. A grievance is a complaint that has been formally presented to the supervisor, union steward, or some other union official under the provisions of a grievance procedure, alleging a violation of the labor agreement.

[3]From 1989–92 Agreement between Western Auto Supply Company and Local No. 618 of the Automotive, Petroleum, and Allied Industries Employees' Union, Teamsters, St. Louis, Missouri.

Section 2.   The term "grievance" shall mean a dispute or difference involving the application or interpretation of any of the provisions of this Agreement. No grievance shall be accepted, adjusted, or acted upon unless it shall have first been presented in writing within five (5) calendar days from the date the act occurred which constituted the grievance, except when an employee is absent on any vacation or sick leave in which case the time limit may be extended, not to exceed a total of thirty (30) calendar days from the date the act occurred.

Step A.   The disputed question shall first be discussed by the employee and the employee's immediate supervisor within forty-eight (48) hours of the time of occurrence, Saturdays, Sundays, holidays, and absence due to illness excluded. If not resolved in this Step, it shall be referred to Step B.

Step B.   The grievance shall be discussed by an official representative of the Union and the District Sales Manager. The District Sales Manager shall give an answer in writing to the Union. If the grievance is not resolved within five (5) working days, it shall then be referred to Step C.

Step C.   The grievance shall be discussed by an official representative of the Local Union and the Regional Employee Relations Representative. If the grievance is not resolved within fifteen (15) days (this time limit may be extended by mutual agreement), the grievance shall then be referred to Step D.

Step D.   The grievance shall be discussed by an official representative of the Local Union and a representative of the Home Office Personnel Department. If the grievance is not resolved at this level within fifteen (15) days (this time limit may be extended by mutual agreement), the grievance shall then be submitted to arbitration as provided in Step E.

Step E.   Disciplinary action for failure to meet and maintain the Company's established productivity standards will be processed through arbitration only at the time and if the Company takes discharge action.

Step F.   The parties may agree to a local arbitrator. If the parties cannot mutually agree on a local arbitrator within five (5) days, then the parties shall request the Director of Federal Mediation and Conciliation Service to furnish a list of seven (7) names from which each party shall strike off three (3) and the person whose name remains shall become the arbitrator. While the grievance is being handled pending the decision, there shall be no strike or lockout, and the decision of the arbitrator shall be final and binding on the Union, on all bargaining unit employees, and on the Company. The arbitrator shall render his decision within thirty (30) days after the case is heard. The arbitrator shall not have the authority to add to, subtract from, or modify any of the terms of this Agreement or any supplemental hereto. The arbitrator shall not substitute the discretion of the Company or the Union, where such discretion has been retained by the Company or the Union, nor shall the arbitrator exercise any responsibility or function of the Company or the Union. Only a single grievance may be heard by the arbitrator at any one time, except by mutual agreement of the parties (Union and Company). It is further agreed that the expenses for the witnesses as parties to an arbitration shall be borne by the parties calling the witnesses. The expenses of the arbitrator shall be shared equally by the Company and the Union.

Section 3.   While differences are being considered by the arbitrator, all matters covered by this Agreement shall continue unchanged without interruption or interference with the regular conduct of the Company's business or the work of the employees pending final determination by an arbitrator.

Although used for numerous reasons, the following are among the most important purposes that grievance procedures serve. First, they serve to locate problems that exist in the relationship between the union and the company, and also to locate problems that exist within both organizations. Second, they tend to open the channels of communication between employees and management. They are especially helpful in stimulating communication upward from employees to management, often to the discomfiture of the managers! Third, the grievance procedure is the instrument that enables the parties to initiate action, to interpret provisions of the collective agreement, and to apply the contract to new and changing aspects of daily relations between the employees and management. Finally, it serves as a valuable source of information and data at contract negotiation periods.

Arbitration

Arbitration constitutes the final step in most grievance procedures. It begins where the other procedures leave off, since the parties are presumed to have explored alternatives of settlement and compromise before resorting to an arbitrator. When the parties turn to arbitration, they voluntarily agree to refer their dispute to an impartial third person. The arbitrator's determination will be made on the basis of the evidence and arguments presented by the parties, who agree in advance to accept the decision of the arbitrator as final and binding.

In the United States, grievance arbitration is essentially a voluntary system. Federal labor law does not require the parties to include an arbitration clause in their collective agreement. However, the NLRB and the federal courts normally will defer to private arbitration for the settlement of those disputes that occur during the life of a labor agreement, provided that there is no dispute involving a legal statute.[4] Thus, grievance arbitration is considered a voluntary process in the United States, since an arbitration clause is the result of negotiations between management and a labor union.[5]

Arbitration is usually viewed as a judicial process. However, the parties do influence this process by the internal policies that each has adopted with respect to it. For example, either the company or the union may follow a policy of carefully screening disputes that are referred to arbitration. Their objectives may be to present to arbitration only those cases that have merit and that the appealing party believes it has a good chance of winning. On the other hand, one or both parties may operate on a percentage basis. If they adopt this approach to arbitration, they may elect to appeal doubtful cases on the theory that arbitrators will tend to compromise. According to this reasoning, they expect to win certain points that they might otherwise have conceded. Of course, this approach to arbitration can be shortsighted; the theory that arbitrators will split decisions is generally not valid, since most arbitrators try to judge each case on the specific

---

[4] This principle was enunciated in a series of U.S. Supreme Court decisions in 1960, collectively referred to as the Steelworkers Trilogy. This principle was affirmed in a 1987 U.S. Supreme Court decision, *United Paperworkers' International Union, AFL-CIO,* v. *Misco, Inc.* (108 S.Ct. 364, 1987).

[5] Arbitration of a grievance as the final step of a grievance procedure is referred to as "rights arbitration," meaning arbitration of rights already established within a collective bargaining agreement. If an arbitrator is asked to render a decision that specifies contractual language, that is, that in effect establishes new terms of a contract, this is referred to as "interest arbitration."

issues involved in the case. Thus, while the arbitration process is essentially a judicial one, in certain respects it is an extension of collective bargaining.

Arbitration has become an important means for the resolution of conflict. First, it has prevented open conflict, which tends to be very costly in terms of income lost to workers and profits lost to companies. Second, arbitration creates a better climate for the resolution of disputes. The parties resolve, as a matter of principle, to settle their disputes amicably. It can promote a spirit of cooperation that tends to pervade the entire grievance-handling process. Third, the parties know in advance that if they do not settle a dispute between themselves, it will ultimately be settled by a third party. While this may, in a few instances, prevent the parties from behaving in a responsible manner, as a general rule arbitration helps foster mature dispute settlements. Finally, no-strike and no-lockout provisions in a collective agreement are possible only if an alternative means for final settlement exists. If a union gives up the right to strike and if a company gives up the right to lock out employees over a grievance during the life of the agreement, both must be assured that some other method for settlement of disputes is available.

Many years ago, Harry Shulman, former dean of the Yale School of Law and a distinguished labor arbitrator, summarized the role of arbitration and of the arbitrator in a classic statement:

> The arbitration is an integral part of the system of self-government. And the system is designed to aid management in its quest for efficiency, to assist union leadership in its participation in the enterprise, and to secure justice for the employees. It is a means of making collective bargaining work and thus preserving private enterprise in a free government . . .
>
> The important question is not whether the parties agree with the award but rather whether they accept it, not resentfully, but cordially and willingly. Again, it is not to be expected that each decision will be accepted with the same degree of cordiality. But general acceptance and satisfaction is an attainable ideal. Its attainment depends upon the parties' seriousness of purpose to make their system of self-government work, and their confidence in the arbitrator. That confidence will ensue if the arbitrator's work inspires the feeling that he has integrity, independence, and courage so that he is not susceptible to pressure, blandishment, or threat of economic loss; that he is intelligent enough to comprehend the parties' contentions and empathetic enough to understand their significance to them; that he is not easily hoodwinked by bluff or histrionics; that he makes earnest effort to inform himself fully and does not go off half-cocked; and that his final judgment is the product of deliberation and reason so applied on the basis of the standards and the authority which they entrusted to him.[6]

Limits and Objections to Arbitration

Voluntary arbitration is a valuable device for settling disputes during the life of a contract, when the arbitrator's function is primarily that of interpreting the language or intent of the parties. Both management and unions generally reject arbitration as a

---

[6]Harry Shulman, "Reason, Contract, and Law in Labor Relations," *Harvard Law Review* 68 (1955), p. 999.

method for determining the language of the contract. The contract is "law," since it represents critical areas of managerial and union decision making. Matters in dispute often are considered by the parties to involve issues of principle, rights, or prerogatives. Neither management nor unions wish to permit an outside third party to resolve such important issues. Not only do they fear losing control over their destinies, but they also fear that a provision of an agreement determined by arbitration could rarely, if ever, be changed. This apprehension is in contrast to their belief that, if an arbitrator's ruling on a clause of an existing contract indicates to a party that the clause is unsatisfactory, that party can hope to change or eliminate that clause in the next contract negotiation.[7]

Arbitration is most useful when the parties resort to its use sparingly and only as a last resort. Constructive conflict can lead to new insights and understandings by the parties. Settlements reached after serious discussion or negotiation also tend to be more acceptable than those imposed from outside. If the parties turn to an arbitrator primarily as a means to avoid a confrontation or to save face, they may be showing a lack of collective bargaining skills and the maturity essential for a satisfactory relationship. In fact, arbitrators often make comments about unsatisfactory grievance handling such as the following: "This case should never have gotten to arbitration," or "The parties should have been able to resolve this case themselves."

Arbitration Procedures

Arbitration clauses in collective agreements usually are individually tailored to meet the needs of each union-management relationship. Some contracts specify the services and procedures of the American Arbitration Association, as the provisions from the following contract demonstrate.[8]

Article IV—Arbitration

Section 2. In the event that either party hereto, within 60 days after completion of the Formal Grievance procedure aforesaid, elects to submit a matter described in the preceding section to arbitration the parties agree that the matter shall be so submitted, and agree that such submission shall be to one arbitrator. The parties shall endeavor in each instance within a three weeks' period to agree upon the arbitrator, but if unable to so agree, the arbitrator shall be designated by the American Arbitration Association upon the written request of either party. In either such event, the arbitration shall be conducted under the then obtaining rules of the Voluntary Labor Arbitration Tribunal of the American Arbitration Association. Each party shall pay for the time consumed by and the expenses of its representatives, and shall be equally responsible for the compensation, if any, of the arbitrator, and any other general administrative expense that may occur.

---

[7]See Frank Elkouri and Edna Asper Elkouri, *How Arbitration Works,* 4th ed. (Washington, D.C.: Bureau of National Affairs, 1985), pp. 342–65.

[8]From 1989–92 Agreement between the Communication Workers of America and Southwestern Bell Telephone Company.

However, the majority of arbitration provisions in collective bargaining agreements are more detailed and specific than the preceding example. The following arbitration provisions specify both the issues subject to arbitration and the authority of the arbitrator.[9]

Section 8—Grievance and Arbitration Procedure.

Step 4.   The employer will answer the grievance in writing after the third step within ten (10) working days. If the parties do not reach a satisfactory solution in Step 3 of the grievance procedure, either party may request that the matter be arbitrated. Such request must be made as follows:

1. Notice in writing of intent to arbitrate shall be delivered by the party seeking arbitration to the opposing party within fifteen (15) calendar days following the decision of Step 4 above. The notice shall set forth the place, date, time and nature of the occurrence upon which the grievance is based, and shall set out the particular portions of the working rules which it is alleged were violated or misinterpreted. If notice of intent to arbitrate is not delivered within fifteen (15) calendar days, the grievance shall be deemed abandoned.
2. Within fifteen (15) calendar days after the above notice is delivered, the parties will mutually agree upon an arbitrator or jointly obtain a list of seven (7) arbitrators from the Federal Mediation and Conciliation Service, and thereafter within twenty (20) calendar days after receipt of the list the parties will alternately and independently strike unacceptable arbitrators from a list with the last remaining arbitrator being selected. Once the arbitrator has been selected, the party requesting arbitration shall have ten (10) calendar days to notify the arbitrator of his selection and request available dates.
3. Employees shall not be paid for the time spent in attending an arbitration proceeding other than as a witness on behalf of the Company.
4. The jurisdiction and authority of the arbitrator shall be bound by the following:
   a. The arbitrator shall have the authority to determine the procedural rules of arbitration, and shall have the ability to make such binding orders as are necessary to enable him to act effectively. He shall observe the rules of evidence, and his decision shall be final and binding on both parties . . .
   b. The arbitrator shall have no power to add to, subtract from, or modify any of the terms of these Working Rules.
   c. In the resolution of disputes between the parties to these Working Rules, the arbitrator shall give no weight or consideration to any matter except the language of these Working Rules and the facts as presented.
   d. The arbitrator shall have discretion to reduce or raise the discipline imposed.
   e. The arbitrator shall have no power to establish or change any wage rates.
   f. The costs of the arbitrator shall be shared equally by the Utility and the Union.

Both the American Arbitration Association and the Federal Mediation and Conciliation Service have developed policies and procedures to govern arbitration cases they

---

[9]From 1987–90 Agreement (Working Rules) between the Board of Public Utilities, Kansas City, Kansas, and Local 53 of the International Brotherhood of Electrical Workers; District 71–Local 92 of the International Association of Machinists and Aerospace Workers; Carpenters District Council; and Painters District Council No. 3.

administer.[10] Further, the arbitration section of a collective agreement usually will contain a statement of policy indicating what types of disputes may be arbitrated and will outline other rules governing the conduct of arbitration proceedings. Issues that must be met in the arbitration clause or by agreement by the parties include:

1. What is arbitrable? Most agreements provide that any dispute arising out of or relating to the interpretation or application of the agreement may be submitted to arbitration. On the other hand, the parties sometimes wish to exclude certain matters from arbitration, such as wage rates or determination of production or piece rate standards.

2. How is the arbitrator appointed, and what procedures shall be followed if the parties are unable to agree upon an arbitrator? Shall the parties appoint a permanent arbitrator or a rotating panel of arbitrators to hear all disputes, or should an ad hoc arbitrator be appointed for each case dispute? Most arbitrators are certified and obtained through either the Federal Mediation and Conciliation Service or the American Arbitration Association.

3. What are the rules and procedures governing the conduct of an arbitration? This issue includes methods for initiating an arbitration, time and place of hearings, swearing of witnesses, representation by legal counsel, recording of the proceedings, filings of briefs, rules of evidence, time within which an award will be made, and to whom it shall be delivered. Most of these issues will be determined by the parties themselves, but sometimes the arbitrator will be asked to rule on such procedural matters.

4. Who bears the cost of an arbitration? Typically, but not always, the parties will agree to share equally in these costs.

Disputes are brought to arbitration by one of two routes: either by a "submission" from the parties, or by a "demand for arbitration" filed by either party. A submission agreement is a statement signed by both parties indicating the specific nature of the issue under contention and the specific relief that the injured party is seeking. A demand for arbitration is a formal request made by either of the two parties to the other for arbitration of an issue in dispute.

Among the major types of evidence and testimony presented and considered by arbitrators are:

1. The language of provisions of the agreement.
2. The intent of the parties in negotiating agreement provisions.
3. Past practice or precedents in handling similar or parallel matters.
4. Practices at other firms in the same industry or in other industries.
5. Equity or fairness in certain matters; "just cause" in disciplinary cases.

---

[10]See pamphlets: *Voluntary Labor Arbitration Rules of the American Arbitration Association* (New York: American Arbitration Association); and *Policies, Functions, and Procedures of the Office of Arbitration Services* (Washington, D.C.: Federal Mediation and Conciliation Service).

6. Arbitration rulings and precedents established by other arbitrators.

7. Industrial relations practices accepted as desirable or undesirable.

The American Arbitration Association has identified 10 common errors committed by parties in arbitration.[11]

1. Using arbitration and arbitration costs as a harassment technique.
2. Overemphasis of the grievance by a union or exaggeration of an employee's fault by management.
3. Reliance on a minimum of facts and a maximum of arguments.
4. Concealing essential facts; distorting the truth.
5. Holding back books, records, or other supporting documents.
6. Typing up proceedings with legal technicalities.
7. Introducing witnesses who have not been properly instructed on demeanor and on the place of their testimony in the entire case.
8. Withholding full cooperation from the arbitrator.
9. Disregarding the ordinary rules of courtesy and decorum.
10. Becoming involved in arguments with the other side. The time to try to convince the other party is before arbitration, during grievance processing. At the arbitration hearing, all efforts should be concentrated on convincing the arbitrator.

The parties to a dispute seek an award from the arbitrator. The purpose of the award is to provide a final and conclusive decision with respect to the controversy. The arbitrator must not exceed the authority given him or her under the terms of the collective agreement. Most agreements, for example, state in some way that the arbitrator may not add to, detract from, or otherwise modify any part of the collective agreement. Even if this is not specifically stated in a collective agreement, this restriction is generally implied in the submission of a dispute to the arbitrator. The award of the arbitrator is to be accepted by both parties, and it will be upheld in the courts unless the arbitrator exceeds the authority granted him or her by the parties, fraud or some other breach of ethics is proved, or the result is contrary to law (e.g., an arbitrator enforces an illegal union security provision).

Expedited Arbitration.   Expedited arbitration is a fairly recent and in some situations still an experimental approach designed to simplify and speed up the arbitration process. A typical arbitration will require several months or more to complete and cost each side thousands of dollars, when costs of personnel, lost time, and attorneys' and the arbitrator's fees and expenses are calculated. In fiscal year 1993, according to FMCS data, an arbitrator's fees and expenses alone averaged over $2,200 per case.

---

[11]American Arbitration Association, *Labor Arbitration, Procedures and Techniques* (New York, 1987), pp. 19–20.

Because of concern about arbitration costs and other factors involved, a number of steel companies and the United Steelworkers Union in 1971 agreed to a three-year experiment that they named "expedited arbitration" or "miniarb." The experiment was successful, and they subsequently incorporated this procedure into their collective agreements. Numerous companies and unions are currently utilizing this procedure. Expedited arbitration is also being utilized in the public sector, as illustrated by the provisions from the following "master agreement."[12]

C. Regional Level Arbitration—Expedited

1. The parties agree to continue the utilization of an expedited arbitration system for disciplinary cases of 14 days suspension or less which do not involve interpretation of the Agreement and for such other cases as the parties may mutually determine. This system may be utilized by agreement of the Union involved through its National President or designee and the Senior Assistant Postmaster General, Employee and Labor Relations Group, or designee. In any case, the FMCS or AAA shall immediately notify the designated arbitrator. The designated arbitrator is that member of the Expedited Panel who, pursuant to a rotation system, is scheduled for the next arbitration hearing. Immediately upon such notification the designated arbitrator shall arrange a place and date for the hearing promptly but within a period of not more than ten (10) working days. If the designated arbitrator is not available to conduct a hearing within the ten (10) working days, the next panel member in rotation shall be notified until an available arbitrator is obtained.
2. If either party concludes that the issues involved are of such complexity or significance as to warrant reference to the Regular Regional Arbitration Panel, that party shall notify the other party of such reference at least twenty-four (24) hours prior to the scheduled time for the expedited arbitration.
3. The hearing shall be conducted in accordance with the following:
    a. The hearing shall be informal.
    b. No brief shall be filed or transcripts made.
    c. There shall be no formal rules of evidence.
    d. The hearing shall normally be completed within one day.
    e. If the arbitrator or the parties mutually conclude at the hearing that the issues involved are of such complexity or significance as to warrant reference to the Regular Regional Arbitration Panel, the case shall be referred to that panel.
    f. The arbitrator may issue a bench decision at the hearing but in any event shall render a decision within forty-eight (48) hours after conclusion of the hearing. Such decision shall be based on the record before the arbitrator and may include a brief written explanation of the basis for such conclusion. These decisions will not be cited as a precedent. The arbitrator's decision shall be final and binding. An arbitrator who issues a bench decision shall furnish a written copy of the award to the parties within forty-eight (48) hours of the close of the hearing.
4. No decision by a member of the Expedited Panel in such a case shall be regarded as a precedent or be cited in any future proceeding, but otherwise will be a final and binding decision.

---

[12]From 1987–90 Collective Bargaining Agreement between American Postal Workers Union, AFL-CIO, and the United States Postal Service.

5. The Expedited Arbitration Panel shall be developed by the National parties, on an area basis, with the aid of the American Arbitration Association and the Federal Mediation and Conciliation Service.

Expedited arbitration is not a substitute for regular arbitration. It is usually employed to settle certain types of disputes at some agreed-upon step of the grievance procedure after the parties have not settled at a previous step, and then only after a joint labor-management committee agrees to the abbreviated procedure.

This arbitration technique is marked by informality. The hearing is usually conducted in the office or shop, sometimes at the workplace, rather than in a hotel room or other neutral site. The arbitrator may interview witnesses on the spot. The rules of evidence often employed in arbitration proceedings are considerably relaxed. The arbitrator normally renders his or her decision within 24 to 48 hours of the hearing. Sometimes the arbitrator renders it the same day, on occasion within minutes after the conclusion of the hearing. This is called a bench decision.

The procedure is more applicable to some cases than others. It has been most useful in settling minor disciplinary cases, although it has also been employed to decide nondisciplinary issues, including compensation and employee rights questions. It is less useful in resolving issues involving interpretation of the meaning of an important contractual clause or questions of principle. Some disputes involve issues so fundamental to the parties that one or both may refuse to submit them to an expedited arbitration. For example, questions involving the meaning of management or union "rights" provisions in the contract, subcontracting, or production standards are more appropriately resolved by a more thorough arbitration procedure.[13]

Although expedited arbitration normally is associated with settlement of rather minor grievances, some companies and unions are utilizing the concept for discharge and other selected cases where the parties wish to bring the arbitration process to a swift conclusion. Here the parties may well have a very thorough and formal arbitration hearing of the case matter, but the selection of the arbitrator, the scheduling of the hearing, and the rendering of the arbitrator's decision are all accomplished within a specified and relatively short period of time. The following "Expedited Procedure" is representative of this type of approach.[14]

Section 4(a). If a grievance involving the discharge of an employee shall have been submitted but not adjusted under Step 3, the following Expedited Procedure shall apply unless the Employer and the Union mutually agree to waive any of these provisions:

1. If the Union wishes to proceed to arbitration, it must give written notice to the Employer of its demand for arbitration within five (5) days after its receipt of the Employer's written reply following the Step 3 meeting.

---

[13]See Arthur A. Sloane and Fred Witney, *Labor Relations,* 8th ed. (Englewood Cliffs, N.J.: Prentice-Hall, 1994), pp. 290–91. Also see pamphlet, *Expedited Labor Arbitration Rules of the American Arbitration Association* (New York: American Arbitration Association).

[14]From 1985–87 Agreement between Anheuser-Busch, Inc., of St. Louis, Missouri, and Bottlers Local Union No. 1187, affiliated with the International Brotherhood of Teamsters, Chauffeurs, Warehousemen, and Helpers of North America.

2. The Employer will promptly notify the appropriate arbitrator selected as set forth below and schedule a hearing which is to take place within the five-day period following the Employer's receipt of the Union's demand for arbitration.
3. The arbitrator shall render a written decision within ten (10) days following the close of the hearing, and within sixty (60) days following the close of the hearing, the arbitrator will render a written opinion explaining the reasons for the decision.

In conjunction with any Expedited Arbitration hereunder, either party may, at its option, submit a pre-hearing brief. And, either party may, at its option, request a court reporter for the hearing at its own cost, unless both parties request a transcript, in which case the cost of the court reporter will be shared equally.

The decision of the arbitrator shall be final and conclusive on both the Employer and the Union. The arbitrator shall have no power to add to, detract from, or alter this agreement in any way. Pending final decision by the arbitrator, there shall be no action taken by either party to the controversy. Any expense incidental to and arising out of the arbitrations shall be borne equally by the Employer and the Union except as otherwise provided in this Article.

(b) Expedited Arbitration Panel—Within thirty (30) days following the effective date of this Agreement, and annually thereafter, the Employer and the Union shall select a panel of five (5) arbitrators designated to decide Expedited Arbitration cases under this Article. The panel of five (5) arbitrators shall be selected as follows: The Federal Mediation and Conciliation Service will be asked to provide five (5) lists of arbitrators with each list containing names of seven (7) names from the Midwest area comprised of the states of Michigan, Illinois, Indiana, Iowa, Arkansas, Kansas, Nebraska, and Missouri. One arbitrator will be chosen from each FMCS list by the procedure of alternating strikes—the party having the first strike on the first list will be determined by a coin flip and thereafter the party having the first strike on the remaining lists will alternate. The five (5) arbitrators thus chosen will constitute the Expedited Panel for proceedings under this Article.

(c) Selection of an Arbitrator from the Expedited Panel—The arbitrator for an Expedited Arbitration shall be selected from the Expedited Panel as follows: The five (5) arbitrators on the Expedited Panel shall be listed in alphabetical order and cases will be referred to the arbitrators in that sequence until a new Expedited Panel is chosen (for example, the first expedited arbitration will be referred to arbitrator No. 1, the second will be referred to arbitrator No. 2, the fifth will be referred to arbitrator No. 5, the sixth will be referred to arbitrator No. 1, the seventh will be referred to arbitrator No. 2, the tenth will be referred to arbitrator No. 5, and so on). However, in the event the arbitrator designated by this procedure is unable to schedule a hearing within the five-day time period provided for above, the case will be referred to the next arbitrator in sequence and so on until an arbitrator is designated who can schedule the hearing within the appropriate time period, and any arbitrator thus bypassed will not be designated again until his name comes up in the regular sequence. Provided further that in the event none of the arbitrators on the Expedited Panel is able to schedule a hearing within the five-day time period described above, then that case will be referred to the arbitrator on the Expedited Panel who is able to schedule the earliest possible hearing, and again the sequence of selection of arbitrators for subsequent cases will start with the next arbitrator on the list and any bypassed arbitrator will not be designated again until his name comes up on the regular sequence.

It is likely that expedited arbitration in one form or another will continue to be utilized in future years. Expedited arbitration that serves the mutual interests of the parties thus represents another form of conflict resolution that can foster a more constructive atmosphere in union-management relationships.

Grievance Mediation.[15] Another relatively new approach for dispute resolution is that of grievance mediation. Grievance mediation is a process by which a union and an employer, assisted by a mediator, seek to resolve grievances without resort to arbitration. It is typically used only after all other prearbitration steps in a contractual grievance procedure have been completed.

Proceedings before a grievance mediator are informal. The facts are brought out in narrative form, the rules of evidence do not apply, and no record is made.

The mediator attempts to settle the grievance by using techniques commonly associated with the mediation process, including private meetings with each party. The mediator encourages the parties to focus not only on the contract, but also on the problems underlying the grievance. If a settlement is not achieved, the mediator gives the parties an on-the-spot oral opinion as to how the grievance is likely to be decided if it goes to arbitration.

If the parties do not accept the mediator's advisory opinion, they are free to arbitrate. If they arbitrate, the mediator will not serve as arbitrator, and nothing said during grievance mediation, including the mediator's advisory opinion, can be used at arbitration.

It is normally recommended that grievance mediation first be tried for an experimental period of 6 to 12 months. During this period, the employer and union can determine from their own experience whether they wish to incorporate mediation into their grievance procedure on a long-term basis.[16]

Selected Statistics on Arbitration as Reported by the American Arbitration Association and the Federal Mediation and Conciliation Service

The American Arbitration Association reported that, of some 9,000 case awards issued through its services in calendar year 1986, 51 percent of the grievances were denied, 32 percent were upheld, and 17 percent were partially upheld and partially denied by the arbitrators. At the arbitration hearings themselves, 77 percent of the employers and 52 percent of the unions were represented by attorneys.[17]

---

[15]Most of this discussion has been excerpted and adapted from the brochure, *Grievance Mediation: An Alternative in the Resolution of Labor/Management Disputes,* as prepared and distributed by the New Spirit of St. Louis Labor/Management Committee and the St. Louis Community College of St. Louis, Missouri. Appendix C to this introductory section for Part II includes material concerning grievance mediation services available through the Federal Mediation and Conciliation Service (FMCS).

[16]See John C. Sigler, "Mediation of Grievances: An Alternative to Arbitration?" *Employee Relations Law Journal* 13 (Autumn 1987), pp. 266–85.

[17]From a letter to members of AAA Labor Panels by Robert Coulson, President of the American Arbitration Association, New York, January 20, 1987.

According to the Federal Mediation and Conciliation Service, in fiscal year 1993 its Office of Arbitration Services assigned some 32,000 arbitration panels, from which arbitrators were appointed in about two-fifths of the case panels assigned. However, the FMCS actually closed only 5,276 cases in FY 93, a number that was not significantly different from those during several previous years. The predominant issues involved in the cases closed were discipline/discharge (48 percent); seniority issues (11 percent); overtime issues (7 percent); and work assignment issues (5 percent). FMCS sample data for FY 93 indicated that the average elapsed time between the date of the filing of a grievance and the date on which the parties requested an FMCS arbitration panel was 96 days. The average elapsed time between the date an FMCS arbitration panel was requested and the date of the arbitrator's award was 217 days. Transcripts were taken at about 11 percent of the hearings, and post-hearing briefs were filed by the parties in slightly over 90 percent of the cases.[18]

Deciding Arbitration Cases from an Arbitrator's Point of View

The cases included in this section all resulted from actual disputes that were processed through grievance procedures in collective bargaining agreements, that remained unsettled, and that then were subsequently submitted to arbitration. In a condensed form, these cases provide the essential information available to the arbitrator. By studying the issues in such cases, one has the opportunity of experiencing actual arbitration situations and of arriving at one's own decisions with respect to the disputes. In so doing, however, it is desirable to follow certain principles that most arbitrators and practitioners of labor relations have come to understand as being appropriate to an arbitrator's decision-making responsibilities.[19]

In general, the three major aspects that an arbitrator must consider, in order of importance, are as follows:

1. What does the labor agreement say?
2. What is the role of past practices or precedents?
3. What standards of fairness or equity should be applied?

What Does the Labor Agreement Say?

It is usually recognized by the parties that a labor agreement is essentially a general outline for handling many problems and situations that arise during the course of an agreement, and that no contract could possibly cover all of them. Nevertheless, an

---

[18]From *Arbitration Statistics—Fiscal Year, 1993* (Washington, D.C.: Federal Mediation and Conciliation Service, March 1994).

[19]Parts of this section were adapted from Raymond L. Hilgert, "An Arbitrator Looks at Grievance Arbitration," *Employee Responsibilities and Rights Journal* 8, no. 1 (April 1995), pp. 67–73.

arbitrator is first of all bound to the wording and general interpretation of the agreement itself. As a rule, most arbitrators take a somewhat restrictive view when applying and interpreting a labor agreement. That is to say, they normally do not expand upon the meaning of a clause in the agreement unless there is some reasonable evidence that this is what the parties had intended.

What Is the Role of Past Practices or Precedents?

If a clause in a labor agreement is not clear, or if it is subject to ambiguous interpretation, most arbitrators will look to past practices or precedents for guidance to determine the intent of the parties. Past practices or precedents can become an extension of a labor agreement almost as if the parties had negotiated additional contract language accordingly. This does not mean that a past practice or precedent always is a permanent fixture and cannot be changed for good reasons. But if the parties have handled a certain problem or parallel problems along consistent lines on a number of occasions, an arbitrator usually is reluctant to make a ruling contrary to such a practice, just as an arbitrator would not choose to change the wording of a labor agreement.

What Standards of Fairness and Equity Should Be Applied?

The third and probably most subjective area of the arbitration process involves standards for fairness and equity to be applied in certain types of cases. This is especially true in discipline and discharge cases, since most labor agreements specify that a company may discipline or discharge an employee for "just cause" or "proper cause."

Over the last several decades, the majority of arbitrators have adopted in one form or another the "Seven Tests for Just Cause," which were first formulated by arbitrator Carroll R. Daugherty in the Enterprise Wire Company case (46 LA 359, 1966). These seven tests were posed in the form of questions that could be applied to the facts of any case involving discipline or discharge. A "no" answer to one or more of these questions presumably would signify that a standard of just (or proper) cause was not met, and the arbitrator, therefore, probably would set aside or modify the employer's disciplinary or discharge action. The seven tests for just cause are as follows:

1. Did the company give to the employee forewarning or foreknowledge of the possible or probable disciplinary consequences of the employee's conduct?
2. Was the company's rule or managerial order reasonably related to *(a)* the orderly, efficient, and safe operation of the company's business; and *(b)* the performance that the company might properly expect of the employee?
3. Did the company, before administering discipline to an employee, make an effort to discover whether the employee did in fact violate or disobey a rule or order of management?
4. Was the company's investigation conducted fairly and objectively?
5. At the investigation, was there substantial evidence or proof that the employee was guilty as charged?

6. Has the company applied its rules, orders, and penalties even-handedly and without discrimination to all employees?

7. Was the degree of discipline administered by the company in a particular case reasonably related to *(a)* the seriousness of the employee's proven offense; and *(b)* the record of the employee in his service with the company?[20]

One aspect that often is crucial in regard to the above tests is the matter of burden of proof in presentation of evidence. Most arbitrators believe that in discipline and discharge cases, the primary burden falls upon management to demonstrate from the preponderance of evidence available that what it did in a particular matter would be considered a reasonable course of action by a neutral or impartial person. Thus, in discharge and disciplinary matters, the cases most likely to go to arbitration, it becomes prudent for management to ask itself how a reasonable, neutral person would view what was done.[21]

APPENDIX C
PREVENTIVE MEDIATION, GRIEVANCE MEDIATION, AND ALTERNATIVE DISPUTE RESOLUTION SERVICES OF THE FEDERAL MEDIATION AND CONCILIATION SERVICE*

Preventive Mediation

Although not as highly visible as dispute mediation, the Service's preventive mediation programs are increasingly used effectively by labor and management. Preventive mediation is used to anticipate problems before they obstruct the collective bargaining relationship from functioning as it should. As the bargaining relationship continues throughout the term of an agreement, the need often arises for FMCS to assist in improving the day-to-day relationships between the union and the employer. The need for preventive mediation has become even more apparent in recent years as a number of influences have placed added stresses on the collective bargaining system.

---

[20]For an expanded discussion of these tests, see Donald S. McPherson, "The Evolving Concept of Just Cause: Carroll R. Daugherty and the Requirement of Disciplinary Due Process," *Labor Law Journal,* July 1987, pp. 387–403. See also, Raymond L. Hilgert, "Reflections of an Arbitrator: The 'Hot Stove Rule' for Imposing Discipline," in *Discipline and Grievances* (Bureau of Business Practice 603, June 1991), p. 9.

[21]In 1991, a national legal commission, called The National Conference of Commissioners on Uniform State Laws, proposed a new employment statute for states that would let most fired employees take their cases to a neutral arbitrator. This commission was a quasi-official body appointed and funded by the states. Under this proposed system of arbitration, an estimated 60 million additional workers could be covered, most of them so-called employment-at-will employees. A number of states already have passed arbitration statutes, and other states are considering the proposal. See "Tell It to the Arbitrator," *Business Week,* November 4, 1991, p. 109.

* Appendix C consists of adapted excerpts from publications of the FMCS, Washington, D.C.

Forces such as economic pressures brought on by recession, increasing competitiveness in the world economy, loss of market share, leveraged buyouts and other factors have changed the goals and strategies of today's employers and their labor forces. Changing technology and upheavals in the leadership of both unions and management have added to the challenges facing the collective bargaining system.

Federal mediators are in a unique position to aid the smooth application of collective bargaining by spending considerable time with both parties during the collective bargaining process. During this time, they are able to see first-hand the real relationships that exist between all parties involved, and are often able to identify problems that could be a source of trouble in the future. These potential obstacles are carefully noted and used later in consultations with both sides.

Often guidance from a respected third-party neutral is necessary to effectively forge better labor-management relationships. Federal mediators are called upon because of their experience with the parties during collective bargaining, and their suggestions are more likely to be accepted than those coming from either side.

Mediators utilize a variety of preventive mediation and training techniques, each designed to meet the differing needs of individual organizations.

Grievance Mediation

While FMCS cannot involve itself in the mediation of routine grievances per se, it can agree to mediate grievances in the context of a full-service approach toward the general improvement of sound relations or within a framework of a larger ongoing program. FMCS will use grievance mediation to help parties adopt better methods of conflict managing and resolution. The grievance mediation process can be used in conjunction with other FMCS services to reduce the stress associated with contract negotiations, particularly when the parties are encumbered by numerous unsettled grievance cases. FMCS's goal is to use the grievance mediation process as another means to fashion improved labor and management relationships.

FMCS Guidelines for Grievance Mediation

1. The parties shall submit a joint request, signed by both parties requesting FMCS assistance. The parties agree that grievance mediation is a supplement to, and not a substitute for, the steps of the contractual grievance procedure.

2. The grievant is entitled to be present at the grievance mediation conference.

3. Any time limits in the parties' labor agreement must be waived to permit the grievance to proceed to arbitration should mediation be unsuccessful.

4. Proceedings before the mediator will be informal and rules of evidence do not apply. No record, stenographic, or tape recordings of the meetings will be made. The mediator's notes are confidential and content shall not be revealed.

5. The mediator shall conduct the mediation conference utilizing all the customary techniques associated with mediation including the use of separate caucuses.

6. The mediator has no authority to compel resolution of the grievance.

7. In the event that no settlement is reached during the mediation conference, the mediator may provide the parties either in separate or joint session with an oral advisory opinion.

8. If either party does not accept an advisory opinion, the matter may then proceed to arbitration in the manner and form provided in their collective bargaining agreement.

Such arbitration hearings will be held as if the grievance mediation effort had not taken place. Nothing said or done by the parties or the mediator during the grievance mediation session can be used against them during arbitration proceedings.

Alternative Dispute Resolution

In late 1990, two pieces of legislation were signed into law by President Bush that have had great impact on FMCS and its expanding role in Alternative Dispute Resolution.

The first Act, the *Administrative Disputes Resolution (ADR) Act of 1990,* required that each Federal agency develop a policy for institutionalizing mediation and other forms of conflict resolution as an alternative to costly litigation proceedings. Along with developing a policy for the use of ADR, all agencies were ordered to appoint a dispute resolution expert and provide ADR training to appropriate staff.

The second Act, the *Negotiated Rulemaking Act of 1990,* encouraged all agencies to utilize the regulatory negotiations, or reg-neg, process in developing agency rules. Both Acts contained specific provisions for FMCS to proffer its personnel for training, consultation, systems design, and third party neutral services to all federal agencies. In particular, the ADR Act also required all agencies to submit their policies to FMCS, along with the Administrative Conference of the United States, for review and comment. While no funds were appropriated for this work, FMCS was allowed to charge for its services via interagency agreements.

FMCS responded to these new responsibilities by appointing the Director of Field Services and Training to design FMCS participation and nine field mediators to act as district coordinators and contact points for the new program. FMCS held an ADR Conference to discuss with the District ADR Coordinators what this new legislation meant to the field mediator and the work of the agency.

Selected Bibliography

Allen, Robert E., and Timothy J. Keaveny. *Contemporary Labor Relations*. 2nd ed. Reading, Mass.: Addison-Wesley, 1988.

Ballot, Michael, with Laurie Lichter-Heath, Thomas Kail, and Ruth Wang. *Labor-Management Relations in a Changing Environment*. New York: John Wiley & Sons, 1992.

Begin, James P., and Edwin F. Beal. *The Practice of Collective Bargaining*. 8th ed. Burr Ridge, Ill.: Richard D. Irwin, 1989.

Bornstein, Tim, and Ann Gosline (gen. eds.), *Labor and Employment Arbitration, Vols. 1, 2, 3*. Albany, N.Y.: Matthew Bender, 1988.

Bowers, Mollie H., and David A. DeCenzo. *Essentials of Labor Relations*. Englewood Cliffs, N.J.: Prentice-Hall, 1992.

Brand, Norman. *Labor Arbitration: The Strategy of Persuasion*. New York: Practising Law Institute, 1987.

Carrell, Michael R., and Christina Heavrin. *Collective Bargaining and Labor Relations: Cases, Practices, and Law*. 3rd ed. New York: MacMillan, 1991.

Code of Professional Responsibility for Arbitrators of Labor-Management Disputes. National Academy of Arbitrators, American Arbitration Association, and Federal Mediation and Conciliation Service.

Colosi, Thomas R., and Arthur Eliot Berkeley. *Collective Bargaining: How It Works and Why*. 2nd ed. New York: American Arbitration Association, 1992.

Coulson, Robert. *Labor Arbitration—What You Need to Know*. Rev. 3rd ed. New York: American Arbitration Association, 1986.

Elkouri, Frank, and Edna A. Elkouri. *How Arbitration Works*. 4th ed. Washington, D.C.: Bureau of National Affairs, 1985.

Fairweather, Owen. *Practice and Procedure in Labor Arbitration*. 3rd ed. Washington, D.C.: Bureau of National Affairs, 1991.

Fossum, John A. *Labor Relations: Development, Structure, Process*. 6th ed. Burr Ridge, Ill.: Richard D. Irwin, 1995.

Fossum, John A., ed. *Employee and Labor Relations—Volume 4 of the SHRM–BNA Series on Human Resource Management*. Washington, D.C.: Bureau of National Affairs, 1990.

Grievance Arbitration in the Federal Service. Huntsville, Ala.: Federal Personnel
   Management Institute, 1987.
Hill, Marvin, Jr., and Anthony V. Sinicropi. *Evidence in Arbitration.* 2nd ed. Washington,
   D.C.: Bureau of National Affairs, 1987.
Hill, Marvin, Jr., and Anthony V. Sinicropi. *Remedies in Arbitration.* 2nd ed. Washington,
   D.C.: Bureau of National Affairs, 1990.
Kagel, Sam. *Anatomy of a Labor Arbitration.* 2nd ed. Washington, D.C.: Bureau of National
   Affairs, 1986.
Kalet, Joseph E. *Primer of Labor Arbitration.* Washington, D.C.: Bureau of National Affairs,
   1989.
Labor Arbitration Awards. Chicago: Commerce Clearing House.
Labor Arbitration in America: The Profession and the Practice. New York: Praeger and the
   American Arbitration Association, 1992.
Labor Arbitration: Procedures and Techniques. New York: American Arbitration Association,
   1987.
Labor Arbitration Reports. Washington, D.C.: Bureau of National Affairs.
Labor Law Course. 26th ed. Chicago: Commerce Clearing House, 1987.
Leap, Terry L. *Collective Bargaining and Labor Relations.* New York: Macmillan, 1991.
Levin, Edward, and Donald Grody. *Witnesses in Arbitration: Selection, Preparation, and
   Presentation.* Washington, D.C.: Bureau of National Affairs, 1987.
Mills, Daniel Quinn. *Labor-Management Relations.* 5th ed. New York: McGraw-Hill, 1994.
Mills, Daniel Quinn, and Janice McCormick. *Industrial Relations in Transition.* New York:
   John Wiley & Sons, 1985.
Redeker, James R. *Employee Discipline: Policies and Practices.* Washington, D.C.: Bureau of
   National Affairs, 1989.
Sandver, Marcus Hart. *Labor Relations: Process and Outcomes.* Boston: Little, Brown, 1987.
Sauer, Robert L., and Keith E. Voelker. *Labor Relations: Structure and Process.* Columbus,
   Ohio: Charles E. Merrill, 1987.
Sloane, Arthur A., and Fred Witney. *Labor Relations.* 8th ed. Englewood Cliffs, N.J.:
   Prentice-Hall, 1994.
Volz, Marlin M., and Edward P. Goggin. *1985–89 Cumulative Supplement to Elkouri and
   Elkouri How Arbitration Works, 4th ed.* Washington, D.C.: Bureau of National Affairs,
   1991.
Zack, Arnold M. *Grievance Arbitration: Issues on the Merits in Discipline, Discharge, and
   Contract Interpretation.* New York: American Arbitration Association, 1992.

Index to Cases for Part II

Index to Cases for Part II (continued)

Index to Cases for Part II (*concluded*)

Case Number and Title	Management Rights	Union Rights and Activities	Seniority and Employee Rights	Discipline and Discharge	Work Assignments/Job Bidding	Job Performance	Change/Past Practices	Wages and Benefits	Employee Health, Safety, and Security	Discrimination/Sexual Harassment
66. Demoted or Reclassified?	X	X	X	X	X	X		X		
67. Voluntary Resignation, or Layoff?	X		X	X				X		
68. No Official "Writing" of Termination	X	X		X		X				
69. Escorting the Union Representatives	X	X					X			
70. Temporary or Probationary?	X	X	X				X			
71. The Doubtful Worker	X		X	X	X	X			X	
72. The Recalled Management Trainee	X	X	X		X					
73. The Right to Bid Down	X		X		X		X			
74. Taking Care of Union Business	X	X		X	X	X				
75. Terminated for Possessing a Gun	X		X	X					X	
76. Forced to Work on a Holiday	X		X		X		X	X		

216

CASE 37
THE DISPUTED TEST

Company:
Star Manufacturing Company, St. Louis, Missouri

Union:
International Brotherhood of Teamsters, Chauffeurs, Warehousemen, and Helpers of America, Local No. 688

On April 14, 1982, Roy Camp,[1] a setup operator at Star Manufacturing Company, submitted the following grievance to his supervisor:

> The company has disqualified me from the model template and sample maker job. I feel that I can effectively perform the duties outlined in the job description.
> Settlement Requested: Granted a 90-day trial period as described in the job bid.

On April 21, plant superintendent Robert Decker replied to Camp and the union as follows:

> After considering testimony given in the grievance hearing of April 20, 1982, with regards to Roy Camp's qualifications for a model maker position, please be advised of the following:
> Consideration was given to Camp's work experience, along with the results of job-related tests that were administered by the company. These were then compared with the qualifications required to be able to perform the duties of the position in question.
> It has been concluded that the grievant lacks the overall ability to fulfill all the requirements of this job. This lack of ability includes areas that are critical to the basic performance of the job.
> Therefore, the grievant's job bid and grievance are being denied.

The parties were unable to resolve the dispute and, as provided in the collective agreement, they submitted the case to an arbitrator for a final and binding decision. The parties agreed that the arbitrator should address the following issue:

> Did the Company violate the Agreement by not awarding Mr. Camp the position of model maker on which he was senior bidder and by not giving him a reasonable trial period on this job? If so, what should be the appropriate remedy?

Background

Roy Camp had been employed by the company since 1973 and had been a setup operator since 1979. In describing his job he stated that it included such functions as reading and interpreting engineering blueprints, making setups on machines, and operating a number of machines, such as the shearing machine, punch press, and brake press machines. Camp had a good work record with no disciplinary problems. He also

---

[1] The names of all individuals are disguised.

received extra compensation as a "lead man." He was one of 12 setup men performing duties similar to his.

The job of model, template, and sample making[2] was performed in a laboratory area separate from production operations. Camp stated that he had worked in the lab area on a number of occasions and that he had assisted several model makers whom he had known down through the years. While the model maker's job paid the same wage rate as the setup operator's job, Camp had bid on the former job in order that he "might learn something new and different." He said that the model maker operated many of the same machines and tools as a setup operator, and that it would not be difficult to learn the additional machines on which model makers work. He added that he had already operated much of the equipment in the lab. According to Camp, a model maker primarily makes the templates (patterns) used in making the production items and from which a setup operator works in setting up and adjusting machines in the manufacturing process. The model maker develops a "prototype of what is manufactured in the plant."

Camp bid on the model maker's job in April 1982. He was the senior bidder on the list of those who bid on the position. Several days later he was administered a written test by the chief engineer, Joseph Shell.

Shell described the test as one requiring applicants to answer questions about various prints, to read caliper and micrometer measurements, and the like. The test placed special emphasis on visualizing and conceptualizing three-dimensional drawings. There were 10 questions, requiring about 45 minutes to complete. Camp failed the test and was so notified about a week later. Shell later reviewed the test results with Camp, who felt that he had answered 7 of the 10 questions correctly. Shell, however, informed him that he lacked an essential skill in that he didn't have "the visual concept."

At the request of the union, Shell administered a second test to Camp. This test included a number of exercises in which he was required to make forms, shapes, and items from drawings. Shell informed Camp that he had also failed the second test and that he had "no visual concept for form or views." Camp disagreed with Shell's evaluation of his abilities because he had "to work from blueprints as a setup person." He stated that he did have to visualize three dimensions from drawings in his present job. Further, as a setup operator it was necessary for him on occasion to make new parts or modify existing parts and dies. He claimed that a setup operator must be able to visualize and that he could learn the visualization that was necessary for the model maker's job.

Testimony and Position of the Union

The union contended that the positions of setup operator and model maker were quite similar, although there were some important differences. For example, the model maker works from "beginning to end on each new model, puts the parts together, and tests the model to ensure that it functions as originally conceived." The union steward, Gino Bertelli, argued that the best experience for becoming a model maker would be to work as a setup operator. He also stated that to his knowledge, no black employee, such as

---

[2]See the appendix to this case for job description and relevant contractual provisions.

Camp, had ever risen to the position of model maker. Bertelli stated that he had reviewed Camp's test results and felt that he had performed adequately to warrant a 90-day trial in that position. He also reviewed the test results of Robert Peters, the second most senior setup operator who successfully passed the test, and felt that he had done "only about equal" to the test performance of Camp. The steward noted that a model maker could readily obtain assistance and help from the engineers and inspectors if a model maker had a problem with a job assignment. While he minimized the significance of the test results, he acknowledged that tests had been used for many years for the model maker's job. Bertelli pointed out that the company had also used a similar test for the position of inspector since 1968. Camp had taken that test in 1975 when he had bid on the job of inspector. He had failed that test; the company, nevertheless, gave him a trial period to qualify for the job. He successfully completed the probationary period for the position of inspector. And, subsequently, he was promoted to the job as a fully qualified inspector. Bertelli argued that Camp would qualify as a model maker, if given the 90-day trial period, in the same fashion as he had earlier qualified for the inspector's position. He claimed that Camp had earned the opportunity to try out for the position of model maker and should not be denied that opportunity because of race.

The position of the union was summarized in a post-hearing brief. Relevant excerpts from this brief follow:

> Roy Camp was the senior qualified person bidding on the model maker job. The company's entire case is based on the subjective opinion of Joseph Shell that Camp was unqualified because he failed to prove on the tests to Mr. Shell that he had the ability to "visualize" properly. They did not in any manner contend that "relative" ability played a part in the management's decision to place the recently hired Leo Kelly in the model maker job since the collective bargaining agreement clearly is of the modified type which provides that the senior employee shall be given preference if he possesses sufficient ability. Under this clause the question simply is, "Can the employee in fact do the job?" In this case the company has admitted that no employee can step immediately into the model maker job and perform it. Training is necessary.
>
> The union strongly believes that the company violated the intent of Article VIII by *solely* relying on the test results to determine that Camp was not qualified. The union has never contested the right of the company to administer a test to employees to aid management in determining an employee's ability to do a job. The key is that the test results must be *only one* of various methods and means of determining the issue of ability. In the instant case the company *solely* relied on the test results as judged by Mr. Shell.
>
> Elkouri and Elkouri in *How Arbitration Works* (1973 edition) state: "It must be kept in mind that arbitrators generally take the view that while the test may be used as an aid in judging ability or as a "verification" of ability, the employer may not base his determination of ability solely upon the results of a test but must consider other factors and other evidence."
>
> The union believes that the company failed to consider the grievant's excellent past performance in the job of "setup" which admittedly is one of the best training grounds for a model maker job. Mr. Camp's past experience was not given due consideration. Because the grievant on a couple of questions failed to convince Mr. Shell that he had the "visualization" ability, the company has unfairly prevented him from expanding his job future. The evidence is clear that the model maker position is a stepping-stone to a management position. Mr. Camp believed he had all the qualities and abilities to become a good model

maker just as he had become a good setup person. Undoubtedly had Mr. Camp been required in 1975 to pass a test for "setup" he would have failed, just as he failed an identical type test for the inspector's job.

Elkouri and Elkouri in their book *How Arbitration Works* state on page 583: "Agreements sometimes provide for a trial or break-in period on the job to determine ability, and questions in connection with the interpretation and application of such provisions are frequently arbitrated. In the absence of contractual provision, the question arises as to whether management must give the senior employee a trial. Obviously, ability to perform the job, or the lack of it, may be demonstrated by a trial or break-in period on the job. As stated by arbitrator Carl A. Warns, "The best evidence as to whether an employee can do a job is to give him a fair trial on it." Arbitrator Vernon L. Stouffer stated, "The purpose of a trial period is to afford an employee the opportunity to demonstrate that he has the ability for the job in question or can with some familiarization therewith achieve the necessary skills within a reasonable period of time to perform the job in an acceptable manner."

The grievant and the union have from the very beginning of this dispute only asked that the company give Mr. Camp a trial period. Article VIII, Section (e) of the contract clearly protects both parties and contemplates the use of such a trial period. The union urges that the company has been unfair in not utilizing the trial period provision.

Thus, arbitrators generally are inclined to the view that if there is a reasonable doubt as to the ability of the senior employee and if the trial would cause no serious inconvenience, it should be granted, but that a trial should not be required in all cases.

In order for management to fairly use test results, the test itself must be prepared, administered, and graded fairly and objectively. It is the union's belief that in the instant case the company has failed to prove that the above criteria were observed. Mr. Shell continually used the phrases "lack of ability to visualize" or "no visual concept" as demonstrating why he considered that Mr. Camp failed the test. But this observation by Mr. Shell is his subjective *opinion.*

For all of the above reasons, the union strenuously urges the sustaining of this grievance.

Testimony and Position of the Company

The company first made considerable effort to establish the credibility and testimony of chief engineer Joseph Shell by pointing out that he had been employed by Star for 26 years, that he was an electrical engineer, that he had served as plant manager for several years, and that he had been "accepted as an expert in numerous federal and state trials as a professional engineer."

In discussing Camp's performance on the test, Shell described the test as made up of 10 questions. Six of the questions were concerned with flat planes; Camp answered five of the six correctly. Three of the questions involved three-dimensional drawings and prints; Camp answered all three incorrectly. He stated that from the test results, he concluded that Camp was unable to "visualize parts in total and accumulate the kind of information necessary to perform the model maker's job adequately."

Shell stated that the model maker's job was different from the setup operator's job in three major respects: (1) the model maker must take sketches, prints, and verbal instructions from an engineer and convert these into parts (including their assembly) that had never before been produced; (2) a model maker must be able to make templates from a part and convert these to flat view sketches from which setup men adjust and set up various machines to produce items for production; (3) the model maker on occasion must also test various items produced from the sketches and drawings for electrical, chemical, and other properties. The test administered to Camp primarily addressed the first area, not the other two, which Shell claimed contained the primary differences between a model maker's and setup operator's job. The test primarily attempted to determine whether or not the applicant possessed the basic visualization skills necessary to perform the job. Management felt that it lacked the expertise to train a person to acquire conceptual skills and felt that this type of skill would be most difficult to teach under the best of circumstances.

Shell stated that after Camp and the union complained about the results of the first test, he agreed to give him a second test, although he had never done so before in this kind of situation. The second test contained five problems, of which Camp correctly answered two and correctly answered a third in part. Shell stated that the results of the second test confirmed those of the first—that Camp could not "visualize spatial dimensions," an ability that was absolutely essential for a model maker.

The company stated that Shell had administered basically the same test or tests to all other model makers in the plant since 1968. Those who were awarded the job of model maker had all passed the same test or tests as those given to Camp. These tests were "very practical and directly job related"; they included several blueprints and sketches typical of the work performed by a model maker.

Shell stated that applicants who failed the test were not promoted to the position of model maker. No one who had failed the test had ever filed a grievance in the 14 years that the testing procedure had been in effect.

The company pointed out that, as a result of Camp's grievance, it had employed an outside consultant to review the procedures and tests involved in this case. The consultant's report stated:

> In my opinion the testing procedure covers the various phases of the work which is to be accomplished, particularly since test questions are based upon common production parts, and is therefore fair.

Shell testified that Robert Peters, the second most senior setup operator, was awarded the vacant position of model maker, but he stayed on that job only a week before deciding to return to his former job as setup operator. Subsequently, Leo Kelly, who was also on the bid list, was given the same two tests as Camp and Peters. Kelly passed both tests successfully and was currently a model maker.

The position of the company was summarized in a post-hearing brief. Relevant excerpts from this brief follow:

> The contract is clear that this position is to be awarded, not on strict seniority, but to the senior "qualified" bidder. Consistent past practice has given this provision the meaning that, for the model maker position, the bidder "qualifies" by passing a test. This same practice has also consistently applied to the inspector position and was in 1980 extended to the setup position. On these facts it is difficult to see how the union can challenge the company's right to test model maker bidders.
>
> Therefore the union must be challenging, not the company's right to test, but the result in the particular case of grievant Camp. Fundamentally the integrity of the tests depends upon

the competence and integrity of the tester. The qualifications of Shell as an expert engineer were unrebutted and his testimony was unchallenged by any union witness with similar expertise. Normally judges and arbitrators accept the testimony of lay witnesses only as to what they saw or heard but not as to what they opine. The point of qualifying someone as an expert is that a tribunal is entitled to rely on that expert's opinion. The company submits that in an industrial setting both it and the arbitrator are entitled to rely on an engineer's opinion as to whether Camp passed tests within the engineer's competence to devise and judge. The union offered no expert testimony to the contrary.

The union noted that Camp failed the test for the position of inspector, at which he ably performed. But this does not show that the tests are unreliable. Camp's inspector test was taken in May 1975, over a year and a half before he was awarded the inspector position on January 20, 1977. Apparently he learned enough in that year and a half to become a successful inspector.

The union also argues that Camp's performance was similar to that of Peters, who passed. First, the company feels that it and the arbitrator are entitled to rely on the judgment of chief engineer Shell that Peters passed and that Camp failed. Moreover, we wish to point out that Peters did not exhibit the same consistent deficiency as Camp had. We concede that Peters' results were closer to those of Camp than to those of Kelly. Perhaps this is why Kelly is still on the job and Peters begged off after a mere week. If Peters, who tested better than Camp, lasted but a week, surely Camp was unqualified.

The union argued that Camp does not test well but he worked well. But chief engineer Shell took the test procedures from day-to-day work performed at the company. Therefore, if you can't do the test, you can't do the work. If Camp could not do the relatively simple visualization required on common production parts used in the test, how could he produce parts from more complex prints? An independent industrial engineer validated the job relatedness and fairness of its tests. The union offered no such evidence to the contrary.

Chief engineer Shell's tests and judgment of them were considered fair by all employees who passed and failed them since 1968. At least no one grieved until now. Moreover when the union in 1980 agreed to testing for the setup position, they knew that chief engineer Shell would conduct these tests as he had all others. If he or his tests had been considered unfair, the union would never have agreed to expanding his testing jurisdiction to yet another position.

The union made an unworthy effort to claim racial discrimination. The truth is that these same tests have been given to employees, black and white, for years. When a black passed the test, no white grieved his being awarded the position. When a white failed the test, he accepted this result. Only Camp has grieved. In fact the only racial discrimination here is that, for the first time in its history, the company gave a bidder (Camp) two tests, something it had never done for a white employee. Instead of discriminating against Camp, the company bent over backward for him.

Moreover if one compared the union's description of the model maker's duties with Shell's description, one would never guess they were the same position. For purposes of this grievance the union portrayed the model maker as a glorified setup man. If that is all the model maker was, there would be no separate classification. Shell's description of the model maker's duties shows both the importance of the position and the reason for testing.

Finally, the union bore and failed to carry its burden of proof that the company violated the contract.

The company urged the arbitrator to deny the grievance.

APPENDIX
RELEVANT PROVISIONS OF THE CONTRACT

Article VIII—Job Vacancies

(a) All job vacancies or new positions and the number thereof shall be posted for a period of two (2) working days. Eligible employees not at work at the time of posting shall be notified by registered mail or telegram of the opening and will have two working days after receipt of such notice in which to notify the company of their intention to bid for such opening, provided that they return to work within 30 calendar days of the original posting of such an opening.

*   *   *   *   *

(c) Employees shall be entitled to bid on such jobs, and the job shall be awarded to the senior qualified employee bidding therefor within a period of five (5) working days and shall be paid at the appropriate rate of pay. If the senior employee bidding for the opening is not qualified to perform the work satisfactorily, the job shall be awarded to the next senior qualified employee who has bid for the job, subject to the grievance procedure. No employee's bid for an opening will be considered unless it would represent a movement to a job of the same or higher rate of pay, except by mutual agreement of the parties.

*   *   *   *   *

(e) An employee awarded a job through the foregoing bidding procedure shall be given a fair trial for a period not to exceed 90 days, but it shall at the end of a fair trial be decided by the Employer (subject to the grievance procedure) that such employee cannot adapt to the new position, or if the employee desires, he or she shall be returned to his or her former position at the rate of pay for that position.

RELEVANT JOB DESCRIPTION

Model, Template, and Sample Making.   Under the direction of his supervisor, the model, template, and sample maker performs duties including, but not limited to, the following:

1. Uses hand tools, power tools, power machinery, spot-welders, grinders, etc., and employs soldering and brazing and other techniques to produce models, templates and samples as required.
2. Reads drawings and is able to make parts and templates from prints, sketches, and verbal instructions or sample parts.
3. Performs other experimental and testing work as directed by the Chief Engineer and his assistants.
4. Must furnish and be proficient in the use of his own tools.
5. Keeps daily time card.
6. Maintains orderly working area.

THE JOB BID POSTED ON THE COMPANY BULLETIN BOARD

JOB BID

DATE POSTED_____4-06-82_____
TIME POSTED_____11 A.M._____
If qualifications are in doubt test will be given.
PROGRESSION RATE SCHEDULE
$6.67–$8.31

HOURS OF WORK * Unless otherwise stated, the hours of work will be the same as those worked by the general factory work force.

TRIAL PERIOD * Unless otherwise stated, the trial period will be from five (5) to ninety (90) days.

BIDS ARE TO BE TURNED IN TO A FOREMAN OR TO THE PRODUCTION OFFICE.

Questions

1. Is the job of model maker different from that of setup operator? If so, how? Are these differences significant to this case?

2. What was the skill that the company contended that Camp lacked?

3. Arbitrators often have applied the "head and shoulders" principle in some of their cases. This principle advocates that in certain selection or promotion decisions, the seniority of an employee should be the decisive criterion, unless a junior-seniority employee is significantly superior to a higher-seniority employee in ability and merit. Should this principle be applied to the circumstances of this case? Why, or why not?

4. Did the company have a duty to grant Camp a 90-day trial period? Why, or why not?

CASE 38
THE FORBIDDEN NUPTIALS

Company:
Distribution Center of Columbus, Inc., Columbus, Ohio

Union:
Columbus Warehouseman's Union, Local No. 102

Mark Fuller[1] was hired by the Distribution Center of Columbus in February 1978. He was terminated on November 22, 1983, because on October 22, 1983, he had married a fellow employee, Irene Fraser. Fraser had been hired by the company in June 1976; on November 22, 1983, she had seven years and five months' seniority, while her spouse had five years and nine months' seniority. The company terminated Fuller, the less senior of the two, for having violated an administrative policy prohibiting the employment of related persons.[2]

Background

Having met while employed by Distribution Center, Fuller and Fraser began dating, and in April 1983 began living together with full knowledge of the company both informal in that their supervisor knew of it, and formal by reason of Fraser's changing her address on company personnel records to Fuller's.

The administrative policy in question was an internal management document. It was not collectively bargained, nor was it part of the published work rules that were made available to employees when hired and that were posted, but its existence had been rumored among employees, including Fuller and Fraser. However, it had never been seen in written form by any of the employees, nor by any union official, until Fuller made a formal inquiry to his supervisor. He was furnished a copy on October 19, only a few days before the couple was married.

Both Fuller and Fraser were classified as warehousemen. Neither supervised the other. Both had received awards for attendance for the first six months of 1983, and neither presented any disciplinary problems. Both were considered very good employees. If Fuller had not married Fraser, he would not have been terminated by the company.

Position of the Union

The union argued that the company had no right to enforce its policy when that policy had not been clearly communicated to employees. The union also argued that the policy was unreasonable, unjust, and contrary to public policy. Fuller and Fraser did not learn

---

[1]The names of all individuals are disguised.
[2]See the appendix for relevant provisions of both the contract and the administrative policy.

of the policy until they made formal inquiry and even then they received a copy only three days before their marriage. The right of management to make reasonable rules does not override the "just cause" protection provided in the collective bargaining agreement.

The union urged the arbitrator to order the company to rehire Fuller with full back pay and seniority, to restore any rights and privileges lost as a result of the company's action, and to remove all reference to this disciplinary action from his personnel records.

Position of the Company

The company contended that the discharge of Fuller was for "just cause," because he had knowingly violated the company's long-standing "no-spouse," antinepotism policy. The policy was a reasonable one and was supported by substantial business considerations. Further, the policy had been enforced in the past and should also be enforced in this instance. The labor agreement itself provided that the company could make and enforce reasonable rules and regulations.

The company argued that, if the union's position were sustained in this case, this decision would abrogate the policy with respect to all present employees and seriously jeopardize the company's ability to protect itself against the detrimental effects of spouses working together.

The company urged the arbitrator to deny this grievance in its entirety.

Appendix
Relevant Provisions of the Contract

Article III—Management Rights

The company retains the right to make and enforce reasonable rules of conduct and regulations not inconsistent with the provisions of this Agreement. However, such rights can only be exercised to the extent that the express provisions of this Agreement do not specifically limit or qualify this right.

The company agrees that disciplinary action, including discharge, shall be only for just cause.

Relevant Provisions of the Administrative Policy Manual

Distribution Centers, Inc., has a policy which prohibits the employment of anyone who is related to another Distribution Centers Associate. This policy is a common practice which many companies adopt for a number of sound reasons, some of which are as follows:

1. Avoiding difficulties in scheduling work where two relatives desire the same hours of work.
2. Preventing family matters from distracting Distribution Centers Associates from their job duties.

3. Minimizing absenteeism, where one relative must take time off to care for another.

4. Avoiding conflicts involving the Associate's loyalties to the spouse or other relatives and his obligation to the Company.

This policy was initiated in January of 1970 and exceptions were made for any relative on the payroll at that time.

For these reasons, the company will not hire or continue the employment of relatives of any existing Distribution Centers Associates or of their spouses regardless of location or facility involved excepting those hired prior to January 1970, as indicated above. The term relatives includes those related by blood or marriage, and if used in this policy, means spouse, parent, children (including foster and adopted), brother, or sister. Should two Distribution Center Associates become related to each other, whether by marriage, adoption, or otherwise, one must resign within 30 days thereafter. If neither employee resigns, the one with the least seniority with the company will be discharged.

Questions

1. Why did the company enact a rule prohibiting the employment of related persons?

2. Do you agree with the company's position on this issue? Why, or why not?

3. Were Fraser and Fuller adequately advised of the rule?

4. Regardless of its outcome, why is a case of this type difficult for management from a policy point of view?

CASE 39
THE PAYROLL ERROR

Company:
   Hermann Oak Leather Company, St. Louis, Missouri

Union:
   International Molders and Allied Workers Union, Local No. 59

Background

On December 7, 1982, foreman Charles Johnson[1] received written notice of a grievance from John Coffman, which stated:

> Company said they overpaid me for 22 weeks. They said I should have caught it and reported it to them. I feel that they fired me unjustly. I want to be paid average for all time lost.

And on the same date, Johnson received an almost identical grievance from Roger Bickford:

> Company said they overpaid me for 24 weeks. They said I should have caught it and reported it to them. I feel that they fired me unjustly. I want to be paid average for all time lost.

Both employees worked in the shipping area of the finishing department of Hermann Oak. Their jobs included measuring, rolling, binding, and shipping leather that had been processed from raw hides to finished leather. The company primarily was involved in tanning and finishing leather for sales to manufacturers. It employed about 50 persons in the tanning and finishing departments.

On Thursday morning, December 2, 1982, Anne Beck, payroll manager, informed Plant Manager Jack Rand that there had been a major error in piecework rates paid to two employees in the shipping department. It had been discovered while new piecework rates, to be effective in January 1983, were being programmed into the computer. Five different piece rates involving Bickford and Coffman had been programmed in error, resulting in overpayment to them. On the following day Beck reported to Rand that the overpayments had extended from June 1982 and averaged $35 per week but were as large as $67. Bickford had been overpaid a total of $840.88 during the 24-week period, and Coffman $780.64 during the 22-week period. (Coffman had been on two weeks vacation during that time.)

Rand met with Bickford and Coffman later that day and informed them they had been overpaid and would be told later what would be done. According to Rand, Bickford then turned to Coffman and said, "I told you so." Neither man denied receiving the overpayment. On the following Monday, both were presented copies of a compilation prepared by Payroll Manager Beck.

Subsequently that day, Rand and Beck met with Robert Henkle, president of Hermann Oak, and the company attorney to determine what action should be taken. A decision was made to terminate both Bickford and Coffman because both were considered guilty of major dishonesty.

---

[1]The names of all individuals are disguised.

The union appealed the company's action through the established grievance procedure without agreement. The case was submitted to arbitration. The parties agreed that the issue to be decided was as follows:

> Were the grievants, Coffman and Bickford, discharged for just cause? If not, what should be the appropriate remedy?

Testimony of the Grievants

Coffman testified that he had been employed by the company for 14 years, during 12 of which he had served as a union committeeperson and steward. He indicated that during those years he had been involved in contract negotiations and grievance meetings, and that he had engaged in many "heated discussions" and "yelling contests" with management. However, he claimed that he had never received any disciplinary actions for his work. He felt that the company had terminated him for his union activity. To support this contention, he claimed that on one occasion Rand had said "he'd get me" following a heated grievance meeting.

Coffman admitted that he had pleaded guilty of embezzlement of union funds in the U.S. District Court and had been placed on probation in return for 200 hours of community service and restoration of the monies to the union.

According to Coffman, he "didn't know anything" about being overpaid for 22 weeks in 1982 until he was informed by the plant manager to this effect on December 3, 1982. He acknowledged that he had lodged several complaints during the earlier months about not being paid enough. But he said that he and Bickford had checked their pay only for about the first five months of 1982; since most of the time company calculations were correct, both he and Bickford stopped challenging their paychecks rather than engage in "aggravating" the company.

He claimed that, during the meeting with Rand on December 3, the plant manager had said that "the company would figure out some plan of restitution," but that this opportunity had never been offered to him and Bickford. He further claimed that during a grievance meeting protesting his discharge, he offered to pay the money back on a weekly installment basis if he could get his job back, but his offer was not acceptable to the company.

Bickford stated that he had been with Hermann Oak for 16 years, during 10 of which he had served as a union committeeperson and steward. He, too, felt that he had been treated unusually harshly by management because of his union activities. He said that he had participated in many heated arguments during grievance meetings, and that he was not liked by several members of management because of his assertive behavior on behalf of his fellow union members. He stated that he had a good work record with the company.

Bickford testified that he had never been indicted nor charged with a crime by the grand jury, although he had been investigated by the U.S. Department of Labor for allegedly claiming and receiving more money from the union for negotiating time than he was entitled to collect.

He testified that he kept "a little black book" in which he kept detailed records of his piecerate earnings, but that he kept such records only at the beginning of each year until such time as he felt assured the company was correctly calculating piece rates. In 1982 he had stopped keeping records after satisfying himself that the company's calculations were generally accurate. He said that he was "not a good mathematician" and that his paychecks varied by as much as $50 from one week to another.

He said it was only reasonable that he attempted to determine his earnings on a daily basis, especially when errors in company records were likely to occur, but he claimed that he had stopped maintaining accurate records of daily earnings late in May 1982, and that he had no personal knowledge of the overpayments from June through December. Like Coffman, Bickford stated that during his first meeting with Rand on December 3, the plant manager had suggested that he would be allowed to make some form of restitution. However, subsequently the company refused to offer him this opportunity in exchange for reinstatement to his former job.

Position of the Union

Lester Norvell, international union vice president, argued on behalf of Coffman and Bickford, as well as for the interests of all other members of the union. He pointed out that two other employees were also overpaid during the two weeks that Coffman was on vacation, but that they had not been asked to refund the overpayments or disciplined in any manner. Neither Coffman nor Bickford had falsified their time cards. The principal problem with the miscalculation of their pay was the incompetence of management in programming the computer and the failure of the company to monitor the operation of its bookkeeping system. This was not only a classic case of "garbage in, garbage out" but also of slovenly attention to what was happening in the bookkeeping department. Neither Coffman nor Bickford was either a computer expert or an accountant. They had kept track of their earnings during the first few months of 1982, but did so with difficulty and the devotion of much time to the activity. They had uncovered several errors in payroll calculations, one as small as $1.33, but usually in the $5 to $10 range; after all, even $1.33 was important to a working man. However, after determining that their pay was being accurately calculated, they had been only too happy to stop keeping detailed records, which they did toward the end of May 1982.

Norvell pointed out that the collective bargaining agreement contained no provision, or even an implication, that required an employee to either compute his own pay or report an overpayment. He argued that the company discharged Bickford and Coffman because of their tenacious defense of the rights of their fellow union members under the terms of the collective agreement.

The union urged that both Bickford and Coffman be reinstated to their former jobs, that they be paid for all time lost, that all references to the company's unwarranted disciplinary action be removed from their personnel files, and that their seniority remain uninterrupted.

Position of the Company

The company charged that Bickford and Coffman were guilty of major dishonesty because both men clearly knew for an extended period of time about the overpayments. In support of this contention, Thomas Howell, assistant plant manager and superintendent of the finishing department, stated that he had observed both Coffman and Bickford figuring and maintaining a record of their pay. According to him, they maintained a "little black book" in which they recorded their pay; he had seen this book in discussions with them. He said they calculated their pay each day at the end of their shift and knew what was due them "to the penny." Both men had discussed discrepancies in their pay at least a dozen times, and when they did so, they always claimed underpayment. These discussions took place during the period of January to June 1982. During the period June to December 1982, they raised questions about wages paid to other employees, but did not question Howell about their own checks. Howell indicated that he had heard Bickford tell a fellow employee following the meeting of December 3, "Didn't I tell you I was being overpaid?"

Payroll Manager Anne Beck also indicated that she had discussed payroll matters with both Bickford and Coffman at least a half dozen times during the year. She claimed that both men calculated their pay on a regular weekly basis, and she cited several examples from payroll records when they had contested alleged payroll errors prior to June 1982. All of the amounts were less than $10. Three examples were:

1. April 1979: $1.33 due Bickford.
2. October 1979: $8.26 due Coffman and $8.54 due Bickford.
3. April 1981: $6.40 due Bickford and $6.25 due Coffman.

Beck also claimed that on many instances they had brought to her attention payroll matters in which they were proven wrong. These, too, were minor discrepancies, usually involving less than $10.

The company stated that only Bickford and Coffman had been disciplined because they were the only persons who had known they were being overpaid over a long period of time. Coffman and Bickford were the only two persons who were overpaid excessively during this period. Two other employees who had served as vacation fill-ins, for one week each, had had no reason to know of the overpayments. The company considered them innocent of dishonesty. Beck stated that she was not sure who had made the computer error, but she held that it was an "innocent mistake."

The company supported its contention that both men were dishonest by noting that Coffman had been found guilty of embezzling union funds in U.S. Circuit Court. And Bickford was under investigation by the U.S. Department of Labor for allegedly padding his expense account, potentially defrauding the union of a considerable amount of money; the charge was that he had claimed payment for more time spent in negotiations than he had actually devoted to that union activity.

The company acknowledged that both Coffman and Bickford were union officers, and that management found both men somewhat contentious in arguing the terms of the collective bargaining agreement and aggressive in supporting perceived rights of other union members. However, Plant Manager Rand stated that on no occasion had he or any other member of management ever said to either man, "I'll get your job." On the other hand, Rand admitted that he had written an official warning to Bickford, dated March 15, 1976, which placed him on final warning for his part in supporting a work stoppage. The company maintained that dishonesty, not union activity, had caused the company to terminate both employees.

The company argued that it was absolutely essential that employees in the shipping area be honest, since they measured and weighed valuable materials shipped to customers. Both men were responsible for reporting rate figures to the company on which the company relied.

In summary, the company argued that since both men calculated their own pay on a regular basis and had challenged the company on numerous occasions for errors, since they knew how to calculate their pay and regularly did so, they had knowingly accepted for many months overpayments to which they were not entitled. Such gross dishonesty could not be permitted in such responsible positions as held by both Bickford and Coffman.

The company urged the arbitrator to find the company's action reasonable and the discharge to be for just cause, and to uphold the termination of both Bickford and Coffman.

APPENDIX
RELEVANT PROVISIONS OF THE CONTRACT

Article VI—Management Rights

The direction of the work and the selection, promotion, and transfer of employees, except as limited in this Agreement or by law, shall lie with the Company. All employees shall observe rules and regulations made by the Company for the conduct of its operations. Any employee shall perform any service at any time in the Company's operations which he is required to and is in the opinion of the Company qualified to perform. Except as herein limited, the hours of labor, the assignment of duties and tasks and the general conduct and management of the Company and of its production processes and facilities, rest with the Company. Nothing herein shall be so construed as to impair or abate the right of the Company to change, modify, or cease its operations, processes, or production in its discretion; and in the event of such change, modifications, or cessations, the Company shall be the sole judge of all factors involved, including, but not limited to, the efficiency, usefulness, and practicability of machinery, processes, location of business, and personnel required by it. The Company will, however, discuss with the Union, on its request, any such change, modification, or cessation which would affect the wages, hours, or working conditions of the employees. The Union will not interfere with the sales policies of the Company or with its source of supplies of raw materials, equipment, supplies, power, services, or other articles and services required by it in its unlimited discretion.

Article VII—Seniority

4. Seniority shall be lost and employment may be terminated for any of the following:
A. Discharge for cause.

Questions

1. Did Coffman and Bickford knowingly accept monies to which they were not entitled? Discuss.
2. Should the responsibility for these payroll errors be attributed to the payroll manager? To Coffman and Bickford?
3. Are the past backgrounds of Coffman and Bickford of any direct relevance to the issues in this case?
4. Were the discharge actions justified? Why, or why not?

CASE 40
DO NEW HIRES INCLUDE REHIRES?

Company:
   Owens-Illinois, Inc. (Libbey Glass Division), Los Angeles, California

Union:
   American Flint Glass Workers, Local No. 705

Negotiating Background

During negotiations in 1983 for a new collective bargaining agreement that was to take effect November 16, 1983, the company presented a "two-tier" wage-scale proposal for all new hires. The union initially rejected the company proposal, and there was little or no discussion of the specific language in the company proposal. Throughout the negotiations, however, the company continued to press the union to accept the two-tier wage proposal. The chief negotiator for the company, Gus Triplett,[1] argued that the proposal did not affect any current employees, but would impact only "nameless, faceless people."

In the final agreement, the union reluctantly agreed to the two-tier wage provision, since it would be difficult for the union membership to take a strike over this issue, which did not affect current employees. Union negotiators, however, said they were opposed in principle to inclusion of the two-tier wage provision, because of the potential problems it could cause among employees in the future.

As drafted by the company and as included in the new collective bargaining agreement, the two-tier wage contractual provision was as follows:

Article 50—New Hire Wage Progression

All new hires in Schedule A (Excluding the Forming Department) shall be paid at a rate of $1.50 per hour less than the qualified rate for the job that they are performing. Such employees shall be increased by 25¢ per hour in each succeeding six months period. They shall also receive contractual increases as they occur.

Such an employee, who is laid off prior to having attained the maximum base rates of the job classification and who is reemployed at the plant within two years from the last day worked, shall receive a rate upon reemployment which has the same relative position to the maximum base rate of the job classification as had been attained by the employee prior to layoff.

Upon such reemployment, the credited rate progression period of the employee's prior period of employment at the plant shall be applied toward his rate progression the maximum base rates of the job classification.

An employee who has received the New Hire Rate Progression, is assigned or continues to be assigned to a job classification that has an extended training period, but has not completed the required time in such classification to receive the maximum base rate, will

---

[1]The names of all individuals are disguised.

continue at the current rate or the rate specified for time worked in such classification, whichever is higher. Thereafter, the specified time limits and rate schedule will be the same as those in the labor agreement for other than new hires.

The Grievance Dispute

In April 1984, Local Union President Miller Brooks first became aware of the problem that led to this grievance dispute. Brooks was contacted by employee Ellen Ferguson, who asked him, "What is going on?" She told Brooks that she had just recently been rehired and that she was making $1.50 less per hour than the other employees who were working in the same jobs. She indicated that there was a man in the warehouse at the same wage grade level who also had just been rehired by the company, and who was being paid $1.50 more per hour than she was getting. Brooks then visited the warehouse facility and talked with Willy Smith, the rehire that Ellen Ferguson had mentioned. Smith stated that he had been rehired by the company, and he was being paid the old rate of pay for the job.

Brooks next approached the company personnel director, Collin Miles, and informed her of the difference in pay between Ferguson and Smith. Miles then went to Willy Smith, and she told him that his pay would be reduced by $1.50 per hour in accordance with Article 50 of the labor-management agreement between the company and union.

About a week or so later, Emily Parker, another employee of the company, quit to take a test for the California State Highway Patrol. Ms. Parker failed the test, and two weeks later she returned and reapplied for a job. Upon rehire, Ms. Parker was informed that she would receive $1.50 less per hour. Several days later, Miller Brooks was approached by employee Penny Ward, who stated that her job was at the same wage level as the other three employees (i.e., Ferguson, Smith, and Parker). Ward reported that she had worked for the company, quit, and subsequently was rehired at a $1.50 per hour less rate of pay.

On July 19, 1984, Miller Brooks filed a grievance on behalf of the four employees; Brooks also inquired of company management to determine whether he had identified all the grievants in this dispute. Brooks was advised that the four grievants constituted all the rehires of the company at this time. After exhausting the grievance procedure, the matter was placed before an arbitrator for a final and binding resolution.

Position of the Union

Union witnesses pointed out that Article 50, the "new hire wage progression" provision in the contract, had been opposed by the union to the very end of the previous negotiations. The union finally gave in, because it would have been a difficult strike issue. Present employees were unwilling to strike about an issue that would not affect their wages.

Counsel for the union claimed that the words *new hire* did not mean or include *rehires*. Since 1965 the company had utilized the word *rehire* in the contract to identify those employees who were hired more than once. Article 22 in the present contract stated as follows:

Article 22—Retirement Program

*   *   *   *   *

Section 14.   Restoration of Service—An employee who is rehired by the Company and who then works at least three (3) years from the date of such rehiring shall be given credit toward pension rights for prior service with the Company provided such prior service with the Company was at least two (2) years.

Thus, an employee who was rehired and who worked at least three years from the date of such rehiring was given credit toward pension rights for prior service, provided such service was at least two years.

Counsel for the union pointed out that company management had proposed and written Article 50. During negotiations, reference was made by the company's chief negotiator to "nameless, faceless people," that is, people who had never worked at the company. The union submitted that the term *new hires* in Article 50 meant exactly that, hires that were new to the plant, not rehires. The grievance should be sustained, and the company should be ordered to reimburse the four grievants the full amount of lost wages as appropriate, which should be revealed by company records.

Position of the Company

Counsel for the company argued that the union was trying to read something into Article 50 that was never intended to be there. The company had drafted Article 50, but the parties really did not bargain about its wording. The union was not as diligent in regard to this matter as it should have been. The company claimed that a *new hire* and a *rehire* were the same thing. That is to say, the purpose of the two-tier wage system under Article 50 was to have a lower wage rate for all employees who were to be hired after the effective date of the new contract, irrespective of whether or not they previously had worked at the company.

Since the union had failed to negotiate any specific wage considerations for so-called rehires under the new two-tier wage system, rehires must be treated the same as new hires. This was the company's intent in developing Article 50. If the union desired to achieve certain rights and privileges for rehires, these should come through the collective bargaining process and not through the grievance-arbitration mechanism.

The company urged that the union grievance be denied.

Questions

1. Evaluate the union's position that the term *new hires* did not include *rehires.*
2. Evaluate the company's position that the term *new hires* was meant to include *rehires* under the new labor agreement.
3. Why is the negotiating background of this dispute somewhat contradictory to the resolution of the grievance? Discuss.
4. Does it make any difference in interpreting Article 50 that the current and previous contracts between the parties contained special provisions for rehires? Why, or why not?

CASE 41
THE PREGNANT LABORATORY ANALYST

Company:
   Cities Service Company, Lube Plant, Lake Charles, Louisiana

Union:
   Oil, Chemical, and Atomic Workers International Union, Local No. 4-500

Background

Lisa Hall[1] was first employed by the Cities Service Company (hereafter referred to as CITGO) in July 1979, as a laborer in the Lake Charles plant. About two years later, she bid on and was awarded a job in the laboratory department. There was only one job classification in the laboratory, that of *analyst*. This job, however, was divided into three job assignments—*tester, sampler,* and *utility pool*—and such assignments were based on seniority progression. The most desirable job was a tester, who worked at a laboratory table using various chemicals. The tester's job required little physical exertion. It was also the most interesting and challenging of the three jobs. On the other hand, it also presented a potential health hazard to those few persons who were allergic to certain toxic chemicals utilized in the tests, even though the laboratory was well ventilated, was outfitted with modern safety equipment, and utilized state-of-the-art safety procedures. The sampler's duties required considerable physical exertion as the samples had to be collected throughout the plant and brought to the laboratory. The utility pool employees worked as samplers, on the sampler truck, or at the testing table to fill in as needed.

Exercising her seniority rights, Ms. Hall had bid for and been awarded the position of analyst on July 1, 1981. She was assigned to duties as a sampler. In August or September 1981, Hall became pregnant. After becoming pregnant, she attempted to continue her work on the sampler truck, but soon discovered that the physical exertion, climbing and lifting, caused her to have cramps and to bleed. She approached her supervisor, Robert Jenkins, and requested that she be allowed to transfer into the utility pool, where there were some vacancies at the time. Hall said that she felt that she could perform the job assignments in utility without difficulty, since she had previously worked in that area and knew that a sustained level of physical exertion was not required. Furthermore, she knew of two other women who had worked in the utility pool almost the entire term of their pregnancies.

Hall's request was denied by supervision on the grounds that Article III, Section 6(i), of the labor agreement stated, "After an employee is awarded and/or accepts a permanent job vacancy, he is not eligible to bid for one (1) year unless he is disqualified from his new assignment."[2] Ms. Hall then requested a transfer as a hardship case. This request was likewise denied.

Hall then requested that she be scheduled to work at the laboratory testing table, which required less physical exertion than the sampler position, and that a more senior

---

[1]The names of all individuals are disguised.
[2]See the appendix for relevant clauses of the contract.

person work the truck until an anticipated opening at the table occurred. Her supervisor likewise refused this request.

The only remaining alternative for Lisa Hall was to request sick leave. She and her union steward claimed that she was advised by her supervisor, Jenkins, that the only way that she could obtain sick leave was to secure a doctor's statement certifying that she could not work around toxic chemicals because of possible damage to the unborn child. Her supervisor later disputed her statement about this, saying that he did not give her such instructions. In any event, Hall secured a medical statement from her doctor, and she then applied for and was granted sick pay, which she subsequently exhausted along with all vacation pay benefits. After depletion of these benefits, Hall was without a source of income during the remaining months of her pregnancy. She was off work because of her pregnancy from October 1981 until August 1982.

In October 1983, Hall and her union steward discovered that another employee, Roy Ruger, had requested an accommodation similar to that which Hall had requested in 1981. The difference, however, was that his request had been granted. Ruger had had a gallbladder operation in August 1983. As he was nearing exhaustion of his full sick pay benefits, his supervisor, again Robert Jenkins, arranged for him to return to the laboratory and work on the testing table, and a more senior employee, Mary Okum, was assigned from the testing table to the sampler truck. There was a dispute as to how the switch was actually accomplished. The union contended that it was a simple case of "inverted seniority." The senior tester, Okum, without her consent, was scheduled to work the more junior sampler job, and Ruger was temporarily assigned to the table. The company, however, maintained that the switch was made by mutual consent. Ms. Hall further discovered at this time that Ruger, as well as other employees, had been permitted to transfer into the utility pool, even though they had held their previous assignments for less than one year.

Lisa Hall and the union concluded that she had been discriminated against by the company, and a grievance was filed on October 28, 1983. On November 14, 1983, the company, through her supervisor, Robert Jenkins, responded that:

> This grievance is not timely and the validity of this complaint as a grievance is questionable.
>
> In answer to the complaint as filed, the company's position on limited duty is that it does not accommodate non-job-related medical conditions and has historically only allowed employees to return to work when they can return to full duty. In Mr. Ruger's case, however, supervision deviated from its position due to the short period that Mr. Ruger needed a special assignment to accommodate his condition (1 week). The company, however, now fully realizes that it erred in its judgment and wishes to assure the union that it will not again occur.
>
> This complaint refers to "Inverted Seniority," however, the current labor agreement contains no provisions for artificial separation of duties in the analyst classification. As negotiated in 1977, an employee within the analyst classification is subject to perform any job to which he/she may be assigned.
>
> In conclusion no discrimination or other violations of the labor agreement occurred in this case.

The parties failed to resolve the dispute through the various steps of the grievance procedure. The union issued a demand for final and binding arbitration as provided in the collective agreement.

The parties were unable to stipulate the wording of the issue and requested that the arbitrator determine the exact wording of the issue(s) to be resolved. The union version of the issue was:

Whether Ms. Lisa Hall had been discriminated against by CITGO in contravention of Article XVI, the antidiscrimination article. This would be . . . on the basis of her sex . . . If so, what would the remedy be?

The company's version of the issue was:

1. Was the grievance filed timely?
2. Does grievant have standing to complain about action the company took concerning Mr. Ruger?
3. Did the company discriminate against Ms. Hall on the basis of sex in 1981 by refusing to assign her the lighter duty of tester?

Position of the Union

The union argued that Lisa Hall, a pregnant woman, was denied her requests to bid into the utility pool and/or be scheduled to the laboratory table, where the job duties were relatively less strenuous than on the sampler truck. Her requests were based on her physical inability to work the truck due to her condition. Hall was treated unequally in that the same or similar requests were granted to others, particularly Roy Ruger. The company had failed to establish a legitimate reason for these disparities. Accordingly, the grievance should be sustained.

In support of this position the union offered the following evidence and conclusions:

First, Article XVI of the agreement prohibited any kind of discrimination based on sex. Lisa Hall was pregnant in late 1981. She was unable to perform her regularly assigned sampler duties because of the physical exertion that was involved in working on the truck. She requested that she be allowed to bid into the utility pool. There was no credible evidence that she could not have performed utility duties; indeed, two other employees had successfully performed utility duties during the full term of their pregnancies. Despite the fact that the agreement stated that a permanent employee in the laboratory or in another department could not bid into utility until she or he had held a prior position for one year, Mr. Ruger—as well as other employees—was allowed to do so. This contention was not refuted by the company. Thus, Ms. Hall was discriminated against because of her pregnancy.

Second, although the company contended that the cases of Ms. Hall and Mr. Ruger were quite dissimilar, such was not actually the case. Mr. Ruger was scheduled to work on the laboratory testing table, while a more senior employee was scheduled to leave the table and work on the sampler truck. This was not a voluntary swap in positions mutually agreed to by the employees involved. The union also noted that Mr. Ruger was medically incapable of lifting heavy objects for a four-week period. Ms. Hall was offered no help by Mr. Jenkins in her time of distress. Yet he readily accommodated a male employee.

The union offered the following exchange during the grievance hearings in support of its position:

Union Attorney: Mr. Jenkins, you didn't attempt to get a volunteer or even suggest that. However, you were ready, willing, and able to suggest that with respect to Mr. Ruger. And not only that, you didn't ask. You just told Ms. Okum that you were going to do that, and she just shrugged. Correct?
Jenkins: That's correct.

The union also referred to the following conversation involving Roy Ruger from the grievance hearings:

Union Attorney: Relate to me what occurred when you came back to work. How did you arrange to work on the testing table?
Ruger: Well, I can't remember who called who, but I remember the conversation between myself and Mr. Jenkins. The conversation was basically that my doctor was not going to release me to do heavy lifting for another two weeks, that's what Dr. Visser had told me. And Mr. Jenkins said, if it's the truck keeping me from coming back to work, that we could work around that. I believe that is just about exactly what he said. I said, yes, it was the truck keeping me from coming back to work. He said, get a release from your doctor and see the company doctor, which is exactly what I did. And the doctor wrote across the release, no heavy lifting. I believe it said for two weeks, if I am not mistaken.

Third, while the company contended that Lisa Hall could not work as a tester because of a potential toxic chemical danger, the union argued, "The truth is that when her requests were denied, she had no alternative but to request sick leave. And the only way she could obtain sick leave, as she was instructed by her supervisor, was to secure a doctor's certificate that she could not work around the chemicals. Thus, the doctor's certificate only reflected instructions from Mr. Jenkins. Nor was management able, through the testimony of the company doctor, to prove that the chemicals listed were fetal-toxic. Actually, the employer had no policy which would have prevented Ms. Hall from working at the laboratory testing table."

Fourth, the union maintained that the company's argument that the grievance was untimely had no merit. A person could not be expected to file a grievance until he or she was aware of the action upon which the grievance was based. Hall's requests were denied in 1981; however, the circumstances creating the basis of her charge of unequal treatment were not apparent until October 1983. Upon discovery of these circumstances, the grievance was filed within the ten-day grace period and thus was timely.

The union held that the grievance was fully meritorious; that Lisa Hall should have been given a position within the classification of analyst that she was able to perform during her pregnancy; and that she should be made whole for all losses sustained as a result of the company's action.

Position of the Company

Both in the arbitration hearing and in its post-hearing brief, the company contended that the evidence clearly indicated that Hall's supervisor, Robert Jenkins, dealt with Hall in an honest and open manner, doing everything he could to help her at the time. In Mr.

Ruger's case, Mr. Jenkins did everything he could to help him. That was equal treatment, not sexual discrimination. There had been no evidence presented by the union to establish that the company intended to discriminate on the basis of sex.

Ms. Hall failed to file her grievance within the time limits established by the agreement. She had no basis for complaining about any company action taken in regard to Mr. Ruger. Additionally, she was not able to prove her prima facie case because, according to the medical report in evidence, she was physically and medically unable to do the work. Further, even if she had been able to work, there was no one willing to trade functions with her for seven months.

The company maintained that Hall did not prove that there was sexual discrimination in her case, and in fact, there was sufficient evidence to show that there was, in fact, no sexual discrimination.

In its post-hearing brief, the company requested that the arbitrator take particular note of the following:

> First, the grievance was certainly untimely in that it was filed in November 1983, yet Ms. Hall complained about an incident which occurred in September 1981. In September 1981 the employee suffered no loss of seniority or loss of pay. The agreement requires that a grievance be filed "within ten (10) working days after the occurrence." This the union failed to do.
>
> Second, Lisa Hall had no standing to complain about the company action in regard to Mr. Ruger when the assignments were switched between Okum and Ruger. Ms. Hall was not adversely affected in any way. The only person who was possibly damaged was Ms. Okum, and since she had agreed to the change no grievance was filed.
>
> Third, the company did not discriminate against the employee on the basis of her sex by refusing to assign her to the light duty as a tester. Ms. Hall cannot even show a *prima facie* case of sexual discrimination. She simply was not qualified to work as a tester for a number of reasons. Her own physician stated that she could not work around toxic chemicals because of the effect of chemicals on the fetus. Furthermore, supervision could not force a senior tester off the table and allow Ms. Hall to claim that job. No one volunteered to trade with her, and management could not force a change in work assignment. In the Ruger case, Ms. Okum volunteered to make the change, thus this case has no bearing on the charge of sexual discrimination. The truth is Mr. Jenkins did everything that he could do to help Ms. Hall. The grievance, therefore, is completely without merit. It should be denied and dismissed in its entirety.

Appendix
Relevant Provisions of the Agreement

Article III—Seniority

Section 6(i).   After an employee is awarded and/or accepts a permanent job vacancy, he is not eligible to bid for one (1) year unless he is disqualified from his new assignment.

Article XVI—Discrimination

Section 1.   Discrimination—There shall be no discrimination against any applicant for employment or against any employee in regard to promotion, discharge, layoff, sickness, accident, insurance, thrift plan, or retirement plan benefits, on account of sex, race, national origin, creed, or color or on account of any activity undertaken in good faith in his capacity as a union representative of other employees.

Article XVIII—Grievances and Arbitration

Section 1.   If any differences, disputes or complaints arise over the interpretation or application of the contents of this agreement, there shall be an earnest effort on the part of the parties to settle such promptly through the following steps:.

*   *   *   *   *

Section 6.   No grievance may be presented later than ten (10) calendar days after the occurrence from which such grievance arose.

Questions

1. The parties were unable to stipulate the wording of the issue to be decided by the arbitrator. If you were the arbitrator, how would you word the issue?
2. Had Lisa Hall been treated differently from other employees under similar circumstances? Why, or why not?
3. Why is a case of this nature of particular concern to both the company and the union? Discuss.
4. If you were the arbitrator, how would you rule in this case? Explain your reasoning.

CASE 42
THE REVISED PAYROLL PERIOD

Company:
    Creative Data Services, Inc., St. Louis, Missouri

Union:
    International Brotherhood of Teamsters, Chauffeurs, Warehousemen, and Helpers of America, Local No. 688

Background

On December 3, 1985, Jeb Wilcox,[1] a printer in the production department, filed the following grievance on behalf of the union bargaining unit employees:

> The company is in violation of the contract by changing the pay period from one week to two. This violates ARTICLE 25.02, Hours of Work, and also ARTICLE 33, Maintenance of Standards, and any other article that may apply.[2]
>   Settlement Requested. Change back to one week pay period.

The grievance was also signed by the union shop steward, Will Davis.
    The company's answer, dated December 6, 1985, and signed by Plant Manager Max Ulrich, was as follows:

> The company has reviewed Article 25.02, Hours of Work, and Article 33, Maintenance of Standards, and changing the pay period is not in violation of these articles.

The union grievance was eventually carried to arbitration.

Position of the Company

The company explained that during the third or fourth week of November 1985, management had decided that it would change to a biweekly basis for paying employees in its St. Louis facility. The company had another facility in Los Angeles, whose employees had always been paid on a biweekly basis; St. Louis employees had always been paid on a weekly basis. According to the company's chief financial officer, Joseph Mills, his review of accounting and administrative functions revealed that in 1985 three employees in St. Louis were involved in payroll work. He testified that there had been numerous payroll errors and expenses that were excessive for the size of the facility in St. Louis. St. Louis employees were paid on a direct-deposit basis with the Commerce Bank of St. Louis; employees received notice of direct deposits of their wages and salaries to their individual accounts at the bank. Mr. Mills stated that there had been many errors and corrections in forms and journal entries, and therefore the company had decided to go to a biweekly payroll for all employees in the St. Louis operation.

---

[1]The names of all individuals are disguised.
[2]See the appendix for relevant provisions of the agreement.

The bargaining unit represented by the union contained from 29 to 34 employees, depending on production levels; additionally there were approximately 75 to 80 non-union employees at the St. Louis facility.

The change to the biweekly pay schedule was made in the second week of January 1986. The company stated that it now had a "streamlined" payroll system that was free from the many errors in the past and that functioned with one fewer employee.

The company pointed out that on November 26, 1985, Mr. Mills had sent a memorandum to all employees apprising them of the impending change to a biweekly payroll schedule beginning December 30, 1985. In addition, Mr. Mills sent a memorandum to all employees on December 2, 1985, offering to prepare an analysis as to what an individual employee's take-home pay would be on a biweekly basis. However, no one sought information or help from him.

Mr. Mills acknowledged that it was his understanding that St. Louis employees had been paid on a weekly basis ever since the union had been organized in about 1976. He further testified that there had been a number of management meetings concerning the payroll question and that Rob Pinter, director of human resources, and Janis Gueriny, vice president for planning and administration, both had assured him that a change to a biweekly payroll schedule would not violate the labor agreement. Mr. Mills also acknowledged that Article 25.02 of the agreement used the term "payroll period," and that the company was now using a "work week" definition that was also in the agreement as a basis for paying people biweekly. Mr. Mills emphasized that the change from a weekly to a biweekly pay period did not affect anything other than the frequency of payment of employees.

The position of the company was summarized in its post-hearing brief, the relevant portions of which follow:

> The grievance and the union's presentation of the grievance reflect a fundamental confusion about payroll periods, work weeks, and paydays. Paragraph 25.02 follows:
>
> 25.02 The payroll period shall be the seven day period from 12:01 A.M. Sunday through 12:00 midnight of the following Saturday. A "work day" shall mean the twenty-four (24) hour period beginning with an employee's starting time. "Work week" means a period of seven (7) consecutive days, beginning with an employee's starting time on the employee's first work day of any payroll period. A "shift" shall be deemed to be worked on the day the shift starts.
>
> Paragraph 25.02 does not contain the term "payday," nor does it, in any way, state when an employee will be paid. This paragraph defines the "payroll period" and defines a "work week" in order to fix the appropriate periods for determining an employee's right to overtime in two (2) ways. There are contractual rules, and there is the Fair Labor Standards Act. The definitions make it easier to determine when the employee is eligible for overtime or premium pay. This section does not fix the time or frequency of payment of wages.
>
> The union also relies on Article 33, Maintenance of Standards, for the proposition that the company could not change when employees are paid. That Article states:
>
> "All conditions of employment relating to wages, . . . shall be maintained at not less than the highest standard in effect at the time of the signing of this Agreement . . . "
>
> This article is a catch-all clause to cover various benefits not contained in the agreement which are too numerous for the union to set forth in detail. Such individuals are frequently referred to as "red circle rate" employees. The union will argue that payday is a benefit or

condition of employment relating to "wages." The company, of course, does not agree. While the frequency has changed, there has not been a reduction in wages—only the frequency of paydays has been changed.

The decision to go to biweekly paydays was based upon sound accounting and good business reasons and was beneficial to the employees. One of the unacceptable circumstances existing at the time of the decision was an excessive error rate in the preparation of the payroll. The company believes that the number of errors was affected by the weekly payday and the fact that three different employees were involved in preparing the payroll. These employees were experienced and competent employees; nevertheless, there were excessive errors. The errors increased the cost of preparing the payroll. The errors also caused problems for the employees—getting the right amount of money and, on occasions, any money at all. Since the company consolidated the payroll function and went to the biweekly payday the errors have been reduced, costs have been reduced, and the company is one system.

Prior to doing its own payroll, the company had two operations: one in St. Louis, and one in Los Angeles. The West Coast operation had been on a biweekly payday from its inception. The bargaining unit is slightly less than a third of the total payroll. The change to paydays biweekly consolidated the whole company on one system, resulting in a smoother operation subject to fewer errors, and made it less costly.

Joseph Mills was asked on cross-examination if his estimates of savings included the use of money for the period of the first week in the two (2) week cycle of paydays. He replied that it did not.

In making an interpretation of the contract, we cite the familiar concept that the contract must be viewed as a whole. A careful examination of the contract reveals that the company and union have gone to great effort to detail the rights and obligations of the company, union, and employees. Thus, the absence of a specific reference to a specific payday is significant. Where there are limits to the company's authority, they are enumerated. Surely, if the parties intended to restrict the company's right to change the paydays, they would have been specific in making such limitations.

The grievance should be denied.

Position of the Union

The union did not present any witnesses at the arbitration hearing. The union only argued its position that the company had violated the agreement when the company decided in late 1985 to change the basis of payment of bargaining unit employees from a weekly period to a biweekly period. The union pointed out that the company had paid bargaining unit employees on a weekly basis throughout the history of the collective bargaining relationship between the parties. The union further indicated that the union grievance predated the actual change in the basis of payment, that is to say, the union filed its grievance when the company announced such a change but before it was actually implemented.

The union position was summarized in its post-hearing brief, the relevant portions of which follow:

> The union submits the issue as: Did the company violate the collective bargaining agreement by converting from a weekly to a biweekly payroll period?
> The undisputed facts are that the company, through its chief financial officer, unilaterally decided to reformulate the payment policy at Creative Data Services. The employees were notified of the policy change through correspondence dated November 26, 1985. Neither the

union's representatives nor the members were notified of any intent to alter the payment policy until the decision was finalized.

The aforementioned decision directly violates Article 25.02 of the collective bargaining agreement, which defines "payroll period" as "the seven day period from 12:01 A.M. Sunday through 12:00 midnight of the following Saturday." Until January 1986, the company's employees had been paid weekly, receiving a payroll check on each Wednesday in compensation for the previous payroll period. Thus, "payroll period" was the period for which each employee was paid and prior to January 1986, the company and the union had always interpreted "payroll period" in this way. In fact the language in Article 25.02 has been in existence since the original collective bargaining agreement negotiated in 1977, and the employees have always been paid based on the contractual definition of the payroll period. The language is clear and a definite standard has been established.

The company now claims that "payroll period" is not used to determine when employees are paid, and that changing to a biweekly payment basis does not violate Article 25.02. However, if in fact, the company does not use the definition of "payroll period" in Article 25.02 as the determination of when employees are paid, then the term "payroll period" becomes meaningless. The collective bargaining agreement provides for other defined periods for every other calculation necessary in Article 25. In his testimony, Joseph Mills admitted that since January 1986, the "payroll period" as defined in the collective bargaining agreement has not been used for any calculation at all and this is meaningless according to the company's current practice.

Accepted principles of contract interpretation dictate that all agreements be construed as a whole, and that all words used in an agreement be given an effect.

$$*\quad*\quad*\quad*\quad*$$

The company also argues that the "payroll period" has not changed. They contend that the company is merely paying employees for two payroll periods in each paycheck rather than one. However, this argument still does avoid the aforementioned alteration or disregard of the Article 25.02 definition of "payroll period." Indeed, in answering the grievance the company acknowledged that it changed the payroll period.

The collective bargaining agreement also contains a section on "Maintenance of Standards." This Article states that: "All conditions of employment relating to wages, hours of work, overtime differentials, and general working conditions shall be maintained at not less than the highest standard in effect at the time of the signing of this agreement."

Through their past practice of paying each employee weekly, according to the payroll period, the company had established a standard. Clearly, the company violated this standard by changing the payroll period and failing to maintain Article 25.02 on "Hours of Work."

Joseph Mills testified, and stated in his November 26 correspondence, that the decision to convert to a biweekly payroll period was made to "reduce the number of people and hours it takes to process payroll." In turn, the company would save money. Thus, the company contends that cost efficiency is justification to alter the terms of the collective bargaining agreement. The union does not deny that the company could save money by adjusting the payroll period. But the fact remains that the company entered into an agreement with the union and it is bound to uphold those terms. Certainly the company could avoid numerous other costs by ignoring the collective bargaining agreement. However, both parties bargained in good faith, have agreed to abide by the terms of the contract, and are therefore obligated to do so regardless of the cost or inconvenience. The employees have a right to be involved in decisions affecting or changing the collective bargaining agreement. In this case, the company ignored that right.

For the reasons stated above, the union urges the arbitrator to sustain the grievance and to enforce the payroll period as defined in the collective bargaining agreement.

APPENDIX
RELEVANT PROVISIONS OF THE AGREEMENT

Article 11—Management

11.01 The management of the company and the direction of the working force, including the right to hire, promote, discipline, suspend, transfer, or discharge for cause, the right to schedule hours, schedule overtime work, and the right to relieve employees from duty because of lack of work or for other reasonable causes, is vested exclusively in the company; provided, however, that no action may be taken by the company which is contrary to the provisions of this agreement.

11.02 The company shall have the sole right to establish reasonable rules, decide the processes and types, kind and amount of machinery and equipment to be used, types and quantity of products to be made, quality of material and workmanship required, number of employees required for various operations, selling prices of product, method of making and selling products, personnel to be employed in supervisory, clerical, and management positions and policies. The foregoing is intended by way of illustration and not in limitation of any customary or usual function of management, all of which are expressly retained by the company; provided, however, that no action may be taken by the company which is contrary to the provisions of this agreement.

Article 25—Hours of Work

25.01 All references in this agreement to "days" refers to calendar days unless the context in which the word is used clearly indicates a different meaning; and the term "working day" refers to days on which the company's plant is actually engaged in production work, regardless of the calendar on which such working day may occur, or refers to the days on which an employee actually works, as the context may require.

25.02 The payroll period shall be the seven day period from 12:01 A.M. Sunday through 12:00 midnight of the following Saturday. A "work day" shall mean the twenty-four (24) hour period beginning with an employee's starting time. "Work week" means a period of seven (7) consecutive days, beginning with an employee's starting time on the employee's first work day of any payroll period. A "shift" shall be deemed to be worked on the day the shift starts.

25.03 The work week shall consist of forty (40) hours a week, which may be five (5) days of eight (8) hours per day or four (4) days of ten (10) hours per day or both a five (5) day and a four (4) day work week. This provision is subject to certain limitations in paragraph 25.12. The company may have multiple work week schedules. An employee may select a work schedule by seniority. An employee's starting time may be changed by notice given at least seventy-two (72) hours in advance. The company may schedule shifts and work weeks in order to meet customer requirements. A schedule of individual starting time may be established by mutual agreement between the company and the employee. An employee's scheduled off days will include Sunday. An employee working four (4) ten (10) hour days will have three consecutive days off, one of which will be Sunday.

Article 33—Maintenance of Standards

33.01 All conditions of employment relating to wages, hours of work, overtime differentials, and general working conditions shall be maintained at not less than the highest standard in effect at the time of the signing of this agreement, and the conditions of employment shall be improved wherever specific provisions of this section shall not apply to inadvertent or bona fide errors made by the company or the union in applying the terms and conditions of this agreement if such error is corrected within ninety (90) days from the date of knowledge or error.

33.02 This provision does not give the company the right to impose or continue wages, hours, and working conditions less than those contained in this agreement, nor does this provision apply to terms or conditions substituted or changed during the course of negotiations for this agreement.

Questions

1. What was the issue to be decided by the arbitrator? Do you agree with the union's statement of the issue? Discuss.
2. Did the company's action violate Article 25.02? Article 33?
3. The parties did not discuss Article 11. If you were the company representative in this case, would you have cited Article 11? Why, or why not?
4. How would you have ruled in this case, if you had been the arbitrator?

Case 43
The Lunch-Time Tipplers

Employer:
   Kalamazoo County Road Commission, Kalamazoo, Michigan

Union:
   Teamsters State, County, and Municipal Workers, Local No. 214

Background

On July 8, 1986, two employees of the Kalamazoo County Road Commission were patching roads adjacent to a public golf course. During their lunch period, which was from 11:30 A.M. to 12:00 noon, they drove their truck to the restaurant at the golf course for lunch. During the course of lunch, Paul Grainger[1] consumed two to four bottles of beer and Roy Steen consumed one or two wine coolers. The precise amount consumed later became a matter of dispute between the two employees and Herbert Larger, manager of the Road Commission. When the two employees returned to the Commission yard shortly after 3:00 P.M. (their work day started at 7:30 A.M. and ended at 4:00 P.M.), they were each handed the following written disciplinary suspension, signed by Larger:

> You are hereby suspended under the provisions of Article III, Section 1 of our current Union contract. This disciplinary action is assessed for violation of Art. XV, Sec. 2(a), Rule (h), "Drinking, possession, or use of any alcoholic beverage or controlled substance without a doctor's prescription on Commission's time, premises, or equipment, or reporting to work while under the influence of alcoholic beverages or controlled substances without a doctor's prescription."
>
> On 7/8/86 you consumed alcoholic beverages during working hours at the golf course on East C Avenue. This was reported to us by the owner of this facility. A determination as to further disciplinary action, including possible discharge, will be made within the next five (5) regularly scheduled working days.[2]

This matter came to Larger's attention on the afternoon of July 8 when he received a message that the owner of the golf course had telephoned to complain that two Road Commission employees working nearby had tracked tar onto the clubhouse carpet. During the conversation, the golf course owner asked if the Road Commission had a policy of allowing its employees to drink alcoholic beverages with their lunch. Larger was out of the office at the time, but when he returned from lunch at 1:20 P.M., he called the club owner, who was out of his office. They were able to arrange a telephone conversation at approximately 2:30 P.M. In the conversation, the club owner confirmed that the two individuals had been in the club for lunch, and he said that they had consumed three or four beers and a couple of wine coolers. Larger immediately wrote up the notice of suspension that he handed Grainger and Steen when they returned to the yard.

---

[1]The names of all individuals are disguised.
[2]See the appendix for relevant contract provisions.

On July 11, following a brief meeting on July 9 that included Larger, Grainger, Steen, and the union business agent, Larger issued the following notice of termination to both employees:

> I have reviewed the situation and occurrences which resulted in your suspension under the provisions of Article III, Section 1 of our contract on July 8, 1986. I have also reviewed your work record.
>
> The decision reached as a result of these reviews is that your employment with this Commission will be and is terminated as of 4:00 P.M., July 11, 1986.

Both Grainger and Steen protested the action taken by the Commission. Grainger filed the following grievance on July 14:

> On 7/8/86 Roy Steen and I were assigned to patch East C Avenue from 40th Street to the County Line. At 11:30 we were close to the Maple Golf Course. I suggested to Steen we have a hot sandwich; with the sandwich I consumed two beers and Steen had one wine cooler. This was reported to KCRC by the owner of the facility—though the KCRC never verified this statement by calling or visiting the golf course.
>
> At a meeting with Herbert Larger and my Union representative on 7/9/86, Herbert stated that the half hour for lunch was "our" half hour, not the KCRC's, but returning to work under the "influence of alcoholic beverages" was his concern. If KCRC thought Steen who was drinking or myself were "under the influence of alcoholic beverages," why didn't they come out to talk to us or relieve us of the equipment? Three and a half hours later we were handed reprimand notices back at the KCRC offices. This was done without any questions asked about what we did or didn't do for lunch. The KCRC had taken it upon themselves to convict us of "under the influence of alcoholic beverages" without a question being asked about the incident. No one seemed to care about the persons using the equipment until three and a half hours later, after we had driven from Gull Lake to Kilgore Road. I am requesting immediate reinstatement of my job at KCRC and all seniority rights and back pay without any reprisals due to the actions taken by the KCRC in my above statement. Signed: Paul Grainger

Steen filed a similar grievance on July 12:

> On July 8, 1986, I was suspended from work for supposedly drinking on the job. I was not drinking on the job. With my lunch I had one bottle of wine cooler at the golf course on C Avenue east of 46th St. on my 30 minute lunch—one-half hour for which I'm not paid.
>
> Article X, Section 3 paragraph (a) does not define our lunch period as paid hours of work. Therefore, I was not working at the time. I did not drink on Commission property or in a Commission vehicle or on the job or Commission time. If the Commission was so concerned about the condition I was in after lunch, why didn't my foreman come out and check us out on the job? The one drink I had with my lunch did not in any way, shape, form, or fashion keep me from doing my job as it had to be performed after lunch was over.
>
> I feel it is only right to reinstate my employment with full back pay. Signed: Roy Steen

The grievances were processed through the grievance procedure and were eventually submitted to arbitration. The parties presented the following issues to the arbitrator:

1. Was the dismissal of Paul Grainger from his employment with the Kalamazoo County Road Commission for "cause"? If not, what shall the remedy be?
2. Was the dismissal of Roy Steen from his employment with the Kalamazoo County Road Commission for "cause"? If not, what shall the remedy be?

Position of the Union

The union argued that the Commission failed to show that Grainger and Steen were "drinking on Commission time, premises, or equipment." The unpaid lunch period was not work time or the Commission's time. The two employees worked the full 8 hours on July 8 and the full 40 hours during that week. The eight hours worked on July 8 did not include the one-half-hour lunch period. Article X, Section 3(a) specifically provided for an "unpaid lunch period at or near the mid-point of their eight (8) hours shift."

The union claimed that the Commission did not support the charge that Grainger and Steen were guilty of reporting to work under the influence of an alcoholic beverage, since Larger did not discuss the matter with them when they returned at 3:00 P.M. and did not test them. No one from management visited the work site between 12:00 noon and 3:00 P.M., and no one prevented them from operating the equipment during that period of time.

The union contended that there was a difference between "consuming alcoholic beverages" and "being under the influence of alcoholic beverages." In fact, the Commission had recognized this difference in the past, when it called crews in to work overtime on emergency snow removal. It permitted employees to operate equipment, even though it was known to management that some employees had consumed alcoholic beverages between the end of their regular work shift and the time at which they were recalled to operate snow removal equipment.

The union pointed out that a 0.10 percent blood alcohol level must be shown in the State of Michigan to prove that an individual was "operating a vehicle under the influence" of alcohol. A blood alcohol level of 0.07 percent indicated that the individual was "impaired." Any reading below the level of 0.07 percent indicated that alcohol had been consumed, but such consumption did not violate the statutes of the State of Michigan. The union also cited the ruling of the court in the *City of Lansing, Michigan*, case that "under the influence" was synonymous with the terms "drunk" or "intoxicated." The Commission had not supported the charge that Grainger and Steen were either drunk or intoxicated.

The union further pointed out that the courts in the state of Michigan had determined that one element in determining whether an individual is "under the influence" is the effect of the substance on the individual, and that for an individual to be shown to be "under the influence," it must be shown that the ability of the individual to operate a vehicle was "substantially and materially affected." The Commission had failed to prove that the ability of the two employees to operate a vehicle was less than that of an ordinary, careful, and prudent driver.

The union asserted that no one in management had noticed anything wrong with the behavior of Grainger and Steen or indicated that they observed any signs that they were "impaired," such as slurred speech or unsteady gait. Larger was not aware that the two men had been drinking until he received a call from the bar owner. Larger did not then take action to observe the two men, nor did he drive to the scene to take charge. In any event, even if the men had been "impaired" in any way, the effects of the alcohol would have worn off during the three hours that they had worked unobserved by management.

The union contended that the Alcohol Awareness Calculator, on which the Commission relied for much of its case (a technique for estimating the alcohol level in the blood), was an unreliable method for determining the state of sobriety of an individual who had consumed alcohol. At best, it provided only a very rough estimate based upon estimated weight of the individual, rate at which the alcohol is consumed, and several other variables. However, the union pointed out that a given quantity of alcohol affected each individual differently, depending on rate of consumption, type and quantity of food consumed during the period in question, and individual body tolerance for alcohol. Furthermore, there was no scientific proof that the blood alcohol level of an individual consuming two drinks in one-half hour would be double that of the same individual consuming two drinks in one hour, as the Commission contended.

Finally, the union argued that the statements made by the golf course owner must be dismissed as hearsay, since he had admitted that he did not personally observe Grainger and Steen consume the alcoholic beverages; rather, he was told by the person serving the drinks how many drinks had been consumed by the two men. Further, neither the golf course owner nor the persons serving the drinks were available to testify as to the amount of alcohol consumed by the two employees.

The union contended that the Kalamazoo County Road Commission did not sustain the burden of proof that Paul Grainger and Roy Steen were guilty of violating Article XV, Section 2(a), Rule (h) of the contract as charged, and they should be restored to their former positions and be made whole for all losses sustained as a consequence of the Commission's action.

Position of the Road Commission

The Commission took strong issue with Grainger's and Steen's claim that they did not violate Article XV, Section 2(a), Rule (h) because they did not drink on the "Commission's time," but were rather free to do as they wished, since they were on their unpaid lunch period. The Commission argued that even though the lunch period was unpaid, it "was a part of the work day and shift" during which the Commission was responsible for the actions of its employees. If the Commission allowed its employees to drink alcoholic beverages during their unpaid lunch period and someone were injured as a consequence, the Commission would be liable. Rule (h) had been negotiated into the contract for this very purpose precisely because of the Commission's liability for the conduct of its employees during the workday.

With reference to the rule, the Commission pointed out that it stated that employees shall not possess or use alcoholic beverages on the Commission's time. Technically, the alcoholic beverage is in the employee's possession after being ingested because it is in his or her stomach and is being "used" for the next 40 to 70 minutes per drink as it is being assimilated into the blood stream. Therefore, since Grainger and Steen consumed somewhere between two and four drinks during a half-hour lunch period, they were in possession of and using alcoholic beverages on the Commission's time.

The Commission contended that these two employees were under the influence of alcohol when they returned to work, since the club owner had stated that they had consumed three or four beers and a couple of wine coolers and the employees admitted to having had at least two beers and one wine cooler.

The Commission argued that according to the Alcohol Awareness Calculator, both employees had blood alcohol levels between 0.06 and 0.08 percent, which put their condition, according to the Calculator, in the category of "Reflexes, vision, judgment, and powers of concentration affected. Driving should not be attempted."

The Commission's claim that these two employees were "under the influence of alcohol" was based on their admission that they had consumed two beers and one wine cooler, although the golf course owner claimed that they had consumed about twice that amount. According to the Commission, the Alcohol Awareness Calculator indicated that, since each of the two men weighed about 200 pounds, their blood alcohol level would have been between 0.04 and 0.03 percent if each had consumed two drinks in one hour. However, since each had consumed the alcohol in a period of 30 minutes, the blood alcohol level should be doubled, to 0.08 and 0.06 percent. This higher level of blood alcohol, according to the Calculator, put them in the range of being "under the influence of alcohol."

The Commission contended that the negotiated term in Rule (h), "under the influence," was intended to mean that the use or consumption of any alcohol or controlled substance by any Road Commission employee was prohibited in the interests of safety to the employee, his or her fellow workers, and the general public. Many employees, such as Grainger and Steen in this instance, must often work without close supervision for lengthy periods of time at considerable distances from the Commission yard. Management must be able to depend upon responsible behavior from these employees. They worked under conditions where the potential for injury to themselves and others was very high. They must be in full possession of all their faculties at all times. They must be alert, careful, and sensitive to situations that carry with them a high potential for an accident that may result in damage to property and equipment, injury, and even death. Larger stated most emphatically that there was no justifiable reason for any employee driving Road Commission vehicles to use alcohol or a controlled substance during the workday, and the unpaid lunch period was a part of the workday.

The Commission admitted, however, that on occasion emergencies had arisen when it had not been possible to monitor its policy on the consumption of alcohol as closely as it felt necessary. These emergencies had arisen during the winter, when sudden snow storms required management to call in crews to operate snow removal equipment. On occasion, one or more of these employees had consumed alcoholic beverages before returning to the job. The Commission stated that in those rare instances, it relied on its observation of the behavior of the employees and their good judgment. It was a situation that it recognized to be undesirable, but one in which it had to weigh the danger of a possible accident from the failure to remove snow against the danger from an occasional employee's escaping detection and becoming involved in an accident because he or she was less than fully alert.

Larger admitted that no one in management noted any "impairment" of Grainger or Steen when they returned to the yard at about 3:00 P.M. on July 8. He pointed out, however, that any ill effects of the alcohol would probably have disappeared during the three-hour lapse between the consumption of the alcohol and the time they returned to the yard. He further admitted that he did not observe them on the job that afternoon. His duties required that he visit job sites at various locations where job difficulties necessitated his presence. He was out of his office at the time the golf course owner telephoned; by the time he heard directly of the incident, Grainger and Steen were already returning to the yard.

The Commission reported that the consumption of alcohol or other controlled substances was not a problem and that no other cases of drinking during the workday had come to its attention. The Commission had made no arrangements for testing employees suspected of having consumed alcohol or other controlled substances during the workday, and it had not discussed the issue of possible testing with the union up to this time.

The Commission contended that both Grainger and Steen were well aware of Rule (h) and knew that the consumption of alcohol during the workday was a violation of the rule.

The Commission urged that the grievances submitted by Paul Grainger and Roy Steen be denied in their entirety.

Appendix
Relevant Provisions of the Agreement

Article II—Grievance Procedure, Arbitration

Section 6(a).   All matters submitted to arbitration shall be submitted to the Michigan Employment Relations Commission in accordance with its procedures, within the time specified above and such procedures shall govern the arbitration hearing. The arbitrator shall have no power or authority to alter, amend, add to or subtract from the terms of this Agreement, and shall be required to render his decision within thirty (30) days after the close of said hearing.

Both parties agree to be bound by a proper award of the arbitrator and that the costs of any arbitration proceeding under this provision shall be borne equally between the parties. The expenses and salaries of witnesses and representatives of the Employer shall be borne by the Commission and the expenses and salaries of witnesses and representatives of the Union shall be borne by the Union.

Article III—Discharge/Discipline

Section 1.   The Commission agrees that employees shall not be discharged without cause from and after the date of this Agreement, and the Union will be furnished with a copy of such notice, but that in all instances in which the Commission may conclude that an employee's conduct may justify discharge or discipline, such employee shall first be suspended.

In all cases of suspension, the Commission shall allow the suspended employee an opportunity to discuss his suspension with his steward before being required to leave the property of the Commission. Such initial suspension shall be for not more than five (5) regularly scheduled working days. If the suspension is converted into a discharge, the decision of whether to discharge will be made within five (5) days after the initial suspension. During the period of initial suspension, the employee may, if he believes he has been unjustly dealt with, request a hearing in a meeting between the Union Grievance Committee, the Superintendent, and the Engineer-Manager. After such hearing or if no such hearing is requested, the Engineer-Manager shall decide dependent upon the facts of the case, whether the suspension without pay already given is considered sufficient, should be extended, should be converted into a discharge, or that no discipline should have been given. In the event the employee believes he has been unjustly disciplined, it shall be a proper subject for the Grievance Procedure, provided a written grievance with respect thereto is presented to the Engineer-Manager pursuant to the Second Step of the Grievance Procedure within two (2) working days after the Engineer-Manager makes his decision as set forth above.

Section 2.   In the event it should be decided under the Grievance Procedure that the employee was unjustly discharged or suspended, the Commission shall reinstate such employee and pay full compensation, partial, or no compensation as may be decided under the Grievance Procedure, which compensation, if any, shall be at the rate of the employee's straight time earnings during the pay period immediately preceding the date of the discharge, less such compensation as he may have earned at other employment during such period and less any worker's or unemployment compensation received.

Article X—Hours of Work

Section 1.   *Day/Week Defined:* The normal work day shall consist of eight (8) hours and the normal work week shall consist of forty (40) hours.

Section 3(a).   Employees shall be required to be ready to start work at the start of their shift and shall be required to remain at work until the end of their shift except for one fifteen (15) minute rest period at about the mid-point of the morning and another at about the mid-point of the afternoon, and except for the unpaid lunch period at or near the mid-point of their eight (8) hours shift.

Article XV—Miscellaneous

Section 2(a), Rule (h).   Drinking, possession, or use of any alcoholic beverage or controlled substance without a doctor's prescription on Commission's time, premises, or equipment, or reporting to work while under the influence of alcoholic beverages or controlled substance without a doctor's prescription is strictly forbidden. Employees violating this rule will be subject to discharge.

Questions

1. Was the Road Commission responsible for the actions of Grainger and Steen during their unpaid lunch period? Did it make any difference whether or not they used the Commission's truck to go to the restaurant? Discuss.
2. How do you assess Larger's decision-making process? Does his handling of this case meet the requirements for taking disciplinary action? Discuss.

3. How do you evaluate the Commission's reliance upon the Alcohol Awareness Calculator to support its claim that the two employees "were under the influence"?

4. Does it make any difference that Road Commission employees often must work for long periods of time without close supervision?

5. Section 2(a), Rule (h) is very specific and stringent in its prohibition against the drinking, possession, or use of alcoholic beverages and drugs during working hours. How do you evaluate the Commission's action in the light of this section?

CASE 44
THE "REHABILITATED" EMPLOYEE

Company:
Navistar International Corporation, Indianapolis, Indiana

Union:
International Union, United Plant Guard Workers of America

Background

On November 19, 1985, Anna Pelton[1] was working the second shift (3:00 P.M. to 11:00 P.M.) as a plant guard. At approximately 4:50 P.M., she was working in the gatehouse, which housed the plant protection headquarters. At that time, her supervisor, Lieutenant Raymond Varley, observed her slurred speech and abnormal behavior and became convinced that she was under the influence of either drugs or alcohol. He consulted the company's medical director, Dr. R. K. Dobson, who also observed her. In response to Dr. Dobson's questions, she denied that she had been drinking.

After being informed that she would be considered intoxicated, on the basis of observations of plant personnel, Pelton agreed to submit to a laboratory test for intoxication at Community Hospital. She was driven to the hospital by another plant guard.

A blood alcohol test administered to Pelton at approximately 6:29 P.M. on November 19, 1985, showed an alcohol reading of 22 milligrams per deciliter, or 0.232 percent of alcohol in the blood. Under Indiana law, prima facie evidence of intoxication is evidence of 0.10 percent or greater of alcohol in the blood (Ind. Code §9-11-1-7). Pelton was thereafter driven from the hospital to the plant accompanied by an acquaintance at approximately 7:52 P.M. Dr. Dobson received the results of the blood alcohol test by telephone on November 20, 1985, and he received the written results of the test shortly thereafter. On November 20, 1985, Pelton was discharged by the company for being intoxicated while on duty, in violation of Company Rule 3.

The union did not refute the company's contention that Anna Pelton was under the influence of alcohol while at work on November 19, 1985. Rather it contended that the company treated her unfairly in comparison with its treatment of other company employees under like circumstances, who were represented by the United Auto Workers (UAW).

Company Rule 3 provided as follows:

> Any employee who is under the influence of alcohol and/or drugs on company property, including parking lots, will be discharged.

Despite the specific language of Rule 3, labor relations director Stanley Poindexter stated that Navistar's treatment of other union-represented employees who had been found guilty of being intoxicated had been much different. While they had been discharged for the first offense, as provided by the rule, the company would reinstate

---

[1]The names of all individuals are disguised.

an employee after six months to a year if he or she filed a grievance and, after discharge, successfully completed a company-approved alcohol rehabilitation program. The employee received no pay during the time off the job. Further, the employee, the union, and the company all had to sign a "last-chance" letter of agreement setting forth the terms under which the employee would be permitted to return to work for the company.

Typically, the last-chance agreement verified the company's rule concerning intoxication while on company property, as well as its rules concerning absenteeism, lateness, safety, and work performance. The agreement also required the discharged employee to conform to a continuous rehabilitation program tailored to the particular employee. The agreement concluded with a provision stating that if the employee were again observed on company property in an intoxicated condition, he or she would be required to undergo an alcohol test; if the individual refused or if this test evidenced the presence of alcohol in his or her system, the employee would be summarily discharged. In the case of those employees represented by the UAW who had been discharged for intoxication on company premises, the company also paid the employee's rehabilitation expenses for the first full month following the employee's discharge.

The company had followed this practice for six employees who had been represented by the UAW. The company did not argue that this practice was not applicable to plant guards represented by the United Guard Workers as well. Rather, it contended that it had complied with this practice when it discharged Anna Pelton.

Anna Pelton had previously been discharged by the company on April 28, 1985, under a charge that she had been intoxicated on the company's premises. She had filed a grievance, denying that she had been intoxicated, contending instead that she had been under medication. She did not attend an alcohol rehabilitation program at that time. The parties settled her grievance on August 22, 1985, when they entered an agreement that provided in its entirety as follows:

> This grievance is resolved effective today, August 22, 1985, as follows:
> Anna Pelton will be reinstated effective Monday, August 26, 1985.
> Anna Pelton will receive eight (8) weeks back pay at the straight time rate with payment being made as soon as practicable.

According to Pelton, her discharge on November 20, 1985, made her aware for the first time that she had lost control over her alcohol consumption and she needed help. She then voluntarily entered the Koala Center rehabilitation program in Lebanon, Indiana, a 30-day inpatient program followed by extensive, ongoing outpatient care.

The Koala program was one of the programs that was approved by the company, but the company did not participate in Pelton's rehabilitation program as it had in the rehabilitation programs for the UAW employees. In the case of the UAW employees, the company closely monitored their rehabilitation through continuous progress reports it received directly from the Koala Center. In Pelton's case, the company was not apprised of her participation in the Koala program, until after she had filed a grievance requesting reinstatement.

Pelton admitted at the grievance proceedings that she was currently a recovering alcoholic. She stated that she had not taken an alcoholic drink since her discharge on November 20, 1985. She was currently taking Antabuse and could not state whether she would be directed by her doctor to continue taking it for the rest of her life. She testified that she regularly attended Alcoholics Anonymous from three to six times per month. She also said that she remained under the care of Dr. Daniel Black, who provided her with a letter dated October 22, 1986, which stated in part that:

> She has been cooperative in treatment with me. She is taking Antabuse and cannot drink even very small amounts of alcohol without becoming deathly ill.

The parties were unable to resolve the issues raised by Anna Pelton's grievance, and they requested that the arbitrator determine the issue(s) and render a decision.

Position of the Union

The union acknowledged that the company practice regarding the rehabilitation of employees was a fair and just one. The union particularly commended the company for reinstating employees after a first offense of intoxication on company property, subject to their undertaking a rehabilitation program and thereafter being reinstated under the terms of a last-chance letter. However, the union argued that the company did not follow this practice in Pelton's case, and that she was, in effect, denied this second opportunity. In that regard, it contended that her discharge on April 28, 1985, was not a first occasion of intoxication on company property. Intoxication was never admitted by the employee or substantiated by the company. The final settlement of the April 28 incident was arrived at on August 22, 1985, and this made no mention of discharge for intoxication, nor did it contain any of the provisions included in last-chance letters provided the six UAW members.

The union pointed out that the labor-management agreement required that the company must show "just cause" to discharge an employee. The union held that the company, by its previous consistent past practice, had defined "just cause" for discharge because of intoxication. The company strayed from that past practice in the case of Anna Pelton; hence, the company had failed to establish that it had "just cause" to terminate her employment.

The union requested that the company reinstate Anna Pelton with full back pay and restore to her all other rights lost as a consequence of the company's action.

Position of the Company

The company stated that it was sympathetic with Anna Pelton's battle with alcoholism, but the company held that the relevant question in this case was whether or not the company was obligated to provide its employees with an alcohol rehabilitation program.

The company argued that it had not treated Pelton differently in this case from the UAW employees who had been charged with intoxication on company premises. The company described the union's argument as creating a "revolving door" that would require the company to fire and rehire an employee until the employee was rehabilitated.

The company further argued that its practice gave an employee a second chance after a first discharge for intoxication, and that the UAW employees had taken it upon themselves to seek rehabilitation. In view of its reinstatement of Pelton on August 26, 1985, the company felt that it had given her as many chances to seek rehabilitation as it had given the UAW employees.

Finally, the company contended that as a result of her work as a plant guard, Pelton was fully aware of Rule 3; she was responsible for her own behavior and had a special duty to abide by company rules, including Rule 3. The company took the only action it could, considering that it had reinstated her after her first discharge for intoxication on the job.

The company requested that the arbitrator deny Anna Pelton's grievance.

Questions

1. What is the issue to be decided? If you were the union representative, how would you word the issue? How would you want to word the issue if you were the management representative? How would you state the issue if you were the arbitrator in this case?
2. Did the agreement signed by the union and the company on August 22, 1985, constitute Anna Pelton's "last chance"? Why, or why not?
3. Had the company treated Anna Pelton differently from other employees?
4. As a plant guard, should she have known of the seriousness of being intoxicated on the job? Does it make any difference that she was a plant guard, rather than a production employee? Why, or why not?
5. How would you rule in this case?

CASE 45
REFUSAL TO SIGN A "SAFETY TRAINING" DOCUMENT

Company:
   James B. Beam Distilling Company, Cincinnati, Ohio

Union:
   Distillery, Wine, and Allied Workers International Union, Local No. 32

Background

The current collective bargaining agreement[1] between the parties became effective on May 1, 1985, for a period of three years. Some 500 production and maintenance employees were represented by the union at the company's Cincinnati, Ohio, plant.

This dispute had its origin during the week of April 21, 1986, when supervisors met with small groups of employees allegedly to train them about the hazards of workplace chemicals with which they might come into contact. The meetings were held to fulfill the company's obligation under the Occupational Safety and Health Administration's "Health Hazard Communication Standard," 29 C.F.R. §1910.1200.

One such meeting was conducted on April 24, 1986, by Richard Crayton,[2] assistant superintendent of the DeKuiper bottling plant. Among the seven employees present were Alex Cox, Norman Locks, Rosemary Wamser, and Karl Steiner.

Utilizing a "Supervisors' Discussion Guide," Crayton provided information about three products common to their workplace which contained hazardous chemicals—a glue, a concentrated soap solution detergent, and a wash-out solution for cleaning product lines and tanks. He discussed hazardous chemical labeling codes and how to interpret OSHA "Material Safety Data Sheets" maintained in the plant office. He also distributed a hazard communication training booklet entitled, "About Handling Hazardous Chemicals."

The meeting lasted about 12 minutes; the employees were given the opportunity to ask questions. When it ended, the employees were asked to sign a form headed, "Hazard Communication Training." This form identified their supervisor and department and the date and time of the meeting, and it stated as follows:

> I hereby acknowledge receipt of the Hazard Communication Training book "About Handling Hazardous Chemicals" and acknowledge that I have received training concerning the handling of hazardous chemicals in my work area.

However, four of the seven employees—Cox, Locks, Wamser, and Steiner—refused to sign the form. They all indicated that they did not feel that they had been trained, and they were concerned that if they signed they would waive their "legal rights."

A few minutes later, Alex Cox and Norman Locks were called to a meeting about the matter in Crayton's office. Also present were Eunice Probst, safety supervisor; Ryan

---

[1]See the appendix for relevant contractual provisions.
[2]The names of all individuals are disguised.

Dobbins, assistant safety supervisor; and Walter Hastings, industrial relations manager. Alex Cox remained adamant against signing the form. Walter Hastings told Cox and Norman Locks that if they did not sign the paper, they would be subject to suspension for insubordination.

At this point, Gino Spano, vice president of the union, was called in to attend the meeting. After some discussion, Hastings asked Cox and Locks if they would be willing to sign the form if the following rider was added to the text:

> The Company recognizes that an employee is not waiving any rights by signing these meeting minutes.

Cox agreed that this language was "more acceptable." After Hastings authenticated the disclaimer by his signature, Cox, at the recommendation of union vice president Spano, signed the form.

Locks initially asked to take the document home to "study it, think about it." But when Hastings declined this request, Locks, too, signed the form.

Employees Wamser and Steiner were then sequentially called into the office and, after similar discussion, they signed the form.

On the following day, however, Cox, Locks, Wamser, and Steiner, along with another employee, Evelyn Bilge, filed the following group grievance, identified as Grievance No. 26:

> On April 24th, 1986, we were forced to sign our names under scare tactics of being discharged. We feel that management has deprived us of our civil rights and if so, we expect to be compensated.

Company management initially denied the grievance on the ground that it had the right to document that the company had met its training obligations under OSHA. At the third step, Plant Manager Sherman Duckworth gave the following written answer:

> The Company is obligated under OSHA to train employees under the "Hazard Communication Standard." In order to document the training, employees were required to sign the meeting minutes acknowledging that they have been trained and that they received the booklet on handling hazardous materials. There appears to be misunderstanding concerning the meaning of the word "training" as some employees feel that even though they have been through the classroom session, they have not really been "trained." The Company feels that this does constitute training as defined in the OSHA standard; however, there is no need to engage in a debate over the OSHA definition of "training."
>
> Thus, to alleviate the concerns of the grieving employees, we will allow them to sign meeting minutes that state they were in attendance, received the booklet, and were given an opportunity to have their questions answered concerning the "Hazard Communication Standard." They can strike their signature from the original sheets. This will also apply to employees who did not file a grievance. By signing this revised statement, employees will only be acknowledging the facts, and we will not be asking them to agree to a definition of "training."
>
> The Company will again provide repeat sessions where necessary to get everyone informed on the new OSHA standard and any employee who feels he needs further instructions will be accommodated.

Duckworth's response, permitting the grievants to strike their signatures from the original sheet and sign minutes that stated they were in attendance, received the informational booklet, and were given an opportunity to have their questions answered, did not satisfy the union. Accordingly, Delbert Jordan, the union's president and business agent, notified Walter Hastings on July 17, 1986, that:

> The Union does not agree that an employee must sign anything that they do not wish to sign. This should not cause the Company a problem.
>
> If this is agreeable, the Union will table Grievance 26.

Because the grievance remained unresolved, the case eventually was carried to arbitration.

Testimony and Position of the Union

At the arbitration hearing, Alex Cox testified that he signed the company's form under duress, and because he feared disciplinary action would be taken against him if he refused to sign. Cox objected to signing a form that stated he had received "training" when, in his view, the presentation was perfunctory. He was concerned that, by signing the form, it might be used against him should he subsequently become involved in a hazardous chemical mishap. Cox stated that he would not have had a problem signing a form that did no more than simply acknowledge his attendance at the informational meeting, receipt of the hazard communication training book, and opportunity to ask questions.

Rosemary Wamser similarly testified that she did not have a problem with signing documents tendered to her by the company so long as she understood what she was signing. However, when she was asked to sign the acknowledgment of "training," she refused because she "could not understand that." Wamser indicated that she would have had no objection to signing the minutes if the document had merely stated that she had attended a meeting, received the informational booklet, and was given an opportunity to have questions answered concerning handling hazardous chemicals. Although Wamser signed the "training" form, she did so "under protest" to avoid being disciplined.

During the arbitration hearing, Delbert Jordan for the union took the position that the company had no right to require employees to sign any document. In his post-hearing brief, however, Jordan argued that the decisional issue was more narrowly whether the company could require an employee to sign a document that affirmed a "debatable fact" or "the truth of a representation against the employee's contrary belief." In the union's view, the company did not have a right to require an employee to sign such a document, and the arbitrator's decision should prohibit the company from this and any such future practice.

Testimony and Position of the Company

Testifying for the company was Industrial Relations Manager Walter Hastings. He claimed that the signature requirement served the purpose of documenting that employees had been provided with training in the event of a subsequent investigation by

OSHA during which an employee might experience a "memory lapse" and claim that he or she had never been advised about hazardous chemicals, and the instructing supervisor was no longer available at the plant to give evidence to the contrary.

Hastings asserted that the company long had had the right to require employees to sign forms such as identification cards, receipts for paychecks, applications for transfers and leaves, materials processing reports, verifications of training to operate a fork-lift truck, and forms by which employees consented to being searched at all times when leaving or entering the plant.

In his post-hearing brief, counsel for the company contended that it would be difficult to identify a single industrial employment context in which bargaining unit members were not required to sign some document. From time cards to inspection reports, from materials receipts to grievance forms, employees were required "to affix their signatures as an affirmation of the accuracy of the information set forth." Management's right to make and enforce reasonable rules embraced the right to require employees to sign documents appropriate to the administration of the business that did not unduly prejudice an employee or unnecessarily call on an employee to sacrifice a significant interest.

In the company's view, management had the right to require the employees to sign the contested "training" document. The union grievance was without merit and should be dismissed in its entirety.

APPENDIX
RELEVANT CONTRACTUAL PROVISIONS

Article VII—Management Rights

Section 1.   The management and direction of the working forces, including the right to suspend, discipline, or discharge an employee for just cause, which shall include the employee's failure strictly to observe shop or working rules, and the right to hire, transfer, promote, or reduce forces because of working requirements, are vested exclusively in the Company, provided that any such action shall not violate the terms of this Agreement.

* * *

Article XVI—Grievance Procedure

Section 1.   Any and all matters of dispute, difference, disagreement, or controversy of any kind or character between the Union, its members, individually or collectively, and the Company, involving or relating to the interpretation or application of the provisions of this Agreement are subject to the Grievance Procedure.

Questions

1. The parties could not agree on the framing of the issue(s) before the arbitrator. If you were the arbitrator, how would you frame the issue(s) for determination?

2. Did the company have the right to require employees to sign all forms "appropriate to the administration of the business"? Why, or why not?

3. If the company had the right to require employees to sign mandated forms (see Question 2 above), would an employee have any recourse? Discuss.

4. Much of the dispute in this case revolved around the meaning and application of the word "training." Were the employees justified in their concerns, or were they just being overly cautious and contentious? Discuss.

CASE 46
OFF-DUTY SALE OF MARIJUANA

Company:
Lockheed Aeronautical Systems Company (a Division of Lockheed Corporation),
Meridian, Mississippi

Union:
Local Lodge No. 2386, International Association of Machinists and Aerospace Workers

Background

The grievant in this case was Tony Travice,[1] who at the time of his termination had for about two years been employed as a production assembler at the company's Meridian, Mississippi, facility. On the night of December 7, 1987, Mississippi Bureau of Narcotics (MBN) Agent Gertrude Yarber purchased an ounce of marijuana from Travice and a friend.

Yarber testified that she and other MBN agents arranged with Travice and his friend, Del Lavy, to make the "buy" while at Johnny B's, a lounge on Highway 45 South in Meridian. Agent Yarber and another agent left Johnny B's and went to a house trailer owned by Travice to complete the sale. Yarber asked Travice for an ounce of marijuana. According to her testimony,

> Travice went to the back of his trailer to a black box. He weighed out one ounce of marijuana. I paid $120 for 26 grams of marijuana. Travice put the marijuana in my hand. Del Lavy received the money; Travice did not receive any money while I was there.

Yarber paid for the marijuana with state funds. She and the other agent departed the trailer and the ounce of substance was sent to the Mississippi Crime Bureau for analysis, where it was verified as marijuana.

Charges were filed against Travice and Lavy. The charges filed against Travice were unknown to company management until August 2, 1988, when a plant supervisor, Willis Gabel, heard on a radio news broadcast that Tony Travice had been indicted by the local grand jury for possessing and selling marijuana. Gabel reported this to the plant manager, Bradley Broze. Company management then conducted an investigation of the situation. On August 8, 1988, Travice was terminated for "misconduct of a serious nature," that is, for the sale of narcotics to an agent of the Mississippi Bureau of Narcotics.

Subsequent to his termination, Travice filed the following grievance on August 9, 1988:

> ACTION REQUESTED BY EMPLOYEE: To be immediately reinstated to my present employment at Lockheed with all back pay and benefits and to be made whole. BASIS OF REQUEST: Article I, Section 4. I was unjustly terminated on August 8 when the company

---

[1]The names of all individuals are disguised.

charged me with misconduct. Other employees had more serious charges against them and not been terminated. I have not been allowed due process.[2]

On October 17, 1988, Tony Travice appeared in the Circuit Court of Lauderdale County, Mississippi, to plead guilty to a charge reduced from "sale of less than an ounce of marijuana" to "misdemeanor possession of less than an ounce of marijuana." In pleading guilty to the lesser charge, Travice was questioned by the Court to ascertain that his plea was voluntary and that he understood the consequences of his plea. He agreed that he did.

The union grievance on behalf of Travice was processed without settlement, and it was eventually carried to arbitration.

Position of the Company

The primary contentions of the company can be summarized as follows:

1. Tony Travice was dismissed for misconduct of a serious nature. This was supported by *Management Directive* J-90, effective 7-6-85, in paragraph D, *Dismissal,* subparagraph 8, which stated that termination would be imposed for:

   Other misconduct of a serious nature; for example, moral turpitude, falsifying Company documents, willful destruction or defacing of Company property, fighting, threatening another employee and continued harassment or abuse of one employee by another, etc.

2. Travice was positively identified by Agent Yarber as having been in Johnny B's lounge, as having been the one who weighed out an ounce of marijuana and put the marijuana in her hand. Yarber paid the money to Del Lavy in the presence of Travice. In circuit court, Travice plead guilty to possession of marijuana.

3. It had been the company's firm policy always to dismiss employees charged and convicted of possession or selling illegal drugs.

4. The company was a defense contractor performing work of a sensitive nature that affected national security. The charges against Travice could jeopardize the company's reputation and ability to gain defense contracts. The termination was for just cause, and the grievance should be denied.

Position of the Union

The chief contentions of the union can be summarized as follows:

1. Tony Travice was not a dealer in illegal drugs; he was only a casual user of marijuana. Travice was "entrapped" by MBN Agent Yarber to participate in the sale of a small amount of marijuana. His friend, Del Lavy, received the money; Lavy was in serious debt and needed money desperately at the time.

---

[2]Article I, Section 4, of the labor-management agreement was a management-rights provision that the company could discipline/discharge employees "for just cause."

2. The company's name and reputation were not identified with what happened. The incident occurred off the job. The company did not learn about the incident until some eight months later, and then only because of a radio report that identified Travice but did not mention the company.

3. On October 17, 1988, the charge against Travice was reduced to a misdemeanor possession of less than one ounce of marijuana. No evidence was presented that: (*a*) any of his fellow employees had complained about Travice; (*b*) any contracts were lost or canceled because of the incident; (*c*) the company had suffered any adverse effects to its reputation.

4. Travice's two supervisors in the plant both testified that they had never had any problems with Travice concerning his work, either before or after the date of the incident that had caused his discharge.

In summary, the union contended that there was not a sufficient basis for the company to justify termination of Tony Travice for a minor violation that had occurred off the job. The grievance should be sustained, and Tony Travice should be reinstated and made whole for all lost income, benefits, and seniority.

Questions

1. Could the company's rule on misconduct of a serious nature be applied to cover the circumstances of this case? Discuss.

2. Should it make any difference to the outcome of this case that the grievant, Tony Travice, plead guilty only to a misdemeanor possession of marijuana, rather than a more serious charge of selling it? Why, or why not?

3. Examine each of the contentions made by the respective parties. Which are the most and which the least compelling?

4. At what point does off-duty (off-the-job) misconduct of an employee become sufficiently serious and relevant to justify his or her discharge? Discuss.

CASE 47
HOW MUCH FUNERAL LEAVE PAY?

Company:
 Georgia-Pacific Corporation, Crossett Plywood Plant, Crossett, Georgia

Union:
 International Woodworkers of America, AFL-CIO-CLC and Local No. 5-475

Walter Grainge[1] was a motor mechanic–millwright who had been employed at the Crossett plant since November 24, 1978. On Saturday, September 10, 1988, he was excused from work after completing six hours to be with his mother who was critically ill and who died that day at a local hospital. Grainge was off work September 11 and September 12, the day of his mother's funeral. Grainge requested three days' funeral leave as provided in Section 6 of the collective bargaining agreement.[2]

The payroll office paid Grainge for his funeral leave as follows: 2 hours for September 10, 8 hours for September 11, and 8 hours for September 12, a total of 18 hours at his straight-time rate of $10.91 per hour.

The union filed a grievance on behalf of Walter Grainge contending that he was entitled to four hours' pay for September 10 and 10 hours' pay for each of the days September 11 and September 12. The grievance stated that Grainge was entitled to 24 hours' pay at his straight-time hourly rate, rather than for 18 hours as determined by the company.

The parties could not resolve their differences through meetings under terms of the grievance procedure. They submitted jointly the following statement of the issue to the arbitrator:

> Did the company violate the agreement when it paid Walter Grainge on the basis of eight (8) hours per day for the funeral leave? If so, what shall the remedy be?

Position of the Union

The union provided a company work schedule indicating that Walter Grainge was scheduled to work 10 hours on each of the three days. Neither the company nor the union disputed that he was entitled to funeral pay for these days. However, the union argued that his funeral pay should have been based on his 10-hour work schedule rather than the 8 hours per day the company utilized in its calculations. When referring to "losses in wages" in Section 15.04, the reference was to the hours the employee was scheduled to work. In Grainge's case it was 10 hours. If he had worked those three days and not taken funeral leave, he would have been paid for 10 hours for each of those three days.

---

[1]The names of all individuals are disguised.
[2]See the appendix for relevant contractual provisions.

The union asserted that Sections 15.04 and 6.07 were similar, and that in each instance the pay should have been computed on the basis of scheduled work hours.

The union urged that the arbitrator sustain the grievance and award Walter Grainge pay for an additional six hours of funeral leave.

Position of the Company

The company showed that Section 15.04 pertaining to funeral leave had been negotiated more than 20 years earlier and that the terms of this clause had not been altered since that time. The company produced data supporting the company's position that it had always paid funeral pay computed on the basis of eight hours per day, and Harold Fletcher, hourly payroll supervisor, testified to this effect. He added that he had served as assistant payroll supervisor for nine years and as payroll supervisor for four years. During those 13 years, funeral leave had always been calculated at the rate of 8 hours, even if the employee had been scheduled to work 10 hours.

The company requested that the arbitrator deny the grievance.

APPENDIX
RELEVANT CONTRACTUAL PROVISIONS

Section 6. 6:07. Paid Holidays.   Subject to the following conditions, all employees covered by this agreement shall be paid for the following holidays ...

Each hourly paid employee shall be paid for the number of hours in the employee's normal scheduled work day (but not less than eight (8) hours) at his regular basic straight time hourly rate for each of the nine (9) above holidays which he is not scheduled to work.

Section 15. 15:04. Funeral Leave.   When an employee is required to be absent as a result of a death in his immediate family, he will be reimbursed for losses in wages at straight time hourly rate up to a maximum of three (3) consecutive days, one of which must be the day of the funeral. The immediate family shall include: spouse, children, father, mother, brother, sister, mother-in-law, and father-in-law of the employee.

Questions

1. Is there any difference between the language and application of Section 6:07 and those of Section 15:04? Discuss.
2. Why would the union raise this issue after some 20 years of the same funeral leave contractual provision?
3. On what basis should the arbitrator make a decision in this case: wording of the agreement, past practice, equity?
4. What are the precedent implications of the arbitrator's decision in this case?

CASE 48
STANDBY PAY FOR THE OFF-DUTY POLICE OFFICER

Employer:
City of Wayzata, Minnesota

Union:
Law Enforcement Labor Services, Inc., of Bloomington, Minnesota

Background

The essential facts in this case were not in dispute. In 1985, a new provision was added to the collective bargaining agreement between the parties. This provision (Article XX) provided for "standby pay" as follows:

Article XX—Standby Pay

Employees required to be on call or on standby shall receive one-half (½) hours' pay for each hour on such status.

Following implementation of the 1985–86 agreement and also during the 1987–88 agreement, no member of the bargaining unit had received standby pay up to and through the time the instant grievance was filed.

In January 1988, Police Officer Morton Beam[1] received two subpoenas from the Hennepin County Attorney's office requiring him to be available to testify in District Court on January 7th and January 14th. Following receipt of the first subpoena, Officer Beam notified the Court that departmental policy, as expressed by Wayzata Chief of Police Russell Caldwell, required that the Court notify the Police Department directly concerning any scheduled court appearance. A copy of the subpoena was then submitted to Chief Caldwell. Subsequently, Officer Beam was notified that he was to be placed on "standby" by the Court, because a settlement of the case scheduled for January 7th was under consideration. Police Chief Caldwell phoned Beam on the morning of January 7th (Beam's day off) and told Beam that he should carry a "pager" so that he would be available if he was called to appear in court that day. Beam told Caldwell that he would prefer to remain at his home near his telephone rather than carry the pager. This procedure was acceptable to Caldwell, and Beam remained at home for a period of four hours that day (i.e., January 7, 1988).

On January 14th, Officer Beam was again subpoenaed to appear in District Court in connection with another case that was scheduled for trial. Again the Police Department was notified by the Court. On January 13th, Beam received a note from Chief Caldwell asking that he carry a pager with him whenever he might be away from his phone on January 14th, since Beam was not scheduled for duty on that date.

Subsequently, Officer Beam put in a request for standby pay for both January 7th and the 14th, claiming six hours at one-half time pursuant to Article XX. When this

---

[1]The names of all individuals are disguised.

request was denied by Chief Caldwell, Officer Beam filed a formal written grievance, which eventually was carried to arbitration.

Statements of the Issue

The parties could not agree on the proper framing of the issue(s) before the arbitrator. The union posed the issue as:

Was Article XX of the Collective Bargaining Agreement violated when the Grievant was denied standby or on-call pay for January 7th and 14th, 1988?

However, the city proposed the following statement of the issues:

1. Did authorized city management personnel place the Grievant on standby duty?
2. Is the "Hennepin County Attorney's Office" the employer of the Grievant under the Labor Agreement between the parties?

Position of the Union

The union maintained that the city had violated Article XX of the collective bargaining agreement when Officer Morton Beam was denied standby pay for January 7th and 14th, 1988. The union contended that court appearances for police officers were an integral part of their job duties and that they were required to appear if subpoenaed. If a police officer failed to make a court appearance after being subpoenaed or directed to do so by superiors, then he or she was subject to discipline by the city administration. Further, the union maintained that on the two days in question in January, Officer Beam was either required to remain near a telephone for a specified period of time, or to carry a pager. Both instances limited Beam's activities during the specified times; therefore he was on standby and entitled to the pay as set forth in Article XX. In addition, the union argued that had Beam not responded to a phone call on January 7th or to the pager on the 14th, he would have been subject to discipline. This was further evidence that Officer Beam had been placed on constructive standby on those dates. The court appearances were a direct result of Officer Beam's performing his assigned job duties and intrinsically related to the standard work assignment of a police officer.

Finally, the union argued that the city's position concerning who was the employer in this instance was without merit, because even if an officer was summoned to appear in court by someone other than the city attorney (i.e., the county attorney), then he or she had routinely and consistently been compensated by the city of Wayzata. For all these reasons, therefore, the union claimed that the grievant should be reimbursed for a total of six hours standby pay at the appropriate rate.

Position of the City

The city of Wayzata was represented by its city attorney, who took the position that the city (i.e., Chief Caldwell) had never authorized Officer Morton Beam to be on standby duty on either January 7th or the 14th. Rather, the subpoena was issued by the Hennepin County Attorney's office, which was not a party to the labor agreement. The city maintained that it had the sole right to schedule employees for work or to make decisions under the bargaining agreement's provisions calling for any payment to bargaining unit members. The practice of the parties clearly indicated that, since the inception of Article XX in 1985, the city had routinely and consistently refrained from making any payments to bargaining unit members under Article XX in circumstances such as those in this case. Further, on the days in question, the city asserted that at no time was Officer Beam instructed that he was being placed on "standby." Finally, the city noted that it had notified the Hennepin County Attorney's office in writing that if the county sought the appearance of any of its police officers in District Court, they must expressly direct the request to the city administration concerning the appearance of an officer, and that the city would then make the final determination as to whether or not the employee could appear on the day specified.

In summary, the city argued that to grant the union grievance would open up a "Pandora's Box" by which employees could abuse the standby provision to claim pay for situations for which standby pay was never intended.

For all these reasons, the city asked that the grievance be dismissed in its entirety.

Questions

1. Look up a dictionary definition of the word "standby." How does this definition apply to the circumstances of this case?
2. Evaluate the respective contentions of the parties. Which are the most persuasive, and which the least persuasive?
3. Does the fact that the city had not previously paid standby pay to any employee mean that a past practice existed that should not be disturbed by the arbitrator? Why, or why not?
4. Why would the city be concerned about a "Pandora's Box" of possible abuse if the union's grievance were sustained? Discuss.

CASE 49
REVOCATION OF DUES CHECKOFF IN A RIGHT-TO-WORK STATE

Company:
Gerland's Food Fair, Inc., Houston, Texas

Union:
United Food and Commercial Workers, Local No. 455

Background

Since 1973, Gerland's Food Fair, Inc., and Local No. 455, United Food and Commercial Workers Union, had had a collective bargaining agreement. Since 1978, all the parties' collective bargaining agreements contained a union security section identified as Section 3.01, which included the following dues checkoff provision: *"No deductions shall be discontinued until the Employer has verified through the Union that the employee's request for revocation is timely and proper."*[1]

For a number of years, the union had used a checkoff authorization form that stated as follows:

I, _____, hereby voluntarily authorize _____, in the State of Texas to deduct my initiation fee, and regular monthly dues as duly established from time to time by United Food & Commercial Workers Union, Local No. 455, United Food & Commercial Workers International Union, AFL-CIO, from my pay check on the _____ week of each month, in advance, and deliver such initiation fees and dues to the aforementioned Local No. 455.

This authorization shall continue in effect for the term of the contract between the Employer and the Union, or one year, whichever occurs sooner, and shall continue in effect for successive periods of one year unless revoked in writing by the undersigned to the Employer and the Union, within fifteen (15) days prior to the expiration of each term of one year or prior to the termination of the Agreement, whichever occurs sooner.

It is understood that the Employer's responsibility for the performance of this service is strictly limited to the delivery of such dues and initiation fees to the UFCW Local Union No. 455.

In 1988, the union revised its dues checkoff authorization form to read as follows:

TO: Any Employer under Contract with United Food and Commercial Workers Union, Local 455, AFL-CIO.

You are hereby authorized and directed to deduct from my wages, commencing with the next payroll period, an amount equivalent to dues and initiation fees as shall be certified by the Secretary-Treasurer of Local 455 of the United Food and Commercial Workers International Union, AFL-CIO, and remit same to said Secretary-Treasurer.

This authorization and assignment is voluntarily made in consideration for the cost of representation and collective bargaining and is not contingent upon my present or future membership in the Union. This authorization and assignment shall be irrevocable for a period of one (1) year from the date of execution or until the termination date of the agreement

---

[1]See the appendix for relevant contractual provisions.

between the Employer and Local 455, whichever occurs sooner, and from year to year thereafter, unless not less than thirty (30) days and not more than forty-five (45) days prior to the end of any subsequent yearly period I give the Employer and Union written notice of revocation bearing my signature therein.

In early 1989, seven employees who had been union members gave the local union written notices that they were resigning their union memberships and wanted their union dues checkoff to be revoked.[2] These employees and the dates of their letters were Nancy Ray and Beatrice Walls (February 24, 1989); James Neal and Paula Mertz (February 28, 1989); Rachel Munger and Marcella Charo (March 1, 1989); and Isabella Gilpin (March 22, 1989).

Between February 27 and March 10, 1989, the union wrote each of the seven that their requests for withdrawal of their union memberships were accepted. However, the union wrote Ray, Walls, Neal, Mertz, Munger, and Charo that their requests to have their dues checkoff revoked were deemed untimely, because their requests were not made "within fifteen (15) days prior to the effective date of execution or fifteen (15) days prior to the termination date of the agreement between the Employer and Local 455, whichever occurs sooner. The checkoff agreement is separate from your membership in the local." Gilpin's request to withdraw her checkoff authorization also was found untimely, because it was not made "not less than thirty (30) days and not more than forty-five (45) days prior to the end of any subsequent yearly period." The union considered the dues checkoff still in force for all seven employees.

Copies of the union response letters to the seven employees were forwarded to Derrick Curtis, the company's Director of Industrial Relations. Curtis did not verify the checkoff revocation requests through the union, but he did review the union's responses to the affected employees. Curtis also briefly discussed the matter with each of the seven employees. On March 10, 1989, Curtis wrote Raleigh Eugene, the local union president, that the company would no longer deduct union dues from the payroll checks of the seven employees until such time as they might rejoin the union. Curtis' letter to the union was based, at least in part, upon advice from Natasha Bingham of the Regional Office of the NLRB. Eugene contacted Curtis by telephone to protest the company's decision. Curtis agreed that until the matter was finally settled, the company would continue to deduct union dues from the checks of the seven employees and put the money in an escrow account.

On April 19, 1989, the union filed unfair labor practice charges against the company. The union claimed that the company had violated Sections 8(a) (1) and 8(a) (5) of the National Labor Relations Act, because the company had refused to give the union the dues from those who had resigned from membership and because it had engaged in individual bargaining. The NLRB regional director refused to issue a complaint; this decision was appealed and the appeal was denied by the General Counsel of the NLRB on July 18, 1989.

Earlier, however, on March 21, 1989, the union also had filed a written general grievance complaining that the company had ceased forwarding the dues. The grievance read, in part:

---

[2]The names of all individuals are disguised.

The Employer has violated the Agreement by ceasing these deductions, since the Union has at no point notified the Employer that these revocations are timely and proper, or that the employee should be removed from the checkoff authorization.

. . . We are requesting that the Union be made whole, that the Employer be responsible for all monies which would have been deducted under the checkoff authorization, and that the employer be required to pay reasonable interest until the matter has been resolved.

The union grievance was not resolved by the parties, and the grievance was eventually carried to arbitration.

Framing of the Issue(s)

There was little factual dispute about the case, but the parties differed considerably in their proposed statements of the issue(s) before the arbitrator.

The union proposed the following statement of the issue(s):

Did the Employer violate the contract when it discontinued dues checkoffs on behalf of certain employees without first verifying through the union that the employees' requests for revocation were timely and proper?

And if so, what should be the remedy?

However, the company proposed a series of questions/issues the arbitrator should resolve. These were:

1. Whether the arbitrator should defer his decision to the NLRB, since the facts herein involve a statutory interpretation of the NLRA.
2. Without waiving issue No. 1, whether the Company verified that the employees' request for revocation of their dues checkoff was timely and proper.
3. Without waiving issue No. 1, whether the Company was excused from verifying directly with the Union whether certain employees' requests for withdrawal from union membership and cessation of their dues checkoff was in conformity with their checkoff authorization.
4. Whether the Company was excused from honoring the Union's request to continue dues checkoff for employees whose revocation requests were untimely.

Because the parties could not agree on the framing of the issue(s), they gave the arbitrator authority to frame the issue(s) as he saw fit. The arbitrator decided on the following statement:

What is the proper disposition of the grievance raised in the Union letter of March 21, 1989?

Position of the Union

In summary arguments, the union contended that its grievance should be sustained because:

1. Clear and unambiguous contract language required the company to verify through the union that requests to discontinue checkoff were timely and proper before honoring such requests. This was not done despite the employer's contractual obligation to do so.

2. Union membership was not a quid pro quo for checkoff. The obligation to fulfill checkoff commitments was between an employee and the union. Derrick Curtis improperly injected the company into that relationship by verifying checkoff discontinuation requests directly with employees.

3. Advice from the NLRB about this matter and NLRB dismissal of the union's unfair labor practice charges did not constitute rulings of a "court of final jurisdiction." If the company felt that the agreement's checkoff language violated federal law, they could have asked the union to renegotiate the problematic language.

4. The arbitrator was enjoined from altering the language of the agreement.

5. The grievance was arbitrable. It was settled labor law that where dual jurisdictions arise, both arbitration and NLRB proceedings may occur. The Supreme Court has long held that the NLRB and the courts should defer to arbitration so long as an arbitration award "draws its essence from the collective bargaining agreement."[3]

Position of the Company

The company contended that the union grievance should be denied, because:

1. The language of the collective bargaining agreement and the checkoff authorization forms showed that dues were a quid pro quo for union membership. This was particularly true since there were no agency shop or financial-core membership provisions. The NLRB has ruled that where dues payment is a quid pro quo for union membership, resignation from the union revokes checkoff authorization regardless of the timing of the resignation. The company was obligated under current labor law to honor employee requests.

2. External law should be applied to the instant case so that the company would not be subjected to inconsistent rulings from the arbitrator and the NLRB.

3. Section 3.01 of the agreement did not specify the manner or method by which the company must verify employee requests for revocation of checkoff authorization. The company did verify these requests by reviewing union letters to the affected employees. The information obtained from that review would have been the same as that given by the union had it been asked directly. Since the employee requests complied with applicable labor law, the company did not have to verify with the union whether the requests were proper or timely.

---

[3]*United Steelworkers* v. *Enterprise Wheel & Car Corp.*, 80 S. Ct. 1358 (46 LRRM 2423), (1960). For a review of the legal status of arbitration, see Frank Elkouri and Edna Asper Elkouri, *How Arbitration Works,* 4th ed. (Washington, D.C.: Bureau of National Affairs, 1985), pp. 23–95.

APPENDIX
RELEVANT CONTRACTUAL PROVISIONS

Article 3—Union Security

Section 3.01.   During the life of this Agreement, the Employer shall deduct initiation fees and regular dues weekly from employees who individually and voluntarily certify in writing on the checkoff authorization form for such deductions. Such authorizations shall be binding on the employees for the duration of this Agreement unless the authorization is revoked in accordance with the provisions of the Taft-Hartley Act of 1947, as amended. No deductions shall be discontinued until the Employer has verified through the Union that the employee's request for revocation is timely and proper. The Union shall certify in writing a list of its new members, together with signed authorization cards with an itemized list of such initiation fees and dues to be deducted from such members. Timing for such deductions may be worked out locally between the Employer and the Union.

Article 19—Dispute Procedure

Section 19.03.   The arbitrator shall have no power to add to, subtract from, alter, amend, modify or project beyond its meaning any of the terms and provisions of this Agreement.

Article 21—Separability

Any provision of this Agreement which may be adjudged by a court of final jurisdiction to be in conflict with any Federal, State or Local Law shall become inoperative to the extent and duration of such conflict. Since it is not the intent of either party hereto to violate any such laws, it is agreed that in the event of a conflict between any law and any provision of this Agreement, the balance of the Agreement shall remain in full force and effect. The Employer and the Union agree that substitute provisions shall be negotiated promptly to replace those provisions coming into conflict with the laws herein described. The Employer and the Union further agree if they are unable to reach an agreement on the substitute provisions to arbitrate any differences concerning a substitute provision.

Questions

1. Should the arbitrator defer disposition of this case to the National Labor Relations Board? Why, or why not?
2. Compare the issues in this case with those in Case 29, "The Grievance-Processing Fee for Nonmembers in a Right-to-Work State." What similarities and differences are involved?
3. Evaluate the company's contention that it did verify the employees' requests, even though the company did not do so directly through the union. Is this a major or a minor issue to be resolved by the arbitrator?
4. Can the arbitrator fashion a decision in this case that "draws its essence from the collective bargaining agreement"? Discuss.

CASE 50
VANDALISM ON THE SCHOOL PARKING LOT

Employer:
Milwaukee Board of School Directors, Milwaukee, Wisconsin

Union:
Milwaukee Teachers Education Association

Background

The employer operated a large metropolitan school district, and the union represented the teachers employed in the district.

One of the benefits provided in the collective bargaining agreement between the parties was a provision stating that teachers would be "reimbursed against loss or damage to their personal property incurred during the course of employment while on duty at their school." That clause, however, also stated that the loss or damage had to be incurred "without negligence on the part of the teacher" and was "not to exceed $150."

Another benefit provided by the collective bargaining agreement was one in which the employer provided financial protection to cover "malicious damage" to employees' cars parked at school during school hours. Unlike the clause on personal property, the auto vandalism provision did not specifically state that coverage was restricted to claims where the teacher making the claim was free from personal negligence.[1] To administer claims for auto vandalism, the employer hired an outside claims adjustment firm called Self Insurers Service, Inc.

Harvey Diehl,[2] a seventh-grade teacher, had been employed in the Milwaukee school system for 17 years. At the time of this case, he was the owner of three automobiles—1971, 1974, and 1975 Gremlins.

On March 31, 1987, Diehl had a nonfactory hood ornament known as a "naked lady" stolen from his 1971 Gremlin automobile while it was parked on the premises of the Kosciuszko Middle School. His car suffered some hood scratches during the theft, but Diehl did not file for hood repairs because he was going to use that particular vehicle for parts. He did, however, file a vandalism claim for $13.75 for the replacement of the ornament itself. Diehl was reimbursed $3.75 after the $10 deductible was applied.

On September 14, 1988, another "naked lady" ornament was stolen from one of Diehl's cars, the 1975 Gremlin, while it was parked at the school. This time the hood was dented and scratched; Diehl was reimbursed the cost of the repairs minus the $20 deductible as per the provision in the collective bargaining contract.

---

[1] Both of these provisions were included under a section of the collective bargaining agreement entitled "Insurance."

[2] Name is disguised.

On February 7, 1989, Diehl suffered the third removal of a "naked lady" hood ornament from his 1975 Gremlin while it was parked in the parking lot of the Kosciuszko Middle School. Again in this vandalism claim, Diehl stated that the ornament was missing, and there were dents and scratches on the hood requiring straightening and painting.

Following the receipt of the third claim, the outside insurance adjuster denied coverage for the replacement value of the hood ornament on the grounds that the nonfactory ornament was an "attractive enticement" to middle-school-aged children.

Two weeks later the union filed a grievance on behalf of Harvey Diehl for reimbursement for the theft of the hood ornament and damage to the car's hood that had been denied. However, after learning that the letter warning that the "naked lady" ornament was an "attractive enticement" did not reach Diehl until after the theft, the employer agreed to pay the third claim. When he was paid the third time, however, Diehl was warned that if he were to install another "naked lady" hood ornament on his automobile, he would be personally responsible for its theft.

On March 16, 1989, Diehl experienced a fourth theft of the "naked lady" hood ornament and car damage to his 1975 Gremlin. Diehl again filed a claim. This time, both the insurance adjuster and the employer denied the claim citing the fact that Diehl had been warned that if he were to install the "naked lady" hood ornament for a fourth time, it would be solely his responsibility.

The union grieved the matter, and it eventually went to arbitration.

Position of the Union

The union claimed that the collective bargaining contract provided that Harvey Diehl be reimbursed for any vandalism done to his car whether he had been warned by the employer or not. The language of the contract had no limitation for negligence or the lack of due care, or because the ornament was an "attractive enticement," or for any other reason.

According to the union, the negligence bar mentioned in the contract applied only to the loss or damage of personal property. In the case of auto vandalism, that section of the contract was separate and distinct and contained no limitation barring a claim involving negligence by a teacher.

The union argued that the two separate provisions of the contract were negotiated specifically concerning separate and distinct things, that is, protection against theft of personal property and protection for automobile vandalism. In one section, the contract specifically declared that there could be no recovery if the teacher was negligent (loss or damage to personal property); but in the other clause there was no such limitation (malicious damage to automobiles). If the employer wanted to change the contract, the union contended it must seek such a change through negotiation. The employer could not alter a specific provision of a contract on its own whim. It especially could not do so, the union argued, on the declaration of an outside third party who had not even taken part in negotiating the contract.

The union urged that the grievance be sustained, and that Harvey Diehl be reimbursed the appropriate amount for repairs to his car.[3]

Position of the Employer

The employer acknowledged that the insurance provision of the parties' collective bargaining contract provided for reimbursement for two types of losses. One dealt with personal property, and the other dealt with auto vandalism. The personal property provision specifically included a standard of negligence as a way of limiting the employer's liability.

Although "negligence" was not explicitly stated in the auto vandalism portion of the contract, this did not mean the employer could not curtail its liability if damage was done to a teacher's automobile due to a teacher's carelessness. The parties did not have to incorporate the term "negligence" in the auto vandalism clause, the employer argued, because it was common insurance practice that auto insurance provisions contained an implicit standard of negligence.

The personal property reimbursement provision of the contract explicitly contained a negligence standard, because it was not an insurance product as was the auto vandalism provision. The personal property reimbursement provision was not administered by an independent insurance adjuster. For this reason, the parties while negotiating the contract felt compelled to incorporate a negligence standard in that provision of the contract. Such a provision was unnecessary when the auto vandalism provision was negotiated into the contract, because a negligence standard is implicit in every insurance policy in order to limit the liability for claims that are the fault of the insured. In other words, argued the employer, an insurance company does not automatically honor every claim once it is submitted. As damage appraisers, the outside adjuster bears the responsibility of determining whether a claim is valid. Therefore, there always was a negligence standard implied under the auto vandalism provision of the contract.

The employer argued that this particular auto vandalism claim should be denied because the claim was caused by the grievant's obvious gross negligence, namely, Harvey Diehl's persistent placing of a "naked lady" hood ornament on his automobile. It was especially negligent behavior considering the time and place where the car was parked. After the second claim was paid, Diehl again mounted the "naked lady" ornament on his automobile. Not more than six months later the "naked lady" hood ornament was stolen from the grievant's car again. This incident prompted the employer to send a letter to Diehl informing him that the "naked lady" hood ornament was an "attractive enticement," and that any further claims submitted by Diehl for the theft of the "naked lady" would not be honored. However, because the third incident of theft had occurred prior to Diehl's receiving notice that his ornament constituted an "attractive enticement," the employer honored the third claim. When the fourth claim was filed, the letter of warning had been received by Diehl, so the claim was justifiably denied by the outside adjuster.

---

[3]According to Harvey Diehl and the union, the net amount due him was $127.05.

The employer argued that the grievant could not repeatedly place a "naked lady" hood ornament on his automobile and submit endless claims and be compensated for damage resulting from the theft of the ornament. If all insureds took this position, insurance companies would be inundated with claims. If private insurance companies honored those claims, they would be in business for a short time only.

It was the joint decision of the outside insurance adjuster and the employer that the theft of the "naked lady" hood ornament resulted from Harvey Diehl's carelessness and negligence. They decided to dishonor his fourth claim; such a decision on the part of the outside adjuster and the employer did not constitute an unreasonable action, nor did it constitute a violation of the contract. Accordingly, the employer declared, the union grievance on behalf of Harvey Diehl should be denied in its entirety.

Questions

1. Evaluate the union's position that the automotive vandalism provision contained no limitation barring a claim involving negligence by a teacher.
2. Evaluate the employer's position that negligence and carelessness on the part of a teacher were valid bases for denying a teacher's claim for damages resulting from auto vandalism.
3. When Harvey Diehl was warned about his auto ornament being an "attractive enticement" for which no further claims of loss would be honored, did this relieve the insurance adjuster and the employer from paying Diehl's fourth claim? Why, or why not?
4. Why does a case of this nature pose a difficult dilemma for the arbitrator?

CASE 51
HOLIDAY PAY WHILE RECEIVING SICK PAY

Company:
Dahlgren's Incorporated, Oglesby, Illinois

Union:
United Brotherhood of Carpenters and Joiners of America, Northwest Illinois District Council and Local Union No. 195

Background

The company was a manufacturer of windows and doors. The collective bargaining agreement at the time of this case was effective for the period May 1, 1987, through April 30, 1990. Under this collective bargaining agreement, employees would receive sick pay if they injured themselves off the job and were unable to report to work.[1]

In mid-November 1988, employee Gregory Zeiss[2] was injured in a motorcycle accident near his home. Because of his injuries, he was unable to work. He applied for and received a medical excuse from the company to extend from November 14 through November 28, 1988. Since Zeiss was classified as a lead man, he was entitled to receive sick pay benefits of $180 weekly during that period.

However, during that period there were two contractual holidays, Thanksgiving and the Friday following. Zeiss applied for two days of holiday pay, and a grievance arose when his application for holiday pay was rejected by the company. Zeiss claimed that he should receive two days of holiday pay at his regular rate multiplied by eight hours for each day. He suggested that his weekly sick pay should be reduced by a formula of proration under which he would receive not $180 for the week, but $36 for each of the three days for which he did not receive compensation and for which the holiday pay provision did not apply. The parties were unable to resolve the grievance, and it was carried to arbitration.

Positions of the Parties

The union urged that just as there was no dispute that Gregory Zeiss was entitled to weekly sick pay for what it termed a "self-inflicted weekend accident," there should be no dispute under the holiday provision regarding his holiday pay. Zeiss had a valid doctor's statement, and he was excused from working. The union argued that the contract clearly specified that the requirement that an employee work the day before and after a holiday to be eligible for extra holiday compensation did not apply "in cases of accident or sickness supported by a doctor's statement." The union noted that it was

---

[1]See the appendix for relevant contractual provisions.
[2]Name is disguised.

not asking for both holiday pay and sick pay; instead, by prorating the sick pay benefit on a daily basis, it was recognizing that an employee could not benefit under both the holiday provision and the sick pay provision. Zeiss's straight-time hourly wage was $10.54; thus, under the contract he was entitled to eight hours of pay for each holiday regardless of whether or not he was also entitled on other days for sick pay.

However, the company contended that the holiday provision in the contract was written around the issue of absences immediately before and after holidays to prevent employees' skipping days of work and extending absence from work while receiving holiday pay. This provision was long-standing, and it had been in several previous collective bargaining agreements. During prior years there had never been an application for holiday pay during a period in which an employee was eligible for sick pay. The company argued that if the holiday provision had been intended to operate as the union was contending, there surely would have been contractual language indicating some kind of control or limitation; for example, there would be nothing to prevent an employee off sick even beyond the 13-week sick pay benefit from applying for holiday pay.

In rebutting the last point, the union urged that in fact there were limitations, 13 weeks being defined as the sick pay benefit limit. Although this situation had never come up, presumably upon the expiration of that period the company would have to decide whether someone remained an employee (i.e., had an expectation of returning) or not. As to the fact that holiday pay had not heretofore been requested under circumstances such as those of Gregory Zeiss, this was not something that could be charged to the union, which did not have knowledge of who was sick or, more particularly, who received what pay while sick.

The company urged that the lack of applications for holiday pay during sick leaves indicated a past practice or understanding. One employee had been absent on sick pay from 5/13/87 to 6/3/87, over the Memorial Day holiday but had not received or asked for holiday pay. Another had been absent from 6/19/87 to 7/20/87, receiving sick pay but not receiving and not applying for Fourth of July pay. Another employee had been ill from 8/17/87 to 10/8/87, receiving sick pay but not receiving or applying for holiday Labor Day pay. Another was sick from October 1986 until some time in January 1987, and did not receive or ask for the four days of Christmas/New Year holiday pay. Still another was off from 6/30/86 to 7/20/86 and did not receive or ask for Fourth of July pay. Another was off from 12/17/84 to 1/21/85, and did not receive or ask for the four days of holiday pay occurring during that period. The company urged that these examples showed that to award the grievant's request would be to give the union something for which it had not bargained.

At the conclusion of the arbitration hearing, the parties described the case as one in which, "despite their best efforts at discussion, they were simply unable to come to agreement." They mutually urged the arbitrator to decide the issue in a manner that would follow the contract's intent as best the arbitrator could objectively determine it.

APPENDIX
RELEVANT CONTRACTUAL PROVISIONS

Article VIII, Section 4—Group Insurance (in Part):

Life & Accidental Death & Dismemberment
All Employees—$5,000.00.
Benefits will terminate at age 70 or retirement, whichever occurs first.
Short Term Disability—Benefits are payable after the Employee waits:
0 Days for an accident.
7 Days for an illness.
Sick Pay
Benefits will continue for 13 weeks.
The amount of Benefits will be: Laborers $150.00 per week. Progressive rate through Journeyman $165.00, lead man $180.00 per week.

Article VIII, Section 1—Paid Holidays (in Part):

For the purposes of determining Holiday pay, the following days shall be considered as legal Holidays: New Year's Day, Decoration Day, Fourth of July, Labor Day, Thanksgiving Day, Christmas Day, Day preceding Christmas, the Day preceding New Year's Day, the Friday after Thanksgiving and Good Friday.

Subject to the following provisions, all Employees, whether or not scheduled to work on any of the aforementioned Holidays or days celebrated as such, shall receive, as extra Holiday compensation, one (1) day's pay at straight time for eight (8) hours.

Extra Holiday compensation, as above provided, will apply only to such Employees as do report and work the customary full work period not only on the day such Employee is scheduled to work that immediately precedes the Holiday, but also reports and works the customary full work period on the day such Employee is scheduled to work immediately after the Holiday. (Except in cases of accident or sickness supported by a doctor's statement.)

The work period that precedes and the work period after each Holiday must be within fifteen (15) working days of the Holiday, or the Company is relieved of its obligation for Holiday pay.

Questions

1. Examine carefully the relevant contractual provisions. Which provisions are most supportive of the parties' respective positions?
2. Did a past practice or understanding exist that would preclude the claim of the grievant for holiday pay while receiving sick pay benefits? Discuss.
3. Should the union grievance's being the first dispute of this type be a basis for denying the union's (Gregory Zeiss's) claim? Why, or why not?
4. On what basis can the arbitrator determine the contract's intent, as urged by both the company and union? Discuss.

CASE 52
THE GROSS SAFETY VIOLATION

Company:
  Gold Kist, Inc., Northwest Georgia Poultry Division, Athens, Georgia

Union:
  Local No. 442, United Food & Commercial Workers District Union

Background

The company operated a poultry processing plant in Athens, Georgia. Production and maintenance employees were represented by the United Food and Commercial Workers District Union, Local No. 442.

This grievance-arbitration case developed as a result of the February 28, 1989, termination of Rose Ross[1] for a "gross safety violation." Ross was first hired by the company in 1974, and at the time of her discharge was a first-shift saw operator. As such, Ross operated a saw with a nine and one-half inch blade revolving at 1,725 revolutions per minute. It was her responsibility to obtain the poultry from the line and guide it through the saw. She was required to wear steel mesh gloves on both hands while performing her duties.

Rose Ross had received two prior warnings in her record relevant to her termination.[2] The first was an oral warning dated August 24, 1982, for failing to wear steel gloves. The second warning, dated October 28, 1986, was a written warning for a similar failure to wear steel gloves.

On February 28, 1989, Rose Ross was observed by her supervisor, Lester Boswell, operating the saw with her gloved right hand. Ross had her bare left hand in her mouth. Boswell immediately turned off the processing line and asked Ross to accompany him to his office. In the presence of a union shop steward, Amanda Dee, Ross was discharged from her job.

On March 9, 1989, a grievance was filed by the union contesting Ross's termination and asking that she be reinstated with back pay. The grievance eventually was carried to arbitration. Both parties agreed that the issue for the arbitrator's determination was: Did the company have just cause under the labor agreement[3] to terminate Rose Ross? If not, what should be the appropriate remedy?

Position of the Company

The company contended that Rose Ross's failure to wear one of her steel gloves while continuing to operate the saw constituted a gross safety violation punishable by discharge, especially since Ross had twice before been warned about this same violation.

---

[1]The names of all individuals are disguised.

[2]The company also offered as evidence a 1985 warning to Ross for failure to wear hearing protection. However, this warning was not presented during the earlier steps of the grievance procedure, nor was it a consideration in Ross's discharge.

[3]See the appendix for the relevant contractual provision.

The testimony of both Lester Boswell and another supervisor, Arno Hammett, demonstrated that the saw job was an extremely dangerous job requiring 100 percent concentration at all times. The saw blade was so sharp that it easily could cut through flesh and bone. Ross admitted not wearing the left-hand glove while continuing to process the poultry. Her own statements had revealed that she was aware of the company's requirement for her to wear steel gloves on both hands while using the saw. Despite two prior warnings, Ross continued to show a blatant disregard for company safety rules and safety policies.

The company's "Work Rules" delineated certain rules violations considered serious enough to warrant major disciplinary action, including discharge. One such rule was the following: "Disregard of safety rules that endanger the safety of the employee or other employees." The company had consistently enforced its safety rules as evidenced by warnings, suspensions, and terminations of other employees. In one case an employee was discharged for failure to wear steel gloves while operating a saw, and that discharge was upheld in arbitration.

The company expected strict adherence to safety rules, particularly in jobs where failure to follow the rules could result in irreparable harm to the employee. The company noted that it must comply with all regulations of the Occupational Safety and Health Administration (OSHA) formulated and enforced under the federal law requiring a safe workplace. In this regard, the company cited the arbitral opinion of Arbitrator Alexander B. Porter in *Bethlehem Steel Co.* (41 LA 1152, 1153), who reasoned that employees may not exercise individual discretion regarding the need to comply with safety rules.

In conclusion, the company urged the arbitrator not to substitute her discretion for that of company management in this matter. The company had the contractual right to formulate and enforce safety policies and rules designed to protect all employees. Ross was discharged after two prior warnings for the same serious offense. Hers was a blatant disregard for company safety rules and safety policies. The company had ample just cause to terminate Ross, and this decision should not be disturbed by the arbitrator.

Position of the Union

The union contended that Rose Ross's actions on February 28, 1989, did not constitute a gross safety violation. According to Ross's testimony, the processing line was shut down when she realized that her temporary false tooth had become loose. She removed her glove and, while she was attempting to remove the tooth, someone turned on the line. She began to process the poultry with her right hand and completed removing the tooth with her left hand. At no time did her left hand come in contact with the poultry or the saw.

The union contended that the circumstances of the other discharge case were considerably different from those in Ross's case. The other discharged employee had injured herself 27 times during only eight years of employment with the company. Further, she had received three warnings for failure to wear protective gloves during the three years prior to her discharge. By contrast, Rose Ross had been warned on only two occasions, occurring two and a half and six and a half years previously. In total, Ross had made only three mistakes warranting a warning during her 14 years with the company. The union further contended that everyone in the workplace was responsible for safety. Therefore, the person who started the processing line without checking the positions of those employees working on the line must bear part of the responsibility for the incident. The company had failed to investigate this aspect of the situation and had simply chosen to single out Rose Ross for discharge.

The union asked the arbitrator to sustain the grievance and to reinstate Rose Ross with full back pay and all other rights under the contract.

APPENDIX
RELEVANT CONTRACTUAL PROVISION

Article 1—Management Rights

Section 1.   The rights of management shall be limited only to the extent necessary to carry out the terms and conditions set out in this Agreement. The management of the Company and its operations, and the direction of its working force, including the right to hire, promote, suspend, or discharge employees for just cause and the maintenance of efficiency are vested exclusively in the Company. The Company may, in its judgment, increase or decrease operations, remove or install machinery or appliances, determine work processes and procedures, maintain discipline, and enact reasonable Company policies and plant rules and regulations, which are not in conflict with the provisions of this Agreement or legal rights of employees.

Questions

1. Assuming that company supervisors believed Rose Ross's explanation of what happened, why would the company terminate her for a "gross safety violation"? Discuss.
2. Evaluate the company's contention supported by a prior arbitral decision that an employee may not exercise individual discretion regarding compliance with safety rules.
3. Evaluate the union's contention that the circumstances involving the discharge of another employee were considerably different from those involving Rose Ross and should be weighed in favor of reinstatement of Ross.
4. Was the company justified in terminating Rose Ross? Why, or why not?

CASE 53
NO MORE MINORITY PREFERENTIAL HIRING?

City:

City of Pontiac, Pontiac, Michigan

Union:

Pontiac Firefighters Union, Local No. 376

In 1986, the city and firefighters union had voluntarily agreed upon an affirmative action plan, the terms of which they included in their collective bargaining agreement in Article V, Section 4(D)(1).[1] The agreement provided that the city would hire minorities into the department on a two-to-one ratio. This procedure was to be in force until the end of the contract, December 31, 1989.

In June 1988, the city's human rights officer, Roger Samuels,[2] determined that the minority hiring goal had been achieved. He reported this to the city attorney who then advised the fire civil service commission to disregard the minority civil service roster and to select candidates solely on the basis of their employment test scores.

On October 4, 1988, the civil service commission adopted the city attorney's recommendation, disregarding the provisions of the agreement. The union submitted a grievance, which was processed to the third step of the grievance procedure. The parties held a meeting on December 29, 1988. On January 13, 1989, 15 days after the third-step meeting, the city issued its reply denying the union's grievance. The union appealed the city's decision to arbitration. The parties agreed that the arbitrator should rule on the following issues:

1. Did the city file a timely response to the grievance at step three level?
2. Did the city act improperly or in violation of the contract by its refusal to continue to implement the minority hiring provisions of the contract? If so, what should be the appropriate remedy?

Position of the Union

The union argued that the grievance was not arbitrable since the city had replied 15 days after the third-step meeting, rather than 10 days as provided in Article III, Sections 1(D) and 1(F) of the agreement. Therefore, as stated in the agreement, the arbitrator should find for the union and grant the remedy it requested in this matter.

The union also held that, even if the arbitrator found that the city's reply had been timely at the third step of the grievance procedure, the city had acted improperly in unilaterally discontinuing the application of the clear and unambigu-

---

[1] See the appendix for relevant provisions of the collective bargaining agreement.
[2] Name is disguised.

ous terms of the agreement. The arbitrator should decide the case based only on the agreement. The arbitrator should also require that the city comply with the terms of the agreement.

The union insisted that the city be directed to cease and desist from unilaterally making changes in the agreement without discussion with and approval of the union. Further, the union requested that the city make appropriate adjustment to the seniority dates of affected employees. Finally, the union sought reimbursement for all costs incurred, including attorney's fees.

The union urged that the arbitrator rule in its favor on all of its requests.

Position of the City

The city contended that the grievance was arbitrable and not subject to forfeiture. The city maintained that its reply was appropriate and timely at the third step of the grievance procedure, since it responded within 10 working days as was intended by the contract. Any other interpretation of the agreement would mean that either party would be required on many occasions to submit a reply on a holiday or on a Saturday or Sunday. In fact, this would always occur whenever a grievance occurred on a Wednesday or Thursday. The union had not been damaged by this interpretation of the agreement, which was the original intent of Article III, Sections 1(D) and 1(F).

The city held that it had every right to eliminate the separate minority hiring roster, because to do otherwise would violate Title VII of the Civil Rights Act as interpreted by the U.S. Supreme Court in *Steelworkers* v. *Weber* (443 U.S. 193) and *Wygant* v. *Jackson Board of Education* (476 U.S. 267). The *Steelworkers* v. *Weber* decision stated, in summary:

> Title VII race bias prohibitions did not outlaw an affirmative action agreement between the employer and union that reserved 50 percent of in-plant craft training openings for black employees until the percentage of black craft workers approximated that in the local labor force;
>
> ... The plan did not require displacement of white workers or create an absolute bar to their advancement. Also, the plan was temporary in nature, was intended to eliminate a manifest racial imbalance and would end when the percentage of black craft workers was commensurate with that in the local labor force.[3]

The *Wygant* v. *Jackson Board of Education* decision stated, in summary:

> Affirmative action provisions of a public school board collective bargaining agreement violated equal protection guarantees by allowing layoff of white teachers while more junior teachers were retained. Governmental use of racial classification could not be justified by the need to correct societal discrimination alone, but required convincing evidence of prior discrimination by the governmental unit involved. The plan was not sufficiently narrowly tailored, because it imposed the entire burden of achieving racial equality on particular

_____

[3]*Fair Employment Practices Cases* (Washington, D.C.: Bureau of National Affairs, 1979), 20, p. 1.

individuals in a disruptive manner while less intrusive means of accomplishing the same purpose, such as hiring goals, were available.[4]

The city argued that once racial balance had been achieved, it was legally required to terminate the two-to-one provision of the collective bargaining agreement. The city, therefore, requested that the arbitrator uphold its position and dismiss the union grievance.

APPENDIX
RELEVANT PROVISIONS OF THE COLLECTIVE BARGAINING AGREEMENT

Article III, Section 1(D)

* * * * *

Third Step if not settled in (second step). Failing settlement within ten (10) days, the grievance shall be processed for appeal to the city's representative by the Grievance Committee. Receipt of the grievance shall be set for a hearing within ten (10) days from receipt. At the hearing the employee and/or the Grievance Committee and the city may be represented by person (or persons) of their own choice. The city shall submit a written answer to grievance to the Grievance Committee within ten (10 days) of the grievance hearing. Time may be extended by mutual agreement.

Article III, Section 1(F)

Failure of the Union to appeal the grievance to the next highest step shall constitute acceptance of the city's last response, while failure by the city to act upon a grievance within the specified contract time shall result in a grant of the relief requested in the grievance.

Article V, Section 4(D)(1)

Effective at the signing of this Agreement, the amended Civil Service procedures will be as follows: Dual lists will be established with one list being all candidates in total score order and the second list a special list of the minorities, including women, in total score order. Hiring will be made from the first list in order except that at least one (1) minority must be hired for every three (3) hires. In order to achieve this the second list will be used if there is not at least one (1) minority for every three (3) hires from the first list. This dual list procedure will be in effect through 1989.

Article IX, Section 7(B)

The city will make no unilateral changes in wages, hours, and conditions of employment during the term of this Agreement either contrary to the provisions of this Agreement or established past practices.

---

[4]*Fair Employment Practices Cases* (Washington, D.C.: Bureau of National Affairs, 1986), 40, p. 1321.

Questions

1. Was the union grievance arbitrable?
2. Why didn't the parties to the agreement spell out exactly what they intended in writing the timeliness provisions of Article III, Section 1(F)? Discuss.
3. Does Title VII of the Civil Rights Act apply in this case?
4. What does the U.S. Supreme Court say in the Steelworkers and the Wygant decisions? Should the arbitrator base his decision of this case on these court decisions, or on the agreement between the parties, or on both? Discuss.

CASE 54
OUT OF LEAVE TIME

Company:
Witte Hardware Corporation, Vandalia, Illinois

Union:
Amalgamated Clothing and Textile Workers Union, Local No. 208A

On August 24, 1989, Henry Breske,[1] vice president for distribution services at Witte Hardware Corporation, sent Mary Easton a letter saying:

> You have been on a personal leave of absence. As discussed with you on Monday, August 14, 1989, and again on Monday, August 21, 1989, company policy allows for a total leave of absence for personal reasons not to exceed ten weeks or fifty working days over a two-year period. Since April 13, 1989, you have been granted excused, personal leave of absence days up to and including fifty working days. As was also discussed with you on those two aforementioned days, you had to make the decision as to whether you were going to return to work at the end of your approved leave or not. You were expected to return to work on Monday, August 21, 1989.
>
> You have not returned to work as of this date. We must, therefore, assume that you have elected to terminate your employment with Witte Hardware Corporation, per Article VII, Section 5(c) of the current Agreement between the Union and the Company.

Easton filed a grievance on August 28 claiming:

> I was unjustly discharged. I am requesting reinstatement with full seniority and back pay.

The company's initial reply to the grievance stated:

> You were given a personal leave of absence through August 21, 1989. You failed to return to work after that leave of absence. Your grievance is denied.

The grievance was eventually carried to arbitration.[2]

Background

Witte Hardware Corporation was a wholly owned subsidiary of Central Hardware Corporation headquartered in St. Louis, Missouri. The Vandalia distribution center was a two-shift operation employing approximately 100 bargaining unit personnel. The distribution center was essentially a warehouse and order-filling facility serving company-owned retail hardware stores in that region.

The grievant, Mary Easton, had been initially hired by Witte Hardware in 1972 when it was owned by another firm. Witte became a subsidiary of Central Hardware in 1985, at which time Easton had been officially "hired" by the new Witte Hardware

---

[1]The names of all individuals are disguised.
[2]See the appendixes for relevant provisions of the collective bargaining agreement and the company policy on personal leaves of absence.

Company. However, by agreement with the union, she retained her original seniority dating back to 1972.

Vice President Breske had been with the company since it had been purchased by Central Hardware four and one-half years earlier. He had served in his present position for three and one-half years; in this capacity he had overall responsibility for Witte Hardware's operation.

The labor-management agreement was silent on the matter of personal leaves of absence, although it did provide that absence in excess of an approved leave of absence without reasonable cause would result in termination and loss of seniority. (See Appendix A.)

The company had adopted a new personal leave policy on June 1, 1989, which provided for up to 10 weeks of personal leave over a two-year period. (See Appendix B.) This new policy replaced one adopted March 1, 1984, which left the granting of personal leaves to "the sole discretion of the director of personnel." The company changed its policy without either consulting or informing the union of its action.

The facts leading up to the arbitration were not in dispute, although the parties presented them from different points of view.

Testimony of the Union   Mary Easton was the sole witness for the union. In the course of her testimony in November 1989, she stated that on April 13, 1989, her son had been in a motorcycle accident in which he was severely injured. He was helicoptered from Vandalia, Illinois, to St. Louis University Hospital in critical condition with head injuries. Easton stayed at the hospital until April 24, when she applied for a leave of absence from Witte Hardware. At that time she told management that her son's recovery had been very slow. She also said that her physician had told her that her son required constant care and supervision. In a subsequent conversation with management in July, she told management that it was necessary for her to be with her son constantly because his doctor had stated that the brain injury was such that her son could be suicidal. She emphasized that she had become a very important part of the therapy essential for her son and that she had to be with him constantly.

At the present time her son was in a medical facility in Benton, Arkansas, where he was receiving therapy. It was necessary for her and her husband to go to Benton twice a month on weekends to see and care for their son. Her husband had been unemployed since October due to an injury.

Testimony of the Company   Henry Breske was the sole witness for the company. Breske stated that he had received a telephone call from Easton's husband on April 14, 1989, concerning the Eastons' son's critical condition as the result of a motorcycle accident. After being absent for several days and following several telephone calls, Mary Easton came in and requested a personal leave of absence on April 24, 1989. The company granted her request for a leave to extend through May 14. Easton then took her annual three-week vacation from the middle of May to early June. She then returned to work until the end of July. The company later received a letter from her son's physician, Dr. A. Nabor, who suggested that she be granted a leave of absence for three months to care for her son. Breske stated that he discussed this with the personnel director, Robert Crompton, and they agreed to grant Easton a 30-day leave of absence;

this meant that she would have to return to work on August 21, 1989. After attempting to contact Dr. Nabor on several occasions and discussing the matter with the international union representative, Roy Brophy, Breske again informed Easton that she was expected to return to work on August 21. Easton grieved the company's decision and requested that she be granted a leave until October 22. The company denied her grievance. Easton did not return to work on August 21, and the company sent her a letter on August 24 notifying her of her termination as of August 21, 1989. Easton then filed a grievance protesting the company's action.

Breske testified that, as a result of Easton's August 26 grievance, he had again tried to contact Dr. Nabor on several occasions without result. He also spoke with the international union representative, Roy Brophy. Breske eventually received a letter from Dr. Nabor on September 12 in which the doctor stated that Easton should be granted a leave of absence in order to care for her son. However, this letter did not identify any time limit or date when she could report back to work. On September 26 Breske was able to arrange a telephone conference call with both Dr. Nabor and Roy Brophy. During that conversation, the physician stated that he did not believe that Easton would be able to return to work on October 17 because of the necessity for her to care for her son. Basing his decision on this conversation, Henry Breske wrote another letter to Easton on September 27 reaffirming his previous decision to terminate her employment as of August 21:

> On September 26, 1989, Witte Hardware was finally able to make contact with Dr. Nabor regarding your son's case. Witte specifically addressed the question of your son's recovery time to which the doctor indicated that his recovery was not imminent. Furthermore, the date of October 17 was unrealistic.
>
> Based on these facts, Witte Hardware will have to maintain its original decision.
>
> If your son should sufficiently recover from his infirmities and you consider returning to the work force, please call me.

Position of the Union

The union pointed out that the critical illness of Mary Easton's son constituted reasonable cause for a lengthy leave of absence. Her physical presence was required as a part of his therapy; it was not sufficient that she employ a caretaker, even if she were financially able to do so. For such a traumatic injury, the length of care must be taken into account by the company.

Further, the union argued that her son's physicians, therapists, and general knowledge had furnished the company with sufficient verification to extend Easton's leave under Article VII, Section 5(c) of the collective bargaining agreement.

The union also contended that Vice President Breske had made a large issue of the fact that, according to written company policy, he could not extend her leave beyond the time granted. However, Article VII, Section 5(c), suggested otherwise. The union cited this article, which read that loss of seniority can be interrupted by "absence in excess of leave of absence without reasonable cause acceptable to the company." This would suggest strongly that as long as the employee proved "reasonable cause," Vice President Breske could have extended the leave for as long as necessary.

The union submitted that the company policy implemented on June 1, 1989, after Easton had begun her leave, was in direct conflict with the collective bargaining agreement. The former policy provided that her leave would have been adjudicated "in the sole discretion of the director of personnel." This policy was more flexible than the one implemented on June 1. Easton's application for leave properly fell under the terms of the former policy, since she had begun her leaves of absence in April.

The union asked that Mary Easton be reinstated with full seniority rights, benefits, back pay, and privileges as though her employment had never been severed by Witte Hardware Corporation.

Position of the Company

The company contended that it had not violated the agreement because the contract was silent on the matter of leave of absence for personal reasons. The statement of company policy provided for granting of leaves up to a maximum of 50 work days during any two-year period. Easton had no right to a leave of absence—she had only a privilege of one.

The company maintained that Easton had used all the leave time for which she was eligible between mid-April and mid-August 1989. When she requested an extension of her last leave of absence and it was denied, she had stayed on leave anyway and was terminated under Article VII, Section 5(c) of the agreement. Easton's request for an extension of her leave amounted to an additional 94 working days of leave, which was unreasonable to the company, especially since her son's physician could not assure her return to work at the end of that extended leave.

The company stated that it had attempted to accommodate Easton's request for additional leave time. However, her request was unreasonable. The company also pointed out that Easton's husband had been on layoff starting in October, and the union had not shown that he was unable to attend to their son during the following period. Easton should have requested to return to work, which she had not done.

The company requested that the arbitrator uphold its action and not grant the relief sought by the union.

APPENDIX A
RELEVANT PROVISIONS OF THE AGREEMENT

Article VII—Seniority

Section 5.   Seniority shall be lost and the employment relationship and continuous service of an employee shall be considered terminated and subsequent reemployment shall be deemed to be new employment in the following events:

  (a) Voluntary quit;
  (b) Discharge for just cause;
  (c) Absence in excess of leave of absence without reasonable cause acceptable to the
      company;

*   *   *   *   *

Article IX

A. DISCHARGES AND DISCIPLINE

Section 1. The union recognizes the company's right at any time to discharge, suspend, or otherwise discipline an employee for cause, including but not limited to insubordination (which shall include failure to comply promptly with management instructions), drinking, dishonesty, use of drugs, fighting, inefficiency, repeated tardiness or excessive absenteeism, willful or negligent damaging of merchandise, equipment, or other property of the company, or failure to comply with company rules and regulations. In the event of company action in such cases, the union and the employee shall be limited to the right to present the case solely as a grievance under the grievance procedure.

B. GRIEVANCE PROCEDURE—ARBITRATION

Section 7. The arbitrator shall interpret the agreement in accordance with the reserved rights theory of labor agreements whereby all rights not expressly limited by the agreement are reserved to the company. The arbitrator shall not have power to restrict the rights of management beyond the restrictions expressly imposed by this agreement, but shall be limited in power and jurisdiction to determine whether there has been a violation of this agreement, and shall have the power to determine the consequences thereof, and to provide a remedy for violation of this agreement.

APPENDIX B

COMPANY POLICY—PERSONAL LEAVE OF ABSENCE: STANDARD OPERATING PROCEDURE (EFFECTIVE JUNE 1, 1989)

1. Purpose: To define personal leave of absence as it pertains to all company employees—be it union or salaried.
2. General: Personal leaves of absence may be granted where humanitarian reasons warrant. All requests shall be in writing. An employee shall not request a leave to take other employment. If an employee is employed by another company while on a personal leave of absence, such breach of faith will constitute grounds for immediate termination.

Such leaves will be limited to 10 calendar weeks or 50 working days during a 2-year period. Vacation accrual will be reduced in the subsequent year proportionate to the time granted.

Specific Guidelines for Personal Leaves of Absence:

1. Formal written request.
2. Approval by management and where necessary, union concurrence.
3. Limited in duration, not more than 10 calendar weeks or 50 working days during a 2-year period.
4. Employee must have 1 year service or more to qualify.
5. Other nonqualifying events:
   a. To stay home.
   b. To take care of children while school is out.

    c. To avoid transfer.
    d. To extend vacation.
    e. To avoid specific job assignment.

Questions

1. What is the significance of Article VII, Section 5(c) of the agreement? What weight should be attached to the company's statement of policy?

2. Why was the company unrelenting in the application of its new 50-day, two-year leave policy?

3. What constraints, if any, apply to the decision an arbitrator may make?

4. In your view, was the company lacking in compassion, or was Easton being unreasonable in her request for an extension of leave? Discuss.

5. In 1993, the Family and Medical Leave Act (FMLA) was passed, which—among other requirements—mandates certain employers to grant annually up to 120 days of unpaid leave to cover situations of conflict between various types of family and work obligations. Obtain and review a copy of FMLA (the Act is administered by the U.S. Department of Labor). How would FMLA affect the company policy in this case? Would the company be required to grant employees an "open-ended" leave such as was requested by the grievant, Mary Easton?

CASE 55
A FOUL AND ABUSIVE MATTER

Company:
  Pacific Union Club, San Francisco, California

Union:
  Hotel Employees & Restaurant Employees, Local No. 2

On the morning of August 23, 1989, waitress Mabel Weston[1] and waiter Kyle Tyson were eating in the club cafeteria when waiter Tom Rijad burst into the room and loudly greeted Walter Ford, a cook, sitting at an adjoining table. Ford had just returned from a vacation in Los Angeles, and he and Rijad carried on a very animated discussion about the trip. Weston told her companion that she wished that Rijad would shut up. Rijad heard her remark.

Rijad left the cafeteria briefly to answer the telephone and returned to carry on his noisy conversation with the cook. At that point, Weston turned around and commanded, "Shut your mouth!" Rijad became angry, strode over to her table, and shouted at her to mind her own business. He called her an "old ugly b_____," "dirty a_____," "w_____," and worse. Weston was visibly shaken and began to cry.

At Tyson's prompting, Weston reported the incident to the club manager, Robert Kling, who promptly interviewed Weston, Tyson, and Ford. He then instructed the assistant manager, Paula Rabbitt, to dismiss Rijad for his obscene and foul language and for harassing Weston.

After receiving notice of his discharge, Rijad asked to meet with Manager Kling. Kling explained to Rijad that he had been terminated because of Weston's complaint. Kling also told Rijad that his behavior could cause the club to be charged with sexual harassment under federal law.[2] Rijad denied the allegations and stated that Weston had gotten what she deserved. Rijad and the union filed a grievance.

The union and club management could not agree on the appropriate action to be taken in this case, and so they mutually agreed to refer the case to an arbitrator as provided in the collective bargaining agreement.

They agreed that the issue to be resolved was:

Whether just cause supports the termination of the grievant. If not, what is the appropriate remedy?

Background

The Pacific Club was a private gentlemen's organization that operated dining, banquet, and sports facilities for its members. The club had been in existence since 1919 and presently had about 450 members. It employed approximately 80 persons, of whom 30

---

[1]The names of all individuals are disguised.
[2]See the appendix for the relevant contractual provision and the employer's policy statement on sexual harassment.

were part-time. About 35 employees were associated with the dining and banquet facilities; about 20 of these were part-time. The grievant, Tom Rijad, had worked for the club as a part-time waiter for approximately five years. Mabel Weston had been employed as a full-time waitress for almost two years.

Shortly after the discharge, at Rijad's request, Manager Robert Kling called a meeting of all participants and witnesses in the incident. A considerable amount of information concerning the behavior of Weston, Rijad, and other employees surfaced at the meeting.

Discussion among participants revealed that this had not been the first altercation between Rijad and Weston. Rijad brought up at the meeting an incident in which Weston had called him an "s.o.b." about a month earlier. Weston conceded that she had made this comment to another waiter when Rijad was not present, because she believed that he had caused another waitress to receive a parking ticket. It was also revealed that about three weeks earlier Weston had become "exasperated" by Rijad's advice as to how she should perform her job. She threw wine in his face and told him to leave her alone. Rijad responded by filling a glass with water and pouring it on her head. The pair had not spoken to each other from that time to this most recent dispute in the cafeteria. The assistant manager, Rabbitt, had witnessed this wine-throwing incident, but taken no action.

Weston also acknowledged that Rijad had shouted and cursed at her when she first came to work at the club. She said she had not complained at that time because she had felt that his behavior was an "understandable" reaction to her accidentally burning him with a hot casserole.

It came to light during the meeting that Rijad had had difficulties with some other employees. In January 1989, the chef had complained to Kling about Rijad's foul language and abusive behavior toward him and the cooks. Kling had met with Rijad and warned him that he would be terminated if there were any further episodes. Rijad, however, maintained that Kling had only cautioned him that the chef could bar him from the kitchen for being disruptive.

Rijad testified that he had explained to Kling that the chef had treated him badly, yelled at him, and addressed him as "ayatolah." Several witnesses confirmed that the chef was autocratic, intimidating, and discourteous toward the staff. One waiter stated that the chef was allowed to "rule his own domain" because he was of great importance to the club.

The assistant manager, Paula Rabbitt, stated that she had heard Rijad call his co-workers "idiot," "p_____," and "b_____" on several occasions. She said that she had reminded Rijad about being "nice" to other employees. Rabbitt stated that Rijad had even addressed her as "a_____" on several occasions, but she said that she had not paid any attention to this.

At the meeting, Rijad denied that the assistant manager, Paula Rabbitt, had ever warned him about using foul language. However, he did recall receiving counseling from Rabbitt for being argumentative.

Several employees testified that they often used loud and boisterous voices when talking with each other. They agreed that profanity was frequently used to tease co-workers. They reported that Rijad was known at the club for "carrying on," and most employees, including Weston, did not take his conduct seriously. They also indicated that Rijad habitually spoke in a loud voice and used his hands flamboyantly for emphasis.

The discussion at the meeting revealed two other foul language incidents, both involving another employee. In October 1988, a waitress had called the assistant manager "a_____" and "stupid" in the dining room while club members were present. About two months later, she called the dining room captain "a_____." Kling had previously warned the waitress about using foul language. She received a formal written warning for this conduct and for taking food from the club. The notice had been removed from her personnel file and destroyed after she had apologized to Manager Kling and promised not to take food out of the club again. She never apologized to the assistant manager or captain.

Position of the Union

The union argued that Rijad's termination was unjustified because he did not sexually harass Weston. A single vulgar remark did not constitute sexual harassment, especially in an organization like the club where crude language was customary and tolerated. Rijad did not single out the waitress because of her sex or create a persistently hostile environment through sexual behavior.

The union asserted that the club had not had just cause to discharge Rijad. It had not conducted a fair investigation of the facts prior to making the decision to discharge. Kling did not talk to Rijad, although he met with other witnesses to the altercation. He did not consider the fact that the waiter had improved after his earlier dispute with the chef. He did not take into account mitigating factors such as Weston's provocation and the prevalence of the use of foul language in the club.

The club had failed to provide Rijad advance notice of the consequences of his behavior. There was no rule prohibiting vulgar, even obscene, language and warning employees that abusive verbal barrages might lead to discharge. The club had failed to provide adequate notice of the charges against him. Nor did it submit a written statement of the charges. Employees did not have a clear understanding of behavior that was off limits; thus, Rijad had no clear understanding of the reasons for his discharge. The club condoned the use of abusive language, which was a common and accepted form of speech among employees. Management even accepted the use of this mode of behavior when it was directed against its supervisors.

The union claimed that, in the general atmosphere of the language used by other employees, the termination was unduly harsh. A waitress had been given a written warning for two instances of abusive language directed against her supervisors in a public area and in the presence of members of the club. In contrast, Rijad's outburst had been provoked by a co-worker in the employee cafeteria.

The union requested that the arbitrator uphold the grievance.

Position of the Company

The club held that Rijad's discharge was appropriate considering his repeated abusive behavior toward other employees. He had been counseled on numerous occasions by the assistant manager that he must not argue or use foul or abusive language. In January 1989, the manager had warned him about being argumentative and profane in speaking to the chef and cooks. Rijad was specifically told that he would be terminated if there were further episodes. Just seven months later, after receiving a warning that such behavior would not be tolerated, Rijad was again abusive, insulting, and offensive. He lost control of himself and yelled vulgarities at Weston. His abuse was intended as a personal attack on a co-worker.

Rijad had demonstrated that he was unable to improve his conduct. He had previously used obscenities in addressing management. He refused to acknowledge any wrongdoing during his termination interview, and he refused to apologize to Weston for his outburst. Management could not tolerate behavior such as Rijad's. Employees, especially in a club such as this, must work together cooperatively and in good spirit.

Discharge was also warranted by the specific language used by Rijad in his attack on Weston. In calling her a "b_____," "w_____," and worse, terms with an obvious sexual connotation, he violated the bounds of acceptable speech. These terms could be perceived as harassment, and created a hostile environment for which the club could be held liable.

The club maintained that Rijad's termination was consistent with other discipline for the same offense. Each time an incident of profane or abusive speech was brought to the attention of management, it took action. The manager, for example, had verbally warned the employee who called a co-worker a "f_____." He had also issued a reprimand to the waitress who called the assistant manager and captain "a_____." When the chef complained about Rijad's conduct in the kitchen, the manager gave Rijad a verbal warning. All these incidents were for a first offense. The disputed discharge was for a second offense.

Finally, the club pointed out that it had thoroughly investigated the complaints against Rijad. The manager, Kling, had spoken to two witnesses who corroborated Weston's account of the events. Since the reports provided by the two witnesses were consistent, it had been unnecessary to interview Rijad. However, the manager had given him the opportunity to give his version of the dispute at the meeting. In other words, the club's action was reasonable and proper.

The club urged the arbitrator to deny the union's grievance and to uphold the discharge of Tom Rijad.

Appendix
Relevant Provision of the Collective Bargaining Agreement

Article IX—Discipline

Section 1.   The Club agrees that it will not discharge or discipline employees without just cause.

Pacific Club Policy on Sexual Harassment, April 1, 1986

It is the position of the Club that sexual harassment on the premises will not be tolerated. Immediate action shall be taken against any individual who sexually harasses anyone. Some obvious examples of sexual harassment are when anyone requires sexual favors as a condition for favored treatment, or when anyone persists in making unwelcome sexual propositions or lewd comments to anyone. Conduct which is less obvious can also be sexual harassment. It includes any conduct which is sexual in origin and is unwelcome. It is not a question of what is intended, but the employee's perception of what is offensive that determines harassment. What may be regarded as an innocent statement by some, may be perceived as offensive by others.

Employees who feel they have been sexually harassed by anyone must inform the Manager or Assistant Manager immediately. A complete, confidential investigation of any such charges will be conducted immediately. Reprisals will not be tolerated.

The Club does not condone and will not tolerate any type of sexual harassment. Anyone who sexually harasses an employee will be subject to disciplinary measures.

Questions

1. Comment on the club's procedure for processing the complaint made by Mabel Weston.
2. Did Rijad's behavior amount to sexual harassment under the provisions of the law? Why, or why not?
3. Were there "mitigating circumstances" that would excuse Rijad from being found guilty of sexual harassment? Discuss.
4. What responsibility, if any, must the management of the club bear for this incident?
5. If you were the arbitrator, how would you decide this dispute? Give your reasoning.

CASE 56
NO PAY FOR TRAVEL TIME

Company:
Raytheon Service Company, Chicago, Illinois

Union:
International Brotherhood of Electrical Workers, Local No. 2347

Electrical Technician John Stark[1] attended an industry-sponsored electrical safety conference in Baltimore from Monday, December 5, through Friday, December 9, 1988. The company paid all costs associated with the conference, including transportation between Chicago and Baltimore, and paid Stark for his normal work hours while at the conference. However, Stark was not compensated for travel time between the cities. Travel time from his home to the conference totaled six hours, and for his return trip, seven and one-half hours.

Stark applied for reimbursement at the overtime rate for the 13½ hours he spent in transit. The company denied his request, and the union filed a grievance, which eventually was processed to arbitration. The parties agreed that the issue was:

> Did the company violate the collective bargaining agreement by not paying John Stark for travel time in both directions between his home and a training program in Maryland? If so, what shall be the remedy?

Position of the Union

The union argued that John Stark was on company business while making the trip and attending the conference. As an hourly employee, he should be compensated for all the time he committed to that activity. According to the union, his hourly wage compensation should be based on all the hours that he "sold" to the company for his services. Stark had devoted 13½ hours to company business for which he had not been paid.

The union also contended that Stark attended the conference at the company's request. He felt he was given no choice but to attend.

The union asserted that the terms of hours and pay were those written into the labor agreement between the union and a predecessor employer.[2] The company had agreed to accept the terms of the existing agreement, and these terms had not been revised by the parties. The predecessor employer regularly paid for the total time in transit when it asked hourly employees to travel.

The union pointed out that in October 1988, Stark and five other employees were sent to a safety course for which they were paid for total transit time in addition to all other expenses. This, the union claimed, had established a precedent it must follow.

---

[1]Name is disguised.
[2]Raytheon purchased the company in 1987. See the appendix for relevant contractual provisions.

By not paying for John Stark's travel time, the company had violated Article XII, Hours of Work and Overtime. The company should compensate him for all the time he used in carrying out its business at the appropriate overtime rate. The union urged that the arbitrator uphold the grievance.

Position of the Company

The company responded by pointing out that wages for travel were not provided for by company policy and procedures; the collective bargaining agreement was silent on the matter. The company admitted paying for travel time for the group that had attended the October 1988 safety course. But payment for travel time on that occasion had been an error in the implementation of policy; the company was not obligated to repeat an error.

Although the predecessor employer had generally paid for travel time, the Raytheon company had no established policy of doing so. The company was not bound to follow or honor policies or practices of the predecessor employer.

The company stated that the union and the company had not bargained on the matter. There had been no other grievances filed on this subject. The company's past practice had always been not to pay for travel time.

The company urged that the grievance be denied.

APPENDIX
RELEVANT PROVISIONS OF THE AGREEMENT

Article XII—Hours of Work and Overtime

E. Definitions
1. Work Week: For the purpose of this Agreement, the work week will begin at 12:01 A.M. Monday and will end at 12:00 midnight the following Sunday.

Article XXVIII—Temporary Off-Site Assignments

Employees temporarily assigned to a location other than the (HOME) facility will be eligible for:

1. Mileage at the rate of twenty-two and one half cents ($.22.5) per mile or the current applicable rate provided by Company Policy, whichever is higher, for all travel to and from the location of the temporary assignment by the most direct and practical route, if they use their personal automobile, or economy air transportation from their point of departure to the location of the temporary assignment and return.
2. Local transportation as determined by the Company if required.
3. A daily allowance at the authorized rate for all such days the employees are required to remain at the temporary assignment.

The authorized daily allowance rate referred to above will be in accordance with the appropriate provisions of the contract between the Department of Defense and Raytheon Support Services Company.

Questions

1. Did the bargaining agreement require that the company pay for travel time? Discuss.
2. Since the company had paid travel time for one previous group attending a safety course, was it now bound to do so in this case? Why, or why not?
3. In taking over the agreement of the predecessor company, did the Raytheon Service Company also assume past practices of that company?
4. Even if the collective bargaining agreement was silent on the matter, was the company ethically obligated to pay John Stark for his travel time to and from the safety conference?

CASE 57
TOO MUCH UNION BUSINESS TIME

Agency:
U.S. Veterans Administration, Extended Care Center, St. Albans, N.Y.

Union:
American Federation of Government Employees, Local No. 1988, AFL-CIO

Background

The Veterans Administration Extended Care Center at St. Albans was a large medical facility designed to provide long-term care to military veterans requiring medical attention as a result of either war-inflicted or subsequent peacetime injuries. The St. Albans Center (to be referred to as the agency) was located in St. Albans, County of Queens, New York, about 25 miles from Manhattan.

On April 6, 1989, employee Victor Dunbar[1] and Chief Union Steward Cynthia Jones requested and were granted eight hours of administrative leave time to attend a Merit Systems Protection Board (MSPB) hearing. These requests, like all such requests to appear before the MSPB or the Federal Labor Relations Authority (FLRA), were routinely granted by the agency.

The hearing was held on April 26, 1989, at 26 Federal Plaza in Manhattan. The hearing began at 8:00 A.M. and concluded at 11:00 A.M. Neither Dunbar nor Jones returned to St. Albans following the conclusion of the hearing. Both claimed they met that afternoon with Casey Lawton, the union's international representative, to discuss "strategy," because the union anticipated an adverse ruling from the MSPB. Dunbar was the appellant at the hearing and Jones was his union representative. They stated that the "strategy" discussions took place following the hearing on the benches of Thomas Paine Park across the street from 26 Federal Plaza. They did not return to the V.A. Center that day.

James Farrell, director of St. Albans, charged Dunbar and Jones with having been three hours absent without leave, claiming that they should have returned to work following the hearing. The union filed a grievance on July 10, 1989. By letter dated July 24, 1989, Farrell offered to convert the three hours of AWOL into three hours of annual leave time, but both Dunbar and Jones declined the offer.

The case was processed through the grievance procedure without arriving at agreement. The union and the agency decided to submit their differences to arbitration, agreeing that the issue was:

Were the grievants properly charged with three (3) hours of AWOL for failing to return to the St. Albans Center upon conclusion of an MSPB hearing at 11:00 A.M. on April 26, 1989? If not, what shall the remedy be?

---

[1]The names of all individuals are disguised.

Position of the Union

The union took the position that once the agency had granted eight hours of administrative leave to Dunbar and Jones, they had discretion as to how they used those eight hours so long as they were used for work-related representational activities. The agency should not be permitted to first approve eight hours leave, and then retroactively reverse its position and levy a penalty of three hours AWOL. The agency initially had determined that these two employees could be spared from their jobs for eight hours without placing any conditions or stipulations on its approval. That is, the agency did not specify that Dunbar and Jones were to return to St. Albans immediately following the MSPB hearing.

Relying upon its interpretation of agency policy and past practice, these employees felt it was entirely proper that they meet with Casey Lawton, union international representative, following the termination of the MSPB hearing. In fact, this meeting was an important one in that Lawton was seldom available for such meetings and the union felt that a strategy conference was very important under the circumstances.

The union further argued that there was no clear policy or past practice requiring an employee to telephone his or her supervisor at the conclusion of an MSPB or FLRA hearing. To support this argument, Glynda Hill, first vice president of the local union, stated that following any labor-management meetings or similar activity, she would return to her union office for the remainder of her administrative leave without ever being questioned about this by her supervisor, Jim Walsh. She claimed that she had discretion to return to the Extended Care Center or to work at the union office as she saw fit.

The union held that the use of the full eight hours was legitimate in that both employees had engaged in necessary union business. Victor Dunbar and Cynthia Jones had met all agency requirements in obtaining this leave. Dunbar completed Form SF-71 (Request for Excused Leave) as required. His supervisor, Joseph Winston, did not mention any exact time that Dunbar was to return following the conclusion of the MSPB hearing; however, Dunbar did call his supervisor at the conclusion of the MSPB hearing. The chief union steward, Cynthia Jones, testified that she was not required to sign Form SF-71, and her supervisor had not required her to return directly to work following the MSPB hearing.

The union pointed out that the local agreement signed by the parties specifically stated that both union representatives and other employees had the right to administrative leave for the purpose of carrying out appropriate representational activities. Further, both the Civil Service Reform Act of 1978, which governs labor-management relations in the federal government, and the Master Agreement between the Veterans Administration and the union provide for administrative leave.[2]

The agency had not established a written policy concerning this matter, leaving employees and the union with the burden of second-guessing the intent of management.

---

[2]See the appendixes for relevant provisions from the Civil Service Reform Act and the collective bargaining agreements.

Dunbar and Jones used their best judgment in interpreting the policies and practices of the agency.

Finally, the union contended that the agency could not decide for itself what amount of administrative time was "reasonable and necessary" for representational activities. If Dunbar and Jones and their union representative decided to utilize the full eight hours of administrative leave, the agency should not be allowed to determine that their post-hearing discussions were not in the public interest, or that the discussions were not reasonable and necessary.

The union requested that the arbitrator uphold the grievance in total.

Position of the Agency

The agency agreed that Dunbar and Jones had been entitled to receive contractual administrative leave to attend the MSPB hearing. On the other hand, they had also had a duty to comply with instructions of their supervisors to return to work on completion of the purposes for which the leave had been granted. Dunbar knew this because he telephoned his supervisor for additional leave time, which the supervisor denied him. Jones's supervisor had told her to return to work at the time he signed Form SF-71 granting her the leave.

The administrative leave had been specifically granted for the MSPB hearing. When that hearing concluded at 11:00 A.M., both employees were expected to return to work. Employees who attended MSPB hearings remained in an on-duty status and were compensated during that time. They were, in effect, granted up to eight hours to participate in the hearing. In this case, the two employees had more than ample time to return to work, even taking into account a one-hour lunch period.

The agency disagreed with the union concerning the use of the full eight hours if that time was used for representational purposes. Such an approach would permit an employee to use the administrative leave for any purposes with full pay and without an obligation to return to work once the purpose for which the leave had been granted was met.

The agency also questioned the credibility of the statements made by Jones and Dunbar concerning their activities following the MSPB hearing. What was the purpose of the meeting on the park bench? Was this meeting necessary? Could it have been carried out at another time under different circumstances with different participants? Why did the two employees not telephone to state specifically the purpose and need for the conference following the hearing?

The agency held that there was no past practice permitting employees to use the full time granted for purposes other than those specifically stated on Form SF-71. While Glynda Hill used her leave time for all types of union business, this was not general practice. If she were a designated district representative, as well as union vice president, she was entitled to use 12 hours per pay period for union representation purposes under the terms of Article I, Section 2, of the Master Agreement; however if she were not a designated district representative, she had been granted this time in error.

The agency urged that the arbitrator deny the union's grievance.

APPENDIXES

A. RELEVANT PROVISIONS OF THE CIVIL SERVICE REFORM ACT OF 1978, AS AMENDED

§7131 (d) (2): ... any employee in an appropriate unit represented by an exclusive representative, shall be granted official time in any amount the agency and the exclusive representative involved agree to be reasonable, necessary, and in the public interest.

B. RELEVANT PROVISIONS OF THE MASTER AGREEMENT—VETERANS ADMINISTRATION AND A.F.G.E., AFL-CIO

Article 8—Official Time

Section 1.   The parties recognize that good communications are vital to positive and constructive relationships between the Union and VA management.

* * * * *

Fifteen Union Designated District Representatives—12 hours [of official time] per pay period.

* * * * *

NOTE 2—Union officials must obtain prior clearance from the Personnel Officer before engaging in any representational activities at a facility other than where they are employed.

* * * * *

Section 2.   The 12 hours per pay period authorized for district representatives may be used as needed: however, upon request, the district representatives will be advanced official time from future time accrual for that leave year. Any time not used during any pay period will be accumulated for the remainder of the leave year ...

C. SUPPLEMENTAL AGREEMENT TO THE MASTER AGREEMENT—LOCAL 1988 (A.F.G.E.) AND V.A. EXTENDED CARE CENTER, ST. ALBANS, NEW YORK

Article S-6—Rights and Responsibilities

Section 1.   Union Representatives.

* * * * *

B. The Employer will authorize a reasonable amount of official time for Union Representatives on all shifts to perform their function. Before leaving his worksite for union business, the Union Representative will request permission of his immediate supervisor and advise said Supervisor of his destination, and estimated time of absence . . . Upon return to his worksite, the Union Representative will check in with his supervisor . . .

C. An employee shall request the permission of his Supervisor to call a Union Representative, to devote time to discussing his problem with a Union Representative, or to leave his worksite for that purpose. The Supervisor will not arbitrarily or capriciously deny any such request.

* * * * *

Section 6. Administrative Leave.   Union representatives will be allowed a reasonable amount of official time to carry out appropriate representational functions at MSPB, FLRA, and other divisions of this medical center. There may be a unique situation when a union representative may have to request a reasonable amount of time to go to another federal agency to carry out appropriate representational functions for the bargaining unit covered by this agreement.

Questions

1. Provisions from the Civil Service Reform Act and two agreements pertain to this grievance. Which, if any, takes precedence?

2. Should Dunbar and Jones have telephoned their supervisors to obtain permission to meet with Casey Lawton following the MSPB meeting?

3. Were Dunbar and Jones entitled to be absent for the entire eight hours, or were they granted up to eight hours only to attend the MSPB meeting? Discuss.

4. What do the master and local agreements say about absence for purposes of union business? Are the agreements clear? If not, how could they have been worded to make them more specific?

5. What credibility should be attached to Jones' and Dunbar's statements that they met with Lawton on the park bench to discuss union business?

6. How would you rule if you were the arbitrator? Give your reasoning.

CASE 58
A CUTBACK IN OVERTIME PAY

Employer:
Margaret Wagner House, Cleveland Heights, Ohio

Union:
Service Hospital Nursing Home & Public Employee Union, Local No. 47

The Margaret Wagner House was a nursing home facility with 184 beds. It provided a range of nursing, physical therapy, occupational therapy, day programs, and medical and cosmetic services to the elderly. While most of its clients resided permanently at the facility, some were accommodated on a temporary basis. The nursing home had been in operation in Cleveland Heights since 1961. Since 1975, the union had been the exclusive bargaining representative for all licensed practical nurses, laundry department employees, food service employees, maids and porters in the housekeeping department, and nurse assistants and nurse assistant coordinators.

From December 1980 to summer 1989, unit employees who worked a double shift received 16 hours of pay—8 hours of regular pay and 8 hours of overtime pay at the rate of time and one-half—even though they worked a total of 15½ hours. While each shift was eight hours, one-half hour was lost in the double shift because of overlap between shifts.

Early in 1989, Mary Norris,[1] the new personnel director at the nursing home, noticed the one-half hour discrepancy. She also learned that the director of nursing knew that employees who worked a double shift had received 16 hours of pay, including 8 hours at the overtime rate. Norris further discovered that the director of nursing was aware of these payments as early as June 1985. In early 1989, Norris called this discrepancy to the attention of the nursing home's executive administrator, Roberta Magness. Magness decided that starting August 1, 1989, compensation would be reduced to reflect the actual number of hours worked. After that date those employees who worked a double shift would be paid eight hours at their regular rate and seven and one-half hours at the overtime rate.

The union protested the nursing home's new method of compensating employees who worked a double shift, and insisted that they be paid for 16 hours, even though they actually worked only 15½ hours. The parties could not agree on the grievance and the case was appealed to an arbitrator for a final and binding decision.

Position of the Union

The union did not dispute the meaning and intent of Article XIII, Section 1, of the collective bargaining agreement, which stated that premium pay for overtime hours be limited to the hours "actually worked." Nor did the union contend that bargaining unit

---

[1]The names of all individuals are disguised.

employees working double shifts actually worked eight rather than seven and one-half hours of overtime work. Rather, the union held that the nursing home's practice of making such payments had amended the language of Article XIII, Section 1. The nursing home could not now amend the contract again unilaterally by changing a procedure that had been operative for almost nine years.[2]

The union held that Article XXIII, Section 2, did not apply in this instance. By past practice the parties had expressly modified the terms of the agreement. In other words, the overtime compensation system in effect during the past years constituted one of the terms "relative to rates of pay" set forth in this article. The agreement had been opened for renegotiation twice since the practice began in 1980. The union had every right to expect that the overtime compensation arrangement had been mutually accepted by both parties.

The union contended that over the years employees had built the one-half hour of overtime pay into their expectations. This was especially important to them in their financial planning. These payments amounted to several hundred dollars per year, and eliminating them would create an unusually difficult financial situation for them. For example, they had made decisions to work for the nursing home, and to remain with it during those nine years, based on the overtime pay arrangement. The practice also determined, in part, their expenditure patterns and their lifestyle. Although the loss of one-half hour at the overtime rate seemed small, over the period of one year the sum of money was sizable.

Finally, the union held that the nursing home's action violated the terms of Article XXIII, Section 2. The intent of this article was to prevent the parties from introducing new issues for bargaining during the life of the agreement. The contract had been renegotiated twice during the previous nine years. The nursing home had not introduced the issue of compensation structure at either of those negotiations. The nursing home had paid the extra half hour at the overtime rate for a long time. The union believed that the overtime practice was not an issue for negotiation since the nursing home had not mentioned any desire to change it.

The union requested that the arbitrator uphold the grievance, including payment for all wages lost since August 1, 1989.

Position of the Employer

The nursing home contended that no amount of practice contrary to the clear language of a written contractual provision could prevail over the latter. Because the nursing home's current method of compensating employees for overtime work since August 1, 1989, was consistent with Article XIII, Section 1, of the agreement and its former practice was inconsistent, the change in the method of compensation was permitted by the agreement.

The nursing home argued that, if the union were concerned about past practice and the language of the contract, it should have called this discrepancy to the attention of management a long time ago.

---

[2]See the appendix for relevant provisions of the contract.

The nursing home held that any change of the agreement through past practice was prohibited by the zipper clause, Article XXIII, Section 2, of the agreement. This clause stated that the terms of the agreement were final and binding during the life of the contract. Neither party could request that the contract be reopened to bargain on new issues or modify existing ones during the life of the collective bargaining agreement.

Finally, the nursing home argued that it had not intended to amend the agreement, since the director of nursing, who permitted the practice to continue until it was changed in August 1989, was not aware that the practice conflicted with the agreement. As soon as the executive administrator, Roberta Magness, learned of the discrepancy, she ordered the practice changed. Changes in the agreement may be made only when the parties mutually agree to a change; no mutuality existed here.

For the reasons cited above, the nursing home urged that the arbitrator deny the grievance.

APPENDIX
RELEVANT PROVISIONS OF THE AGREEMENT, SEPTEMBER 7, 1987— SEPTEMBER 6, 1990

Article XIII—Overtime and Shift Differential Pay

Section 1.   Employees shall be paid at the rate of one and one-half (1½) times their straight-time pay for all hours authorized by the employer which are actually worked in excess of forty (40) in any scheduled work week of seven (7) days or in excess of eight (8) in any scheduled work day. Nothing in this Section shall be construed as authorizing overtime pyramiding. "Pyramiding" is defined as either the payment of more than one premium rate for the same hours worked (i.e., the payment of overtime on overtime) or the counting of hours payable at the premium rate under one overtime provision in computing the hours payable at the premium rate under another overtime provision.

Article XXIII

*   *   *

Separability; Waiver

Section 2.   This agreement sets forth all the terms and provisions relative to rates of pay, hours of work, and all other conditions of employment within the scope of collective bargaining on or concerning which the parties intend to bargain or contract during the life of this agreement. Neither party shall have a duty to bargain nor shall be requested to bargain on any subject during the life of this agreement except as may be expressly provided herein above.

Questions

1. Is past practice more, or less, important than the written language of the agreement in determining an arbitrator's decision? Discuss.
2. Does nine years of past practice affect the applicability of Article XIII, Section 1? Why, or why not?
3. What is a "zipper" clause in a contract? What is its purpose? How does it affect the agreement during its life?
4. Both parties invoked Article XXIII, Section 2, to bolster their arguments. Why?

CASE 59
VANDALIZING THE SIGN

Company:
Joerns Healthcare, Inc., Newark, New Jersey

Union:
United Steelworkers of America, Local No. 333-U

Background

During the afternoon of August 31, 1989, the company posted a framed plexiglass-covered sign, described as the "Pursuit of Excellence" sign, near the main aisle in the plant. September 1 was the first full day that the sign was posted. The sign was specifically located near a workstation used by both the tube benders and the welders. The area around the sign was accessible to both hourly employees and management.

At about 7:45 A.M. on September 1, Tim Halsey,[1] a department head, noticed that someone had drawn a swastika on a piece of cardboard covering the sign. Halsey earlier that morning had seen some of the welders standing near the sign. When he had the cardboard swastika removed at about 9:00 A.M., he noticed that the sign was also covered with a blue oil, similar to the type of oil used by the tube benders. He discussed this with the tube benders' lead man and directed him to clean the sign.

At 10:00 A.M. Halsey noticed that two holes had been punched into the back of the sign and one in the plexiglass covering. In order to have punched the holes, it would have been necessary for the vandal to have climbed onto a desk and filing cabinet in the welding station and intentionally struck the sign with a pointed metal object.

At 11:30 A.M., Tim Halsey called a meeting of the tube benders and welders. At that meeting, Harry Mohr, company vice president and operations manager, informed the employees that if the culprit or culprits who damaged the sign were not identified before noon, all 32 employees would be sent home for the balance of the day.

No one admitted damaging the sign or identified anyone else who had done so. The employees were sent home at noon, although they had been scheduled to work from one to three and one-half additional hours that day.

The union filed a grievance on behalf of all affected employees, asking for compensation for the hours not worked on that day. The grievance was not settled at the lower levels of the grievance procedure and was submitted to a jointly agreed upon arbitrator.

The parties agreed that the issue at hand was:

Did the company have the authority, under the terms of the labor agreement, to discipline 32 workers because an unidentified person or group of persons vandalized a sign in the plant?

---

[1]The names of all individuals are disguised.

Position of the Union

The union argued that the company had taken action exceeding its authority under the contract. The contract stated that an employee may be disciplined only for "just cause," and this provision in the agreement prevented the company from imposing discipline on a group for an act that was not committed by all members of the group.[2] In other words, the union held that "just cause" limited the company to disciplining only those individuals who had damaged the sign.

The union maintained that, although the company could discipline each individual who damaged the sign, it erred in applying group discipline to everyone in the hope that it might catch the guilty person or persons.

The union pointed out that the company had not proven that the vandalism had been committed by union members. It held that it was equally plausible that the act had been committed by a member of management. Therefore, to punish only persons in the bargaining unit was patently unjust.

Since the company lacked "just cause" for disciplining the whole group of employees, the union sought pay for all employees for time lost on September 1.

Position of the Company

The company contended that vandalism was a serious breach of discipline, and failure to punish it encouraged other acts of willful damage to company property.

The company stated that it would have been impossible for anyone to damage the sign without knowledge of one or more of the other welders. To reach the sign required that the culprit climb on both a desk and a filing cabinet. The person responsible for the act of vandalism must have been observed by one or more employees in the area. It must be concluded that employees had engaged in a conspiracy of silence, preventing the company from properly punishing the person or persons who actually committed the acts. Further, the company held that employees had a duty to protest, prevent if possible, and report to management any willful acts of vandalism to company property.

The company contended that it possessed authority to punish all 32 employees under Article IV, Section 1, and Article 1A of the contract. It, therefore, requested that the arbitrator deny the grievance.

APPENDIX
RELEVANT PROVISIONS OF THE AGREEMENT

Article IV—Hours of Work and Overtime Pay

Section 1.   The regular work week shall consist of five (5) eight (8) hour days from Monday to Friday inclusive. This definition of work week shall in no way require the employer to guarantee any number of hours of work per week, except as hereinafter provided.

---

[2]See the appendix for relevant contract provisions.

Article IA—Management Rights

Section 1.   Management of the plant, plant operations, and the direction of the work force, including but not limited to the right to introduce new products, machinery, operations and methods; the right to hire, suspend, discipline, or discharge for proper cause as provided herein; to transfer associates, the right to schedule work to be performed and when it will be performed; the right to make and enforce such reasonable rules of conduct and regulations as it may deem necessary for the purpose of maintaining order, safety, and efficiency (all such rules to be posted throughout the plant); to increase or decrease the work force; to determine job content, including the right to assign an associate to more than one type of work, consistent with accepted safety standards, shall be exclusively the function of the employer provided that these will not be used for the purpose of discrimination against any associate. All rules and regulations posted by the employer shall be subject to the grievance procedure of the agreement.

Article V—Discharge

Section 1.   No associate shall be discriminated against for union activities or in any way as to violate the letter or spirit of this agreement.

The employer shall not discharge, discipline, or demote any regular associate without just cause, and shall give at least one (1) warning notice of complaint to both the associate involved and to the union, in writing against such associate (except for a violation of a company rule that is subject to discharge without warning). Discharge shall be made by written notice, giving cause for such discharge to both the associate involved and the union.

Questions

1. Why did the company discipline everyone in the group?
2. What are the purposes and consequences of disciplining the entire group?
3. Did the acts of vandalism constitute "just cause" to discipline everyone on the presumption that members of the group knew the identity of the vandal(s)?
4. How would you rule if you were the arbitrator? Give your reasoning.

CASE 60
WHO SHOULD MAINTAIN THE PARKS AND BALLFIELDS?

Employer:
Town of Lee, Massachusetts

Union:
Local No. 404, General Teamsters, Warehousemen & Helpers, Building Materials, Heavy and Highway Construction Employees

Background

In early 1990, the town's Department of Public Works had a bargaining unit of five employees. As permitted by the parties' collective bargaining agreement,[1] the town also had employed two temporary employees, Joe and Carl Judson,[2] who were not members of the bargaining unit.

In accordance with paragraph 91 of the agreement, the Truck Drivers/ Laborers did the grass and lawn maintenance along the town's roads. For the past dozen years or so, various students had been hired as spring and summer help and assigned the grass and lawn maintenance of the town's seven parks and ballfields. The regular crew of union workers and the two temporaries did this work during the periods before and after the availability of the temporary student help. The Judson brothers were assigned this work in 1987 when the summer help became unreliable. By the summer of 1988, the Judson brothers had left the payroll and the work was again done by students. In 1989, two major maintenance vehicles and other equipment were inoperative. Without sufficient working equipment, neither the students nor the bargaining unit employees could do the work. Therefore, all park maintenance was contracted out for that year to a local tree and lawn service firm.

In early 1990, the town council decided to contract out the park and ballfields work again. The proposed contract called for work to be done periodically between May 1, 1990, and October 9, 1990. Also, the town council decided that it would contract out that portion of the road work that involved side slopes, ditches, and brush clearance. This latter work was not done regularly by anyone, but every four or five years a regular crew or the Judsons would do it.

The superintendent of public works, Abner Collins, informed the union steward, Bill Phillips, of his intent to contract. This notice took place verbally, after the contractual bid had been advertised in a local newspaper.

Phillips notified Wilson Billingham, president of Local 404 of the union, about the town's decision to contract out the various maintenance work. Subsequently, the union filed a grievance, which was eventually submitted to arbitration.[3] The parties agreed on the following framing of the issue to be decided:

---

[1] See the appendix for relevant contractual provisions.
[2] The names of all individuals are disguised.
[3] The dispute was submitted to the Massachusetts Board of Conciliation and Arbitration in accordance with Article VII of the collective bargaining agreement between the parties. An arbitrator was appointed by the MBCA to hear and decide the case.

Is the maintenance of lawns and ballfields in the town parks bargaining unit work? If so, is subcontracting of the maintenance of town lawns and ballfields a violation of the agreement? If so, what shall the remedy be?

Position of the Union

The union contended that paragraph 91 of the parties' labor agreement guaranteed that park maintenance be done solely by bargaining unit members. The only permissible exception was that paragraph 43 allowed assignment of temporary employees, which had been done with the Judson brothers or with summer student help.

The union claimed that paragraph 43 of the agreement was intended to permit the town to have temporary workers who would not be in the bargaining unit, but this was the only exception to the union's work jurisdiction. This exception had been utilized each summer, and there had been no contracting out except in 1989 when maintenance vehicles and equipment had broken down. Therefore, the union claimed the labor agreement did not permit contracting out.

In addition, the union complained that notice of the intent to contract out the disputed work should have been given to the union office, not to the shop steward.

The union urged that the grievance be sustained by the arbitrator, that the arbitrator issue a "cease and desist" order on the town, and that the town be directed to negotiate the matter with the union. Absent any agreement with the union, the arbitrator should direct that the contested work be performed only by bargaining unit members.

Position of the Employer

Counsel for the town contended that the collective bargaining agreement was silent on the question of contracting out. Further, contracting out had taken place the previous summer (1989) when necessary vehicles and equipment were not working.

The town saw no difference between a temporary employee and a contractor. In either case, the disputed work had been done each year by non–bargaining unit members. Therefore, there was no practice or precedent to prevent the town from contracting out.

The town believed that it could contract out for the slopes, ditches, and brush clearance, because it did not have the appropriate equipment to accomplish those tasks.

As to the notice, the superintendent, Abner Collins, had always notified the union informally by talking with the shop steward. This complaint of the union was a "red herring" with no relevance to the merits of the case.

Counsel for the town urged the arbitrator to totally dismiss the union grievance.

APPENDIX
RELEVANT CONTRACTUAL PROVISIONS

Article I—Union Recognition

Paragraph 10.   Pursuant to the certification of representation ... the Employer hereby recognizes the Union as the sole and exclusive bargaining agency ... for all truck drivers/laborers ... employed by the Highway and Landfill Division ...

Article IX—Wages and Classifications

Paragraph 91. Classification Descriptions ... Truck Driver/Laborer. A truck driver/laborer ... will perform a variety of maintenance and construction repair duties related to public works projects including, but not limited to highway ... recreation, forestry work ...

Article IV—Seniority

Paragraph 43. The provisions of this agreement do not apply to temporary employees ... However, in order that the Union may determine which new hires may acquire seniority, the Employer ... will notify the Union, within ten (10) days after hiring any new employee, whether he was hired as a temporary or probationary. Any temporary employee will not work in excess of one hundred and twenty (120) days within a calendar year.

Questions

1. Carefully examine the relevant contractual provisions. Which (if any) provisions are supportive of the union's position? Of the employer's position?

2. Is there any real difference between a "temporary employee" and a "contractor" in this case? Discuss.

3. Should the employer have sent its notice of proposed contracting out to the union office, or is this not a real issue? Why would the union local complain about this notification procedure?

4. What should the arbitrator decide? (Evaluate the union's suggested remedy if the arbitrator should find for the union's position.)

CASE 61
THE STOLEN OR MISSING TOOLS

Company:
Centrex Corporation, Inc., Findlay, Ohio

Union:
United Rubber Workers of America, Local No. 627

The Grievance

On March 14, 1990, Calvin Marshall[1] filed the following grievance:

Contract Violation   Theft of Calvin Marshall's tools 3/3/90 from Co. premises. Calvin's tools are a condition of his employment and the company has the responsibility to provide a reasonably secure place to keep them.

Settlement Required   Company will replace Calvin's tools.

The company's response to the grievance was as follows:

As the company has done in the past we will replace broken tools, but not tools that come up missing. The company has to see what it is replacing. If tools are stolen that you need to have to do your job, the company will pay for the tools and it will be deducted from your check accordingly.

The union followed up the second-step grievance hearing between the parties with the following statement:

Calvin and the union do not agree with this answer. Carry on to third step. Calvin's tools are a condition of his employment and they should be replaced since they were taken on company property.

The union appealed the grievance to the third step of the grievance procedure. The company again denied the grievance, stating:

The union spent most of their time discussing the events leading up to the reported theft, the items reported stolen, the events following the reported thefts, the company's broken tool policy, the type of tool required by the company, the type of tools actually used by the maintenance department and numerous other maintenance related subjects. At no time during this step 3 did the union specify as to what section of the contract union feels the company has violated.

Based on the above, the company can only restate what has already been stated in all of the previous answers to this grievance. Our policy has always been and will continue to be, Centrex Corporation is not responsible for lost or stolen items on company premises.

Grievance denied.

The union appealed the grievance to arbitration.

---

[1]The names of all individuals are disguised.

Background

On March 3, 1990, Calvin Marshall arrived at work at approximately 12:00 midnight to start his third-shift turn. After clocking in, he walked to the maintenance area with Hal Jones, the second-shift mechanic. There he discovered that his toolbox had been moved and that the lock had been cut with bolt cutters. Opening the toolbox, he discovered that several tools were missing.

Marshall immediately contacted both the second- and third-shift foremen, who searched the area for the missing tools and to determine whether other toolboxes had also been rifled. At that point Marshall asked that the police be called, but both foremen dissuaded him from this course of action, suggesting that they wait until morning when the maintenance supervisor and production manager would be available. Since Marshall had no tools, he was sent home at about 3:00 A.M.

The company's security department searched the area again the following morning. No tools were found. The production manager then contacted the local police, who made still another search without success. The police made out a theft report and left.

The company later that day posted a notice on the bulletin boards stating that it would give a reward to anyone who came forward with information regarding the missing tools. The tools were never recovered, and the thief was never apprehended.

Position of the Union

The union held that since it was a condition of employment that maintenance mechanics furnish their own tools, the company had a duty to protect the tools while they were on company property. The toolboxes were large and the tools were very heavy. The company provided an area for their storage. Marshall's toolbox was locked and in the designated area. The company had provided inadequate security, as evidenced by the theft of the tools.

The union argued that Marshall should have been paid for the five hours he was not permitted to work the morning of March 4. By sending him home without compensation, the company had unfairly penalized him for a situation over which he had no control and which had resulted from the company's failure to provide adequate security.

The union requested that the arbitrator uphold the grievance by requiring the company to replace Marshall's tools and compensate him for lost time on the morning of March 4, 1990.

Position of the Company

The company took the position that the requirements on the parties had been clearly spelled out in Article 1, Section 18.7, of the agreement.[2] The agreement specifically and precisely stated when the employer was obliged to reimburse employees for their tools.

---

[2]See the appendix for relevant contractual provisions.

That obligation extended to their replacement only when the tools were worn or broken on the job. The agreement made no provision for the replacement of tools that were stolen. Since the language of the agreement was very precise about replacing worn out or broken tools, it was evident that the parties had not intended that the company replace stolen tools.

The company contended that no one had proven that the tools had been stolen. They were missing. Anyone could have removed them from the toolbox, including Marshall himself.

The company argued that it should not be required to compensate Marshall for his lost time on the morning of March 4. While he may not have been responsible for being unable to work because of the absence of his tools, neither was the company. It was an unfortunate situation for which the company must not be held responsible.

The company requested that the arbitrator deny the grievance in its entirety.

APPENDIX
RELEVANT PROVISIONS OF THE AGREEMENT

* * * * *

Article I—Recognition

Section 1.1.   (b) The Company agrees to meet with and bargain with the accredited representatives of the Union on all matters pertaining to rates of pay, wages, hours of employment, and other conditions of employment.

18.7. Replacement of Tools.   The Company will promptly replace tools that are worn out or broken on the job. New personal tools which may be required by the employee will be furnished at cost.

Article VI—Grievance Procedure

6.1. Definition of Grievance.   A grievance is a complaint, dispute, or controversy in which it is claimed that the Company or the Union has failed to comply with an obligation assumed by it under the terms of this Agreement, which involves either (1) a dispute as to facts involved; (2) a question concerning the meaning, interpretation, scope, or application of this Agreement; or (3) both.

* * * * *

6.5   Arbitration.   (f) The arbitrator's jurisdiction and authority shall be limited to the particular issue presented to him and he shall have no jurisdiction or authority to add to, subtract from, or modify in any way the terms of this Agreement. The general wage scale shall not be subject to arbitration.

Questions

1. What, if any, responsibility did the company bear for the loss of the tools? Discuss.
2. Were the tools missing or stolen? Should this make any difference in the outcome of the case?
3. Why did the union not mention Article I, Section 18.7, in its arguments before the arbitrator?
4. What is the significance of Article VI, Section 6.1?
5. How should the arbitrator decide this case? Discuss.

CASE 62
A CHANGED REMEDY FOR MISASSIGNMENTS

Company:
   Pierce Company, Upland, Indiana

Union:
   Retail, Wholesale & Department Store Union, Unit D

Background

On April 24, 1990, the company's human resources manager, Esther Daly,[1] sent a letter to Viola Musgrove, president of the union, which stated in part:

> This will serve to confirm items discussed in our meeting Tuesday, April 17, 1990.
>   Should the company erroneously assign overtime, the injured party will be made whole in the following manner: Within thirty days after the matter is brought to the Company's attention, the Company, at the employee's request, will make available the same amount of overtime work to the employee.

The union filed a grievance on April 26, 1990, charging that the company had violated provisions of the collective bargaining agreement including, but not limited to, Article 7—Seniority, Section 2.[2] The union requested that the company "rescind the policy on overtime as stated in your letter of April 24, 1990."

In denying the grievance, the company responded that its "policy on overtime will be administered in a fair and equal way." The grievance was not resolved and eventually was carried to arbitration.

Testimony and Position of the Union

Union President Viola Musgrove testified that at a grievance meeting on April 17, 1990, Giles Holiday, general manager, had announced that the company intended to change the practice on overtime payments that were to be made to rectify errors in overtime assignments. Holiday had stated that, if overtime was available and the senior employee was overlooked, that employee would not be paid automatically. Rather, he or she would be offered overtime on a makeup basis within the next 30 days, if the employee advised the company of the error in overtime assignment within three days of the error. According to Musgrove, this was the first time in 24 years that the company had announced such a policy. In the past, the company had always paid the senior employee for overtime assignment errors and did not remedy them by makeup overtime.

---

[1]The names of all individuals are disguised.
[2]See the appendix for relevant contractual provisions.

Musgrove testified that at the April 17 meeting the company's human resources manager, Esther Daly, had stated that the company did not have a big problem with errors in overtime assignments, but she wanted to have a better and fairer policy in place.

Dorsey Alexander, a full-time union staff representative who had serviced the company for 13 months, was also at the April 17, 1990, grievance meeting. He testified substantially to the same effect as union President Musgrove. Alexander noted that when Ms. Daly had indicated that overtime misassignments were "not much of a problem," she had stated that in the previous 10 years there had been only two erroneous overtime assignments, and the eligible senior employees were paid for these errors.

In its post-hearing brief, the union argued that the company was bound by past practice to continue paying for erroneous overtime assignments, rather than giving makeup overtime assignments as a remedy. The union claimed that simply offering an employee an opportunity to make up improperly lost hours at a later date would not be an adequate remedy. The injured employee was entitled to work those hours at the time the hours were available. The injured employee should not be expected to work at a time more convenient to the employer, or at the discretion of a supervisor. The proper way to discourage supervisory errors, or favoritism in making overtime assignments, was to hold the company liable for breaches of contract by awarding pay to the employee who failed to get his or her proper assignment.

The union urged that its grievance be sustained, and that the company be directed to rescind the new overtime misassignment policy asserted in its letter of April 24, 1990.

Testimony and Position of the Company

General Manager Giles Holiday testified that at the April 17 meeting the company had notified the union that it intended to change the manner of paying for erroneously assigned overtime, but there was no intent whatsoever to change the collective bargaining agreement with respect to the manner of making overtime assignments.

Human Resources Manager Esther Daly testified that the company was not bound to any so-called past practice, since—to her knowledge—there had been only two erroneous overtime assignments during the past 10 years. The company felt that it had the reserved right under the contract to change the remedy for mistaken overtime assignments. It made no economic sense to pay an employee for not working just because there had been an unintentional supervisory error. The company's new policy, which was provided to the union in April 1990, would be a fair and equitable remedy, and this new policy did not in any way alter the contract. In its post-hearing brief, the company contended:

> The Company does not propose to change any overtime policy but only proposes a different remedy for aggrieved employees who erroneously were not assigned overtime.
>
> The Company on April 17, 1990, notified the union committee that in the future employees erroneously assigned overtime would be made whole as follows:

"Should the Company erroneously assign overtime the injured party will be made whole in the following manner: Within thirty days after the matter is brought to the Company's attention, the Company, at the employee's request, will make available the same amount of overtime work to the employee."

This was confirmed in a letter to the union dated April 24th. The union presented a grievance dated April 26th citing Article VII, Section 2. This article states the Company agrees to invoke the rule of seniority in a reasonable and equal way, giving preference to the senior employee where he possesses the necessary qualifications to do the work.

By making available the overtime within 30 days the Company is not violating Article 7, Section 2. Nor is the Company violating any section of the current contract as the contract is silent on the remedy to correct overtime errors.

The company urged that the union grievance be denied.

APPENDIX
RELEVANT CONTRACTUAL PROVISIONS

Article 4—Hours of Work and Overtime

Section 7.   When overtime work is necessary the overtime work shall be offered to senior employees currently holding the classification and the work to be performed in the department. A shift overtime will be performed by employees working on the A shift, unless declined. B shift overtime will be performed by the employees working on the B shift, unless declined. C shift overtime will be performed by the employees working on the C shift, unless declined. If these employees refuse the overtime, the following will apply.

STEP 1: Saturday overtime for less than three shifts shall be offered to employees currently holding classification in department by seniority.

STEP 2: From the qualified coded availability list by plant seniority.

STEP 3: Qualified probationary employees.

STEP 4: The company can require the least senior qualified employees on the plant seniority list to work the overtime starting with qualified probationary employees.

Section 8.   The above procedure will be followed except that employees will be permitted to continue working on work being performed at the end of their shift irrespective of seniority, not to exceed forty-five (45) minutes. When this work exceeds forty-five (45) minutes the above procedure will be followed except where it is impractical for the company to follow this procedure, either through the inability to contact employees, available employees are not qualified to do the work involved, or an emergency occurs.

Section 9.   Scheduled overtime will be posted by 11:00 A.M. of the third day of the work week. Employees affected by the overtime will advise the company on the fourth day of the work week of their intent to work by their first break.

Article 7—Seniority

Section 2.   The Company agrees to continue to invoke the rule of seniority for employees in a reasonable and equal way, giving preference to the senior employee where he possesses the necessary qualifications to do the work. The qualifications of any employee to do the work shall continue to be determined by the Company in accordance with the following factors: skill on work previously performed for the Company, job knowledge, attendance, and physical fitness. Any determination made by the Company as to an employee's qualifications may be challenged through the grievance procedure.

Questions

1. Why would the company and union pursue this case to arbitration when the problem involved occurred quite infrequently? Discuss.
2. Analyze the union's arguments and the company's arguments. Which are the most, and which the least persuasive?
3. Arbitrators have often differed concerning the weight that should be afforded to past practices in interpretation and application of contract language.[3] Was the company bound to continue its previous practice (policy) concerning payments for erroneous overtime assignments? Why, or why not?

---

[3]See Frank Elkouri and Edna Asper Elkouri, *How Arbitration Works,* 4th ed. (Washington, D.C.: Bureau of National Affairs, 1985), pp. 437–56.

CASE 63
PROBATION FOR THE TEACHER

Employer:
Jefferson County Board of Education (Kentucky)

Union:
Jefferson County Teachers' Association

Background

During the 1989–90 school year, Roy Hastings,[1] a middle-school teacher with 19 years' experience in the system who had been recently transferred from teaching in an elementary school, was involved in a classroom incident during which he overturned a desk and threw a stapler. No one was injured and no property damage occurred. Following an investigation, the school principal, Helen Frieman, issued a report called an E-2 report, dated May 31, 1990. Hastings received a copy, which read:

> We discussed the outcome of Mr. Rupert Tuttle's investigation dated May 30, 1990. While you did admit throwing the stapler, you stated that you do not throw objects when you become upset as stated in the writeup. You also wanted to make it clear that you attempted to set up the desk with one hand and it lost its balance.
>
> I then told you that you need to refrain from throwing anything in the classroom or acting in any way other than professional which will only serve to downgrade your reputation. We then discussed the need for more alternatives to student conduct.

Hastings disputed some of the statements contained in the E-2 report. However, because of the intervening summer recess, he did not meet with his principal to discuss the matter until September 5, 1990, at a Level 1-B grievance meeting.[2] The meeting was attended by his union representative, Jane Seeger, and Principal Frieman. The meeting was apparently successful and the matter appeared to be resolved to everyone's satisfaction. Seeger followed up with a letter to the principal, dated October 11, 1990, summarizing her notes of the meeting:

> This letter is to verify the agreement we reached on September 5, 1990, concerning the grievance initiated by Hastings. This was a Level 1-B meeting to resolve the issue of an E-2 dated 5/31/90 which Hastings received at the end of the 1989–90 school year.
>
> We agreed that you would keep this E-2 in your school file for the 1990–91 school year. If there are no incidents during this time, the E-2 dated 5/31/90 will be destroyed; i.e., it will *never* be sent to his permanent employee personnel file.
>
> If this does not meet with your understanding of our agreement, please notify me immediately. Thank you for your cooperation in this matter.

---

[1]The names of all individuals are disguised.
[2]See the appendix for relevant contractual clauses.

However, while this first incident was being resolved, Hastings was involved in a second classroom incident. A student's parent telephoned the principal complaining that his son had been mistreated by Hastings. At Frieman's recommendation, the complaint was reduced to writing in a letter from the child's father, dated October 19, 1990. The principal met with Hastings on October 24. Hastings was informed of the complaint, but he did not admit to the event in question. He volunteered to phone the parent and resolve the problem. On October 30, Frieman sent Hastings the following letter summarizing the matter:

> This letter serves as a summary of parent concern disposition. On October 22, 1990, the attached letter was received from Mr. John McDonald. On October 24, 1990, you and I met to address the complaint. You told me at that time you did not recall the incident. I reminded you to keep your hands off the students. You offered to call Mr. McDonald to discuss the letter. I asked you to call by the end of the day on 10/25/90. I called the John McDonald residence and spoke with the grandmother. I told her that you and I had a conference and asked her to tell Mr. McDonald to expect a call from you.
>
> On October 29, I met with you to bring closure to the complaint. You told me you had called Mr. McDonald and he seemed "satisfied" with the call.
>
> We concluded our conference with me reminding you to watch how you talk to students and to watch your contact with students.

Subsequently, Roy Hastings had occasion to review the contents of his permanent personnel file. He discovered that the E-2 document of May 31, 1990, had been inserted into this file. After discussing this with his union representative, he filed the following grievance:

> The Board, through its agents, violated the JCTA/JCBE Agreement by taking adverse action against the grievant, improperly disciplining the grievant, and placing improper material in the employee's personnel file. Such actions are in direct violation of Article IX, Employee Discipline; and Article XXIX, Grievance Procedure.

The parties were unable to resolve the grievance in the first three steps of the grievance procedure. The union, therefore, exercised its right to arbitrate under the terms of the agreement. The parties agreed on the following submission:

> Did the Jefferson County School Board, through its representative, Principal Helen Frieman, violate the Collective Bargaining Agreement by placing a Form E-2, which recorded a classroom incident, in the grievant's personnel file, and if so, what shall the remedy be?

Position of the Union

The union argued that the testimony of both Jane Seeger and Roy Hastings proved that, following the September 5, 1990, meeting, they understood that the E-2 report would be held in the principal's office. Thus, the form should never have found its way into Hastings' personnel file. The union also held that the E-2 was apparently already in his file at the time of the September 5 meeting, and that Frieman had deliberately withheld that information from them. Placing the E-2 in Hastings' file constituted a violation of the Level 1-B resolution of his first grievance.

The union asserted that Hastings had not been informed that the October 1990, McDonald incident constituted a violation of his probation. As a consequence, he had no way of defending himself with respect to the parent's accusation and Frieman's decision. Following his meeting with Principal Frieman on October 29, 1990, he was convinced that the matter had been handled appropriately and was closed. The union argued that Hastings had complied with the conditions of the first grievance settlement, and thus the E-2 report should have been destroyed.

Finally, the union pointed out that the purpose of the E-2 form was to record the notes taken during a conference or investigation and should not have been used as an instrument for adding a disciplinary action to an employee's personnel file.

The union requested that the arbitrator order the removal of the E-2 report from Hastings' file, remove him from a probationary status, and expunge from his files all references to the McDonald incident.

Position of the Board

The Board held that it had not violated either the collective bargaining agreement or the resolution of the Level 1-B meeting on September 5, 1990.

Principal Helen Frieman testified that in consideration of Hastings' 19 years as a teacher in the system and in order to provide him with an opportunity to adjust to the new classroom environment in the middle school, she had agreed to expunge the record of the incident from his file, provided he completed the 1990–91 year without further incident. She admitted that she accepted the letter of October 11, 1990, from union representative, Jane Seeger, without having read it. She stated that they had reached complete agreement regarding the probationary period.

Frieman testified that following the October 29 meeting with Hastings concerning the second 1990 (or McDonald) incident, she had interviewed two other children from the class, and she had determined that this incident did constitute a violation of Hastings' probationary period.

In addressing the use of the E-2 report, the principal stated that the form was routinely used as a record in an employee's personnel file, such as it was used in this case. She said that she did not remember when the E-2 report had been placed in Hastings' file.

The Board argued that whether or not the E-2 form resided in the principal's office or the grievant's personnel file was irrelevant, since the desired outcome was that it would be destroyed if Hastings behaved appropriately during his probationary period.

Finally, the Board pointed out that the principal was the individual charged with the responsibility of judging whether or not the second incident constituted a violation of the Level 1-B meeting held on September 5, 1990, and that she alone should determine whether Hastings had complied with the probation or not.

The Board urged that the arbitrator deny the grievance in its entirety.

APPENDIX
RELEVANT PROVISIONS OF THE AGREEMENT

Article IX—Employee Discipline

Section A. Conditions for Just Cause.   A.1. The employee has had opportunity to have foreknowledge of the possible or probable disciplinary consequences of the conduct or performance;

*   *   *   *   *

A.3. Before disciplining or terminating the employee, a fair and objective investigation was made . . . and the decision was based on substantial evidence or proof;

*   *   *   *   *

A.5. The degree of formal discipline . . . reasonably relates to (*a*) the seriousness of the employee's proven offense and (*b*) the record of the employee's service with the Employer.

*   *   *   *   *

Section C.   The employee must be afforded an opportunity to answer the complaint and meet with the complainant within two weeks of receipt of the complaint.

Article XXIX—Grievance Procedure

A. Any employee covered by this Contract who feels that Management has violated the terms of the Contract or who believes that he/she has been treated unjustly, may file a grievance which shall be in writing and presented to that individual's immediate supervisor . . .
B. The first step of the grievance procedure (Level 1-B) . . .
C. The second step . . .
D. The third step . . .
E. If the parties are unable to resolve the grievance, either party may request that it be submitted to arbitration . . .

Questions

1. Did the principal, Helen Frieman, follow appropriate contractual due process in handling this case? Why, or why not?
2. The Board held that it was Frieman's sole responsibility to determine whether or not Hastings had violated his probationary period. Are there any limitations to this right? If so, what are they?
3. Did Frieman improperly discipline Hastings in violation of the just cause provisions of the contract? Why, or why not?
4. How should the arbitrator rule in this case? Explain.

CASE 64
ARBITRABILITY OF THE REVISED SALARY STEP INCREASE AWARD

Agency:
Internal Revenue Service, Austin, Texas

Union:
National Treasury Employees Union

Background

Beginning in October 1989, the Internal Revenue Service (Agency) established guidelines allowing employees who had earned an "all fives" rating on their performance appraisals ("five" meaning "superior") the option of receiving either a cash award, or a High Quality Step Increase (QSI). A QSI represented a substantial award, for it provided that an employee would receive for one year a salary increase one pay step higher than what he or she would have otherwise received. For example, an employee who might normally have received a 4 percent increase would receive an additional increase equal to the increase awarded to the next step, say 3 percent, for a total of 7 percent.

The award guidelines were established unilaterally by the Agency without consultation with the union. The Agency established this policy in an attempt to maximize the number of awards given to employees. About a year later, management concluded that the awarding of the QSIs was having a detrimental effect on the Austin Agency's overall budget. Accordingly, the guidelines for earning a QSI were unilaterally revised by the Agency effective November 1990. The revised guidelines provided that (1) a QSI would not be given to any employee in consecutive years; and (2) an employee must receive an "all fives" rating for two consecutive years to be eligible for a QSI.

Two employees, Robert Watkins and Harold Layman,[1] received the results of their annual performance appraisals in February 1991, for the 1990–91 appraisal period. Both had earned "all fives" ratings. They had also earned "all fives" for the previous year, 1989–90. For that earlier period they had been given the option of a QSI or a cash award. Both chose the QSI.

Shortly after receiving notice of their 1990–91 ratings, they were informed by the Agency that they were entitled only to the cash award under the revised guidelines. The union thereupon filed the following individual grievances on behalf of Watkins and Layman:

> Robert Watkins (Harold Layman) was improperly denied a QSI award, as he requested, after earning "all fives" on his annual performance appraisal. The Agency, based on past practice, improperly denied him his choice. Robert Watkins (Harold Layman) to be offered a QSI.

---

[1]The names of all individuals are disguised.

The parties were unable to resolve their differences at either the first or second steps of the grievance procedure. At the third step, the union formally charged that the Agency had not provided it with advance notice of the revision in November 1990, and had denied it the opportunity to bargain over the revision. The Agency refused to modify the grievance, claiming that the union should have included that issue in its grievance at the first step of the grievance procedure.[2] Since it had failed to do so, the union pursuant to Article 41, Section 8(C), was barred from raising this issue at that late date.

The parties were unable to resolve the grievance. They agreed that the arbitrator should rule on the following issue:

> Whether the issue of the Agency's failure to provide the Union with notice and an opportunity to bargain over the procedure for awarding High Quality Step Increases (QSI) is properly before the Arbitrator. If so, what is the appropriate remedy?

Position of the Union

The union claimed that it did, in fact, raise the question of notice and opportunity to bargain during the first-step proceedings. It presented four witnesses, each of whom testified that the union steward, Ruth Carlton, had raised the issue of notice and opportunity to bargain. The grievance, in effect, was amended at the first-step hearing. The union also held that nothing in the National Agreement between the Internal Revenue Service and the National Treasury Employees Union mandated that the additional issues raised during the first-step hearing be put into writing.

The Agency had acknowledged that the union formally raised the matter in the third-step proceedings. The Agency had never asserted that it would not consider the question of notice and failure to bargain. While it might be argued that the Agency did not respond to the union in negotiations on this issue because it felt no need to do so, it was more likely that the Agency, in not responding, was actually acquiescing to the union's position with respect to notice and opportunity to bargain. The issue was properly raised during the grievance procedure and the matter was arbitrable.

The union argued that when the Agency unilaterally implemented changes to the procedure for granting QSI awards, it violated provisions of Title VIII of the Civil Service Reform Act that make it an unfair labor practice to refuse to consult or negotiate with the employee's exclusive representative. The QSI policy was a condition of employment under this act, which covers federal government employees. The policy was unilaterally changed by the Agency without either notifying the union or providing it with the opportunity to negotiate a proposed change in the policy.

The union asked the arbitrator to hold that a *status quo ante* remedy[3] be imposed on the Agency.

---

[2]See the appendix in this case for relevant contractual clauses.

[3]For this case, this meant a return to the original guidelines that the Agency had issued in October 1989.

Position of the Agency

The Agency held that the union was barred from raising the issue of notice and opportunity to bargain because it had not raised the issue in the first step of the grievance proceedings. At the first step, union steward Carlton had raised only the issue that was on the face of the written grievance. Further, the recorded testimony of the union representatives during the hearing made no reference to notice and opportunity to bargain. Four management representatives present at the first- and second-step hearings swore that no verbal statements were made about notice and opportunity to bargain by the union representatives. Written documentation of these hearings and of Agency responses to the union grievance made no mention whatsoever of the union's charges about notice and opportunity to bargain. It was not until the third step that the union raised the new issues, that is, notice and opportunity to bargain over QSIs. At no time did any Agency official agree to join the new issues raised at the third step.

The Agency argued that the union had not established that there had been a change in a negotiable condition of employment, nor had the union introduced any evidence that special circumstances existed to warrant a *status quo ante* remedy in this case. The change in awarding QSIs, according to the Agency, was outside its duty to bargain. In the third-step proceedings the Agency's chief spokesperson had asserted that:

> ... the procedures to which you refer for considering an employee for a QSI are considered to be guidelines for managers. Therefore, it was not necessary to share any changes with NTEU.

The Agency stated that imposition of a *status quo ante* remedy would require that it offer a QSI to every employee who had earned "all fives" on his or her performance appraisal for the past year. Such a remedy would place an unduly heavy financial burden on the Austin office of the Internal Revenue Service.

The Agency asked the arbitrator to deny the grievance in its entirety.

APPENDIX
RELEVANT PROVISIONS OF THE AGREEMENT

Article 41—Employee Grievance Procedure

Section 1.   B. The purpose of this article is to provide an orderly method for the disposition and processing of grievances brought by employees or by the Union on behalf of employees. Nothing in this article shall apply to institutional grievances brought by employees concerning the effect or interpretation, or a claim of breach of the provisions, of this Agreement relating to the rights and benefits accruing to the Union as the exclusive representative of bargaining unit employees.

*   *   *   *   *

Section 7. Step 1.   The matter will be reduced to writing and submitted to the attention of the unit manager by the aggrieved and/or the aggrieved's Union steward. The written grievance will provide information concerning the nature of the grievance, the article(s) and section(s) of the Agreement alleged to have been violated, and the remedy sought. Either party may then request that a meeting be held on the matter, or the parties may agree that no meeting be held. If either party elects a meeting, it shall take place within three (3) days of the submission of the grievance.

The foregoing meeting will be between the unit manager and any other management representative the Employer deems necessary, the grievant and/or the grievant's steward.

The unit manager's decision will be given to the aggrieved within five (5) days of the close of the meeting, if one is held, or within five (5) days of the submission if no meeting is held.

Steps 2–3.

*   *   *   *   *

Section 8.   A. The Parties will have the obligation of making a complete record during steps of the grievance procedure, including the obligation to produce any and all witnesses who have information relevant to the matter at issue.

*   *   *   *   *

C. With the exception of subsection D below, new issues may not be raised by either party unless they have been raised at Step 1 of the grievance procedure; provided, however, that the parties may agree to join the new issues with a grievance in process . . .

D. If the Employer raises question of grievability or arbitrability, the grievance will be amended to include a resolution of this question in the processing of the grievance.

Section 9.   A. The arbitrator may not amend, modify, or add to the provisions of the Agreement. The decision must be based upon an interpretation of the express relevant language of the Agreement.

B. The Arbitrator shall render a decision as soon as possible, but no later than 60 days following the termination of the proceedings.

*   *   *   *   *

Questions

1. Why would the parties agree to include Article 41, Section 8(C) in the agreement?
2. The union claimed that it had included the issue of notice and opportunity to bargain at the first step of the grievance procedure. On the other hand, the Agency insisted that the union had not raised this issue at the first step. Explain the likely reasons for these different claims.
3. Evaluate the union's charge that the Agency had violated provisions of the Civil Service Reform Act. How should the arbitrator handle this contention? Evaluate the Agency's response to the effect that the QSI

procedures were only guidelines to aid managers in making pay increases and not subject to negotiation.

4. If you were an arbitrator and were unable to determine from the testimony of the parties whether or not the contested issue had been properly raised, what would you do?
5. If you were the arbitrator, how would you rule? Give your reasoning.

CASE 65
DENIAL OF THE SAFETY INCENTIVE PRIZE

Company:
   Chevron Chemical Company (Ortho Division), Maryland Heights, Missouri

Union:
   Automotive, Petroleum, and Allied Industries Employees Union, Teamsters Local No. 618

Background

The company plant produced consumer products under the Ortho product line; some 120 operations and maintenance employees in the plant were represented by the union.

The union grievance heard in arbitration in this case had been filed on February 13, 1991, by Jack Cason,[1] a production operator. The grievance included in relevant part the following complaint:

> Failure to comply with safety program. People that had OSHA recordable injuries still received their full safety award money while others did not.

Introduced in the arbitration hearing was a copy of a document entitled, "1990 Safety Incentive Programs."[2] The administration of these programs was the focal point of the dispute before the arbitrator. The parties stipulated that there was no provision in the labor-management agreement directly covering this matter. However, the parties also stipulated that the matter was properly before the arbitrator for determination as provided in the grievance-arbitration procedure in the collective bargaining agreement.

The issue for the arbitrator was submitted as follows:

> Did the company violate the terms of its "1990 Safety Incentive Programs" when it denied Jack Cason a 1990 monetary prize?
> If so, what should be the appropriate remedy?

Testimony and Position of the Union

Giving primary testimony for the union was the grievant, Jack Cason, who said that he had been employed by the company for approximately 12 years. According to Cason, he had incurred an OSHA recordable incident in 1990, but still he should have received an incentive prize under the company's "Safety Incentive Programs," yet he did not. Cason's injury was to his right elbow area; it was identified as "ulnar tunnel syndrome" (somewhat similar to carpal tunnel syndrome) caused by repetitive motions.

The injury was work-related and caused by repetitive arm movements in his job. Cason said he had filed his grievance because another employee, John Alvino, had

---

[1]The names of all individuals are disguised.
[2]See the appendix for relevant provisions of this program.

received a $160 safety prize for 1990, despite the fact that Alvino also had an OSHA recordable incident. Cason said that the company had told him that Alvino was not personally responsible for his injury, and therefore Alvino was still eligible for the safety incentive prize.

Testifying next for the union was Dorothy Dobbs, union shop steward. She stated that in contrast to John Alvino's receiving a prize despite his OSHA recordable incident, other employees were denied a monthly incentive prize of $40 for which by the same logic they should have been eligible. She indicated that this had occurred in March or May of 1990. Dobbs said she believed that Alvino had received favorable treatment because Alvino was very active in a movement attempting to decertify the union in 1990. She stated that Alvino had "bragged" about his role in attempting to have the union decertified. A decertification election was held by the National Labor Relations Board in early 1991, but the union won the election. Dobbs stated that Alvino was one of the observers at the decertification election as part of the group that was trying to decertify the union.

Summarizing the union position, Jeffrey Cage, union assistant business representative, stated that neither he nor other union officers had ever received copies of the company's "Safety Incentive Programs" until Jack Cason's grievance was filed. This was a clear example of disparate and discriminatory treatment. The company had used its own safety program to show direct favoritism for John Alvino, who had been involved in an attempt to decertify the union. The union requested the arbitrator to grant Jack Cason $160 for equitable treatment under the "Safety Incentive Programs," and to direct the company to treat employees equally in the future.

Testimony and Position of the Company

Giving testimony for the company was Bradley Genther, operations supervisor, who stated that he was responsible for production and warehouse facilities. Jack Cason reported to a first-line supervisor who in turn reported to Genther. Genther stated that the "1990 Safety Incentive Programs" were implemented in an effort to reduce frequency of accidents. The programs were developed with the participation of a safety committee. Seven of the 10 members of this committee were employees in the bargaining unit. Genther stated that an occupational injury absence caused by repetitive work motions was an OSHA recordable incident; this excluded Jack Cason from a 1990 safety award. Cason had been absent for a period as a consequence of his injury, and had received payment from the state workers' compensation system.

Genther testified that John Alvino did have an absence period in 1990. This had come about when he was sent to a training department facility to have blood drawn as part of a blood test monitoring program. Alvino developed an infection that caused him to be absent for several weeks. This had been defined as an OSHA recordable incident because of OSHA regulations. However, Genther stated, company management had met and decided to pay Alvino the $160 safety incentive award, because his OSHA recordable incident was not in any way a direct result of performing his job duties. No one was penalized because Alvino received this payment. Alvino's absence was technically an OSHA recordable incident, but the company was trying to treat Alvino fairly in regard to the overall intent of the "Safety Incentive Programs."

The position of the company was summarized by Dexter Sohn, labor relations counselor. Sohn contended that the company's "1990 Safety Incentive Programs" had been developed in conjunction with bargaining unit employees. The purpose was to assist in prevention of accidents and illnesses, and the programs were not a contractual matter under the parties' negotiated agreement. Sohn claimed that the company felt that John Alvino was entitled to the safety incentive award of $160, since his OSHA recordable incident was not directly related to performance on the job. Sohn asserted that the reason why some employees had not received the $40 monthly prize in question was that during the same period other employees had incurred OSHA recordable incidents besides Alvino. Sohn contended that he had been unable in his review of the case to find any evidence that indicated Alvino had been treated favorably because of his involvement in the union decertification campaign. The company urged the arbitrator to deny the union grievance.

APPENDIX
RELEVANT PROVISIONS OF THE "SAFETY INCENTIVE PROGRAMS" DOCUMENT

Maryland Heights 1990 Safety Program

X. Safety Incentive Programs—1990   Safety incentive programs are developed and used for the purpose of heightening safety awareness and rewarding exemplary safety performance. The programs that will be used in 1990 were developed by a safety incentive committee made up mostly of O&M employees. The programs are based on individual and plant safety performance.

A. For every *individual* that completes the calendar year of 1990 without having an OSHA recordable injury or illness, $160.00 will be awarded.

B. For each calendar month in which the *entire plant* experiences no OSHA recordable injuries or illnesses, each person will be awarded $40.00.

C. When the entire plant completes the first six months of 1990 with 6 OSHA incidents or less, a $5,000.00 pot will be divided by all employees. The same program will be in effect for the second half of 1990.

Definitions

OCCUPATIONAL INJURY:
Any injury such as a cut, fracture, sprain, amputation, etc., which results from a work accident or from an exposure involving a single incident in the work environment.
OCCUPATIONAL ILLNESS:
Any abnormal condition or disorder, other than one resulting from an occupational injury, caused by exposure to environmental factors associated with employment. It includes acute and

chronic illnesses or diseases which may be caused by inhalation, absorption, ingestion, repetitive motion, or direct contact.

OSHA RECORDABLE INCIDENT:

An occupational illness or injury as stated above that requires treatment by a physician or results in lost workdays, work restrictions, prescription of medicines, or therapeutic measures. This list is not complete but implies the recordability criteria.

Questions

1. Why would the company agree to arbitrate this case when the issue arose under a document that was not part of the parties' collective bargaining agreement?

2. Should the company have denied a safety prize to John Alvino, even though his OSHA recordable incident was not due to his work performance? Explain.

3. To what degree should the fact that John Alvino was openly supportive of the union decertification effort be weighed by the arbitrator? Discuss.

4. How should the arbitrator decide this case? Why?

CASE 66
DEMOTED OR RECLASSIFIED?

Company:
Lord Aerospace Products (Division of Lord Corporation), Erie, Pennsylvania

Union:
International Association of Machinists and Aerospace Workers, District Lodge 83, Local Lodge No. 1968

Background

For several years prior to the grievance in this case, the company had sought to have its toolroom operate in what it characterized as a "self-directed mode." Management had hoped to develop a shop environment in which toolmakers would help manage their own day-to-day activities and develop a greater sense of responsibility for the quality and quantity of their work. Management expected that obtaining greater employee involvement through "participative management" would improve quality and efficiency and achieve greater customer satisfaction.

The company had created four Lead Toolmaker positions at the start of the self-direction project, and four men assumed these positions after bidding for the jobs.[1]

After giving the new organization structure a trial of several years, management came to believe that the Lead Toolmaker position, as it had been conceived, was part of the problem with the project. Self-direction had not worked out as planned. Management concluded that the Lead Toolmakers, in practice, had relieved the majority of the toolmakers of their responsibilities for quality and quantity. Their continuous role as advisors and helpers had prevented the rest of the toolmakers from feeling ownership of their work.

In April 1991, management informed the four Lead Toolmakers of its decision to vacate the position of Lead Toolmaker and to assign them to their former positions as journeyman toolmakers at a rate of $1.02 less than they had received as Lead Toolmakers.

The union on May 16, 1991, filed the following grievance:
The grievance was eventually carried to arbitration.

On April 25, 1991, Dan Goetz, Harold Hannigan, Byron Smith, and Ben Borgatta,[2] were informed by their Facilitator Henry Beecher and their Manager George Hall that effective April 29, 1991, their duties as Lead Toolmakers were no longer needed, and that their rates of pay would be decreased to those of a top "A" Toolmaker. The aforementioned aggrieved members and the Union feel that this action is contrary to the present agreement, and that the Company should do whatever is necessary to make the aggrieved members whole.

---

[1]See the appendix for the job summary of the Lead Toolmaker position and for relevant contractual provisions.
[2]The names of all individuals are disguised.

Position of the Union

The union pointed out that all four grievants possessed the requisite skills, training, and knowledge to perform their jobs. All had graduated from apprentice to journeyman under the job-training program at Lord Aerospace. In fact, two of them, Goetz and Borgatta, had completed their apprenticeship programs in three years, rather than the normal four.

The company's action violated Article I (2) and Article IV (3) (a), which required that it negotiate with the union on matters of wages, hours, and other conditions of employment. In the past, the company had always discussed and negotiated changes that affected employees in the bargaining unit, and the union insisted that it do so in this instance. By reclassifying the Lead Toolmakers as toolmakers, management had demoted them and reduced their wage rate. The company could not do so without the consent of the union.

The union argued that the job classification of Lead Toolmaker had first appeared in the contract in 1975, and that it had remained there to this day. The company could not now eliminate that classification and remove the Lead Toolmakers from the contract without agreement from the union.

Finally, the union argued that if management felt that the Lead Toolmakers were not effective in their role as it had been defined in their job descriptions, management should have given them clear-cut supervisory responsibilities and paid them accordingly.

The union petitioned that the arbitrator uphold the grievance in its entirety. The four demoted grievants should be returned to the classification of Lead Toolmaker and made whole for all losses they had sustained because of the improper demotions.

Position of the Company

The company contended that it had not violated the contract, and that Article V (1) bestowed on management the right to restructure the toolroom and to assign and reassign employees to meet the needs of the organization. The company had always negotiated on matters designated in the contract; this was simply a case where the contract did not apply.

The company stated that the four Lead Toolmakers were not disciplined, demoted, or punished. They were reassigned to their former positions of journeyman toolmakers, because the company had decided that the position of Lead Toolmaker currently was no longer needed. The job classification of Lead Toolmaker had not been eliminated; it was only being vacated at this time. In previous years, the Lead Toolmaker position had not always been filled, depending on the company's needs. What the company had done was to determine again that there was no present need for the Lead Toolmaker position in the toolroom. If in the future the company decided to again fill the position of Lead Toolmaker, the grievants would be afforded the opportunity to apply for and/or bid for the position.

Management reiterated its position that the performance of the grievants was entirely satisfactory. They had not been demoted. While their wage rate had been reduced by $1.02 per hour, they were receiving the top rate for the toolmaker classification.

The company requested that the arbitrator deny the grievance.

APPENDIX
RELEVANT PROVISIONS OF THE AGREEMENT

Article I—Recognition

2. The Company will bargain collectively with the Union with respect to rates of pay, wages, hours, and other conditions of employment involving the employees in the above-stated classifications, provided however, that this Agreement shall finally dispose of all demands of the Company and the Union which have heretofore been made or which might be the subject of collective bargaining throughout the period of this Agreement, not intending, however, to preclude the presentation of or processing of grievances hereunder.

Article IV—Settlement of Grievances

3. a. Only matters concerning the interpretation and application of the terms of this Agreement are subject to arbitration. However, differences with respect to changes in the existing wage structure, or differences with respect to terms of a new Agreement, will not be subject to arbitration. The impartial arbitrator shall have no jurisdiction or power to amend, modify, supplement, vary, disregard, or contravene any provision of this Agreement, or any supplement thereto, in any respect whatsoever.

*   *   *   *   *

Article V—Management Responsibilities

1. The management of the plant and the direction of the working forces, including: the right to direct, plan and control plant operations; the right to select, assign, transfer, suspend, promote, demote, or terminate employees on the basis of knowledge, training, skill, and performance; to terminate or discharge employees for justifiable causes and to relieve employees of duty because of lack of work or for other legitimate reasons; and the right to introduce new and improved methods and facilities and the management of the properties is vested exclusively in the Company. It is also understood that it is the sole responsibility of the Company to use whatever instructional and corrective procedures it deems appropriate in any and all cases involving employee performance that is unsatisfactory in the opinion of Management, provided however, that if an employee is demoted, suspended, or discharged following the application of such procedures, he may file a grievance and the case may be processed through arbitration for a review as to whether the demotion, suspension, or discharge was for just cause. Any action taken under this Article shall not circumvent, supersede, or in any manner conflict with the expressed terms of this Agreement.

JOB SUMMARY FOR LEAD TOOLMAKER

Assume complete responsibility for the manufacture of any complex tooling. Set up and operate all machines involved. Perform necessary assembly and bench work. Direct other Tool Room personnel when assigned to him by the Supervisor. Heat treat as needed. Also responsible for final assembly and acceptance at inspection by the Gage Room.

Specific Duties.   The duties of the job include, but are not limited to:

1. Make and repair any type of mold, die, gage, jig and fixture, including the most complex.
2. Machine and fabricate complex parts to close tolerances to ensure acceptable final assembly.
3. Direct other Tool Room personnel as required to complete assignments.
4. Usually work from complex prints; may also work from simple prints, models, sketches, and verbal instructions. Use shop and machinist's handbooks.
5. Perform work of toolmakers A, B, and C as required.
6. Perform other similar and related duties.

Questions

1. What limits do Articles I, IV, and V place on the union's right to participate in or contest any decision regarding the reorganization of the toolroom and the transfer of the four grievants out of their jobs as Lead Toolmakers? What limits do these Articles place on management?
2. Were the four grievants demoted or reassigned? Explain.
3. Should company management have discussed the decision with the union prior to implementing it, even if management felt it was not obligated contractually to do so? Discuss.
4. How should the arbitrator rule in the case? Explain.

CASE 67
VOLUNTARY RESIGNATION, OR LAYOFF?

Company:
  Quantum Chemical Corporation/UST Division, Port Arthur, Texas

Union:
  Oil, Chemical, and Atomic Workers International Union (OCAW), Local No. 4-288

Background

On June 27, 1991, the company announced plans to shut down parts of three of its less efficient production units, one of which was located at the Port Arthur, Texas, plant. The human resources manager, Otis Gullion,[1] entered into discussions with the union with regard to the payment of severance pay. He advised the union that each case would be handled on an individual basis.

On August 2, 1991, the company issued a 45-day-notice letter to the employees who were scheduled for layoff. The grievant in this case, Ramona Hawthorne, and other OCAW employees received this letter. Hawthorne's letter indicated a layoff date of September 16, 1991.

On receiving the notice of layoff, Hawthorne commenced looking for a job. She had worked as a laboratory technician for the company, but her efforts to find work in that capacity elsewhere revealed that no such positions were open. Hawthorne had been a teacher prior to coming to work for the company, so she began to look for work in the teaching profession. Most permanent teaching jobs in the area had been filled, since most schools in the area opened August 21, 1991. Hawthorne was eventually offered a substitute teaching job in mathematics at a junior high school, and she worked in that capacity on Wednesday, August 21, Thursday, August 22, and Friday, August 23. Since she was scheduled to work at the company on those days, she called in "sick" to cover her absences when in fact she was performing substitute teaching work. On Monday, August 26, she was offered a permanent job as a teacher at the school; by letter, Hawthorne resigned her employment with the company as of that date.

Ricardo Niechez, company labor relations supervisor, returned from his vacation on August 19, 1991. While reviewing attendance reports, he noticed that Ramona Hawthorne had reported sick on two separate occasions over a short period of time. He subsequently learned that there was some reason to believe that Hawthorne had found other employment. He talked to Hawthorne by telephone on August 23. She admitted that she was working as a substitute school teacher. She also stated that she had reported off sick on several days, even though she was not sick. Niechez advised Hawthorne that he was going to investigate the situation, and that she could be in "serious trouble" for reporting off sick when in fact she was working elsewhere. On

---

[1]The names of all individuals are disguised.

receipt of Hawthorne's resignation letter on August 28, he canceled his investigation into the matter.

Subsequently, Otis Gullion advised Hawthorne that she was not eligible either for severance pay or recall rights, as a consequence of her voluntary resignation. Hawthorne and the union filed a grievance in protest of this management action.

The grievance was not resolved by the parties, and it was eventually submitted to arbitration. The parties stipulated that the issue for the arbitrator's determination was as follows:

> Did the Company violate the Agreement[2] by denying Ramona Hawthorne severance pay? If so, what is the appropriate remedy?

Position of the Union

The union maintained that Ramona Hawthorne was entitled to severance pay under Article XVII, Section C, of the parties' collective agreement. She had met all the requirements for that benefit. She had a minimum of one year continuous employment, and she was laid off through no fault of her own, because of a reduction in work forces. As a result, under the contract's schedule of benefits, having two years of employment, Hawthorne was entitled to two weeks severance pay. The denial of severance pay to her was arbitrary and unjust.

The union advanced arguments as rebuttal to the contentions of the company why it had denied Hawthorne her severance pay. The company had argued that Hawthorne had left prior to the effective day of the layoff, September 16, 1991, and therefore she was not entitled to severance pay. The union pointed out that there was no such requirement in the labor agreement, nor was there any practice to that effect. In fact, in a later layoff in spring 1992, a number of employees had left the company well before the effective date of their layoffs and had been given severance pay.

The company also had argued that Hawthorne had engaged in a false and deceitful act by reporting off sick, when in fact she was working as a substitute school teacher. The union countered that she had not been paid for the days she called in sick, nor did she request pay. No discipline was ever imposed on her. Hawthorne was not terminated for cause. She left the company because of a reduction in force, and she needed to find new employment. She voluntarily resigned on August 26, 1991. There was no provision in the contract barring her right to severance pay because of an early resignation or for improperly calling in sick under such circumstances as these.

Position of the Company

The company contended that under the language of Article XVII, Section C, severance pay was not automatic. Certain eligibility requirements were set forth, and Ramona Hawthorne did not meet these requirements. She had received a contractually mandated

---

[2]See the appendix for relevant contractual provisions.

45-day layoff notice from the company, but she had not fulfilled this requirement because she had not worked until the layoff date. Hawthorne terminated her employment by a voluntary resignation prior to the layoff date of September 16, 1991.

The union had cited the layoff in February 1992, in support of its position. In this particular layoff, the company had determined that the layoff date would be April 16, 1992. However, the company decided to release those employees scheduled for layoff in March 1992, but continued to make them whole in terms of wages and benefits until the layoff date of April 16, 1992. Severance pay and recall rights were given those employees until April 16, 1992. Thus, the affected individuals remained in the company's employment.

The company claimed that the weakness of the union's claim of severance pay for Ramona Hawthorne was a proposal made by the union in contractual negotiations in November 1991. At that time, the union had proposed that employees who were given a 45-day notice of layoff would not lose their rights to severance pay or recall rights, if they found employment elsewhere. This was precisely the Hawthorne case. The company had rejected the union proposal. The company maintained its position that employees who resigned or who left before the layoff date would not be eligible for severance pay.

The imposition of eligibility requirements for severance pay was essential to the company's efficient operation. When a layoff notice was given, the company had every right to expect those employees to remain until the effective date of their layoff. The well-planned and controlled downsizing by the company required that employees remain until their layoff date, so as not to jeopardize production, maintenance, and safety. An employee who resigned his or her employment prior to the effective date of the layoff forfeited severance and recall rights.

The company urged the arbitrator to deny the union grievance.

APPENDIX
RELEVANT PROVISIONS OF THE AGREEMENT

Article XVII—Additional Benefits

Section C. Severance Pay Plan.   1. The Severance Pay Plan has been incorporated herein and made part of this Agreement.

An employee shall be eligible for benefits hereunder, provided:

(1) They have had a minimum of one (1) year continuous employment by the Company immediately prior to the layoff date; and

(2) They are laid off through no fault of their own, because of a reduction in forces.

Amount of Benefits.

An eligible employee shall be entitled to receive severance pay based on their current rate at the time of separation in accordance with the following schedule:

1 yr. but less than 2 yrs. 1 wk's pay.

2 yrs. but less than 4 yrs. 2 wk's pay.

4 yrs. but less than 7 yrs. 3 wk's pay.

7 yrs. but less than 10 yrs. 4 wk's pay.

10 yrs. but less than 15 yrs. 5 wk's pay.

15 yrs. but less than 20 yrs. 7 wk's pay.

20 yrs. and over 9 wk's pay.

Payment of Benefits

Payments under this Plan may be paid in a lump sum or in installments. Lump sums will not be paid when the layoff is presumed temporary.

Reemployment.

Upon recall an employee who has received all severance pay due shall be considered a new employee for severance pay purposes.

Under no conditions will severance pay for any employee exceed the maximum of nine (9) weeks.

Questions

1. Evaluate the arguments presented by the union on behalf of the grievant. Which do you consider the most/least persuasive?

2. Evaluate the arguments presented by the company. Which do you consider the most/least persuasive?

3. Should Ramona Hawthorne's "dishonesty," that is, calling in sick when she was working elsewhere, disqualify her from receiving severance pay?

4. What should the arbitrator decide? Why?

CASE 68
NO OFFICIAL "WRITING" OF TERMINATION

Company:
Jefferson Smurfit Corporation, Middletown, Ohio

Union:
United Paperworkers International Union, Local No. 1973

Background

On July 21, 1991, John Dyer,[1] a fork lift operator in the carton plant warehouse, was discharged for operating his equipment in a "reckless manner" on July 7, 1991, having caused a considerable monetary loss to the company. The company conducted a disciplinary hearing preliminary to discharge, which was summarized in a memorandum that read as follows:

> July 16, 1991
> Memo to File
> RE: Disciplinary Hearing/Dyer
>
> In the presence of Dan Damon and Ian Kelly, union representatives, Joseph Paulsen, Plant Manager, and Donald Wilson, Dept. Manager, John Dyer was informed that he was being suspended for an indefinite period of time due to an incident that occurred on July 7, 1991.
>
> Dyer, when removing a jumbo roll of paper from a stack in the plant warehouse, rearranged one of the rolls to a higher level. When it did not fit properly, Dyer pushed the roll back with the clamps. This roll pushed a roll stored next to the wall out through the concrete block and brick wall making a hole in the wall. The debris from the block and bricks fell on a parked car next to the wall, severely damaging the hood of the car. First estimates of damage to the wall were approximately $10,000. Dyer was informed that further investigation was required to make a final decision on any discipline, but in the interest of plant safety he was suspended. Two reports of running his truck at excessive speeds had been reported on this same date.
>
> Dyer indicated that it had taken a lot of ingenuity and initiative to get that roll out. No one else would have attempted to move it out.
>
> Dyer was informed that moving a wall to make room for movement of a roll was not considered an act of ingenuity or initiative.
>
> Sincerely,
>
> David McDonald
> Employee Relations Manager

On July 18, 1991, Employee Relations Manager David McDonald prepared an incident status report, which contained in the "Reason and Remarks" section the following statement:

---

[1]The names of all individuals are disguised.

John Dyer—Terminated for operating an industrial motor vehicle in an unsafe manner with complete inattention to his job which caused considerable damage to building and personal property.

John Dyer and his union representative, Dan Damon, received copies of both the disciplinary memorandum and the status report. However, neither Dyer nor any union officer or the union itself received a "writing," a formal notice of Dyer's termination in this case, from the company. The union subsequently grieved Dyer's discharge, and the grievance document stated in relevant part:

Nature of Grievance—DISCHARGE. ARTICLE XIII, XV, AND OR ANY OTHER AR-TICLE THAT MAY APPLY. ON 7-21-91 GRIEVANT WAS UNJUSTLY DISCHARGED.
Settlement desired: Reinstate, Full seniority, All Monies To Be Made Whole.

When the parties were unable to resolve their dispute, the case was taken to arbitration. The union proposed that the issue before the arbitrator should be stated as follows:

Did the company violate Article III, Section 3 of the Agreement[2] when it discharged John Dyer? If so, what should be the remedy?

The company did not agree with this statement, and proposed that the issue should be framed by the arbitrator after the testimony and evidence were presented.

During the arbitration hearing, both parties agreed that no official notification of discharge, or "writing," had been mailed to either Dyer or the union pursuant to Article XIII, Section 3 of the contract. They also stipulated that this provision had been in the parties' contracts since 1975, and that neither party had sought to remove or amend it since that time. The union agreed that it had raised the charge of lack of proper due process in regard to Article III, Section 3, on the part of the company for the first time during the arbitration hearing.

Position of the Union

The union claimed that every bargaining unit person previously terminated had received an official "writing" to that effect. The union submitted a copy of a letter sent to another terminated employee to indicate the nature of the information that should have been contained in such a "writing" to Dyer:

Mr. Karl Gregory
1715 Orchard Street
Middletown, Ohio 45044

Dear Karl:

In our meeting with you on January 30, we discussed with you the incident that occurred on the previous afternoon. At that time, we informed you that you would be placed on an indefinite suspension pending further investigation.

We have reviewed your files thoroughly and have discussed your case with all parties involved. Regretfully, we find that we have no alternative but to terminate your employment with this company effective today, February 4, 1991.

---

[2]See the appendix for relevant contractual clauses.

Your termination notice shall read, "Violation of company rules concerning reporting to work under the influence of alcohol."

All monies due you, if any, will be paid to you as soon as possible.

Sincerely,

David McDonald
Employee Relations Manager

The union alleged that the company had failed to meet the conditions of Article XIII, Section 3, of the agreement. The case was straightforward. The arbitrator should uphold the grievance, and Dyer should be reinstated with full accumulated seniority and be made whole for lost wages and all benefits that would have otherwise accrued.

Position of the Company

The company held that John Dyer was terminated for just cause, and that he had received sufficient notice of his termination and the reasons for it. Copies of the memorandum of the disciplinary hearing and of the incident status report were sent to Dyer and the union. These were sufficient, and another "writing" would have stated no more than was already contained in these two documents.

The company contended that Dyer had received every bit of due process required by the contract, and that any such defense raised by the union for the first time at the arbitration hearing was too late, considering that his termination had occurred more than a year ago.

The company responded to the union's allegation that all previously terminated employees had received a "writing" by citing the case of an employee some two years previous who had not received a "writing" at his termination. The union had not raised any issue of notification in that case. The union could not now claim that a "writing" was an absolute requirement in this instance.[3]

The company concluded that it had met the requirements of Article XIII, Section 3, and had ample just cause to terminate John Dyer. The company claimed that the union grievance was without merit and was a desperate effort by the union to have Dyer reinstated on a mere technicality. The company urged the arbitrator to deny the grievance.

Appendix
Relevant Provisions of the Agreement

Article XIII—Report on Discharges

Section 3.   The Company shall promptly furnish the Union in writing the reason for a discharge. Notification will be in addition to a status report.

---

[3]The union countered that it had no knowledge of the case matter to which the company alluded with respect to notification. The union had not grieved or appealed that termination to arbitration. Hence, the union had no record of it.

Questions

1. Was the company position in effect asking the arbitrator to grant it a waiver of Article XIII, Section 3, by stating that the two documents received by the union and the grievant were sufficient and that another "writing" would have added nothing? Explain.
2. Did the company satisfy the requirement of Article XIII, Section 3? Explain.
3. Could the union raise the charge that John Dyer had been denied proper due process at the arbitration hearing when the union had not done so at prior steps of the grievance procedure? Discuss.
4. How should the arbitrator rule? Explain.

CASE 69
ESCORTING THE UNION REPRESENTATIVES

Company:
   Unicare Health Facilities, Inc., St. Petersburg, Florida

Union:
   Nursing Home and Hospital Employees Union, Local No. 1115

Background

Unicare Health Facilities, Inc., operated 20 nursing home facilities in the state of Florida. Nursing Home and Hospital Employees, Local No. 1115, represented certain employees at 7 of these facilities including the company's St. Petersburg facility.

On August 19, 1991, the union assigned Ralph Miller, Jr.,[1] to the position of business representative to service the needs of represented employees in the St. Petersburg region. Miller's assignment constituted part of a substantial change in the union's organization. Previously, two business representatives from South Florida, Martha Ross and Milton Wiedenbaum, had traveled to the St. Petersburg area from time to time to meet with union members.

In September 1991, Ralph Miller visited the Colonial Care Center, a Unicare facility near St. Petersburg, to meet with Administrator Donald Davidson and to conduct union business with union members. Davidson refused to allow Miller to go into the hallways to talk with his people. Davidson did offer to escort Miller through the halls to the breakroom where he could talk with union employees during their scheduled breaks. All attempts by Miller to enter the company's premises without an escort were thwarted by Davidson.

The one exception to this was the laundry. Tim Fredericks, manager of the laundry, let Miller proceed unaccompanied to the breakroom to meet with six union employees.

The union filed a grievance on October 20, 1991, charging that the company was preventing the union from carrying on necessary union business on company premises contrary to the provisions of Article V of the parties' collective bargaining contract.[2] The parties were unable to resolve their differences, and they agreed to submit the grievance to arbitration as provided in the contract. They stipulated to the following statement of the issue:

> Did the Employer violate the Agreement by its conduct? If so, what should be the appropriate remedy?

Testimony of the Union

The union presented several witnesses to support its position that it had been prevented from representing its members, contrary to the provisions of the collective agreement.

---

[1]The names of all individuals are disguised.
[2]See the appendix for relevant contractual clauses.

Testimony of Milton Wiedenbaum. Union witness Milton Wiedenbaum testified that he had visited the company's facilities several times during the period 1988 to 1991 while serving as a union business representative. He said that he had always been allowed to roam freely through the halls, talking with employees and giving out his business card. He said that the policy of requiring "escorts" for union representatives at Unicare constituted a radical change of company policy.

Testimony of Martha Ross. Former union representative and present member of its executive board, Martha Ross, supported the testimony of Wiedenbaum. She, too, had visited company facilities on several occasions from 1988 to 1991, and she had never been escorted by company management.

Testimony of Ralph Miller, Jr. Union business representative Ralph Miller explained how the company's policy affected his ability to service his members. He was not allowed to walk the floors; he was permitted only to speak to employees while on break or after work, not in the hallways or at nurses' stations. As a consequence, he could not see all his union members. Miller testified he felt employees often had a need to "see" him. The company's policy inhibited his ability to speak with employees freely. He explained that he could not resolve grievances at a shop meeting. He wasn't able to speak with employees after work because most of them held a second job and had to leave immediately. The company's rule also hampered the union's ability to collect dues.

Most important of all, according to Miller, the escort policy interfered with the way employees felt about their union. Union members, and those who were not members of the union but were members of the bargaining unit, must see him at the workplace. He must "be there" to be effective. Miller said he wanted to be "where I wanted to be, not where management wanted me to be." He stated that he felt it was vitally important that he not be a "ghost." Walking the facility was crucial. Miller stated emphatically that under no circumstances would he allow his presence to interfere with patient care. He reiterated that he had never let this happen, and he would not let it happen in the future.

Testimony of the Company

The company presented several witnesses who testified concerning the need for an escort policy and its consistency with the wording of Article V of the agreement.

Testimony of Mary Hopkins. Mary Hopkins, director of employee relations, challenged Miller's assertion that he did not interfere with patient care. According to Hopkins, even when escorted to the breakroom, Miller would work his way down the hall saying "hello," kissing and hugging union members. She described him as "rather loud." She stated, "He created a scene when he walked down the hall. He's expressive."

Hopkins testified that she had received a telephone call from a union official, Dan Rogers, early in January 1992, complaining about Unicare's escort policy. She explained that Rogers told her that "walking the halls" was the way union representatives did it "up north." She stated that she told him that this was not the way they did it at Unicare.

Hopkins read from a letter she subsequently had sent to Rogers (the union had entered it as an exhibit). The letter said, among other things, that a union business representative was not allowed to "attempt to organize the company's nonunion staff." Hopkins asserted that the letter was significant because Miller was attempting to organize the nurses.

Hopkins testified concerning the bargaining history of Article V. She explained that the basic part of the provision had been in the contract for many years. The company had sought in the 1987 negotiations to add a provision requiring that a union representative give four hours advance notice of his or her visit. The company dropped this demand after the union president assured management that such notice would be given. Again, during 1990 negotiations management had proposed a provision requiring advance notice. Hopkins explained that the purpose of the proposed provision was to enable the company to prepare for the visit. It could provide someone to escort the business representative, alert employees so that they could be available to speak with the union representative during their breaks, and be available to discuss issues.[3] Hopkins said the parties did agree in the 1991 negotiations to add the words "when possible" to Article V.

Testimony of Georgia Ramsey.   Georgia Ramsey, a licensed practical nurse, testified that in January 1992, Ralph Miller had approached her about joining the union. She stated that when her supervisor, Michael Workman, asked Miller about this, he responded that he was only joking.

Testimony of Marcia Hennings.   Marcia Hennings, a physical therapist, complained of an impromptu meeting conducted by Ralph Miller in the hallway outside her door with five or six employees who were blocking the hallway and using abusive language about their supervisor.

Position of the Union

The union held that the language of Article V was clear and unambiguous. The union's representative had the right to perform his or her duties; management's restrictions unduly interfered with the exercise of that right. Under management's escort policy, the union representative had been "virtually handcuffed."

The union contended that most arbitration cases historically have strongly supported the union's position in this matter. Arbitrators have repeatedly upheld grievances, such as this one, contesting management restriction on union activities. Arbitrators have also upheld reasonable limitations on the exercise of union visitation rights. The union had not abused its visitation rights in this case.

Therefore, the grievance should be granted. Union business representatives should be allowed complete access to the facilities as long as they informed management in advance when possible, and did not interfere with the company's operations.

---

[3]Upon cross-examination by the arbitrator, union witness Milton Wiedenbaum who was a negotiator in 1991 said that he did not recall this company proposal or discussing it at the bargaining table.

Position of the Company

The company held that the union did not possess the contractual right to have unlimited access to the working areas of the company's property for the purpose of conferring with, and engaging in other union business with, employees who were on duty. Although the union had the right of access to work areas, the company had the right to escort union officials in such areas to assure no interference with operations.

Under the long established principle of the "reserved rights doctrine," management had the right to manage the company, limited only by the clear and specific contract language.

The company pointed out that its action in this case was consistent with its past practice and the bargaining history of the 1991 negotiations. The company would not agree to permit any outside party to have complete and unrestricted access to its facilities and employees.

Therefore, the grievance should be denied.

APPENDIX
RELEVANT PROVISIONS OF THE AGREEMENT

Article V—Union Visitation and Bulletin Boards

The Business Representative for the Union or the Union's designee, after advising management of his presence, shall have admission to all properties covered by this Agreement to discharge his duties as representative of the Union, provided that such admission shall not interfere with management's operations. The Union, when possible, shall inform the Facility in advance of its intention to visit the building. The Employer shall make available to the Union in the Nursing Home a bulletin board for the purpose of posting union notices. The Union shall be permitted to conduct union meetings on the Employer's premises with the Employer's consent on the regular employer's time, which shall not be unreasonably withheld.

Questions

1. The company held that it retained all management rights not specifically restricted in the contract. What does this mean in this case? Evaluate the company's position.
2. What is the relevance of past practice and the history of negotiations to Article V?
3. What "reasonable" limitations, if any, might be imposed on the union's access to the facility and to employees?
4. What is the purpose of Article V? Is it clear and unambiguous?
5. Could the company's escort policy be an unfair labor practice under the National Labor Relations Act? Explain. If it might be an unfair labor practice, why did the union appeal its case to arbitration rather than file an unfair labor practice charge with the NLRB?
6. How should the arbitrator rule in this case?

CASE 70
TEMPORARY OR PROBATIONARY?

Company:
   Heiner's Bakery, Inc., Huntington, West Virginia

Union:
   Retail, Wholesale, and Department Store Union, Local No. 21

Background

Heiner's Bakery operated a commercial bakery in Huntington, West Virginia, along with four sales branches in that state and southern Ohio. The company employed approximately 400 men and women of whom about 120 were members of Local 21 of the union. In October 1991, the company contracted with Kelly Temporary Services for several workers, including Roger Spalding,[1] the grievant in this case. Spalding's work was to stock and load trays while a new, automated piece of equipment was being readied for service. On his 30th day on the job, Spalding signed a union card and the union submitted this card to the company.[2] Toward the end of the day, Roy Pellam, personnel director, told Spalding that he could finish his work that day but he should then leave the premises and not return. Spalding did so; but on the following day he filed a grievance charging that the 30 days he had worked at the bakery should be counted as probationary employment time under the terms of the collective bargaining agreement and according to the company's past practice.

The parties failed to resolve their dispute, which they agreed to submit to an arbitrator. They stipulated that Roger Spalding had worked a full 30 days and that the issues were as follows:

1. Whether or not the time worked by the grievant as a Kelly temporary employee counted as probationary employment time with the company under:
   (a) the Agreement, or
   (b) past practice?
2. If the answer to Issue 1 is affirmative, did the grievant complete his probationary period and become an employee of the company?

Testimony of the Union

The union presented three witnesses who testified on behalf of Roger Spalding.

Testimony of Bill Bosch, President of Local No. 21.   Bill Bosch testified that Roger Spalding had never been informed by the company that his work was temporary and for a specific job only. Bosch stated that he had spoken with Personnel Director Roy Pellam about Spalding, but Pellam "didn't act like he knew how long he was going to

---

[1]The names of all individuals are disguised.
[2]See the appendix for relevant contractual clauses.

keep Spalding." Bosch accordingly said he told Spalding, "Just do your work, son. That's the best thing I can say to do."

Bosch testified that the company failed to give the union notice that it was bringing in temporary employees. He asserted, "At no time did the company ever inform or take the position with the union that Spalding was anything but a regularly hired employee."

However, under cross-examination during the arbitration proceedings, Bosch acknowledged:

> He (Roy Pellam) told me that Kelly people were coming, but he never told me how long they were going to work. I never asked him and he never told me.

Union President Bosch said that he was a 41-year employee, and he next testified on the company's past practices with respect to probationary and temporary employees. He stated that some 30 years earlier the company had taken on two people in circumstances like those of Spalding:

> The company . . . used Manpower Temporary Services for a long time . . . back in the 60s . . . They used them for a whole year . . . They had a hiring freeze on for a year there . . . They would work them for 29 days, and then they would get rid of them.

Concerning another precedent, Bosch testified:

> And then when the year (hiring freeze) was up, they had some [two people] working 29 days and then when the 29 days were up, we signed them up and they were accepted . . . In the 60s in that freeze, two of them worked over and we signed them up and they were accepted. They worked the 30th day.

On cross-examination, Bosch elaborated:

Q: The company was bringing them in and turning them over [on a 30 day cycle]?
A: Right.
Q: They were being paid by Heiner's?
A: Right, and I got a copy of their card every week.
Q: Well, if we bring a guy in off the street and we hire him and we pay him?
A: You brought that man in, worked him 30 days, and we signed him.
Q: But we didn't hire him?
A: OK. He worked there 30 days.
Q: I know, but this is different.
A: He was working for Manpower, too, but they didn't have this kind of arrangement then.
Q: How do you know they were working for Manpower?
A: They said they were.
Q: But what was the arrangement?
A: I don't know.
Q: You really can't say for sure because you don't know what their status was back then—if they were employees, or they were being paid some way through Manpower?

A: They said Manpower.

Q: They punched the time clock?

A: They punched the time clock.

Q: Who were these two people?

A: I couldn't say. I don't know.

Q: Well, are you sure that they weren't interviewed and hired and paid directly by the company, rather than through Manpower?

A: Well, they all punched time cards from Heiner's. They didn't have these things here like that then, and Heiner's gave me a copy of the hours they worked.

Testimony of Ron Smothers, Union Shop Steward.   Ron Smothers was a union shop steward and a 19-year employee who testified, "Over the years there have been 30 to 40 temporaries who have become regular employees and union members." Under cross-examination, however, he admitted that he was only guessing at the number. He stated:

> I know definitely of five people who went full-time . . . you have two in maintenance, one in shipping, and two in sanitation . . . They have used temporary services before. So far as I know, this is the first one who has worked 30 days.

Testimony of Roger Spalding, Grievant.   Roger Spalding testified that he had asked his supervisor, Ruth Sampson, how long the job would last, and that Sampson had replied, "If you hang in there, it will be quite a while." Spalding also testified that from the actions of Sampson and his fellow workers, he felt that he would be kept on the job indefinitely and that he would become a regular employee with the company. When Ron Smothers, the union shop steward, spoke to him about joining the union once his 30-day probationary period ended, he was certain that he would be kept on.

Testimony of the Company

The company presented three witnesses who spoke in defense of the discharge of Roger Spalding.

Testimony of Roy Pellam, Personnel Director.   Roy Pellam testified that it was company policy to hire employees for regular work, but the company used "temporaries" for jobs that were "just temporary." Pellam asserted that Spalding was not an employee of the company, but rather of Kelly Temporary Services.

He stated that the company did not inform the union that it was bringing in temporaries because it had no need to do so. The contract was silent on the matter of temporaries, and the company had not done so in the past. Article IV, Section 7.1, of the contract did not apply to temporaries, but rather to regular hires. Pellam asserted that the company had utilized temporary services such as Kelly and Manpower for the past 8 to 10 years; none of them, to his knowledge, had been offered permanent jobs.

Pellam testified that he had no knowledge of what had transpired 30 years ago, since he had been with Heiner's Bakery for about 12 years. He reported that he knew of no current management person who might be knowledgeable on the matter. However, he stated that he had inquired of his predecessor, now retired, who was with the company in the 60s, about the use of temporaries during that time. The former personnel director told him that no temporaries had been hired as described by Bill Bosch.

Testimony of Ruth Sampson, Supervisor.   Ruth Sampson, who had been Roger Spalding's supervisor, asserted that she had made no commitments to Spalding or offered him any hope that he might be kept on as a permanent employee. She stated that she knew that the job was temporary, and that it would end as soon as the new automated equipment had been installed.

Testimony of Marjorie Thiele, Manager, Kelly Temporary Services.   Marjorie Thiele, manager of the local Kelly office, testified that Roger Spalding must have known that he was a temporary. First, she said, he had previously been on two temporary assignments at Marshall University. Second, he had been paid by Kelly; his tax withholding and insurance deductions were made by Kelly; and his time card clearly stated at the top "Kelly Temporary Services." He had received and signed six cards while working at Heiner's Bakery. Thiele further testified that she had told Spalding that the job would be of short duration, and that Kelly would attempt to reassign him when the job expired.

Position of the Union

The union contended that Article IV, Section 7.1, of the agreement required that the company notify it of the employment of Roger Spalding, which it had failed to do in violation of the agreement.

The union argued that the company's past employment practices of making temporary employees permanent employees after completing their probationary period now required that it offer the same opportunity to Spalding. By not making Spalding a permanent employee, it was creating another exception to Article I, Section 3.3, which already exempted office employees, seasonal employees, and managers having the right to hire. The company could not unilaterally add to the agreement in this manner.

The union asserted that the company exercised the same control over Spalding that it exercised over permanent employees. Such exercise of control, in effect, made Spalding a probationary employee eligible to become a permanent employee once he passed the 30-day probationary period.

The union urged that the arbitrator sustain the grievance.

Position of the Company

The company argued that as a temporary employee of Kelly Temporary Services, Roger Spalding never was an employee of the company. The agreement made no mention of temporaries. They simply were not employees; they were employees of independent contractors. As such they were no different from the employees of electrical, plumbing, or construction contractors that the company might employ.

The company pointed out that the testimony of Marjorie Thiele made it very clear that Spalding should not have looked on himself as an employee of Heiner's Bakery. She had stated that Spalding signed six weekly time cards on which the words, "Kelly Temporary Services," were printed at the top. He received his weekly pay check from Kelly, and all payroll deductions were made by that firm. She further stated that she had told Spalding at the time he received the Heiner assignment that it would be of short duration.

As a temporary worker, Spalding was not covered by Article IV, Section 7.1. The company was not required to give the union notice of his arrival.

Finally, the company argued that it had not employed temporaries as permanent personnel within the last 8 to 10 years. No one in management had first-hand knowledge of what had transpired 30 years ago. In any event, if one or two temporaries had been retained to become permanent employees 30 years ago, that would not constitute a past practice pertinent to this case.

The company urged that the arbitrator deny the grievance, since Spalding's work at the company did not make him an employee either under the agreement or by past practice.

APPENDIX
RELEVANT PROVISIONS OF THE AGREEMENT

Article I

3.1 All employees covered by this Agreement shall be members of the Union after thirty . . . working days of employment.

3.2 The Company agrees to recognize the Union as the sole and exclusive bargaining agent for all employees of the Company except those employees described in Section 3.3, for the purpose of collective bargaining, with respect to wages, hours, and working condition.

3.3 The following employees are excluded from all provisions of the Agreement:

(a) Employees having the right to hire.

(b) Office employees.

(c) Any seasonal employees who are employed specifically as such during the period beginning May 1st and ending October 1st.

(d) Part-time employees are those who report for work on some regular or irregular schedule between October 1st and May 1st . . . in the production department; they are not to exceed 25 hours of work in a work week. In other departments, they are not to exceed 18 hours of work in a work week.

Article IV

7.1 The Company agrees to report the hiring of new employees to the Union within . . . 96 hours after . . . start of work.

Article XV

The management of works and the direction of the working forces, including the right to hire, suspend or discharge for proper cause, or transfer . . . is vested exclusively in the Company, provided that this will not be used . . . in violation of any of the terms of this Agreement.

Questions

1. What is the appropriate status of an employee of an independent contractor working on the premises of a company such as Heiner's Bakery? How much control did the company exercise over Roger Spalding?
2. Evaluate the testimony of the union president, Bill Bosch.
3. Did Article IV, Section 7.1, include Roger Spalding? Why, or why not?
4. What normally constitutes a past practice? Assess the union's claim concerning past practices in this case.
5. How should the arbitrator rule in this case? Explain.

CASE 71
THE DOUBTFUL WORKER

Company:
   Fraenkel Company, Olive Branch, Tennessee

Union:
   Furniture Workers Division of the International Union of Electronic, Electrical, Machine, and Furniture Workers, Local No. 282

Background

The company manufactured mattresses, boxsprings, and other bedding materials in Olive Branch, Tennessee, outside Memphis.

Anne Manion,[1] the grievant in this incident, was hired on February 15, 1991, and assigned to a job in sewing supply of the bedding department. She continued to work there until she was laid off on October 28, 1991, along with several others in the plant. She was recalled from layoff on November 22, 1991, but to a different job. Although in the same section and department, the new job was a production rather than a supply job, and it required that she work under output standards.

Manion was first notified of the recall by the assistant manager, Ron Steffin, in a telephone call. Manion immediately focused on the differences between the two jobs. Her supply job had no production standards, and Manion expressed deep fear that she would be unable to meet the production standards.

Manion's reluctance to return to work on the new job was discussed at length during two telephone conversations with Steffin on Friday, November 22. Most of their discussion focused on whether or not she was qualified to perform the work. Manion persisted in arguing that she would be unable to perform the work; Steffin was adamant that she could. He discussed the problem with Alice Moon, her supervisor, who also felt that Manion was qualified, since the duties of the job she had been performing and those of the new job were similar.

Steffin then wrote a letter that was delivered by certified mail on Monday, November 25. Manion neither reported for work on Monday nor otherwise communicated with the company that week. She was terminated on Friday, November 29, 1991.

The union then filed a grievance stating that the company had violated Article XI, Sections 5 and 7, of the labor agreement, and that Anne Manion was unqualified to perform the new job.[2] The union claimed that her termination was improper, and she should be reinstated and remain on layoff until such time as a job for which she was qualified opened up.

The parties were unable to resolve the dispute and selected an arbitrator to render a final and binding decision. The union and company agreed that the issue to be resolved was:

---

[1]The names of all individuals are disguised.

[2]See the appendix for relevant contractual clauses.

Whether the grievant, Anne Manion, was discharged for just cause; if not, what is the proper remedy?

Position of the Union

The union contended that Anne Manion did not possess the ability and qualifications to perform the job of sewing mattress panels, the job she had been recalled to perform. She had never before performed the work, and she could not have been said to be qualified without having had considerable training and experience on this new job.

In discussing the new job with Ron Steffin on Friday, November 22, Manion had asked him what would happen if she couldn't perform the work. According to her, he had told her she would be terminated. She stated that she told him she wanted to pass up this job and stay on layoff until something in supply came up. She told him she could not perform the job of sewing mattress panels, and she was afraid to try since she was sure she would fail at it.

The union argued that rather than being required to take a job she could not perform, Manion should have been offered a job in sewing boxsprings made vacant by the retirement of Debra Gribbons. Gribbons' job had instead been given to Pam Benson, who had less seniority than Manion, and Manion was now being offered Benson's job. The union asserted that the provisions of Article XII of the agreement had been violated.

The union pointed out that Manion had been laid off in October 1991, despite the fact that employees with less seniority who were sewing mattress panels had not been laid off. The company could not have it both ways. It was not proper for the company now to declare that Manion was qualified for this new job when she had not been thought to be sufficiently qualified to avoid layoff.

The union requested that the arbitrator uphold its position, and that Anne Manion be reinstated and made whole in every way.

Position of the Company

Management maintained that Anne Manion was qualified to perform the job to which she had been recalled, sewing mattress panels. Several management witnesses asserted that her old job and the new one were very similar. Jerry Winters, assistant plant manager, testified in response to the question, "What was her former job?" as follows:

> Sewing borders and closing them up . . . It was about a 15-inch-wide strip of quilted material, about a quarter-inch thick, sewn together on the ends where it would have made a complete loop. And put it into a sewing machine and ran it through and it sewed the ends closed and cut off the edge where it would make a nice straight line and take all the threads and everything off and closed it, closed with threads kind of wrapped around it to make it nice and neat and straight . . . and then there was another sewing machine that she had so she could sew the corners up on. It was two processes she did.

When questioned about the new job to which Manion had been recalled, that is, sewing mattress panels, Winters said that supervisor Alice Moon had told him that Manion could do this job. Winters testified:

Well, it's the same machine for doing the borders. It just has one needle added to it for doing the mattress panels. And there's a five-and-a-half-inch strip of cloth that's attached underneath the panel as it's run through the machine. But it's the same process. It's a rectangular panel, and you have to turn corners on it, whereas the other one was just running it straight through. It's the same identical machine used for the other process.

The assistant manager, Ron Steffin, stated that he had never told Manion that she would be terminated if she were unable to meet production standards on the new job. He had not heard Manion state that she wished to remain on layoff until a job opened up in supply. In any event, she did not have that choice.

Finally, the company pointed out that Article XI, Section 8(3) of the collective agreement required that she report for work on Monday, November 25. The contract provided that she must return to work within three days of having received the letter of recall. When she failed to report, the company had justifiably terminated her.

The company reiterated that it had met all the provisions of the collective bargaining agreement, and that the arbitrator should uphold its position and deny the union grievance.

APPENDIX
RELEVANT PROVISIONS OF THE AGREEMENT

Article XI—Seniority

Section 4.   Current departments as established by the Company are:

(a) Bedding plant;

(b) Wholesale plant/Over-The-Road drivers.

Section 5.   When the company determines that it is necessary to lay off employees, employees will be laid off by departments. Layoff of employees in a department will be done as follows:

1. The least senior person in the department will be laid off provided there is another employee in the department who has the qualifications and ability to perform the job of the individual to be laid off.

2. ·If another employee in the department does not have the ability or qualifications to perform the job, the Company will then choose the next least senior person in the department provided there is an employee in the department who has the ability and qualifications to perform the job. Therefore, the least senior person in the department will be laid off provided another employee in the department has the qualifications and ability to perform the job.

Section 6.   Once layoff occurs, the Company has the right to transfer employees in the department to cover any job(s) as the result of the layoff. For the first forty-five (45) days, the employee transferred will be paid his personal rate or the base rate in the classification, whichever is higher. After forty-five (45) days, the transferred employee will be paid at the classification rate of the job he is performing whether higher or lower.

Section 7.

In the event that a job opening becomes available in the department and there are laid-off employees, the Company will recall employees as follows:

1. The employee laid off with the most departmental seniority will be recalled to the job provided the employee has the ability and qualifications to do the job.

2. In the event that a job opening becomes available and individuals on the layoff list do not have the ability and qualifications to perform the job, the Company has the right to transfer personnel in the department to perform the job, and recall the most senior laid-off employee in the department to perform the open job, providing the employee has the ability and qualifications to perform the job.

3. Recalled employees will be paid the classification rate of the job to which they are recalled.

Once an employee is recalled to a classification, there will be no other rights to transfer to another job unless transferred by the Company.

Section 8.   An employee shall be terminated and lose all accumulated seniority upon the occurrence of any of the following events:

1. Voluntary quit.

2. Discharge for just cause.

3. Failure to return to work within 3 days after receipt by certified mail of written notice of recall mailed by the Company to the employee's last known address on the records.

4. The employee is absent for two consecutive working days without written or oral notification to the Company management, the burden of proving notification to be on the employee.

5. The employee is separated from payroll from the Company for any reason for a period of twelve (12) consecutive months.

Article XII—Job Posting and Bidding

In the event of a permanent vacancy, the Company shall post a notice on the bulletin board in the department that has the vacancy (Bedding or Wholesale/OTR) for three working days advising the employees of the vacancy. A vacancy exists when the Company determines that a new job has been created or that an existing job has become permanently vacant. Procedure for filling the job is as follows:

1. All employees in the department have the right to bid on the job.

2. The Company will select the most senior person bidding on the job provided the employee has the qualifications and ability to perform the job. When two or more employees' qualifications and ability are relatively equal, the employee with the most departmental seniority will be awarded the job.

3. Once an employee is awarded the job, the Company shall consider that employee's job vacant and the job will be posted for job bidding.

4. After the second job is bid, the Company no longer has the obligation to post for bid any other job opening created by job bids. The Company may fill any job in its discretion with any employee or hire from an outside source. However, prior to filling the job with another employee or from an outside source, the Company will offer the job to any laid-off employee who has the ability and qualifications to perform the job. In the event a laid-off employee is requested and accepts the job, they lose any recall rights to the job from which they were laid off.

An employee who accepts a job under this Article will be paid the hire-in rate for a period of forty-five (45) days and then will move to the classification rate of the job.

Questions

1. Was Anne Manion qualified to perform the job of sewing mattress panels? How can the arbitrator determine this?
2. Did Article XI, Sections 5 and 7, of the collective agreement protect Manion from disciplinary action if she did not possess the qualifications and ability to perform the job? Explain.
3. Did the company violate the bidding procedure of the contract? Discuss.
4. How should the arbitrator rule? Why?

CASE 72
THE RECALLED MANAGEMENT TRAINEE

Company:
Stacor Corporation, Dunmore, Pennsylvania

Union:
United Brotherhood of Carpenters & Joiners of America, Local No. 2075

Background

The Dunmore facility was one of several installations operated nationwide by Stacor Corporation. In April 1992, the corporation decided to temporarily suspend all production operations and lay off all bargaining unit employees.

Prior to that time, one hourly rated bargaining unit employee, Willis Hussmann,[1] had worked in a part-time capacity as a management trainee. This arrangement had existed for approximately one year prior to the layoff without any objection by the union. During this time, Hussmann performed bargaining unit work, and on a part-time basis he also was being groomed by management to assume a supervisory position at some time in the future.

The layoff was of short duration. Management determined that the situation required additional supervisory personnel preparatory to resuming production. It called Hussmann back to work in a supervisory capacity to assist in making the plant ready for the recall of the other workers and production to begin again. Hussmann had remained on the bargaining unit seniority roster during the year prior to the layoff; he was on it during the layoff; and he was still on the union seniority list at the time the union filed a grievance, April 27, 1992.

The union grievance charged that the company had violated Article XVII, Layoffs, of the agreement,[2] when it recalled Hussmann and failed to recall Henry Porter, a 30-year employee who had considerably more seniority than Hussmann. In all, Hussmann worked some 17 days before Henry Porter, too, was recalled from layoff.

When the parties could not agree on a settlement, the grievance was referred to an arbitrator for a final and binding decision. The parties agreed that the issue was:

Did the company improperly recall Willis Hussmann to work and deny Henry Porter employment and pay for 17 days? If so, what shall the remedy be?

Position of the Union

The union charged that the company had violated the rights of Henry Porter by recalling Hussmann, a less senior employee who had only nine years seniority, before Porter. The layoff and recall language contained in the contract was clear and

---

[1]The names of all individuals are disguised.
[2]See the appendix for this provision.

unequivocal. Hussmann had not been removed from the union's seniority list. He was far down the list from Porter. Further, the union had not agreed to any departure from the language in Article XVII.

In remedy, the union requested that the company award Porter 17 days back pay, as the agreement required. It also requested that such payment not be reduced by the amount of his unemployment earnings during that time.

Position of the Company

The company held that it had not violated the terms of the collective bargaining agreement by placing Willis Hussmann in a supervisory position during the period when all other employees were still on layoff. The company had been grooming him for a supervisory position for more than a year with no objection from the union. The union could not now change a long-standing practice. The company contended that it had needed an additional supervisor in April 1992, and that Hussmann was qualified to serve in that capacity. In this regard, there was nothing in the agreement to prevent management from promoting an hourly rated employee to a supervisory position at its discretion. All management rights not specifically contracted away in the agreement resided with Stacor Corporation.

The company pointed out that by recalling Hussmann to a supervisory position and placing him on the management team, this in effect had shortened the layoff period for all employees by increasing management's ability to get ready for call-back and full production. Even though Hussmann was still on the union seniority roster list when he was recalled and promoted to a supervisory position, this was a technical oversight of no consequence to management's decision in this situation.

Finally, the company argued that the remedy sought by the union, including back pay for 17 days without the deduction of any unemployment income, would constitute punitive damages. To pay Porter the sum sought by the union would unjustly enrich him at the company's expense.

The company requested that the arbitrator deny the grievance.

Appendix
Relevant Provision of the Agreement

Article XVII (Layoffs)

Layoffs will start with the last employee hired plant-wide and proceed, with the exception of Chief Steward previously mentioned, by date of hire; the inverse will be applied on rehire. Any exceptions to this seniority procedure will be mutually agreed to by the Company and Union. New employees shall not be hired until all layoffs are recalled.

Questions

1. Evaluate the union's claim that Article XVII denied the company the right to promote Willis Hussmann.

2. The company employed Hussmann as a part-time management trainee before the layoff. Why didn't the union grieve the company's action?

3. Since the contract was silent on the matter of promotion out of the bargaining unit, why would the union grieve at this time?

4. Evaluate the union's request that Henry Porter be awarded payment for lost time without reduction for unemployment benefits he received.

5. Evaluate the company's claim that by recalling Hussmann into a supervisory position, it was able to recall bargaining unit workers faster.

6. Why had Hussmann remained on the union's membership roster during all this time?

7. How should the arbitrator rule in this case? Explain.

CASE 73
THE RIGHT TO BID DOWN

Company:
Alltel Florida, Inc., Alachua, Florida

Union:
Communications Workers of America, District No. 3

Background

The company was a telephone company that provided telephone service to customers in a wide area of north Florida. Gerardo Thornwall,[1] the grievant in this case, had worked for the company for 16 years. He was classified as a P.B.X. Installer-Repairperson, a labor "Grade 6" job, which was the highest plant grade. His job was repair and service of "private exchange" facilities for large commercial and industrial customers in the company's Alachua, Florida, exchange area.

In summer 1992, the company posted a job vacancy for the position of Installer-Repairperson in its Alachua exchange. This job was a labor "Grade 5" position. Thornwall bid on the job, notwithstanding the fact that it was a lower-paid job, and would involve a demotion (or downgrade) and reduction in pay. Thornwall's stated reasons were personal; he claimed that he did not think the additional pay he received in his current job was sufficient for the added responsibility and stress that it required.

Two other employees also bid on the job. Although Thornwall was the senior bidder and company management recognized that he was well qualified to hold the position of Installer-Repairperson, the job was awarded to another employee with less seniority. Thornwall was told by his supervisor, Alex Claremont, and the director of human resources, Meredith Juniper, that his bid in effect was asking for a downgrade, and that voluntary demotions or downgrades were granted only at the discretion of the company and not by seniority. They also told Thornwall that the company had good reasons to reject his bid in this case.

A union grievance was filed and processed through the steps resulting in arbitration. The parties agreed that the issue before the arbitrator was:

Did the company violate the contract[2] on or about July 9, 1992, in its award of the Installer-Repairperson job on which Gerardo Thornwall had bid? If so, what should be the remedy?

Position of the Union

The union contended that the parties' labor-management agreement did not specify that employees could not bid down. There were several past cases in which qualified employees had bid down and the seniority and qualifications of the bidders were

---

[1]The names of all individuals are disguised.
[2]See the appendix for relevant provisions of the agreement.

determinative in the award of such bids. Thornwall was the most senior qualified bidder; the seniority principle should have been followed in awarding him the position for which he had bid.

The union argued that since the contract was ambiguous in this area, such past practices of awarding by seniority in downward bids should have been followed in this case.

The union asked that the company be directed to rescind its prior decision, and the job in question be awarded to the grievant, Gerardo Thornwall.

Position of the Company

The company contended that there was nothing in the contract that required it to follow seniority in a downward bid. In any downward bids, the selection was solely discretionary with the company.

The company claimed that even if management had on occasion deferred to seniority in downward bids, Articles 29 and 39 of the parties' labor-management agreement made any such practice discretionary on the part of the company.

The company contended that it had valid reasons for not awarding the job in question to Thornwall. He was a valuable and experienced employee whose skills were needed in his higher-rated "P.B.X." position. It would have been an economic waste to have Thornwall working at a lower-skilled position. Further, Thornwall currently was the only employee trained on certain equipment; it would have placed the company in a difficult position with certain customers if his bid down had been permitted.

The company urged the arbitrator to deny the union grievance.

APPENDIX
RELEVANT PROVISIONS OF THE AGREEMENT

Article 1—Definitions

P. *Promotions.* Reassignment to a job having a higher maximum rate or top basic rate within the bargaining unit.

Article 15—Promotions

A. Where qualifications are substantially equal, seniority shall be the controlling factor in all matters of promotion.

B. A classification shall be considered to be higher if the scheduled rate of pay is higher.

C. Seniority shall be determined from the seniority roster posted on the bulletin board.

D. It is recognized that the Company retains the right to conduct oral and/or written tests providing the evaluations are pertinent to the job tested for. The Company will give the employees tested a copy of their grades and evaluation.

E. The Company agrees that it will not promote or transfer any duly certified Union representatives without two (2) weeks' written notice to the local.

Article 17—Job Vacancies

A. A job vacant within the bargaining unit shall be posted by the Company, in each location where employees report for work, at least ten (10) working days prior to the time the job vacancy is to be filled. All such postings shall show the report location of the job. However, such posting of report location shall not restrict the Company's subsequent right to assign reporting locations within work areas and/or to transfer as provided in Articles 11 and 12 of this Agreement.

B. Employees desiring to be considered for the posted job shall submit a written bid within ten (10) working days from the date of the job posting, stating his qualifications, and the reasons he desires the job. Written bids should be sent to the employee's immediate supervisor.

C. The Company will fill the posted job within thirty (30) days after the closing date on the bid and notify, in writing, all who bid, as to the person given the job. Both successful and unsuccessful bidders will be notified on the same date. The successful bidder will be transferred to his new job as soon as practical but within thirty (30) days. The Company may withdraw the job vacancy if it is determined that the vacancy does not exist. The Employee may decline the job if within ten (10) days he notifies the Company in writing of such from the date he is notified of selection.

D. If the Company has not filled a posted job bid within three (3) months by either selection of a bidder, or the hiring of a new employee, the job will again be posted for bidding before the Company can hire into the job.

E. The following jobs shall be considered as entrance jobs and not subject to job posting and bidding: Commercial-Accounting, Grade 2 positions; Janitors; Right-of-Way Person; Lineperson; Cable Helper; Coin Collector.

However, in the event of a vacancy in any such entry level job, consideration shall be given, in order of seniority, to any employees then in other entry level jobs. Notice of such vacancies shall be posted.

F. The Company shall not be required to accord transfer or promotional consideration to any employee who has held his/her job classification for less than one (1) year.

Article 29—Rights of Company

The management of the business and the direction of the working force shall remain with the Company, including the right to hire, promote, and discharge for just cause, to use improved methods or equipment, to determine work assignments and tours, to decide the number of employees needed at any particular time or place and to be the sole judge of the communications service rendered the public; provided, however, that this section will not be used for the purpose of discriminating against members of the Union nor shall it alter the meaning of any provisions of this Agreement.

Nothing contained in this Agreement shall be deemed to limit the Company in any way in the exercise of the regular and generally recognized customary functions and responsibilities of management. Moreover, such functions of management as may be included herein shall not be deemed to exclude other functions of management not specifically included herein.

Article 39—Past Practices

It is recognized by the parties that this agreement contains the entirety of their respective commitments. Any and all past practices not specifically mentioned in this Agreement may be continued, discontinued, or modified by the Company, except as noted below:

The Company will continue its practice of paying employees to climb microwave towers at the rate of $25.00 per climb.

Questions

1. Examine carefully the relevant contractual provisions. Which provisions appear to be most supportive of the union position? Of the company position?
2. Should the seniority principle prevail in a downward bid, if the most senior employee is the most qualified job bidder? Why, or why not?
3. Was the "past practice" of allowing some previous downward bids by seniority binding on the company, or was this type of decision solely discretionary with the company? Discuss.
4. What should the arbitrator decide? Why?

CASE 74
TAKING CARE OF UNION BUSINESS

Employer:
Bloomfield Board of Education, Bloomfield, Connecticut

Union:
National Association of Government Employees (NAGE), Local No. RI-214

Background

Local No. RI-214 represented certain employees in the Bloomfield, Connecticut, educational district who were classified as custodians, bus drivers, maintenance personnel, and other positions. Rocco Mahoney,[1] the grievant in this case, was a licensed electrician who also served as president of the local union.

The grievance heard in arbitration was filed by the union and Rocco Mahoney protesting the employer's 30-day suspension of Mahoney for alleged insubordination in his conducting union business on company time. This suspension was effective September 1, 1992.

As mutually stipulated by the parties, the issue before the arbitrator was:

Did the Bloomfield Board of Education have just cause pursuant to Article XX of the collective bargaining agreement[2] to suspend Rocco Mahoney for 30 days? If not, what shall the remedy be?

Testimony and Evidence Presented in the Arbitration Hearing

Ray Steele, director of facilities, testified that he had given Rocco Mahoney numerous verbal warnings about conducting union business on company time without proper permission. Steele said it was especially important that Mahoney devote his time to his electrical work, since Mahoney was the only licensed electrician working for the Bloomfield district.

Steele said that in September 1990, he had documented his warnings to Mahoney in a written memorandum specifically stating that Mahoney must have management permission to conduct union business during working hours. In relevant part, the memorandum included the following:

September 18, 1990

To: Rocco Mahoney, President
          NAGE Bloomfield local

From: Ray Steele, Director of Facilities
Subject: Role of Union Representative

I am very appreciative that the recent grievance taken by your local was resolved in my office. I must call to your attention, however, what I see as the role of the Union President

---

[1]The names of all individuals are disguised.
[2]See the appendix for relevant contractual provisions.

during working hours. If I or one of my assistants listens to a grievance by an employee during the work day, you or someone in your place has the right to represent the employee at the meeting. This is done by contacting your immediate superior and informing him of your need to be present.

You may not, however, use company time to meet with Union representatives during the work day to discuss Union business unless I personally approve of such a request.

If you have any questions regarding the above, please contact me immediately.

Ray Steele testified that he had received reports from several supervisors that Rocco Mahoney's habit of conducting union business during working hours disrupted the work schedule of other employees. Therefore, he again told Mahoney in late 1991 that he (Steele) was the only person who could give Mahoney permission to discuss union business during working hours. If Steele was not available, Durwood Gable, another management person, was designated to give permission to Mahoney for this purpose.

Durwood Gable, superintendent of highways, testified that on numerous occasions he had heard Rocco Mahoney disrupting workers' job duties during their work time. On two occasions in 1991, he had ordered Mahoney out of the highway department building. Gable testified that he reported these incidents both to Steele and to Ollie Carbol, Mahoney's immediate supervisor, who reported directly to Steele.

Milicent Rohrbach, secretary to Ray Steele, testified that at approximately 9:00 A.M. on September 1, 1992, Mahoney had requested her to contact Ray Steele to get his permission for Mahoney to attend a meeting at the local office of the State Labor Department. She was unable to reach Steele, but she did talk with Durwood Gable, who said he would reach Steele and have him call back. This message was given to Mahoney. However, when Steele eventually called, Mahoney had already left the building without getting the approval of Steele to attend the meeting at the Labor Department.

In his testimony, Rocco Mahoney asserted that he had not known about a hearing at the Labor Department until he was informed by a fellow worker earlier that morning. He immediately spoke with Milicent Rohrbach, Ray Steele's secretary, who advised him that Steele was not available. However, Rohrbach did reach Durwood Gable, and she advised Gable that Mahoney had to attend a hearing. The message relayed to him (Mahoney) by Ms. Rohrbach was that Gable would contact Steele to advise him of (Mahoney's) need to attend a hearing at the Labor Department.

Mahoney testified that he had then contacted Barbara Marchesi, secretary-treasurer of the union. Marchesi said that she was not aware of a hearing at the Labor Department; but she did suggest to him that as union president, he should attend all hearings and meetings where employees' interests were at stake. Mahoney went to the Labor Department building, but found there was no hearing scheduled. With some prior information in mind that he had received from Barbara Marchesi, he then proceeded to a meeting being held at an employer facility in Bloomfield. There he was advised by the NAGE staff attorney that this meeting had been arranged for the purpose of stipulating facts relative to an upcoming arbitration hearing concerning bus drivers. Mahoney said that this meeting lasted several hours. Following the meeting, he returned to his job site where he was informed that he had been suspended for insubordination.

Geofrey Milchrist, a consultant to the Bloomfield Board of Education, testified that he was present at the meeting attended by Mahoney. He said that he had been disturbed that Mahoney was there, since Mahoney's presence was unnecessary. However, Beth Margo, staff attorney of the union present at this meeting, testified that she had explained to Milchrist that Mahoney sincerely believed he was required to be present even though this might not have actually been the case.

Position of the Employer

Counsel for the Bloomfield Board of Education contended that there was ample just cause for the employer to suspend the grievant, Rocco Mahoney, for 30 days for his willful insubordination in the incident of September 1, 1992. As required under Article XX of the agreement, Mahoney had been warned both verbally and in a written memorandum concerning the proper procedures to follow if he wanted to conduct union business on company time. His behavior had caused disruption of work among other employees in the workplace, and he was on ample notice to follow the required procedure.

On September 1, 1992, Rocco Mahoney failed to get permission to attend a hearing or meeting on that date. Even though he may have believed that his presence was necessary at a hearing or meeting, this did not give him the right to leave his job without management permission. As an employee who was also union president, Mahoney had to follow legitimate rules and procedures just like anyone else. His behavior in this situation was inexcusable, and it showed willful insubordination and a reckless lack of concern for his job responsibilities.

Counsel for the Bloomfield Board of Education reiterated that the employer had ample just cause under the agreement to suspend Rocco Mahoney for 30 days. He urged that the union grievance on behalf of Mahoney be denied.

Position of the Union

Counsel for the union urged that Rocco Mahoney had been unjustly suspended for 30 days because of circumstances that were beyond his control. Mahoney had tried diligently to contact Ray Steele for permission to attend a hearing he thought had been scheduled at the State Department of Labor. He was under the impression from the message he received from Milicent Rohrbach, Mr. Steele's secretary, that the permission to attend the meeting would be forthcoming. Mahoney had felt that his duty to represent union members at an important hearing would be understood by Mr. Steele; therefore he had left to go to the hearing, and then to a meeting, even though he had not specifically talked with Mr. Steele.

Counsel for the union claimed that at most Rocco Mahoney was a "victim of communication difficulties" that had placed him in an untenable position where he had had to make a choice of action. He had not recklessly abandoned his job responsibilities, since he had tried to communicate with the proper management persons as he had recognized he was required to do. In the union's view, the employer's 30-day suspension of Rocco Mahoney was totally unjustified given the mitigating circumstances. Counsel for the union asserted that the employer had not had just cause to administer a major suspension on Mr. Mahoney, and urged that the union grievance be sustained, the disciplinary suspension rescinded, and Mr. Mahoney made whole for all lost pay and benefits during the period of unjust suspension.

APPENDIX
RELEVANT PROVISIONS OF THE AGREEMENT

Article XX—Discipline

Section 3.(1)   All disciplinary actions shall be applied in a fair manner and shall not be inconsistent with the infraction for which the disciplinary action is being applied.

(2) All suspensions and discharges must be for just cause and must be stated in writing with the reason given and a copy provided to the employee at the time of the suspension or discharge. A copy shall also be forwarded to the Union at the time it is provided to the employee.

(3) Serious misconduct shall be grounds for immediate suspension or discharge and need not follow the procedure listed in (4) below. Examples of serious misconduct include: theft, moral turpitude, insubordination.

(4) Disciplinary actions shall include:
- *(a)* verbal discussion of problem,
- *(b)* written warning,
- *(c)* suspension without pay,
- *(d)* termination,

and shall follow in this order except as noted in (3) above as serious misconduct.

Questions

1. Was the requirement that Rocco Mahoney receive specific permission to attend to union business a reasonable directive, especially as applied to the circumstances of September 1, 1992? Discuss.

2. Why would the employer want to control the time spent by a union president on union business? Why would the union want to have its union president available to conduct union business as the need might arise, often at unexpected times?

3. Was Rocco Mahoney guilty of willful insubordination, or was he caught between "a rock and a hard place" and forced to make a judgment that caused the employer to react?

4. If you were the arbitrator in this case, how would you decide? Why?

CASE 75
TERMINATED FOR POSSESSING A GUN

Employer:
   City of New Haven, Connecticut

Union:
   American Federation of State, County, and Municipal Employees, Council 4, Local No. 3144

Background

Matthew Kress[1] had been employed for 14 years by the Water Pollution Control Authority (WPCA) in the city of New Haven. At the time of his discharge, he held the title of Wastewater Supervisor I, and he was assigned to the third shift (midnight to 8 A.M.).

On May 8, 1986, WPCA had distributed to all employees a policy concerning weapons on the premises. It included the following:

> Effective immediately—No weapons of any sort shall be allowed on WPCA premises, including lockers and private vehicles parked on WPCA property. No exceptions shall be made to this policy. Anyone caught with a weapon on WPCA property in violation of this policy shall be subject to immediate discharge.

Matthew Kress had received a copy of this policy and signed an acknowledgment form to that effect.

On November 17, 1992, Kress brought a gun onto WPCA premises. Kress had a state permit to carry a weapon. He had previously stated that the neighborhood in which he lived had caused him to purchase and carry a gun for his personal safety. On November 17, he removed his gun from his briefcase and showed it to a co-worker. Two other employees later testified that they also saw the gun that night.

On November 18, 1992, Roger Schienvar, general manager, initiated an investigation of the gun incident. The employees who had seen Kress display the gun stated their observations to WPCA investigators.

In addition to the gun incident investigation, Schienvar reviewed Kress's work history at WPCA. Schienvar found and reported in a memorandum dated November 20, 1992, including as follows:

> There have been a series of continuing and ongoing incidents of failure to perform duties in an appropriate manner, failure to follow orders, failure to follow and apply policies and procedures, failure to display appropriate level of care and judgment to the position of Waste Supervisor I.

Several of these previous incidents had involved difficulties and confrontations with other employees. Concerning Matthew Kress's disciplinary history, Schienvar found and wrote in his memorandum:

He has been given verbal warnings to written warnings to suspensions in increasing terms, and the last discipline prior to this particular incident was a 30-day suspension that was invoked in early July of 1992.

On January 6, 1993, WPCA management provided Kress with a pretermination conference during which he had union representation. After this January 6 conference, management reached a decision to terminate Matthew Kress. In a termination letter to Kress, Roger Schienvar included the following statement:

> There was a request—appeal, if you will—from the union for leniency. But for a number of factors, primarily the seriousness of the offense and the definitive and clear nature of the policy, it was our decision to follow through on the termination.

The union filed a grievance on behalf of Matthew Kress, which was carried to arbitration. The issue was framed as:

Was the discharge of Matthew Kress for just cause?[2] If not, what shall the remedy be?

Position of the Employer

It was WPCA's position that Matthew Kress had been discharged for just cause. Kress had admitted he knew the policy prohibiting bringing weapons to work. He admitted bringing a fully loaded weapon to work, and he admitted showing the gun to at least one employee. Such acts were clear violations of rules and of the contract, and they were extremely dangerous. WPCA could not allow such actions on the part of any employee. Therefore, the discharge of Kress was for ample just cause, and WPCA asked that the grievance be denied.

Position of the Union

It was the union's position that WPCA's policy was not posted anywhere in the Authority's facilities. Matthew Kress had a permit to carry a weapon issued by the state of Connecticut. He obeyed the law concerning his gun. Except for this one incident of showing the gun to another employee, Kress had kept the gun out of sight in his briefcase. He promised never to bring the gun to work or onto the work premises again. Kress had never threatened anyone with the gun. Kress had kept the gun with him because of the high-crime area in which he lived. He couldn't keep it in his car at work because of the numerous break-ins of cars in the parking lot. In this case, the WPCA and the City had overreacted. Their decision to terminate a long-service employee was arbitrary and unreasonable, and it did not meet a just cause standard. The union asked that the grievance be sustained, and that Matthew Kress be reinstated to his position and made appropriately whole.

---

[2]See the appendix for relevant contractual provisions.

APPENDIX
RELEVANT PROVISIONS OF THE AGREEMENT

Article 16—Discharge and Discipline

Section 2.   (a) Disciplinary action shall be consistent with the type of infraction or malfeasance which is the subject of the discipline.

(b) Discipline should be progressive in nature, but where circumstances warrant termination, it need not necessarily have been preceded by lesser disciplinary actions.

Questions

1. Evaluate the employer's and the union's respective arguments. Which do you find the most and which the least persuasive?
2. Should Matthew Kress's prior disciplinary record be a major or minor consideration in the arbitration decision? Explain.
3. Is there a conflict between the statutory right of an employee to obtain a permit to carry a gun, and the employer's policy of no weapons on the premises? Discuss.
4. How should the arbitrator decide? Why?

CASE 76
FORCED TO WORK ON A HOLIDAY

Company:
   Ravarino and Freschi (Division of Borden, Inc.), St. Louis, Missouri
Union:
   Teamsters Local Union No. 688

Background

At the time of this case, there were about 250 employees in the plant bargaining unit represented by Teamsters Local Union No. 688. The company plant manufactured a full line of pasta products.

On January 1, 1994, three virtually identical union grievances were filed by bargaining unit employees. Each protested the company's having required bargaining unit employees to work on January 1, 1994. These grievances were eventually taken to arbitration.

In relevant part, each union grievance stated:

> Forced work on any of the holidays stated in Article 33[1] is a violation of the contract. The contract specifically states that "no work is performed on such holiday." The union membership is owed a day of no work on the nine stated holidays in Article 33. If the company decides to exercise its right to reschedule the holiday, then the membership is still "owed" a day of no work with holiday pay on a different day. We request compliance with Article 33 on every holiday stated therein or a rescheduled day of no work, with holiday pay, on another day. We request that if this grievance is won that it becomes binding on every holiday until the end of the contract.

The issue for the arbitrator was framed somewhat differently by the parties. Counsel for the union submitted that the issue should be stated:

> Does the company have the right to force employees to work on holidays?

Counsel for the company submitted that the issue should be framed:

> Did the company violate the agreement when it scheduled a work day on one of the contractually stipulated holidays?

Testimony in the Arbitration Hearing

Giving brief testimony for the union was Carla Hempelmann,[2] a production employee. She had been with the company since 1986, and she was union chief shop steward after having served previously as a union shop steward. She indicated that Article 15 of the collective bargaining agreement had provided the company with considerable flexibility

---

[1]See the appendix for relevant contractual provisions.
[2]The names of all individuals are disguised.

to transfer and assign employees in order to accommodate the start-up of a new company plant, which had opened in late 1991. In December 1993, company management had moved the Christmas holiday schedule around in a manner that was consistent with the previous agreement, but everyone did get two days off for Christmas as stipulated in the agreement. Hempelmann stated that except for the year when the new plant was involved in the start-up, no one had ever been forced to work a contractual holiday until January 1, 1994.

Giving major testimony for the union was Rafael Decker, union business representative, who said that he serviced the Ravarino and Freschi plant. According to Decker, provisions in the agreement required that the company first seek volunteers before requiring overtime. He stated that for the most part, the company had been able to secure adequate volunteers when the company had had overtime needs. Introduced as union exhibits were several grievances filed by another employee, Martin Dumas, and the settlement of these grievances in the latter part of 1993. Decker said that Dumas' grievances had been granted by higher company management because management had recognized that contractual procedures for seeking volunteers before requiring overtime had not been followed. Thus, Decker stated, when bargaining unit employees were told that they had to work the January 1, 1994, holiday, employees first should have been asked to work on a voluntary basis. Forcing employees to work overtime on a contractually designated holiday was not permitted under the agreement, and it had never been attempted by the company until January 1, 1994.

Decker acknowledged that for overtime needs of the company except on contractual holidays, the company could force employees to work overtime after the company had first sought volunteers, if not enough volunteers were willing to work. If the company wanted to work everyone, the company could do this except for holidays. To Decker's knowledge, there had never been a prior grievance on the subject of forcing employees to work on a contractual holiday. Decker and the union suggested as one remedy for this grievance that employees who had been forced to work on January 1 might be given another day off on a date mutually agreeable to company and employees. Further, a number of employees who had not worked on January 1, 1994, had been given written warnings, and the union wanted all these warnings rescinded and removed from employee records.

Testifying for the company was Albert Gronski, who stated that since early 1993, he had been operations coordinator for the company in Columbus, Ohio. From 1981 until 1986, he had been vice president of manufacturing at the Ravarino and Freschi plant in St. Louis. The company had been purchased by Borden in November 1986, and he had served as operations manager in the St. Louis plant until his move to Columbus, Ohio. Gronski stated that he had been involved in contractual negotiations for the two prior labor-management agreements. The current agreement had been negotiated in May 1990, because the company had been building a new plant in St. Louis and shutting down production operations at its older St. Louis plant and several other facilities. The company had wanted a new labor agreement to provide flexibility for a transition to the new plant which opened in November 1991.

Gronski said he believed the entire plant had worked on Thanksgiving Day 1991, although the plant was shut down for Christmas 1991. As a result of an edict from the former president of the division, all plant bargaining unit employees had worked on January 1, 1992. Gronski said he also thought this had been the case on July 4, 1992. According to Gronski, the decision to require employees to work on January 1, 1994, had been to rectify a situation of very low inventory and high production order requirements. The company had needed to keep the plant running in order to meet the demands of customers. The business was very competitive, and the decision was made to schedule the entire plant on January 1, 1994, because of the inventory and customer concerns. Under cross-examination, Gronski admitted that he was "unsure" whether any employees were forced to work on the Thanksgiving 1991 and July 4, 1992, holidays that he had mentioned earlier in his testimony.

Position of the Union

The position of the union was summarized in a post-hearing brief submitted by counsel for the union. Excerpts from this brief were as follows:

> The holiday clause of the collective bargaining agreement contains the following sentence: "No work is performed on such holiday." That sentence has been in the contract for many years, and during that time employees have never been forced to work on a holiday. The plain meaning of that sentence must be accepted for what it readily implies, i.e., employees cannot be forced to work on a holiday contrary to their wishes. If that interpretation is not given to the language, the sentence has no meaning at all which cannot be the intent of the parties. It is a well-recognized principle of contract construction that a contract must be construed in a way which gives full meaning to all of provisions; and another recognized principle is that the words of the contract must be given their plain and ordinary meaning. Those principles require that the contract be interpreted as not permitting the Employer to require employees to work on a scheduled holiday. Of course, the Employer has the unusual flexibility to schedule when the holidays will be observed in order to meet its business needs.
>
> Furthermore, Article 27, Section 7 of the collective bargaining agreement requires that in order for an employee on vacation or a holiday to be eligible to work on weekend overtime, the employee must make his/her availability known prior to leaving for vacation or holiday. It appears that this language may have been carried over inadvertently after the institution of mandatory overtime and the elimination of personal and birthday holidays; but the language supports the conclusion that the parties intended that work performed on holidays must be voluntary.
>
> The Employer argues that the language of Article 27, Section 2 specifying how employees who work on a holiday are to be paid supports the conclusion that the Employer may force employees to work on a holiday; but that language merely provides for the manner in which employees who agree to work on a holiday will be paid. The Employer also argues that its severe production requirements demand that it be permitted to require employees to work on holidays; but production demands, however severe, may not override the restrictions of the contract. The Employer has been able to satisfy its production demands for many years without forcing employees to work on scheduled holidays; and the Employer has the flexibility of scheduling the holidays on days which accommodate its legitimate business needs. Therefore, the requirements of the contract must be followed, unless and until the Employer is able to negotiate a change, as it did with mandatory overtime.
>
> Therefore, the grievance should be sustained.

Position of the Company

The position of the company was summarized in a post-hearing brief submitted by counsel for the company. Excerpts from this brief were as follows:

The Company maintains they can schedule a holiday as a work day as long as they pay the proper premiums. That is, 8 hours' pay for the holiday plus the additional time and one-half for the hours worked.

There is absolutely nothing in Article 33 that prevents the Company from scheduling one of the contractual holidays as a work day for the entire plant. In addition, there is absolutely nothing in Article 33 that requires the Company to schedule another day as a holiday if they do schedule all the employees to work on one of the days listed in the contract.

The language of Article 27, Section 2, which reads "all work performed on a holiday or the day celebrated in lieu thereof shall be paid for at time and one-half (1½) plus holiday pay." clearly shows the intent was not to keep the Company from scheduling work on a holiday but to require them to pay a premium to the employees if they did so.

Article 27, *Hours of Work,* Section 2(D) specifically buttresses the Company position that mandatory overtime can be required when the Company deems it necessary to schedule the employees to work overtime.

*   *   *   *   *

The management rights clause, Article 23, specifically provides that the management of the business and the direction of the work force is vested exclusively in the employer except as specifically provided in the labor agreement.

*   *   *   *   *

In line with the language contained in the Management Rights Clause, and contra to the Union's position, there is absolutely no language in the agreement that prevents the Company from scheduling full production on a holiday and certainly no language that requires the Company to schedule another day off for the employees when a holiday is worked.

*   *   *   *   *

A reading of Article 33 in the totality shows that the phrase "no work is performed on such holiday" simply sets forth the situation which will entitle the employee to eight (8) hours' pay at straight time. Thus the employee will receive holiday pay if he/she performs no work on a holiday and works the scheduled day before and the scheduled day after the holiday.

Setting forth the requirements that need to be met to receive regular holiday pay does not contractually restrict the Company from scheduling work on a holiday.

*   *   *   *   *

Article 27 of the labor agreement clearly anticipates the Company may need to schedule work on a holiday by spelling out the requirement that "all work performed on a holiday or the day celebrated in lieu thereof, shall be paid for at time and one-half (1½) plus holiday pay."

Therefore, according to the contract, an employee will receive 8 hours' straight time pay if he doesn't work on a holiday and eight (8) hours pay at straight time plus time and one-half if a holiday is worked.

Conversely, nowhere in the contract does it say the Company can't schedule work on a holiday and nowhere does it set forth the requirement that anyone who works on a holiday must be given another day off in lieu of the holiday.

*   *   *   *   *

Frankly, the testimony on past practice was so confusing and conflicting that it was impossible to follow. Parties must knowingly enter into a past practice for it to be binding on the parties. Obviously, such is not the case before the arbitrator.

Then too, the failure to exercise a particular management right for a period of time does not waive the right. From the testimony, it would appear that on most of the holidays in the past, the Company production requirements did not require that all the employees be scheduled to work on a holiday. If you don't need to schedule the employees, that does not mean you have waived the right to schedule when needed.

$$* \quad * \quad * \quad * \quad *$$

We submit that the applicable contractual language and Industrial Common Law permits the scheduling of mandatory overtime on a holiday without requiring the Company to designate another day of non-work in lieu of the holiday worked. This being the case, we respectfully submit the grievance before the arbitrator should be dismissed in the entirety.

Appendix
Relevant Provisions from the Agreement

Article 15—Transfers

The Employer may make temporary transfers from one classification to another as business needs dictate. The senior employee with the ability in a classification (when transfer exceeds one (1) hour) shall be offered the transfer when the transfer involves a higher paying job. The employee transferred shall receive the higher rate for the entire day which he works at the higher rated job. The junior employee in the classification (when transfer exceeds one (1) hour) shall be the one transferred to an equal or lower paying job. The employee transferred shall retain his regular rate. It may be necessary to make double transfers as business needs dictate, however, such double transfers shall be reviewed with the Chief Shop Steward, where the transfer exceeds one hour; EXCEPTION:

During the first year of the start-up phase of the new facility located at Davis Street, the Company will be transferring employees over to the new facility based on production and efficiency requirements without regard to seniority and overtime. Transferring of employees within either operation during the start-up phase will be done with total flexibility without regard to seniority.

Article 23—Management Rights

Except as provided specifically in this Agreement, the management of the Employer's business and the direction of the working force, including the right to hire, suspend, or discharge for cause, or to transfer, to promote or demote, and the right to relieve employees from duty because of lack of work or for other legitimate reasons, is vested exclusively in the Employer, provided, however, that none of the powers herein reserved to the Employer shall be used for the purpose of discrimination because of an employee's membership in the Union.

Article 27—Hours of Work

Section 1. The regular work week shall consist of any eight (8) hours per day, forty (40) hours per week, or four (4) days at ten (10) hours per day or a 4-10 day schedule.

Section 2. Time and one-half shall be paid for work performed in excess of eight (8) per day or ten (10) hours on a 4 day 10 hour schedule or forty (40) hours per week, but no employee will be paid overtime twice for the same hours. Vacation and holidays will be figured as time worked when computing overtime. Time and one-half (1½) will be paid for the sixth consecutive day worked and seventh consecutive day worked.

All hours paid for shall be considered hours worked for the purpose of computing fifth, sixth, and seventh consecutive day overtime.

All work performed on a holiday or the day celebrated in lieu thereof, shall be paid for at time and one-half (1½) plus holiday pay.

Employees who work their vacation shall receive vacation pay plus their regular straight time rate.

This section defines the normal hours of work and shall not be construed as a guarantee of hours per day per week.

* * * * *

Section 6(A). Overtime shall be voluntary by seniority within the classifications to the extent the operation permits (i.e., voluntary first).

(B) If sufficient amount of employees cannot be obtained as stated above, then such overtime shall be offered according to seniority (with the ability) within the department.

(C) If sufficient amount of employees cannot be obtained as stated in "B," then such overtime shall be offered by unit-wide seniority (of the employees in the plant) with the ability to perform the available work.

(D) If the Company can't get employees to work the required overtime, such overtime shall be mandatory within the classification in reverse order of seniority. Overtime shall be posted on the bulletin board at least twenty-four (24) hours in advance of said overtime, whenever reasonably possible.

* * * * *

Section 7. An employee taking vacation, holiday (personal or birthday), or sick leave will be eligible for weekend overtime only if that employee informs his supervisor in writing on a form supplied by the Employer that he or she will be available for work prior to leaving. The employee so informing his supervisor shall be obligated to work the overtime and shall call his supervisor between 2:00 P.M. and 3:00 P.M. on the Friday preceding the weekend to learn whether he has been assigned to that overtime work.

* * * * *

Article 33—Holidays

Employees shall be paid at straight time on the basis of an eight (8) hour day whenever any of the following holidays occur during a work week or not. No work is performed on such holiday. Provided such employee works the scheduled day before and the scheduled day after such holiday unless otherwise agreed to by the Company and the Union. The following holidays shall be observed:

NEW YEAR'S DAY	THANKSGIVING DAY
MEMORIAL DAY	FRIDAY AFTER THANKSGIVING
FOURTH OF JULY	CHRISTMAS DAY
GOOD FRIDAY	DAY AFTER CHRISTMAS
LABOR DAY	

The Company reserves the right to schedule the holiday.

Article 34—Entire Agreement

The parties agree that this Agreement incorporates their full and complete understanding and that prior agreements or practices are superseded by the terms of this Agreement. The parties further agree that no oral understanding will be recognized in the future unless committed to in writing and signed by the parties as a supplement to this hereto.

Questions

1. Examine the various contractual provisions. Which of these most support the union position? Which of these most support the company position?
2. Do the prior grievances of employee Martin Dumas cited by the union have significant relevance to this case? Why, or why not?
3. Why is the outcome of this case of major significance to the company? To the union? Discuss.
4. How should the arbitrator decide? Why?